The essential account of H. H. Holmes, Chicago's most gruesome killer— from Harold Schechter, "America's foremost pop historian of serial murder"

(The

"*DEPRAVED* demon̶̶̶̶̶̶̶̶̶̶̶̶̶̶̶̶̶̶̶̶̶̶ not a modern-day phenomenon. . . . Gruesome, awesome, compelling reporting."
    —Ann Rule, bestselling author of *Without Pity*

"A meticulously researched, brilliantly detailed, and above all riveting account of Dr. H. H. Holmes, a nineteenth-century serial killer who embodied the ferociously dark side of America's seemingly timeless preoccupations with ambition, money, and power. Schechter has done his usual sterling job in resurrecting this amazing tale."
    —Caleb Carr, bestselling author of *The Alienist*

"I unhesitatingly recommend [*DEPRAVED*] . . . to round out your understanding of the true depth, meaning, and perversity of [this] uniquely American brand of mayhem."
    —*The Boston Book Review*

"As chilling as *The Silence of the Lambs* and as blood curdling as the best Stephen King novel. . . . It will deprive you of your sleep, and take your attention away from everything else on your schedule until you finish it."
    —*Flint* (MI) *Journal*

"Schechter's writing keeps you turning the pages. . . . "
    —*Syracuse Herald-American*

THE A TO Z ENCYCLOPEDIA OF SERIAL KILLERS
By Harold Schechter and David Everitt

"The scholarship is both genuine and fascinating."
—The Boston Book Review

"A grisly tome. . . . Schechter knows his subject matter."
—Denver Rocky Mountain News

"The ultimate reference on this fascinating phenomenon."
—PI Magazine

Critical acclaim for Harold Schechter's historical crime fiction featuring Edgar Allan Poe

THE HUM BUG

"A riveting excursion. . . . Poe and his times come across with wonderful credibility and vitality."
—Booklist

"Evocative. . . ."
—Kirkus Reviews

NEVERMORE

"Schechter's entertaining premise is supported by rich period atmospherics. . . . Keeps the finger of suspicion wandering until the very end."
—The New York Times Book Review

"A literary confection. . . . A first-rate mystery."
—Booklist

Pocket Books by Harold Schechter

NONFICTION
The A to Z Encyclopedia of Serial Killers
    (with David Everitt)
Deranged
Depraved
Deviant
Fiend
Bestial
Fatal

FICTION
Nevermore
The Hum Bug
Outcry

HAROLD SCHECHTER

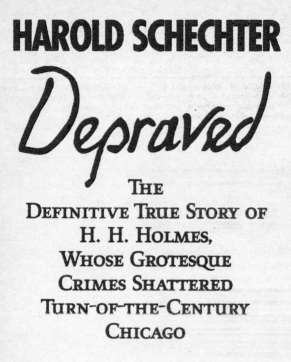

Depraved

THE DEFINITIVE TRUE STORY OF H. H. HOLMES, WHOSE GROTESQUE CRIMES SHATTERED TURN-OF-THE-CENTURY CHICAGO

POCKET STAR BOOKS

New York   London   Toronto   Sydney

A Pocket Star Book published by
POCKET BOOKS, a division of Simon & Schuster, Inc.
1230 Avenue of the Americas, New York, NY 10020

ISBN: 0-7434-9035-5

This Pocket Books printing February 2004

10 9 8 7 6

POCKET STAR BOOKS and colophon are registered
trademarks of Simon & Schuster, Inc.

Cover design by Brigid Pearson
Photos: Columbian Exposition Building in Chicago: ©Bettmann/CORBIS
        sky: Byron Aughenbaugh/The Image Bank

Manufactured in the United States of America

For information regarding special discounts for bulk purchases,
please contact Simon & Schuster Special Sales at 1-800-456-6798 or
business@simonandschuster.com

In memory of
Mildred Voris Kerr

Ourself behind ourself, concealed—
Should startle most—
Assassin hid in our apartment
Be horror's least.

—Emily Dickinson

Prologue

Among the human predators that exist in every period of history, a few become legends. From Gilles de Rais (the original "Bluebeard") to Jack the Ripper to Ted Bundy, these beings assume the status of myth. That status derives partly from the hideous nature of their crimes, which seem less like the product of madness than the handiwork of some supernatural horror—the doings of demons or ghouls.

But their mythic dimension stems from another source, too. These individuals fascinate because they seem to symbolize the darkest impulses of their times—aristocratic depravity, the diseased sexuality spawned by Victorian taboos, the sociopathic appetites of our own "culture of narcissism." As much as any hero or celebrity, such monsters personify their day. In his book *Representative Men,* Ralph Waldo Emerson argues that the divine essence incarnates itself in remarkable figures—Plato, Shakespeare, Napoleon.

The deeds of creatures like de Rais, the Ripper, Bundy, and others suggest that primordial evil does, too.

In the last quarter of the nineteenth century, a fiend roamed through America.

His career coincided with a remarkable time in the life of our nation—with that era of feverish enterprise and gaudy excess that Mark Twain dubbed "The Gilded Age." Titanic energies were afoot in the land. It was a period of sweeping social change, when our country was burgeoning into an industrial and commercial giant, and American technological wizardry—Bell's telephone, Edison's lightbulb, Ford's

1

"horseless carriage"—was altering the very nature of modern life.

Most of all, it was an age when the almighty dollar held sway as never before and a "mania for money-getting" (in Mark Twain's words) gripped the soul of America. In place of the military idols of the Civil War, society now worshiped a new breed of hero—the self-made millionaire, the captain of industry, the financial tycoon. P. T. Barnum publicized "The Rules for Success," Andrew Carnegie preached "The Gospel of Wealth," and Horatio Alger inspired the youth of America with his rags-to-riches dreams.

Hungry for their share of that dream, enormous tides of humanity swept into the cities, swelling their populations to unprecedented size. The United States, formerly a country of small towns, villages, and farms, became the land of the metropolis—New York, Pittsburgh, Cleveland, Detroit. But of all the sprawling cities, none epitomized the spirit of the age—the expansive growth, raw energy, and driving ambition—more completely than Chicago, the "gem of the prairie," the "most American of American cities," as one awestruck visitor described it.

Reduced to ashes by the great fire of 1871, Chicago soared back to life like a phoenix, becoming the world's first skyscraper city in 1885 and passing the million mark in population five years later. Booming with vigor, heady with pride, flush with opportunity—"Hog Butcher, Tool Maker, Stacker of Wheat, Player with Railroads, and Freight Handler to the Nation"—Chicago served as a colossal magnet, drawing newcomers by the thousands.

Pouring out of the countryside in quest of a brighter life, these hopefuls were brimming with spunk and ambition. "How shall one hymn, let alone suggest, a city as great as this in spirit?" rhapsodized Theodore Dreiser, himself one of the legion of "life-hungry" dreamers who swarmed to Chicago. "The American of this time, native, for the most part, of endless backwoods communities, was ignorant and gauche. But how ambitious and courageous! Such bumptiousness! Such assurance!"

And there was another quality, too, that these migrant throngs possessed. They were full of innocence. Fresh from the provinces, they knew little of the corruptions and perils of the big city, of its dark and brutal underside.

For along with the hardworking thousands, the city attracted a very different breed of dweller—creatures lured to the metropolis not by its sparkling promise but by its cloaking shadows, not by the availability of work but by the abundance of prey, not by a hunger for success but by the smell of blood.

For a man of monstrous appetites, Chicago was a land of plenty. It is no wonder, then, that the city became home to the most heinous criminal of the age. Having drifted westward from his birthplace in New England, he arrived in the metropolis in 1886 and, finding it ideal for his purposes, settled in its outskirts.

To all outward appearances, he was a quintessential man of his day, possessed of the prodigious energies characteristic of that bustling era. Doctor, druggist, inventor, get-rich-quick schemer, he consecrated himself to the acquisition of wealth.

But greed was not what drove him. All the wealth of J. P. Morgan could never have gratified his darkest compulsions.

In a booming suburb of Chicago, he erected his stronghold, a place as imposing in its way as Marshall Field's dazzling emporium or the gleaming domes and spires of the Chicago World's Fair—"the Great White City" that would arise on the shores of Lake Michigan within a few years of the monster's arrival. Massively built and bristling with battlements and turrets, the structure served as both business place and residence, though its appearance made it seem more like a medieval fortress. Appropriately, it came to be known as "the Castle."

To the neighborhood residents, the Castle was a source of pride, a symbol of the prominence and prosperity of their thriving suburb. Those who were enticed inside, however, and who glimpsed the Castle's darkest secrets acquired a very different impression. But none of them lived to reveal what lay behind the splendid facade.

The discrepancy between its outward appearance and inner reality mirrored the nature of the owner himself. But in this sense, too, the lord of the Castle was a representative man of his day. After all, in characterizing his time not as a golden but as a gilded age, Mark Twain had meant to emphasize its specious quality.

Of course, Mark Twain could never have imagined a place like the Castle. Theodore Dreiser couldn't have either, in spite of his deep understanding of the city's sordid underside. It would have taken a writer with a far different sort of imagination to conceive of such a place. It would have taken Edgar Allan Poe.

When investigators finally broke into the Castle, they were stunned at what they found—a Gothic labyrinth of trapdoors, secret passageways, soundproof vaults, and torture chambers. And then there were the greased chutes—large enough to accommodate a human body—that led down from the living quarters to a cellar equipped with acid vats, a crematorium, a dissecting table, and cases full of gleaming surgical tools.

As the true character of the Castle's owner came to light, the public struggled to make sense of him. Some saw in him the malignant consequences of Gilded Age rapacity, others diagnosed him as a case of "moral degeneracy," while there were those who spoke in terms of satanic possession. Unacquainted as yet with the language of sociopathology, the American public could only characterize him in the terminology of the day—archfiend, monster, demon. They did not know how else to describe him, since the correct label hadn't yet been invented.

In appearance, manner, and enterprise, he was an epitome of his age. But in respect to his psychopathology, he was very much a man of our own. And for that reason, he is of some historic significance.

An early edition of *The Guinness Book of World Records* lists him as "the most prolific murderer known in recent criminal history." In the era of Henry Lee Lucas and John Wayne Gacy, that record has long since been broken. But he holds another distinction that time can never erase.

His name was Herman Mudgett, though the world knew him as H. H. Holmes—and he was America's first serial killer.

Part 1

The Castle

1

Men said at vespers: "All is well!"
In one wild night the city fell;
Fell shrines of prayer and marts of grain
Before the fiery hurricane.

On threescore spires had sunset shone,
Where ghastly sunrise looked on none.
Men clasped each other's hands and said:
"The City of the West is dead!"

 —John Greenleaf Whittier, "Chicago"

Legend lays the blame for the disaster on Mrs. Patrick O'Leary's cow, though the likelier suspects were a crew of young hooligans—neighborhood boys sneaking a smoke in the hayloft of the O'Leary's ramshackle barn at 137 De Koven Street on Chicago's West Side. There were other explanations, too. Moralizing on the meaning of the catastrophe, the Reverend Granville Moody declared that it was clearly the work of a vengeful Lord, outraged at a citizenry that permitted saloons to do business on the Sabbath.

Whatever the cause, accident or divine retribution, the conflagration—which began early on the evening of Sunday, October 8, 1871—laid waste to the city in just over twenty-four hours. The West Side went first. Glancing out his bedroom window, a neighbor saw the flames rising from the O'Learys' barn and made a beeline for the nearest firebox. But for reasons unknown, his alarm never registered. A full hour passed before a lookout spotted the glow from his post atop the Cook County Courthouse—and even more time was lost when he alerted the wrong engine company after misjudging the fire's location.

The firemen who responded to his call were an exhausted crew, worn down from a battle with a three-alarm blaze that had raged just the evening before. By the time they arrived at the O'Leary place, the fire was racing northward through the neighborhood, a working-class warren of shanties, sheds, stables, and cottages. At ten P.M., when the flames ignited the wooden steeple of St. Paul's Church at Clinton and Mather, the conflagration was officially out of control.

Any hopes that the Chicago River would check the fire's progress were dashed just before midnight when the flames leapt the water, propelled by a parched, gale-force wind, as fierce as a blast from Vulcan's bellows. The Parmalee Stage and Omnibus Company building—a brand-new, block-long, three-story structure—was instantly engulfed by a "sweeping ocean of flame" (in the words of one eyewitness).

For all its claims to grandeur, Chicago was, in fact, a tinderbox city. Almost two-thirds of its sixty-five thousand buildings were constructed completely of wood, and even its most imposing structures were generally wooden buildings with flimsy brick or fake-marble facades. Its slum districts were crammed with wooden tenements, while its wealthy homes featured wood floors, wood window frames, and wood roofs, with tidy wood fences ringing the grounds. Major downtown thoroughfares were paved with pinewood blocks, and over 650 miles of its sidewalks consisted of raised wooden slats. Wooden ships lay anchored in the Chicago River, which was spanned by wooden bridges.

There were some in Chicago who—decrying it as "a city of everlasting pine, shingles, shams, and veneers"—had warned of the potential peril. The situation was made even more hazardous by the worst drought in recent memory. Since the third of July, less than three inches of rain had fallen on Chicago—about a quarter of the usual amount. The parched weather and omnipresent wood made for an explosive combination.

When midnight came and the fire swept eastward into the downtown business district, the result was catastrophic.

One by one, the proudest buildings of the city fell—the Palmer House and the Grand Pacific Hotel, McVicker's Theater and Crosby's Opera House, Field and Lieter's dazzling emporium and the supposedly fireproof stone building of the *Chicago Tribune.* "Everywhere," wrote one reporter describing the calamitous scene, "dust, smoke, flame, heat, thunder of falling walls, crackle of fire, hissing of water, panting of engines, shouts, braying of trumpets, wind, tumult, and uproar." By the time the nightmare ended, every hotel, theater, newspaper office, factory, store, public building, and bank in the business district was gone—reduced to ashes or a blackened shell.

The most devastating loss of all, however, was the destruction of the million-dollar Courthouse, the city's showpiece, where Abraham Lincoln's body had lain in state. Its five-ton bell had rung for countless civic ceremonies and tolled the warning when the conflagration began. At two-fifteen A.M., with the cupola blazing, the great bell crashed into the basement, and its thunderous fall seemed to sound the knell for the city itself.

By then, the flames had already raced across the State Street Bridge and gained a foothold in the North Side, the most prosperous residential district in the city, home to the stately mansions of Chicago's elite—the McCormicks, Trees, Kinzies, Arnolds, Rumseys, and Ogdens. Long before sunrise, their splendid homes lay in smoldering ruins. Also consumed was the neoclassic building of the Chicago Historical Society, which housed, among other treasures, President Lincoln's walking stick and the original draft of the Emancipation Proclamation.

Pandemonium reigned. With tidal waves of flame bearing down on them, frenzied hordes—at least 75,000 of the city's 335,000 residents—took to the streets in desperate flight. The situation was made even more nightmarish by the utter breakdown of social order, as packs of thieves and hoodlums rampaged through the city, looting homes, office buildings, and stores, and preying on the panic-stricken citizenry.

A desperate population turned to Allan Pinkerton and a

special force of men from his famous detective agency to combat this rampant lawlessness. But neither Pinkerton's "Preventive Police" nor the U.S. Army troops brought in under the command of Gen. Philip Sheridan could do much to stop the looting.

Sheridan had more success fighting the fire itself. Under his direction, several blocks of houses were blown up with gunpowder, halting the spread of the conflagration on the South Side.

It wasn't until late Monday, however, that the tide finally turned, thanks to a sudden shift in the weather that seemed, to the beleaguered residents, like an act of Providence. At around eleven that night, the wind died down and a cold drizzle began to fall. By early Tuesday, the rain was pouring steadily, dowsing the last of the flames.

The scenes of devastation that greeted the survivors when sunrise came were almost too vast to comprehend. The vital hub of their metropolis had been transformed into a charred and smoking wasteland. In an area roughly one mile wide and four miles long, over seventeen thousand buildings had been obliterated entirely or reduced to charred walls and rubble.

The incineration of the downtown section was so complete that (as one historian has recorded) when some sight-seers clambered onto the roof of their omnibus for a better view of the ruins, they "gazed across the main streets of the South Division—across what had been the heart of the business district—and saw men standing on the ground three miles away."

The Chicago Fire—"The Greatest Calamity of the Age," as the papers quickly dubbed it—made news around the world and inspired an international outpouring of sympathy and support. Twenty-nine foreign countries contributed close to $1 million in aid. In the United States, money and material flowed in from every part of the nation. New York City donated $600,000, President Grant sent a personal gift of $1,000, the newsboys of Cincinnati volunteered two days' of their earnings. The staff of the Ohio Female College donated sixty suits of ladies' undergarments, while the citizens of Curlew, Nebraska, offered free parcels of land to any Chicagoan who wished to resettle in their town.

New Hampshirites pitched in, too. With the bulk of Chicago's fire equipment disabled or destroyed, the Amoskeag Manufacturing Company of Manchester, N.H., immediately shipped off a brand-new engine to help protect the stricken city.

Of course, not everyone in New Hampshire learned of the disaster right away. While the residents of the big Northeastern cities—New York, Boston, Philadelphia—received word of the fire even as it was blazing, the news took longer to reach the countryside.

Chicago's ruins had already cooled before the tidings hit Gilmanton Academy, a tiny hamlet whose character had changed little since the founding, in 1794, of the venerable institution in whose honor the village was named. Nestled among the Suncook hills at the southern end of New Hampshire's Lake District, Gilmanton Academy was (in the words of the man who would become its most infamous native) "so remote from the outside world that . . . daily newspapers were rare and almost unknown." Even big news, like the burning of Chicago, filtered slowly into the little farming community, largely through the medium of "weekly papers and a few periodicals."

Yet once the villagers got word of the catastrophe, they naturally were as hungry for details as the rest of the country. To the schoolchildren especially, the immolation of the great, faraway city seemed like one of the fabled cataclysms of ancient times—the burning of Rome or the burying of Pompeii.

One eleven-year-old Gilmanton boy was even more spellbound by tales of Chicago's destruction than his schoolmates. His name was Herman, a slightly built boy with blue eyes and brown hair and a glib, peculiarly grown-up manner that revealed nothing of his profound emotional disorder.

From earliest childhood, he had been subjected to the regular brutalities of his father, a fierce disciplinarian who wielded the rod with an unsparing hand. His mother was a pious, submissive woman, incapable of shielding the boy from her husband's cruelties. Though Herman had learned to profess his filial devotion, he detested both his parents and dreamed longingly of their deaths. Hearing of the Great Fire, he imagined them trapped by the hellish flames, their flesh consumed, their bones reduced to ashes. He yearned to be delivered from them, if not by their deaths then by his eventual escape.

Even at eleven, he knew that his will and intelligence required an infinitely larger sphere of operation than New Hampshire could possibly afford. Everyone remarked on his sharpness. "A boy with a head on him," the neighbors would say. "A lad with a future."

Partly because of his delicate stature but also because of his success at school, Herman had often been persecuted by the bigger boys in town, especially during his younger years.

One episode in particular remained with him for the rest of his life. It happened when Herman was five, the year he began school.

The way to the schoolhouse ran past the village doctor's front door, which was rarely closed. Emanating from the gloomy interior were sharp medicinal odors, associated in little Herman's mind with the vile nostrums he was forced to imbibe whenever he was ill. Partly for this reason, and partly because of certain dark stories he had heard from his schoolmates (according to rumor, the doctor's cabinets housed a collection of preserved human heads and amputated limbs), the office had assumed a terrifying dimension in young Herman's imagination.

One day, having learned of Herman's horror of the place, two of his older schoolmates waylaid him while the doctor was out on an errand and dragged him, struggling and weeping, over the terrible threshold.

Through his tears, Herman could make out a ghastly specter—a leering skeleton hovering in the shadows like a demon risen from the grave. Herman's cries turned into terror-crazed shrieks, which only spurred on his tormentors. They wrestled him closer and closer to the looming skeleton, which seemed to reach out its bony hands, as if to seize the boy in a fatal embrace.

At that moment, the doctor came hurrying back to his office and—sizing up the situation at a glance—began shouting at the two bullies, who let go of Herman and raced out the doorway, leaving the hysterical boy gagging and sobbing at the foot of the mounted specimen.

Ironically, it was to this traumatic experience that Herman later attributed his interest in anatomy. By the time he was eleven, he was already conducting his secret medical experiments—first on salamanders and frogs, then on rabbits, cats, and stray dogs. He preferred to perform his operations on living creatures and became skilled at disabling his subjects without killing them. Sometimes, he retained a special part—a rabbit skull or cat's paw—storing his treasure in a metal box, which he kept hidden in the cellar of his house.

Herman never showed his treasures to anyone. There was no one he cared to share them with. For a brief period during his childhood, he did have one close friend—an older boy named Tom, who died under tragic circumstances, falling to his death from an upstairs landing while he and Herman were exploring an abandoned house.

Herman never missed Tom. He much preferred his solitude, which gave him time to plan, scheme, and dream of the day when he would finally leave New Hampshire forever.

Given his great drive and ambition, it was only a matter of time before Herman realized his goal. Eventually, he would put his past behind him and make his way by a circuitous route to the resurrected metropolis of Chicago where he would become a permanent part of the city's lore.

In a booming South Side neighborhood, he would construct a legendary residence. Allan Pinkerton's agents, who had tried so tenaciously to maintain civic order at the height of the Great Conflageration, would come to regard him as one of their most memorable foes. And thanks to him, Chicago would once again find itself on the front pages of newspapers throughout the nation—not, this time, as the site of the "Greatest Calamity of the Age" but as the home of the "Greatest Criminal of the Century."

2

Located twelve feet above the level of the lake, with a perfect water, sewerage and gas system, and an excellent police and fire department, Englewood combines all of the conveniences of the city, with the fresh, healthful air of the country.... We have more enterprising men and less "dead-beats" than any other suburb in the country.

—*Englewood Directory*, 1882

Dr. E. S. Holton's drugstore stood at the corner of Wallace and Sixty-third in the burgeoning business district of Englewood, Illinois, a well-to-do suburb just south of Chicago's city limits. On a murderously hot day in July 1886, the proprietor himself, racked with prostate cancer, lay moaning in the swelter of his second-floor bedroom, while his sixty-year-old, soon-to-be-widowed wife toiled downstairs.

Business was booming. Normally, the constant flow of customers would have been a welcome circumstance. As it was—with a desperately sick husband to tend and no one to assist her in the store—Mrs. Holton was overworked to the point of collapse.

The recent surge in business was due partly to the weather. The wilting midsummer heat had caused a run on such revitalizing elixirs as Parker's Ginger Tonic and Ayer's Sarsaparilla. But the main reason for the Holtons' thriving trade was the dramatic growth of Englewood itself.

Three years before the Great Fire, Englewood's entire

population had consisted of fewer than twenty families. By 1882, nearly two thousand Chicagoans had resettled in the lush, outlying suburb. By the time the decade ended, the *Englewood Directory* listed over forty-five thousand inhabitants, most of them urban refugees seeking the same advantages that would lure city dwellers to the suburbs throughout the coming century—fresh air, country quiet, and easy access to the metropolitan center.

As the Chamber of Commerce boasted, Englewood was "the best locality for suburban residence in the vicinity of Chicago. . . . Seven leading lines of railway furnish forty-five trains each way daily. All of these trains must stop at Englewood. These magnificent facilities give us advantages possessed by no other suburb of Chicago, the majority of which are mere flag stations, dependent upon one or two dummy trains a day, while the regular trains whizz through the town unmindful of its interests."

It was the proximity of Sixty-third and Wallace to the Western Indiana Railway Station (located less than a block away from the Holton's store) that made that intersection a hub of thriving commerce. Eventually—after the suburb was officially annexed by the city in 1889—the Holton's neighborhood would become known as "the most prosperous and best-developed cross street in the great city of Chicago" (according to one local historian).

On that broiling afternoon in 1886, however, there was still a fair amount of undeveloped land along Sixty-third Street. Indeed, looking out through the store's big, pane-glass display window—over the neatly arranged packages of Paine's Celery Compound, the amber bottles of Mrs. Winslow's Soothing Syrup, and the advertising placards for Dr. Moore's Indian Root Pills and Henderson's Digestive Tablets—the druggist's wife would have seen, across the street and catercorner to the store, a large, grassy plot, studded with luxuriant oak trees.

Had Mrs. Holton glanced out the window at a certain point late in the afternoon, she would have seen something else, too—a nattily attired gentleman peering intently at the patent medicines on display and then, after giving his suit

15

vest a small, fastidious tug, striding determinedly through her wide-flung front door.

Mrs. Holton—who knew all of her customers by sight if not by name—did not recognize the strikingly attractive young man who stepped into the store. Weighing a shade under 150 pounds and standing five feet seven inches tall, he had an erect, manly carriage and moved with a quiet grace. His eyes were slate blue, his hair—which showed itself at the temples beneath the brim of his handsome fedora—was a silky chestnut brown. He wore a walrus mustache in the style of the day but kept it carefully trimmed and slightly upcurled at the corners. Beneath the mustache, his lower lip seemed almost feminine in its fullness.

His brown suit was spotlessly clean, his cravat neatly tied, and the linen shirt-cuffs that protruded from his coat sleeves were affixed with gold buttons. A solid-gold watch chain, adorned with a charm of rich design, was strung across his vest-front. All in all, the new customer would have struck any observer—especially, perhaps, one of the opposite sex— as a fine figure of a man.

As it happened, the young man was not a customer at all. Politely doffing his hat and favoring Mrs. Holton with a slight bow, he introduced himself as Dr. H. H. Holmes, a graduate of the University of Michigan, with training and experience as a druggist. He had recently moved to the area, he explained, and was seeking employment in a store such as Mrs. Holton's. He had come to inquire if she might be in need of an assistant.

To the beleaguered, overburdened Mrs. Holton, the young man, appearing at such a difficult moment in her life, must have seemed heaven-sent.

She hired him on the spot.

The wall shelves and display cases of the Holtons' cavernous store were packed with the countless commercial cure-alls—the liver pills and stomach bitters, neuralgia remedies and regulator teas, catarrh ointments and consumption syrups—that flooded the American marketplace in the decades following the Civil War. But a druggist was more than a nostrum peddler. His job required the compounding of medicinal powders and potions, and at that delicate task Dr.

Holmes clearly excelled. His long, delicate fingers moved with marvelous dexterity, and Mrs. Holton—herself not a licensed druggist—was delighted to place the job of filling prescriptions entirely in his deft hands.

Beyond ascertaining that he had worked in a drugstore on Columbia Avenue in Philadelphia, Mrs. Holton never saw the need to inquire very closely into the history of Holmes's employment. His manifest skill was proof enough of his experience. And Holmes himself saw no need to discuss the details of his previous job, particularly its unfortunate denouement. It still pained him to think about the accident that had necessitated his hasty departure from Philadelphia—the sudden, inexplicable poisoning of a woman customer who had died after ingesting a medicine Holmes had prepared for her that morning. Holmes did not hold himself responsible for that tragedy and, understandably enough, was not eager for news of it to get around.

Besides medicine, Holmes was adept at dispensing another commodity, too—a suave, smooth-tongued charm, which he proffered freely to his female customers, many of whom began to patronize the store with surprising frequency. The Holtons' business, already vigorous, prospered as never before.

Unhappily, prosperity was of no avail to the elderly owner, who did not outlive the summer. By the time of the old man's death, Holmes's duties had extended beyond the pharmacological to include handling the store's account books, as the grieving Mrs. Holton grew increasingly remote from the day-to-day operations of the business.

Sometime during the latter part of August, not long after the druggist's death, Holmes approached the widow with a proposal to purchase the store. After giving the matter some thought, the old lady accepted on the condition that she be permitted to remain in her apartment upstairs.

She had nowhere else to go, she explained to Holmes. She had no living relations, and in any case she preferred to spend her declining years in the rooms she had occupied so happily with her late husband.

Holmes agreed to the terms, and the deal was consummated. The deed was signed, the down payment rendered, and the familiar sign above the entranceway replaced with the gold-lettered name of the drugstore's new proprietor, H. H. HOLMES.

Holmes was soon to become a familiar figure in Englewood. When he had first gone to work at the drugstore, he had commuted from his lodgings at some distance from the suburb. Even Mrs. Holton had never been able to ascertain precisely where Holmes made his home, receiving vague and elusive answers on the few occasions she had inquired.

Soon after purchasing the store, however, Holmes took rooms a few blocks away. Early on weekday evenings and on Sunday afternoons, he would stroll around the neighborhood; walking stick in hand, he was the very picture of suave self-possession, tipping his hat to the ladies and pausing to exchange small talk with the men. His fellow merchants along Sixty-third Street regarded the well-spoken, industrious young druggist as an asset to the community.

Mrs. Holton, however, was coming to a very different conclusion about her former employee. Relations between Holmes and the elderly widow had become increasingly bitter over the issue of his purchase payments—or, more precisely, nonpayments. Holmes kept promising to deliver the money and then, with equal consistency, failing to come up with it. The situation became so desperate for Mrs. Holton that she finally threatened Holmes with legal action, and when that tactic failed, filed papers against him.

What happened next remains a mystery, though one fact is indisputable. Shortly after Mrs. Holton brought suit against Holmes, she dropped out of sight.

When her former customers, having noticed her absence from the neighborhood, inquired as to her whereabouts, Holmes informed them that she had moved away from Chicago. With her husband gone, he explained, the apartment had come to seem painfully empty to the lonely widow, and so she had decided to go live with relatives in California.

By then, of course, Holmes had already given up his rooms in the nearby boarding house and moved his belongings into the far more convenient living quarters directly above his store.

*   *   *

DEPRAVED

Just a few years later, the name of H. H. Holmes would be emblazoned on the front pages of newspapers throughout the United States (and beyond). Enterprising reporters would scour the country for anyone who could furnish information on the man. And scores of individuals, even those who had had only the most casual dealings with him, would step forth and volunteer their recollections.

But Mrs. Holton, who had learned so much about the man who called himself H. H. Holmes, remained forever silent. Like so many other women who met and fell prey to his enticements, the elderly widow was never seen or heard from again.

3

Godliness is in league with riches.... Material prosperity is helping to make the national character sweeter, more joyous, more unselfish, more Christlike.... In the long run, it is only to the man of morality that wealth comes.

—Bishop William Lawrence,
"The Relation of Wealth to Morals" (1901)

To the good burghers of Englewood, particularly the mothers of marriageable daughters, it seemed a terrible waste that a gentleman of Dr. Holmes's eminent qualifications should remain a bachelor. Personable, educated, infused with the entrepreneurial spirit of the age, he appeared supremely well suited for matrimony. For such a man to refuse to take a wife seemed vaguely irresponsible, if not unnatural.

It was with markedly mixed emotions, then, that his neighbors reacted to the news, which spread rapidly through the community early in 1887, that Dr. Henry Howard Holmes had gotten married.

His bride, the former Miss Myrta Z. Belknap, was a buxom young woman with long blond curls, placid brown eyes, and a soft, baby-smooth face. Holmes had met her during a business trip to Minneapolis in late December 1886 and, after a whirlwind courtship, wed her there on January 28, 1887.

For several months after their return to Chicago, the new Mrs. Holmes worked contentedly at her husband's side as a salesclerk in the store. Quiet and self-effacing, she had nothing of Holmes's glib, outgoing charm. Customers were struck by the contrast in their personalities—and by the open adoration in the young woman's eyes whenever she gazed at her handsome, successful husband.

After a short period, however, Myrta Holmes was seen only infrequently in the store. At her husband's insistence, she busied herself upstairs with domestic chores or passed the time window-shopping along Sixty-third Street.

It was not that she had proved to be an incompetent clerk. Holmes simply wanted her out of the way. She had quickly become a nuisance to him, cramping his flirtatious style. An incorrigible ladies' man, he refused to modify his behavior merely because he was burdened with a wife. If anything, his manner toward his female patrons grew steadily more seductive in the months immediately following his marriage.

As for Myrta, though she did her best to make light of her husband's behavior—to dismiss it as nothing more than the mark of his natural gallantry—she could not help being pained by it. Eventually she was moved to make mild protests to which Holmes responded snappishly. Tensions mounted. Myrta's meek complaints turned into angry recriminations. By the time a year had passed, visitors to the store witnessed increasingly embarrassing scenes, which generally ended with Holmes hissing sharp imprecations while Myrta stormed tearfully upstairs.

Before long, the situation grew intolerable. Divorce was out of the question. In spite of her husband's faults, which made it impossible for her to continue living with him above the store, Myrta still loved Holmes. Besides, she could not abide the stigma of divorce. And there was another, even more compelling reason why she would not consider ending her marriage.

By the spring of 1888, Myrta Holmes was pregnant.

New living arrangements had to be made. Though Myrta, in her weekly letters home, had bravely concealed the painful truth from her parents, she was finally forced to reveal to them just how dire her situation had become. Her mother and father responded without hesitation. In the summer of 1888, the elder Belknaps moved into a tidy, two-story, red-frame house in Wilmette, Illinois, just north of Chicago, and took Myrta in to live with them. Holmes agreed to provide financial support and pay regular visits to his wife.

Once again, H. H. Holmes found himself living alone on Sixty-third Street—a position that suited him perfectly, given the plan that was taking shape inside his head.

Though Holmes had clearly come to regard Myrta as a serious inconvenience, there are reasons to believe that he cared for her, after his fashion.

The first was a legal action he initiated on February 14, 1887, just a few weeks after his marriage. On that date, Holmes appeared at the Cook County Courthouse to file divorce papers against Clara A. Lovering Mudgett of Alton, New Hampshire—his childhood sweetheart and first wife, to whom he was still wed at the time of his union to Myrta Z. Belknap.

Myrta, of course, did not know of Clara Mudgett's existence—or that her own marriage to Holmes, being bigamous, had no legal validity.

As it happened, Homes never followed through on his divorce from Clara Mudgett, and the suit was eventually dismissed by the court "for default of appearance of complainant." Still, for a fleeting moment, Holmes had at least contemplated doing right by Myrta Belknap—possibly the first time in his life that he had ever experienced such an impulse, and certainly the only time it can be documented.

In the years to come, there would be other indications that Holmes felt something like human warmth for Myrta. But perhaps the most convincing proof is simply this: unlike most of the women who became intimately involved with Holmes during his years in Chicago, Myrta Belknap lived to enjoy her old age and died of natural causes.

With his wife out of the way, Holmes lost no time in putting his master plan into motion. To those customers who inquired after Myrta's whereabouts, he explained that the stresses of her physical condition, combined with prolonged exposure to the din of the nearby railway trains—whose clanging bells, piercing whistles, and chugging engines sounded constantly throughout the day—had left her in a state of nervous exhaustion. Being preoccupied with the demands of his business, he had thought it best to consign her to the care of her parents. His customers conveyed their sympathy and continued to regard the enterprising young druggist as a paragon.

And indeed, in all outward respects, Holmes was the very model of the up-and-coming young businessman. "Say to yourself, 'My place is at the top!'" preached Andrew Carnegie in his popular lecture, "The Road to Business Success." Holmes—an avid devourer of the how-to advice of his day—had clearly taken the message to heart. The Holtons' corner drugstore could not contain his colossal ambitions. Fortunes were to be made by young men of pluck, drive, and vision. Holmes would not be satisfied until he became the owner of a magnificent building that proclaimed his success to the world.

There were other reasons why he desired to construct a building of his own. His lust for wealth was not only undisguised but—given the ethics of the day—widely admired. But beneath his money hunger lurked other, far darker appetites whose gratification demanded a high degree of privacy. The small apartment he inhabited above the drugstore was ludicrously insufficient for the fulfillment of those needs.

It was no coincidence that an ideal spot for his purposes existed so close to the Holtons' store. Holmes had spent a good deal of time scouting various locations before settling on the corner of Sixty-third and Wallace. His shrewd eye for real estate had recognized the intersection as a prime business site. Deeper still, in his mind's eye, he perceived possibilities of another kind.

Even with the money he was making from his store, Holmes did not have adequate funds for his purposes. But that disadvantage had never stopped him before.

By the summer of 1888, he had managed to secure a lease on the vacant property across from the store. In the fall of that year, shortly after Myrta moved in with her parents, he set about making his secret blueprint a reality.

4

The most sensational American case of the same decade was in some ways more sensational than that of Jack the Ripper.... Like the Ripper, Holmes is a kind of grim landmark in social history. But his sadism was far more cold and calculating.

—Colin Wilson, *A Criminal History of Mankind*

At that very moment, half a world away, a maniac was on the loose—a madman whose crimes so unsettled society that the aftershock can still be felt today.

He struck first in the early hours of August 31, 1888. At three-forty A.M., while walking down Buck's Row—a deserted, dimly lit street in London's squalid East End—a market porter named George Cross stumbled upon what he took to be a tarpaulin-wrapped bundle. Peering closer, he saw that the sprawling heap was the butchered body of a woman, later identified as a forty-two-year-old prostitute named Mary Anne Nicholls. Her killer had clamped a powerful hand over her mouth, then slashed her throat so savagely that his blade had cut all the way through to her spinal column. Not until the corpse was laid out in the mortuary, however, did examiners discover her other injuries—belly slit from left to right, vagina mutilated with stab wounds.

The second killing, which occurred a week later, provoked a citywide panic, sending shock waves through every level of London society. At six o'clock in the morning of September 8, the mutilated remains of Annie Chapman, a wasted,

24

forty-seven-year-old prostitute suffering from malnutrition and consumption, were discovered in the rear of a lodging house at 29 Hanbury Street, a half mile from the site of the first murder. The woman's head was barely attached to her body—the killer had severed her neck muscles and nearly succeeded in sawing through her spine before abandoning the effort.

Chapman had also been disemboweled. In a postmortem report published in the medical journal *The Lancet*, the examining surgeon, Dr. Bagster Phillips, graphically described the condition of the corpse: "The abdomen had been entirely laid open and the intestines severed from their mesenteric attachments which had been lifted out and placed on the shoulder of the corpse; whilst from the pelvis, the uterus and its appendages with the upper portions of the vagina and the posterior two-thirds of the bladder had been entirely removed. Obviously the work was that of an expert—or one, at least, who had such knowledge of anatomical or pathological examinations as to be enabled to secure the pelvic organs with one sweep of the knife."

The true identity of the killer would never be known. But on September 28, the Metropolitan Police received a taunting letter by a writer who claimed to be the culprit and signed his note with a sinister nom de plume. The name caught on with the public. From that point on, the mad butcher of Whitechapel would be known throughout the world by his grisly nickname—Jack the Ripper.

On September 30, two days after the police received the "Ripper" letter, the killer cut the throat of a Swedish prostitute named Elizabeth Stride in a courtyard behind the International Working Man's Educational Club in Berner Street. Before he could commit any further atrocities on this unfortunate woman, he was interrupted by the sounds of an approaching horse-drawn wagon, driven by the club's steward.

Hurrying away down Commercial Street, the Ripper encountered Catherine Eddowes, a forty-three-year-old prostitute who had been released only moments before from the Bishopsgate police station, where she had spent several hours sobering up after having been found lying drunk on the pavement. The Ripper lured her into Mitre Square, where he dispatched her in the usual fashion, slitting her windpipe with a single vicious slash. Then, in the grip of a demoniacal frenzy, he proceeded to savage her corpse, disfiguring her face, splitting her body from rectum to breastbone, removing her entrails, and carrying off her left kidney.

Part of that kidney (with an inch of renal artery still attached) was enclosed in a parcel that arrived on October 16 at the home of George Lusk, head of the Whitechapel Vigilance Committee, a group of local tradesmen who had organized to assist in the search for the killer. Accompanying this ghastly artifact was an equally appalling letter, addressed to Mr. Lusk: "Sir I send you half the kidne I took from one woman prasarved it for you tother piece I fried and ate it was very nise I may send you the bloody knif that I took it out if you only wate a whil longer. Signed Catch me when you can Mister Lusk."

The sender's address on the upper-right-hand corner of the letter said simply: "From Hell."

The final crime committed by the Ripper was also the most hideous. On the evening of November 9, he picked up a twenty-five-year-old Irish prostitute named Mary Kelly, three months pregnant, who took him back to her rooms in Miller's Court. Sometime in the middle of the night, he killed her in bed, then spent several leisurely hours butchering her corpse. The next morning, the landlord's assistant, sent to collect Kelly's rent, discovered her body, whose horrific condition was reported in the *Illustrated Police News:*

> The throat had been cut right across with a knife, nearly severing the head from the body. The abdomen had been partially ripped open, and both of the breasts had been cut from the body. The left arm, like the head, hung to the body by the skin only. The nose had been cut off, the forehead skinned, and the thighs, down to the feet, stripped of the flesh. The abdomen had been slashed with a knife across downwards, and the liver and entrails wrenched away. The entrails and other portions of the frame were missing, but the liver, etc., were

found placed between the feet of this poor victim. The flesh from the thighs and legs, together with the breasts and nose, had been placed by the murderer on the table, and one of the hands of the dead woman had been pushed into her stomach.

Following this outrage, the Whitechapel murders came to an abrupt halt. Within the next few years, several more prostitutes were killed, their throats slashed and stomachs sliced open. But police judged these crimes to be the work of copycat killers. The Ripper vanished forever, stepping out of history and into the realm of myth.

The Ripper murders made headlines around the world. To the citizens of Chicago, reading the sensational details in *The Tribune*, *The Times-Herald*, or *The Inter Ocean*, the depredations of the Whitechapel monster, as disturbing as they were, must have seemed reassuringly distant from the realities of their own lives.

They had no way of knowing that even at that moment, in the outskirts of their city, a psychopath who called himself H. H. Holmes was busily laying the groundwork for a murderous career that would rival, and in some ways outmatch, the atrocities of his English counterpart, Jack the Ripper.

5

> My son, if sinners entice thee,
> consent thou not. . . .
> Refrain thy foot from their path:
> for their feet run to evil,
> and make haste to shed blood.
>
> —Proverbs 1:10, 15–16

During the month of February 1879, Benjamin W. Pitezel of Kewanee, Illinois, composed a keepsake for his wayward son, Benjamin, Jr. Known to the family by his middle name, Freelon, the younger Pitezel was paying a rare visit to his parents before returning to his wife and children in Galva.

The keepsake was a miscellany of family anecdotes, meticulously inscribed in a three-by-five-inch notebook with marbled covers. Interspersed with accounts of assorted milestones—births and deaths, marriages and funerals, illnesses and religious conversions—were extended passages of fatherly counsel and heartfelt prayer.

"Freelon," Benjamin, Sr., wrote toward the end of the journal, "I have written some things in this book for you to think about. As you will be going back to your home soon, this may be the last advice that I may ever be permitted to give you in this way, as life is so uncertain and I cannot tell how soon I may fall."

Then, in images and diction drawn from Scripture, he poured out a final appeal:

28

Come with me and I will do the good is the
Saviour's command. Will you go? Listen. I will take
all your old garments and I will put on you a clean
white robe. I will put shoes on your feet and a ring
on your hand. I will take that wicked nature out of
you, and I will wash from you all your stains, and
I will be a father to you and you shall be a son
and an heir.... I love you, although you have gone
far astray. But now come back and let me clothe
you in your right mind.... If you will come to me,
I will take that hard heart of yours and give you a
new heart. All this will I do because I have loved
you.

The urgency of the elder Pitezel's tone attests to his desperate concern for the spiritual well-being of his namesake.
Of his five children, Benjamin, Jr., had turned out to be the
prodigal son. Two years earlier, he had seduced eighteen-
year-old Carrie Canning of Galva, Illinois—the daughter of
a Methodist minister—and gotten her with child. Thanks to
a hastily arranged marriage, the baby—a girl named Dessie—had been born in wedlock. But the scandal had brought
disgrace on both families.

Carrie had recently given birth to a second daughter, Etta
Alice, and the younger Pitezel was about to resume his responsibilities as head of his own household. His father, understanding both the weight of those responsibilities and the
faults in his son's nature, could only pray for the young
man's reform. Benjamin, Jr., was not insensible of his father's gift, and the little notebook remained a treasured
possession.

But however appreciative he might have been of the offering, Benjamin Freelon Pitezel was a fully grown man, and
his weaknesses of character were far too deeply ingrained
to be overcome by even the most fervent of prayers.

To a stranger, those weaknesses would not have been
readily apparent. At twenty-three, Ben Pitezel cut a striking
figure. Six feet tall and muscular, he had the broad back and
square, calloused hands of a working man. But his features

were as fine as those of any highborn hero in a popular romance—clean jaw, straight nose, soft, blue eyes, and sensitive mouth. His hair was thick and raven black, his upper lip adorned with a neatly trimmed mustache. His largest flaw was a warty growth on the back of his neck, just above the top of his shirt collar. It was easy enough to see why a plain-featured girl—even one as piously raised as Carrie Canning—would have succumbed to his blandishments.

But his wastrel's life would soon make its mark on his appearance. Already the air of a perennial ne'er-do-well hung about him. His willful disposition was made infinitely worse by his growing fondness for the bottle. In another few years, the drinking and hard living—including the bar fights that would leave him with a broken nose and several missing teeth—would coarsen his features considerably. Though he never entirely lost his good looks, no one would ever again mistake him for a gentleman. Rawboned and surly, he grew to look like what he was—a chronic hard-luck case with a peevish spirit and a shifty intelligence.

His great redeeming feature was his devotion to his wife and growing brood of children, whose number eventually reached six (though one child, a boy named Nevit Noble, would die of diphtheria just short of his second birthday). But Pitezel's loyalty to his family was offset by the hardships and grief that his alcoholism brought upon them.

For ten grinding years, he dragged his family around the Midwest, drifting from job to job, town to town, always in and out of trouble. He earned honest money when he could, but his drinking made it hard for him to hold on to any work for very long. Throughout the 1880s, he was briefly employed as a circus roustabout, a lumbermill hand, a railroad worker, and a janitor. He'd also spent time in various jails for crimes ranging from petty larceny to forgery to horse stealing.

Exactly when the Pitezels settled in Chicago is unclear, though they must certainly have arrived there no later than the fall of 1889. For in November of that year, Benjamin answered a help-wanted ad in a local newspaper. Carpenters were needed for a new building in Englewood. The ad instructed applicants to contact Dr. H. H. Holmes.

DEPRAVED

No record exists of Pitezel's first, fateful meeting with Holmes. But surely the latter, with his genius for discerning a potential dupe, must have sized Pitezel up at a glance.

In later years, Holmes's cool manipulativeness—his skill at spotting and exploiting the weak points of his victims—would generate a host of wild claims. Countless articles and pamphlets would depict him as a being of nearly supernatural power, possessed of the ability to mesmerize his victims with a single, piercing stare.

Clearly such assertions were nothing more than sensationalistic claptrap. Nevertheless, it is true that the cunning and charismatic Holmes was remarkably adept at playing upon the vulnerabilities of weaker-willed individuals.

Pitezel was a case in point. In November of 1889, he hired on as a construction worker for Holmes. But before very long, he found himself performing a host of other, far more questionable activities.

In the old-fashioned meaning of the word—"one who is actuated by the will of another and is ready to do his bidding"—Benjamin Pitezel became H. H. Holmes's creature.

6

Not by a mountain side, nor on the bank of a rushing river, stands an old and deserted castle; but by the side of a lay of four railroad tracks leading south out of the great city of Chicago ... is a castle of modern construction.

—Robert L. Corbitt, *The Holmes Castle* (1895)

Remarkable feats of architecture were nothing new to Chicagoans in the last decades of the nineteenth century. After all, it had taken only a few years for the entire city to rebuild itself from the wreckage of the Great Conflagration. Reconstruction had begun before the ruins had cooled. Six weeks later, the burned-out districts boasted more than two hundred new buildings of brick and stone. By the end of the 1880s, that number had expanded to nearly one hundred thousand, and brilliant young architects such as Louis Henri Sullivan and John Wellborn Root had turned Chicago into an urban showcase—the world's first city of skyscrapers.

Even so, the construction taking place at Sixty-third and Wallace streets between the fall of 1888 and the spring of 1890 was impressive enough to arouse the excited interest of the local citizenry.

It was not the height of the building that made it so notable. Compared to the ten- and twelve-story office towers springing up in the city's commercial district, the new structure was relatively squat—only three stories tall when completed. But in square footage, the place was imposing, utilizing every inch of the 50-by-162-foot corner lot.

Moreover, the sheer amount of activity involved in its construction was striking. Neighborhood residents, pausing in their daily rounds to watch the magnificent new edifice taking shape, marveled at the number of laborers who swarmed over the site.

Strangely, however, the work seemed to progress at a remarkably slow pace. Even allowing for its massive dimensions, the building should not have taken a skilled work crew more than six months to erect. But for seemingly mysterious reasons, a solid year and a half passed between groundbreaking and completion.

It would have taken an unusually observant onlooker—someone who paid particular attention to the identity of the construction workers—to solve the mystery. Such a person would have noticed that none of the men remained on the job very long. Most of them were fired after a week or two; others lasted only a few days before being replaced.

By the time the final nail was hammered home and the last coat of paint applied, more than five hundred craftsmen and common laborers had come and gone.

For all the neighborhood interest in the project, however, no one seemed to notice this extraordinary turnover. Certainly no one could have guessed that it was a deliberate ploy on the part of the building's owner, architect, general contractor, and construction foreman—Dr. H. H. Holmes.

Though this endless cycle of hiring and firing slowed construction down by at least a year, it served two important purposes for the devious Dr. Holmes. First, it saved him a significant amount of money in wages. A mason or plumber might put in a full two weeks of work before asking to be paid. As soon as he did, Holmes would accuse him of doing substandard work and sack him on the spot, without forking over a nickel.

The second purpose was distinctly more sinister. By insuring that each man worked on only a small part of the structure before being replaced, Holmes was able to conceal its overall layout from the world. A carpenter might be fired after erecting a few doorframes, a bricklayer after putting

33

up a single basement wall. As a result, only one man—Holmes himself—had a clear picture of the building's total design.

The young doctor's caution in this regard is understandable, since anyone privy to the floor plans would certainly have questioned Holmes's architectural qualifications—if not, indeed, his sanity.

Because the construction site was just across the street from his drugstore, Holmes was able to spend hours each day overseeing the project—dictating orders, issuing demands, and of course, dismissing employees on a regular basis. Neighborhood gawkers witnessed more than one angry scene between the imperious young doctor and embittered workers who had been peremptorily fired for their supposed incompetence. Some of the latter eventually filed suits, which Holmes, with his shyster's cunning, managed to mire in protracted litigation.

Those who resorted to more direct physical threats found themselves backing off quickly. Though Holmes was an infinitely more dangerous man than anyone could have guessed at the time, his appearance was not especially intimidating. What gave his enemies pause was the presence of the hard-bitten assistant who seemed to hover constantly at Holmes's side—Benjamin Pitezel.

The construction workers cheated of their pay weren't the only ones who came to regret their dealings with Dr. Holmes. So did the suppliers who provided the new building with its various and often highly peculiar appurtenances.

There was, for example, the enormous safe—as large as a walk-in bank vault—that Holmes purchased on credit before his building was half-completed. When the vault was delivered, Holmes installed it in a vacant area on the third floor of the building, then constructed a room to contain it, making sure that the doorway was so small that the safe couldn't possibly pass through. When Holmes, in typical fashion, failed to meet any of his payments, the safe company dispatched a crew to repossess the vault. Holmes offered to let them remove it but warned that if they damaged his building in any way, he would slap the company with a ruinous lawsuit.

The vault stayed where it was.

Holmes employed a similar stratagem to acquire the other accoutrements he claimed to require as part of his pharmacological pursuits. These included a massive kiln fitted with a cast-iron door and a grate that slid in and out on rollers; a large zinc tank; an assortment of vats designed to store corrosives such as acid and quicklime; and enough asbestos-covered, sheet-iron plates to line the walls of several rooms.

For weeks after construction was completed in May 1890, excited crowds gathered to admire the splendid new addition to their neighborhood. Stretching nearly half the length of Wallace Street, the building—with its turreted roof, tessellated cornices, mullioned bay windows, and sham battlements—was indeed an impressive sight, a perfect reflection of its proud and ambitious young owner.

Of course, the crowds had no way of knowing what the striking facade concealed—any more than they could see behind Dr. Holmes's admirable exterior, into the bizarre and labyrinthine operations of his mind.

To be sure, part of the building was open to the public. The first floor consisted of a string of street-level shops, some run by Holmes, others leased to local merchants, who were delighted to do business in such a prime location. In the coming years, thousands of patrons would enter the property. But, limited to ground level, they couldn't possibly suspect the dire secrets hidden elsewhere in the building—in the depths of the cellar and the dark of the chambers upstairs.

In addition to Holmes's private office, with its curving bay window that overlooked Wallace Street, the third floor contained three dozen rooms. The majority of these were unexceptional. Comfortably furnished with beds, bureaus, rocking chairs, rugs, and wall mirrors, they were indistinguishable from the lodgings available in countless hostelries throughout the city. The guests who eventually stayed in these quarters, however, must have found it peculiarly frustrating to locate their rooms, which were strung along a tortuous network of narrow, weirdly angled hallways. Dimly lit by gas jets mounted on the walls at widely spaced intervals, these corridors took strange and unexpected turns, terminating in dead ends, stairways that seemed to lead nowhere, and perpetually locked doors to which only Holmes possessed the key.

One of these closed-off rooms, adjacent to his office, contained the walk-in bank vault, whose interior had been modified by the addition of a gas pipe. The flow of gas through this conduit was controlled by a cut-off valve concealed inside a closet in Holmes's sleeping chamber.

The second floor of the building was even more mazelike than the third. Indeed, its floor plan was similar to the labyrinthine layout of a carnival funhouse, though the hidden surprises it contained were considerably more frightening. Fifty-one doors lined six shadowy corridors, which zigzagged at crazy angles. Behind the doors lay thirty-five rooms, a few fitted up—like the lodgings upstairs—as ordinary bedchambers.

There was nothing ordinary about the other rooms.

Some were airtight, lined from floor to ceiling with the asbestos-covered steel plates that Holmes had procured. Others had been soundproofed. Still others were so narrow and low-ceilinged that they were little more than closets.

Most of the rooms had been rigged with gas pipes connected to the control panel in Holmes's bedchamber. The doors to these rooms could be locked only from the outside and were equipped with special peepholes that permitted the landlord to keep a close eye on his guests.

And then there were the other, equally sinister features of the second story—the secret passageways, concealed closets accessible through sliding panels, trapdoors opening up into darkness, and large, greased shafts that led straight to the cellar.

Cavernous and dank, the brick-walled cellar had the aspect of a Gothic-horror dungeon—a resemblance reinforced by the grim paraphernalia it contained. It was here that Holmes kept his acid tank, quicklime vats, dissecting table, surgeon's cabinet, and the other gruesome tools of his trade. In years to come, the basement would also house a grotesque contraption dubbed an "elasticity determinator." According to its inventor—Dr. H. H. Holmes—the apparatus was a technological marvel, whose purpose was to produce "a race of giants" by stretching experimental subjects to twice their normal length.

To those who viewed it up close, however, the device did not appear to be a miracle of modern technology.

It appeared to be a medieval torture rack.

It is impossible to say who first christened the building with its byname. Perhaps it was a neighborhood resident, paying tribute to the imposing look of Holmes's creation. Or perhaps it was Holmes himself, whose talent for self-promotion matched his grandiose ambitions. Whatever the case, soon after its completion, Englewood's citizens began referring to the new building as "the Castle."

In later years, of course, that name would be modified, and the looming structure at the corner of Wallace and Sixty-third streets would become known to the world by other phrases:

Bluebeard's Castle. Murder Castle. Nightmare Castle. The Castle of Horror.

Part 2

Ladykiller

7

I told you, you must have confidence, unquestioning confidence, I meant confidence in the genuine medicine, and the genuine *me*.

—Herman Melville, *The Confidence-Man*

In June 1890, a month after the completion of his Castle, Holmes put his drugstore up for sale and quickly found a prospective buyer—an enterprising young Michiganite named A. L. Jones, who had come to Chicago with a new wife, a modest inheritance, and a determination to establish himself as a businessman in the hustling city. At Holmes's invitation, Mr. Jones visited the shop on a prearranged afternoon and was impressed by the constant flow of customers—never realizing that Holmes had ensured an unusually brisk trade by supplementing his regular clientele with hirelings, brought in to make phony purchases.

At the end of the day, the two men sat down to talk business. Why, Mr. Jones inquired, had Dr. Holmes decided to sell such a thriving enterprise?

Holmes had anticipated such a question and was ready with a response. It was the very success of the store that now made it impossible for him to continue running it, he explained. The profits he had reaped during the past few years had permitted him to expand into other activities, which now required his complete attention. With Holmes's departure from the business, Jones would have the neighborhood all to himself.

A bargain was struck. The purchase price amounted to Mr. Jones's entire patrimony, but the young man had little doubt that the investment would soon repay itself. In July 1890, the drugstore originally established by Dr. E. S. Holton changed hands once again.

A few weeks later, a large, horse-drawn delivery truck pulled up in front of Holmes's Castle, just across the street from the little drugstore. As its new owner and his young wife watched with mounting confusion, workmen began uncrating a load of elegant store fixtures—glass-fronted display cases, rich, dark-wood cabinets, marble-topped counters—and hauling them through the semihexagonal entranceway of the vacant corner store of the Castle.

Before long, a magnificent wooden sign, carved in the shape of a mortar and pestle, hung over the entranceway. Glittering gold letters in the center of the ivory-painted icon proclaimed H. H. HOLMES PHARMACY.

The interior of the store did justice to the splendor of the sign. Stepping out of the hectic street, a customer would first pass by a massive column supporting the arched ceiling of the entranceway. Overhead, a dazzling Catherine-wheel design seemed to radiate from the Corinthian capital of the pillar. Moving into the store proper, the visitor's eyes would be dazzled by the frescoed stucco work that graced the ceiling and walls; by the black-and-white diamonds that tiled the floor; by the marbled elegance of the countertops; by the brassy shine of the soda fountain spigots; and by the sparkling elixirs that filled the glass cases and lined the walnut shelves.

Holmes's handsome new pharmacy—which soon became a neighborhood showplace—made his old store seem as dingy as a cowshed. It didn't take long before the hapless Jones was compelled to close up shop and return to his native village, a ruined man.

But, while business was good for Holmes, the Castle required a great deal of upkeep, and even with the money from his tenants, his income proved inadequate for his desires. Living at a time—"The Age of Excess," as it is sometimes called—when the millionaire entrepreneur was the cultural ideal, he lusted for the fortune that he believed was his due.

In the fall of 1890, Holmes was already thirty years old, no longer a particularly young man by the measure of the day. Rapacious by nature, he became increasingly obsessed by money, embarking on a frantic series of commercial ventures. On the ground floor of the Castle, he opened and managed a string of businesses—a jewelry store, a restaurant, a barbershop. He manufactured glycerin soap and invested in a duplicating device called the ABC Copier, a forerunner of the modern-day mimeograph.

That Holmes failed to make his million from these varied enterprises was undoubtedly due to the deformities of his character. Though he possessed all of the attributes that should have guaranteed his success—abundant energy, creativity, ingenuity, and drive—he was undone by his psychopathology.

Dissatisfied with the revenues from his legitimate ventures, he embarked on a series of brazen swindles that revealed the icy underlying arrogance—distinctive of psychopaths—concealed beneath his personable exterior.

There was the time, for example, when Holmes announced that he had invented a revolutionary machine for manufacturing cheap illuminating gas from tap water. Attracting the interest of a group of Canadian investors, Holmes invited the men to the Castle, where he led them down to a remote corner of the cellar, sequestered from the dungeonlike surroundings by a high wooden partition.

Within this enclosure stood Holmes's marvelous Chemical-Water Gas Generator. To one skeptical observer, the bizarre-looking contraption—a small iron tank sprouting a tangle of pipes, shutoff valves, and pressure gauges—resembled "a washing machine on stilts."

Unscrewing a metal cap, Holmes dumped a cupful of water down the spout, added some scoops of mysterious chemicals, turned a few valves, adjusted a knob here and there. An instant later, gas spewed from a vent. With a flourish, Holmes struck a match, held it to the jetting gas, and the little enclosure was aglow with light.

The excited investors immediately agreed to purchase the

patent from Holmes for nearly $10,000. It wasn't until the Chicago Gas Company got wind of the device and sent an inspector to the Castle that the ruse was uncovered. A little pipe, cleverly concealed at the rear of the contraption, disappeared beneath the floor of the Castle and led straight to a public gas main. Holmes had simply tapped into the city supply.

For unknown reasons, the gas company decided not to prosecute, though workmen did confiscate the machine, leaving Holmes with a sizable hole in his cellar floor. But in his own aberrant way, Holmes was a visionary. Staring down at the excavation, he was struck with an inspiration.

Within days, the H. H. Holmes Pharmacy featured a new product—Linden Grove Mineral Water, an elixir presumably pumped from an artesian well that Dr. Holmes had bored in the basement of his Castle. Holmes peddled the potion for five cents a glass, two bits a bottle.

The revivifying liquid proved highly popular with Holmes's customers, who never guessed that they were drinking ordinary tap water doctored with a dash of vanilla extract and a soupçon of bitters.

Even so, they might have counted themselves lucky to be cheated in this way. Vanilla-flavored snake oil was one of Holmes's more harmless concoctions. Previous patrons— such as the unfortunate young Philadelphia woman whose tragic death had necessitated his flight from that city back in 1884—had ingested far worse.

And there were many more victims still to come—men and especially women who would have been happy to lose nothing more than their money to the man they knew as Dr. Henry Howard Holmes.

Only a month or so after the gas company carted away his bogus invention, Holmes came across a newspaper article that described an innovative process for bending plate glass, patented by a man named Warner.

Shortly thereafter, Holmes appeared at the downtown office of a firm that manufactured oil-burning furnaces. Holmes explained to the manager that he was about to embark on a glass-bending venture, but before he could do so, the kiln in the basement of his office building required modification, since it did not generate the requisite heat.

A few days later, a mechanic was dispatched to the Castle and ushered downstairs where, in a remote corner of the basement, the kiln hulked in the shadows. In the course of a long day's work, the mechanic installed a new burner inside the kiln and hooked it to a large oil tank in the alley. At full blast, the kiln was now capable of reaching a temperature of three thousand degrees.

Certainly that was hot enough to bend plate glass. What struck the mechanic as peculiar, however, were the dimensions of the kiln, whose inner chamber, constructed of fire brick, measured three feet high, three feet wide, and eight feet long. A slight man, he had been able to work inside the furnace without any trouble—indeed, it seemed a perfect size for a human being. But it couldn't possibly accommodate a very large sheet of plate glass.

The next day at work, he shared this observation with his supervisor. The kiln just didn't seem very practical for commercial purposes, he reflected. Not unless—and here the two men laughed at the absurdity of the thought—Dr. Holmes was planning to operate a crematory.

8

"Alas, poor child," replied the old woman, "whither
have you come? You are in a murderer's den.
You think you are a bride soon to be married, but
you will keep your wedding with death."

—Grimm, "The Robber Bridegroom"

Full-figured and nearly six feet tall, Julia Smythe would undoubtedly seem buxom by modern standards: handsome
rather than beautiful. But the feminine ideal of her day—
epitomized by the statuesque "Gibson girl"—was considerably more fleshy. In the eyes of her contemporaries, the
eighteen-year-old grocer's daughter, with her thick chestnut
hair and frank green eyes, was a strikingly lovely person.

An uncommonly clever one, too. Even as a child, she was
known for her quickness. "Pretty as a picture," the folks in
Davenport would say of her. "And sharp as a tack." By the
time she was thirteen, she was already keeping the books in
her father's store.

Beauty, brains, ambition—Julia had been blessed with all
three. Everyone who knew her predicted a great future for
the girl and wondered what sort of husband she would settle on.

She could certainly have had the pick of the crop. From
the moment she reached marriageable age, she was besieged
with suitors. Julia enjoyed their attentions and responded
with a free-and-easy friendliness that earned her a reputation, among certain backbiting acquaintances, as a shameless

flirt. But most of the townsfolk took a far more generous view of her character.

There was nothing coquettish about Julia Smythe, they declared. She was simply a healthy, bright, high-spirited girl who took pleasure in male company. The fellow who finally persuaded her to become his wife would obviously have to be somebody special—a man whose intelligence, determination, and spunk were, at the very least, the equal of her own.

And so, when the news got around town in early 1880 that Julia Smythe had become engaged to Icilius T. Conner, the reactions ranged from bafflement to outright shock.

A native of Muscatine, Iowa, the twenty-year-old Conner—known since boyhood by his nickname, Ned—had drifted into Davenport several years earlier. A jeweler and watchmaker by trade, he had set himself up in a small shop on Main Street from which he eked out a meager living.

Few customers ventured into the store. The problem wasn't Ned's skill as a watchmaker; he was a capable enough craftsman. But the shop itself seemed hopelessly glum, from its dingy display window—in which a pair of gold-plated pocket watches dangled forlornly—to its cramped, dusty interior. A sad, shabby air seemed to hang about the place. It hung about the proprietor, too. Though no one ever accused Ned of laziness, he did not impress people as a young man of much promise. With his mousy appearance and diffident manner, he seemed like a person predestined—in spite of his hard work and perseverance—for failure.

Exactly what the radiant young woman saw in him was a mystery to her family and friends. Everyone admitted that Ned had a sweetness about him. But then, so did a dish of milk toast. Folks had just naturally assumed that Julia would want someone with a bit more fiber.

Julia's mother and father—in spite of their disappointment, even dismay, at her choice—thought it best not to voice their reservations. Parental objection, they knew, would only cause their headstrong daughter to dig in her heels. So they held their tongues and silently prayed that Julia would come to her senses before the wedding day arrived.

Their prayers went unanswered. In the summer of 1880, Julia Louise Smythe became Mrs. Ned Conner.

The marriage was troubled from the start. Perhaps Julia had dreamed that—with her at his side to inspire, assist, and advise him—her husband would blossom into a successful tradesman. If so, she quickly discovered how mistaken she was. Ned remained hopelessly inept at business affairs. Money barely trickled in.

Her disappointment deepened into contempt. When she spoke to him, her voice had a cutting edge, which Ned tried his best to ignore. He did, however, grow increasingly resentful over the warm, friendly way she continued to treat other men. Alone, they would retreat into a charged, angry silence, broken only by a few bitter words. When this simmering tension reached the boiling point, they would break into violent, sometimes public, quarrels.

Though Julia's parents had foreseen her unhappiness, they could not condone a divorce. Their daughter would have to live with her mistake and make the best of the situation. They did what they could to smooth things over between the youngsters. For a while, the marriage seemed to go better. Then in the fall of 1882, Julia discovered that she was pregnant. Everyone hoped that the baby would bring the couple closer together.

Unfortunately, the child was stillborn. The tragedy added more strain to the relationship. Soon afterward, Ned and Julia packed up and left Davenport, seeking a fresh start for both their business and their marriage. Over the next seven years, they lived in half a dozen towns in Iowa and Illinois—Columbus Junction, Muscatine, Bradford, and others. In each place, the same pattern of hopeful expectation, gradual disappointment, and ultimate failure repeated itself.

In 1887, Julia gave birth again, this time to a healthy girl she and her husband named Pearl. Two years later—having failed to make a go of yet another small-town jewelry store—Julia and Ned came to a momentous decision. Though both of them were leery of cities, they resolved to try their luck in the place that seemed to hold out the last, best hope for success—Chicago.

Ned had no trouble finding a job in a downtown jewelry

shop, but his wages were pathetically small—barely enough for his family to subsist on. And then, sometime in late 1890, a sudden opportunity presented itself.

Precisely how Ned came to learn of this opening is unclear. According to certain accounts, he came upon it in a newspaper classified. According to others, he was apprised of the position by a business acquaintance. Whatever the case, one fact is indisputable—shortly after his arrival in Chicago, Ned Conner learned that a gentleman named H. H. Holmes was seeking a qualified manager for a jewelry shop he owned in a building located at Wallace and Sixty-third streets in Englewood.

Attired in his fanciest clothing, Ned traveled out to the suburb the very next day to meet Dr. Holmes. The interview proved satisfactory to both parties. Ned was offered the manager's job at a weekly salary of twelve dollars, plus room and board for himself and his family. He accepted without hesitation.

And so it was that, in November 1890, Ned, Julia, and baby Pearl took up residence in the third floor of Dr. Holmes's Castle.

What happened within the next few months was, if not inevitable, then at least unsurprising. Julia Conner was a warm-blooded woman married to a man she despised. Compared to her ineffectual husband, Holmes was a dashing figure—a bold, dynamic businessman, dapper and glib. And the constant presence of the splendid young woman must have been an irresistible temptation to Holmes.

No one can say exactly when Julia became Holmes's mistress, though it is certain that the two were lovers by March 1891.

It is a mark of Ned's haplessness that he did not foresee the affair—particularly given the scandal that preceded it, involving his younger sister, Gertrude.

Eager to see the big city for the first time, the naive eighteen-year-old Gertie had come to visit her older brother shortly after he began working at the Castle. Dark-haired and lovely, she instantly caught the eye of Dr. Holmes. Soon thereafter, he declared his infatuation, volunteering to divorce his wife, Myrta, and take Gertie east with him to live. Shocked at the doctor's impropriety she hastened back to Muscatine, though not before informing Ned of Holmes's proposition.

Soon after his failure with Gertie, Holmes focused his attention on Julia, who proved far more receptive. Before long, Holmes had fired his drugstore cashier—an efficient but plain-featured young woman named Dietz—and installed Julia in her place. Holmes and Julia made little effort to conceal their intimacy, which became an open secret among the drugstore regulars.

Ned alone seemed oblivious of the affair, although given his jealous bent, it was more likely that he turned a willfully blind eye on his wife's infidelity. Perhaps—having found status and contentment for the first time in his career—he was afraid to jeopardize his position as the manager of Holmes's thriving shop. In the end, however, even he could not ignore the situation—particularly after several ostensibly well-meaning acquaintances took him aside one day to alert him of his wife's scandalous behavior.

Forced into an ugly confrontation with Julia, Ned demanded that she break off her relationship with Holmes at once, threatening to leave her unless she complied. When she flatly refused, Ned had no choice.

In March 1891, he moved out of the third-floor flat, spending the first night sleeping downstairs on the floor of Holmes's barbershop. Soon afterward, he took an apartment downtown and secured a new job at the H. Purdy Company.

For a few months, hoping that she would finally come to her senses, he kept in close touch with his wife and their child. When it finally became apparent that she had no intention of ending her affair, he sued for divorce.

A few weeks later, Ned left Chicago to start his life anew. Eventually, he would take another wife and open a series of small-town jewelry shops, whose successive and predictable failure never seemed to discourage him from trying yet again.

Long before Ned Conner remarried, however, Holmes had grown tired of Julia.

Strong-willed and ambitious, Julia had no intention of being relegated to the role of Holmes's kept woman. She regarded herself as his partner, not his concubine, and insisted on taking a more active part in his affairs. She wanted Holmes to make her his bookkeeper and to send her to a local business college so that she could master the intricacies of accounting. Holmes agreed to both proposals.

By then, however, he had already resolved to rid himself of Julia. Her purposeful, independent spirit—so refreshingly different, at first, from the meek submissiveness of the other women he had known—had grown tiresome to him. He was also unhappy about her deepening involvement in his affairs. But most galling of all was a development that occurred sometime in November 1891, when Julia announced that she was pregnant and expected Holmes to marry her.

Evidence suggests that, when Holmes refused, Julia reminded him of how much she already knew about a number of his more questionable dealings. Holmes got the point. He agreed to divorce Myrta and marry Julia—but only on one condition.

He already had a child by Myrta—a two-year-old daughter named Lucy, to whom he paid periodic visits. And, of course, in marrying Julia, he would be adopting little Pearl as his own. He was not prepared to assume any additional burdens.

He would make Julia his wife, he declared. But only if she agreed to a voluntary abortion. He would perform it himself.

Julia was initially horrified at the idea, though Holmes finally won her over, assuring her that the procedure was perfectly safe. He had performed it many times during his medical school days in Ann Arbor, on behalf of fellow students who had gotten local girls pregnant.

Holmes thought it best to proceed at once, though Julia kept finding reasons to delay. Finally, they agreed on a date—December 24, Christmas Eve, 1891.

Holmes spent several hours late that afternoon making his preparations in the basement, where the operation was to take place. By sunset, Julia was in a state of such extreme agitation that she could not bring herself to put Pearl to bed.

Holmes offered to do it.

Leaving Julia huddled in a chair in his bedchamber—a knitted shawl thrown over her shoulders—Holmes proceeded down the dim-lit hallway to the little apartment Pearl and Julia shared.

Before he reached the apartment, however, he stopped at his office, where he removed a bottle of colorless liquid and a cotton cloth from a locked drawer in his desk.

Fifteen minutes later, he returned to his bedchamber. Pearl had gone right to sleep, he assured Julia. He was sure she wouldn't awaken anytime soon.

Then, putting an arm about the shivering woman, he led her to a hidden staircase whose existence she had never suspected and ushered her down to the murk of the cellar, where his subterranean laboratory awaited.

9

But woe to the riches and skill thus obtained,
Woe to the wretch that would injure the dead,
And woe to his portion whose fingers are stained
With the red drops of life that he cruelly shed.

—Anonymous, *Ballad on William Burke*

In January 1892, H. H. Holmes discovered that one of his employees—a machinist named Charles M. Chappell—possessed a highly specialized skill: mounting human skeletons.

Chappell had acquired this unusual ability several years earlier while working for a contractor named A. L. Goode, who had rented an office at 513 State Street—the same building occupied by the Bennett Medical College. Goode later testified that "it was nothing unusual to see bodies brought to that building for dissection, and then the bones articulated." Apparently, Chappell—a jack-of-all-trades with a quenchless curiosity about manual skills—had become fascinated with skeletal articulation and had managed to pick up some firsthand experience in the college anatomy lab.

It had been years since Chappell had worked with anatomical specimens. He had begun doing odd jobs at the Castle in the fall of 1890, after answering an ad Holmes had placed in the papers. Six months later, Holmes broached the subject of the skeletons. When Chappell admitted that he did indeed have some practice at articulating human bones, Holmes led him upstairs to a dimly lit room on the second floor of the Castle.

There, stretched out on a table, was a partially dissected cadaver. Chappell could tell that the corpse was that of a woman, though, to his eyes, it looked more "like a jackrabbit that had been skinned by splitting the skin down the face and rolling it back off the entire body," as he later described it. "In some places," Chappell went on to explain, "considerable flesh had been taken off."

Holmes offered to pay Chappell $36 to finish stripping the corpse of its flesh and to prepare the skeleton. Chappell— who evidently assumed that Dr. Holmes had been performing a postmortem examination on a deceased patient— readily agreed. That night, a steamer trunk containing the corpse was delivered to Chappell's house by Holmes's brusque, rawboned assistant.

A week later, Chappell returned the cleaned and articulated skeleton to Dr. Holmes and collected his money, happy for the extra work.

Holmes was happy, too. Within a week, he had transported the skeleton to the Hahnemann Medical College and sold it for nearly $200.

The skeleton remained at the medical school for only a few months before it was appropriated by a surgeon named Pauling, who proudly displayed it in his private offices at home. The mounted specimen was indeed an exceptional object. In all his years of practice, Dr. Pauling had never seen a female skeleton that stood nearly six feet tall.

She must have been a fine figure of a woman when she was alive, Dr. Pauling occasionally remarked to a visitor. Gazing at her bleached remains, he sometimes found himself wondering what it was—pneumonia? consumption? childbirth?—that had killed her.

10

The bride, after completing her education, was employed as a stenographer in the County Recorder's office. From there she went to Dwight, and from there to Chicago, where she met her fate.

—from the newspaper notice
announcing Emeline Cigrand's
marriage, December 7, 1892

Like other celebrity doctors, before and since, who have grown rich marketing revolutionary health regimens, Leslie Enraught Keeley owed his fame less to the proven virtues of his program than to his talent for self-promotion. Indeed, no evidence exists that his famous Keeley Cure for alcoholism (also known as the Gold Cure) was based on any research or experimentation whatsoever. Nevertheless, nearly a half million Americans eventually subjected themselves to the remedy. Many of them even managed to persuade themselves that the method really worked.

Born in Ireland in 1834, Keeley grew up in New York, graduated from the Rush Medical School in Chicago, and settled permanently in Illinois after serving in the Union Army medical corps during the Civil War. In 1880, he proclaimed that he had not only identified the root cause of alcoholism but also invented a surefire cure.

According to Keeley, problem drinking was a disease produced by alcoholic poisoning of the nerve cells. The remedy consisted of a strict dietary regimen accompanied by regular injections of "bichloride of gold." Though Keeley never revealed the contents of this dubious potion, experts in the history of alcoholism have surmised that it was concocted of gold salts and vegetable compounds.

Shortly after making his announcement, he founded the first Keeley Institute, a prairie sanitarium located in Dwight, Illinois, seventy-five miles southwest of Chicago. Keeley's big break came in 1891, when the *Chicago Tribune* published a glowing series on his Gold Cure. Before long, thousands of alcoholics—desperate to break the hold of "demon rum" on their lives—began flocking to Dwight. Keeley was quick to capitalize on this publicity, sending "graduates" of the Institute (as they were grandiloquently called) on lecture tours around the states, creating a nationwide Keeley League whose detoxicated membership met in annual conventions, and even organizing the wives of former patients into a women's auxiliary group, known as the Ladies' Bichloride of Gold Club. By the turn of the century, every state in the union had at least one Keeley Institute.

The original sanitarium in Dwight, however, remained the hub of his empire, attracting drunkards by the thousands. And among the many patients who checked into the Institute in the spring of 1892, hoping to rid themselves of their ruinous addiction, was Benjamin Freelon Pitezel.

Since a stay at the Institute was not cheap by the standards of the day—$100 for the full, four-week program—it seems likely that Pitezel's treatment was subsidized, if not paid for entirely, by his employer, H. H. Holmes. That Holmes was ready to foot the bill for such a costly procedure is a mark not only of the close personal relationship that the two men had established by then, but also of Pitezel's invaluable worth as Holmes's accomplice and tool.

When Pitezel returned to Englewood in early April 1892, he appeared to be a different man, a walking testimonial to the truth of Keeley's claims—sober, well-groomed, and healthier than he'd looked in years. But like many other presumably gold-cured alcoholics—whose high rate of relapse eventually destroyed Keeley's credibility—he found it impossible to stay on the wagon. Within a few months of his return from Dwight, he looked every bit as seedy as he had before he'd left, and his breath smelled as strongly of drink.

Even so, Holmes may well have felt that his investment in Pitezel's failed reformation had not been entirely wasted. For Ben had brought back something else besides his short-lived sobriety.

He had brought back a description of Emeline Cigrand.

She was (so Pitezel reported) a tall, shapely blonde whose beauty was a match for Julia Conner's. If anything, Emeline Cigrand was even lovelier. After all, when Holmes had met his former mistress, she was already twenty-seven and twice a mother. But Emeline Cigrand was pristine—a dewy twenty-four-year-old whose innocence was nearly as palpable as the perfume of a flower.

A native of Lafayette, Indiana, Emeline had worked for a year as a stenographer at the Tippecanoe County Recorder's office before going to work at Dwight in July, 1891. She had been there for less than a year when Pitezel checked in. Captivated by her beauty, he struck up an acquaintance with the young woman and did his best to dazzle her with his importance. He represented himself as the partner of Dr. H. H. Holmes, one of Chicago's most prominent businessmen. Emeline, who had never visited the great metropolis—indeed, had never been to a city bigger than Lafayette—was suitably impressed.

Back in Englewood, Pitezel rhapsodized about Emeline to Holmes, who wasted little time in luring the young woman to his Castle.

Within a week of Pitezel's return, Holmes wrote to Emeline, offering her a job as his private secretary at a salary of $18 per week—a 50 percent increase over the wage Dr. Keeley was paying her. In May 1892, the young woman bid farewell to her friends at Dwight and journeyed to Englewood, where she rented a room in a boardinghouse only a block away from the Castle.

Holmes set about seducing her with his usual energy and determination. He bought her flowers, took her sight-seeing in the city, treated her to pretty trinkets—hair ribbons, a tortoiseshell comb, a cameo brooch—at Marshall Field's.

Soon, he was squiring her to the theater and springing for costly dinners at fashionable downtown restaurants. They spent Sunday afternoons strolling around Englewood or bicycling in the park. Emeline took to the new sport with such enthusiasm that Holmes presented her with her own Pope two-wheeler.

By the middle of the summer, she had become his mistress. Even a casual observer could see that (as one of the Castle's tenants later testified) "the relations between Holmes and Miss Cigrand were not strictly those of employer and employee."

Apart from such testimony, little is known about the details of their affair, though circumstantial evidence strongly suggests that, by early fall of 1892, she expected him to marry her. Indeed, he appears to have encouraged her to communicate the happy news to her relatives and friends. However, he insisted—presumably for complicated legal reasons involving his divorce from Myrta—that she refer to him by an alias: Robert E. Phelps.

Throughout the fall, Emeline corresponded frequently with her friends back in Dwight, gushing over her husband-to-be—his kindness and generosity, his wealth and position, his fine manners and gentlemanly ways. For their honeymoon, he intended to take her to Europe. To her younger sister, Philomena Ida, Emeline confided that her intended was the son of an English lord, whom they planned to visit during their trip. Possibly, they might even settle permanently abroad.

Early in October 1892, Emeline's cousins, Dr. and Mrs. B. J. Cigrand, visited Chicago and, shortly after their arrival, paid a call on Emeline. Her fiancé was not present, but she spoke warmly of his virtues. Though considerably older than herself, he was, she insisted, a "fine gentleman," "very wealthy," who had treated her with unstinting kindness. To give them a sense of his accomplishments, she took them over to the Castle, showed them the first-floor shops, and led them up to the main office on the third floor.

As it happened, Dr. Cigrand was not as impressed as Emeline had hoped. Indeed, he could not help noticing the poor construction evident throughout the interior. The winding staircase in particular struck him as a particularly shoddy piece of work, and he commented on the bad lumber it had been built with. Emeline, though put out by his response, said nothing.

The wedding of Emeline Cigrand and H. H. Holmes—planned as a strictly private, civil ceremony—was scheduled for the first week in December. Sometime in early November, Holmes presented Emeline with a dozen white envelopes and asked her to address them to her closest relatives and friends. He intended to have formal marriage announcements printed up, he explained, which he would mail out immediately after their wedding. Emeline sat down at once and penned the addresses in her fine, flowing hand.

She had no conceivable way of knowing, of course, the true purpose of Holmes's request, which did not become evident until much later. But in retrospect, its significance is clear.

By the time Holmes asked her to fill out the envelopes, he had already decided to kill her.

Why did Holmes want Emeline Cigrand dead? Like Julia Conner, she may well have known too many of his secrets, having served as his private secretary for over six months. There is also reason to think that Emeline had pressured Holmes into proposing by threatening to leave him. And Holmes was not a man who took kindly to threats.

Or perhaps Holmes's decision to do away with his young mistress signified nothing more than this: he simply felt the urge.

Sometime during the first week of December—probably on the sixth—Holmes, who was working in his office, called Emeline to his side and asked her to fetch a document from the walk-in vault next door. While Emeline searched for the papers in question, Holmes walked up to the vault, swung the heavy door shut, and spun the lock. Then he pulled up a chair, pressed his ear to the steel door, and listened intently as her shock turned to panic and, finally, to pure, primal terror.

As the minutes passed, his excitement grew so acute that he undid his trousers, exposed his rigid member, and masturbated into a pocket handkerchief until—having spent himself repeatedly—he sank back, sated, in the chair.

On December 17, 1892, Emeline's family friends received her handwritten envelopes in the mail. Inside, they found a card, printed with a simple inscription:

Mr. Robert Phelps
Miss Emeline Cigrand
Married
Wednesday, December 7th
1892
Chicago.

Emeline's hometown newspaper had already taken note of her good fortune. Ten days earlier, the paper had published the following item under the headline "Miss Cigrand Weds Robert E. Phelps": "The bride, after completing her education, was employed as a stenographer in the County Recorder's office. From there she went to Dwight, and from there to Chicago, where she met her fate. She is a lady of great intelligence and has a charming manner and a handsome appearance. She is a lady of refinement and possesses a character that is strong and pure. Her many friends see that she has exercised good judgment in selecting a husband and will heartily congratulate her."

It is striking—and grimly ironic—that the writer of this notice chose the phrase "met her fate" to refer to Emeline Cigrand's fiancé, the fictitious Mr. Phelps. Emeline had indeed met her fate in Chicago, though not in the sense that the writer intended.

It is impossible to say whether the young woman was already dead by the time this newspaper announcement appeared, though the oxygen supply in the sealed vault must surely have run out by then—particularly given the high respiration rate induced by uncontrolled hysteria. As Holmes later indicated, from the moment the full horror of her situation finally sank in, Emeline's frenzied cries and pleas continued for hours without letup. In any event, Emeline Cigrand was never seen alive again.

Not many weeks after her disappearance, the LaSalle Medical School became the owner of a new anatomical specimen: a fine female skeleton acquired from Dr. H. H. Holmes.

11

There was one strange thing that troubled me; amid the occupations or amusements of the fair, nothing was more common than for a person—whether at a feast, theatre, or church, or trafficking for wealth and honors, or whatever he might be doing, and however unseasonable the interruption—suddenly to vanish like a soap bubble, and be never more seen of his fellows.

—Nathaniel Hawthorne, "The Celestial Railroad"

A century later, the quincentennial of Columbus's landmark voyage would be marked by dissension and controversy. The master seaman would be portrayed, not as a heroic pioneer—"The Admiral of the Ocean Sea"—but as a brutal invader whose misguided expeditions brought enslavement, despoliation, and disease to the native inhabitants of the Americas.

In 1892, however, the four hundredth anniversary of Columbus's arrival in the New World was a cause for unqualified celebration. And the United States, surging with pride and strength and ambition, intended to commemorate it with the most spectacular bash the world had ever witnessed.

The idea for a World's Columbian Exposition had begun taking shape in the late 1880s. By the last year of that decade, four cities, each eager to host the extravaganza—New York, Washington, St. Louis, and Chicago—were vying hotly for the honor. But the brash Midwestern metropolis, determined to assert its claims to cultural superiority, ultimately carried the day. Supported by a $5-million kitty, a coalition of public-minded businessmen and financiers launched an aggressive lobbying campaign on behalf of their city. On April 25, 1890, President Benjamin Harrison signed a bill designating Chicago as the site of the Exposition. "America's coming-of-age party" would be staged on the shores of Lake Michigan.

To Eastern elitists, Chicago was a provincial upstart, the symbol of the nation's raw, commercial energies, colossal but crude—"hog butcher to the world" (as Carl Sandburg later described it). Cynics predicted the worst. A world's fair that reflected the host city's brazen spirit was bound to be an embarrassment—a huge, vaunting display of American vulgarity.

The skeptics fell silent when the organizers called upon the country's most eminent architects, painters, sculptors, landscapists, and engineers to design the Exposition. Schooled, for the most part, at Paris's École des Beaux-Arts, the participants shared a common ideal of harmony, order, and grandeur. "Look here, old fellow," exclaimed the renowned sculptor Augustus Saint-Gaudens after one planning session. "Do you realize that this is the greatest meeting of artists since the fifteenth century?"

Gaudens's heady belief that he was taking part in a grand aesthetic venture turned out to be fully justified. Within two years, he and his collaborators—among them the great environmental designer Frederick Law Olmsted, muralists John La Farge and Elihu Vedder, sculptor Daniel Chester French, and architects Daniel H. Burnham and Richard Morris Hunt—created a dazzling exhibition that astonished the world and had a lasting impact on the look of American cities.

On a stretch of boggy shoreline, seven miles south of central Chicago, a glorious vision took shape—a dream city of classical grace and proportion, constructed (or so it seemed) of the purest white marble. Work officially commenced in February 1891 with the clearing, filling, and grading of the land. Construction of the first of the glittering exhibition halls was under way by July of that year. All told, seven thousand laborers toiled heroically to meet the October 1892 deadline.

To Chicagoans, this miraculous architectural feat—the erection, in less than two years, of an entire utopian city on a six-hundred-acre plot of swamp—was yet another demonstration of their city's remarkable vigor and determination, a confirmation of its quintessentially American character. "During the storms of summer, through the frosts of winter," declaimed Daniel H. Burnham, chief of construction for the fair, "the little band of American boys ran the race for victory with Father Time, and won it."

Burnham had every reason to be proud, though his claim was a little overstated, since the fair was still unfinished on Dedication Day, October 21, 1892. Even so, the ceremonies were a smashing success. The festivities began with a spectacular, ten-mile-long military parade that passed through the city to the fair site. An estimated 800,000 people turned out to cheer as marching bands played, flags waved, cavalry-steeds pranced, and dignitaries rolled by in their carriages of state.

The dedication itself took place inside the Exposition's most awesome structure, the Manufactures and Liberal Arts Building, whose interior (as fair promoters never tired of pointing out) could have comfortably contained the United States Capitol, Winchester Cathedral, Saint Paul's Cathedral, Madison Square Garden, and the Great Pyramid of Gizeh—with plenty of room to spare.

Following a rousing rendition of "The Columbian March"—composed by Harvard Professor John Knowles Paine and performed by the two-hundred-forty piece Chicago Orchestra—the spectators were treated to several hours of highflown orations, interspersed with other musical selections, including Mendelssohn's "To the Sons of Arts" and the "Hallelujah Chorus" from Handel's *Messiah*. Other highlights included an awards presentation by Harlow N. Higinbotham, head of the World's Columbian Exposition Corporation, and a "light luncheon" for the assembled crowd of 140,000 (only half of whom actually managed to get something to eat in the mad scramble for the food). Not even the absence of President Harrison—who was forced to cancel his appearance when his wife fell gravely ill—detracted from the unparalleled pageantry of the event.

Another six months passed before the World's Columbian Exposition—or Chicago World's Fair, as it was otherwise known—finally opened to the public. Two hundred thousand people braved a heavy downpour to show up for the occasion. By midmorning, the rain had stopped, and the vista that stretched before the surging crowd seemed—even in the dreariness of that overcast day—overwhelming in its splendor.

Like millions of others who poured into the Exposition during the few months of its fleeting existence, the first-day visitors—even those who used language for a living—experienced a common sense of inadequacy, an inability to find words or comparisons that did justice to the grandeur of the fair. Some likened it to classical Rome, others to Venice, still others to the "New Jerusalem." The Exposition was a fairy realm, an Aladdin's wonderland, a "scene of inexpressible splendor reminding one of the gorgeous descriptions in the Arabian nights when Haroun Al Raschid was Caliph." But one particular phrase—suggestive of the celestial glories of the heavenly kingdom itself—became the most popular title by which the fair was known: the White City.

At the heart of the White City lay the Court of Honor. Standing within its awesome precincts, fairgoers beheld a breathtaking vista of glittering palaces, snowy colonnades, soaring arches, and gleaming domes—all flanking a formal basin 2,500 feet long. Colossal statues rose from the water at either end of the basin. To the east stood Daniel Chester French's "The Republic"—a towering, toga-garbed figure, holding aloft an eagle and a victory cap. The opposite end was dominated by Frederick MacMonnies's "Columbia Fountain"—a monumental sculpture depicting the figure of Columbia, sailing triumphantly over the waters in a great barge manned by allegorical representations of Science, Industry, Agriculture, Commerce, and the Arts.

But these splendors of the Court were by no means the only such wonders the fair had to offer. Every acre of the White City was filled with similarly stunning examples of architectural and sculptural opulence—from Louis Henri Sullivan's Transportation Building, with its magnificent Golden Door, to Henry Ives Cobb's "Spanish-Romanesque" Fisheries Building, to Charles B. Atwood's Palace of the Fine Arts, which writer Julian Hawthorne (Nathaniel's son) unequivocally declared "the most beautiful piece of architecture in the world."

For those who craved less enriching fare, the Exposition offered the garish pleasures of the Midway Plaisance, a mile-long sideshow featuring such exotic attractions as a South Sea islands village, a Japanese bazaar, an encampment of Dahomey cannibals, the World Congress of Beauties ("40 Ladies from 40 Nations"), and the Street of Cairo, where an Arabian lovely called Little Egypt performed her notorious *danse du ventre*—more commonly known as the hootchy-kootchy.

Even those moralists most scandalized by Little Egypt's "lascivious contorting," however, would not have missed a visit to the Midway's other main attraction, the giant circle of rotating steel that carried riders 250 feet into the air for a view of the entire White City. An awesome engineering achievement, the colossal wheel would become a staple of amusement parks, where it continues to be known by the name of its inventor, George W. Ferris.

A pilgrimage to the White City became an overriding dream for countless Americans. On some days, as many as three-quarters of a million visitors attended, at fifty cents apiece. People mortgaged their farms and dipped into their life savings for a trip to Chicago. "Well, Susan," one old man reportedly remarked to his wife, "it paid even if it did take all the burial money." After viewing the sights, the novelist Hamlin Garland dashed off an urgent letter to his elderly parents back home in Dakota: "Sell the cook stove and come. You *must* see the Fair." Altogether, more than 27 million people attended the World's Columbian Exposition in the six months of its existence, from May 1 through October 30, 1893.

For the tourists who flocked to the fair from every corner of the nation—and, indeed, from countries throughout the world—Chicago offered all kinds of accommodations. Visitors on a spree could treat themselves to a stay at a luxury hotel such as the Great Northern, the Leland, or the Richelieu. Others, more restricted by their budgets, were happy to settle for a well-kept boardinghouse.

Such was the demand for decent lodgings that anyone with a clean room to spare could pick up a few extra dollars by renting a bed to a desperate out-of-towner. A landlord with even a few empty flats at his disposal could realize a tidy profit in a hurry.

H. H. Holmes had two entire floors of vacant rooms just perfect for transients.

And he meant to make a killing.

For several years—virtually from the moment that Congress selected Chicago as the Exposition site—Holmes had been laying his plans. The third floor of the Castle had undergone extensive renovations in preparation for the big event. As soon as opening day arrived, he began running newspaper advertisements for his "World's Fair Hotel."

No one can say exactly how many fairgoers Holmes lured to the Castle between May and October 1893, though he appears to have filled the place to capacity on most nights. It is also unclear how many of these travelers—slumbering soundly in their rooms after a long day at the fair, perhaps dreaming of its endless enchantments—never awoke again.

We do, however, know something about the likely manner of their deaths.

By means of the control valves hidden in his private quarters, Holmes could fill any of the second- or third-floor bedchambers with asphyxiating gas. Submerged in sleep, the occupants would never have heard the quiet hissing from the wall jets as the deadly vapor suffused the darkness of their rooms.

Chloroform was another important part of Holmes's murder repertoire. To unlock a door with his master key, steal silently across the floor, and extinguish a life with a saturated rag was a skill that Holmes had perfected through long years of practice.

Disposing of the evidence was an equally simple matter of dumping the limp bodies down the greased chute to his basement laboratory. Though some of the corpses ended up as medical specimens, the majority were obliterated in his private crematorium or acid vat, along with whatever personal effects Holmes had no use for. The more profitable items—cash, jewelry, watches, and so on—became part of Holmes's assets.

A few of the corpses—all of them female, none older than twenty-five—served to satisfy those hungers that, for beings like Holmes, the flesh of living women cannot ever allay.

Holmes would eventually confess to only a single slaying of a fairgoer. Others have claimed that the number was significantly higher. According to certain accounts, as many as fifty tourists who took rooms at the Castle never returned home from their trip to the Chicago World's Fair.

The World's Columbian Exposition came to an end at sunset, October 31, 1893, closing to the somber strains of Beethoven's "Funeral March." Gala ceremonies—equivalent to those that had marked Dedication Day—had been planned for the occasion but were canceled at the last moment. Two days earlier, Chicago's sixty-nine-year-old, five-term mayor, Carter Harrison, had delivered a speech foreseeing a glorious future for the city. "Chicago has chosen a star," he proclaimed. "I intend to live for more than half a century still, and at the end of that time, London will be trembling lest Chicago shall surpass her, and New York shall say, 'Let us go to the metropolis of America!'"

That evening, while the weary mayor rested at home in his housecoat and slippers, the doorbell rang. When Harrison answered, he was shot dead by an embittered office-seeker who had failed to receive a political appointment. The killing cast a heavy pall over the fair's official closing.

Just a few months later, on January 8, 1894, a fire destroyed three major Exposition buildings, the Casino, the Peristyle, and the Music Hall. Six months later, an even more devastating blaze reduced its most glorious structures—including the awesome Manufactures and Liberal Arts Building—to ashes.

At the height of the fair, few visitors would have believed just how flimsy the White City really was. Dazzled by its beauty, they would have found it hard to credit that its white-marble wonders—its palaces and pavilions, monuments and museums—were actually made of staff, a compound of plaster and fibrous material laid over a temporary wood-and-metal framework. Among the many lessons that the World's Columbian Exposition taught, one—completely unintended by its creators—had to do with the duplicity of appearances.

But, of course, this was a bitter truth that a number of fair visitors—perhaps as many as fifty—had already discovered in the dark heart of Dr. Holmes's murder castle.

12

Deceit is in the heart of them that imagine evil.

—Proverbs 12:20

Deception was so deeply ingrained in H. H. Holmes's character that he was incapable of telling the truth about the simplest matter. Lies were not merely the tools of his trade, as they are for every con man and swindler. They were the reflection of his profoundly psychopathic nature. Nothing he said could be trusted or taken at face value. Even when it suited his purpose to stick close to the facts, his words were infected with falsehood.

As a result, it is extremely difficult, if not impossible, to establish some of the most basic facts about Holmes's life—such as the precise circumstances under which he first met Minnie Williams.

According to his own testimony, they had been introduced either in New York City in 1888, where he was engaged in some unspecified dealings under the alias Edward Hatch, or in Boston one year later, where he was traveling under the pseudonym Harry Gordon. On other occasions, he claimed that they had gotten to know each other even earlier, during a business trip that had taken him through Mississippi sometime around 1886.

At still another point, he insisted that he had never laid eyes on her until the day a local employment agency dispatched her to his office in response to his request for a stenographer.

One fact, however, is unquestionable. In March 1893, Minnie Williams showed up in Chicago, where she became Holmes's private secretary and, within a matter of weeks, his mistress.

Minnie's readiness to enter into such a relationship with Holmes was not, as some detractors later alleged, a mark of her moral laxity or worldliness. Quite the contrary. Everyone who knew her testified to her extreme naïveté. "She didn't seem to know a great deal," was the way one acquaintance put it. This guilelessness was in keeping with her physical appearance. Short-legged and plump, with light brown ringlets framing her smooth, chubby face, she resembled nothing so much as an overgrown baby.

Minnie's air of simple sweetness was, perhaps, her most appealing feature. Meeting her for the first time, Holmes's confederates—not only Ben Pitezel but also Pat Quinlan, the Castle's janitor and jack-of-all-trades—were struck by her comparative plainness. As far as looks went, they agreed, she simply couldn't hold a candle to Holmes's previous lovers—particularly the splendid Julia Conner and the stunning Emeline Cigrand.

Minnie Williams did, however, possess one attribute that more than compensated for her physical limitations as far as Holmes was concerned.

She was the heiress to a considerable fortune.

Tragedy had struck Minnie's life when she was still a child. Just six years after her birth in 1866, her father had been killed in a train wreck and her heartbroken mother had died shortly thereafter. The orphan had been taken into the household of a kindly uncle in Dallas, Texas, who raised Minnie as though she were his own child. Another uncle living in Jackson, Mississippi—the Reverend C. W. Black, editor of the Methodist *Christian Advocate*—had adopted Minnie's younger sister, Nannie.

When Minnie was twenty, her uncle sent her to study at the Boston Conservatory of Music and Elocution. She graduated three years later, but the occasion was marred by misfortune. Just days before she was to receive her degree, her uncle succumbed to a lingering illness.

Even in death, however, he continued to serve as her

benefactor, bequeathing her some property he owned in Fort Worth, valued at over $40,000.

By May 1893—when Minnie and Holmes were already sharing a furnished flat a 1220 Wrightwood Avenue—even that impressive sum would not have been sufficient to relieve Holmes of his debts. To his Englewood neighbors, he continued to seem like a man of means—a dedicated businessman whose hard work and enterprise had brought him all the trappings of success. They had no way of knowing what corruptions those trappings concealed. Or that the trappings themselves had been acquired through the most devious and underhanded means. Holmes's Castle and all its furnishings, the fixtures in his stores, the very clothing on his back—all were the fruits not, as his neighbors believed, of Holmes's tireless industry, but of his frenzied double-dealings.

Ironically, Holmes possessed the sort of boldness, savvy, and boundless ambition that might well have earned him the financial success he so frantically craved. But the perversions of his nature made it impossible for him to employ his powers for legitimate ends. His colossal energies (when they weren't being misspent on his countless frauds, scams, and far more sinister pursuits) were devoted to outwitting his creditors.

By 1893, however—when hard times hit the country in the wake of a major financial panic—a small army of those creditors had closed ranks and was moving in on him. It would require desperate measures to elude them.

Persuading Minnie to sign over her property to him posed no problem for the smooth-tongued Dr. Holmes. Indeed, the young woman's simple-heartedness was so extreme that even he seemed touched by it, offering tribute on a later occasion to her "innocent and childlike nature." Of course, having title to the Fort Worth real estate still left Holmes with the problem of converting it into cash. More than eight hundred miles of country separated him from his new acquisition.

And another obstacle, too, stood between him and the

money he so urgently needed—Minnie's younger sister, Nannie.

Though the two had been raised in different parts of the country, they had renewed their relationship in the years preceding Minnie's move to Chicago. In 1889, shortly after her graduation from the Boston Conservatory, Minnie had been invited to spend the summer at the home of her surviving uncle, Rev. C. W. Black. There, she and Nannie had become reacquainted, each discovering in the other not only an affectionate sister but a sympathetic friend.

When Minnie was required to return to Dallas to sign some documents relating to her departed uncle's estate, Nannie had traveled with her. Nannie was so taken with Texas that she decided to remain there, while Minnie returned to Boston and later moved to Chicago. That had been in 1890. Since that time, they had visited each other periodically and maintained a steady correspondence.

As a result, Nannie knew all about Holmes. In one of Minnie's very first letters from Chicago, she had rhapsodized over the "handsome, wealthy, and intelligent" gentleman who had hired her as his personal secretary. Within a matter of weeks, she had communicated the remarkable news that she and her employer, Dr. Henry Howard Holmes—or "Harry" as she invariably referred to him—had become engaged.

During their trip together to Dallas, Nannie had been made privy to all the details of Minnie's inheritance. She had also discovered just how unsophisticated a person her sister was. As the ward of a Methodist minister, Nannie had received an upbringing even more sheltered than Minnie's, but she had been blessed with a much shrewder sense of the world. She was keenly aware that her guileless—and suddenly wealthy—older sibling would make an exceptionally easy target for an unscrupulous suitor.

In the evenings—seated across from each other at a restaurant table or sharing some quiet moments alone in their flat—Holmes questioned Minnie closely about her relatives. Minnie was touched by her lover's curiosity about her life and told him all about her family—especially her dear younger sister.

Holmes was quick to realize that Nannie posed a serious threat to his intentions. Should an unfortunate accident befall Minnie Williams, Nannie's suspicions were sure to be aroused.

And so, in May 1893, Holmes suggested to Minnie that she write her younger sister and invite her to come see the fair.

During the second week of June, Nannie made the long trip from Midlothian, Texas, to Chicago, where she was met at the train station by her beaming, moon-faced sister and the dapper Dr. Holmes, who greeted her with a brotherly warmth that immediately disarmed her.

Nannie was so excited by her first glimpse of the great metropolis that she insisted on doing some sightseeing right away. She and her hosts spent several hours taking in the sights of downtown Chicago before Holmes and Minnie escorted her back to Englewood and helped her settle in. To maintain appearances, Holmes had previously moved his personal belongings back to the Castle, so that Minnie could share the Wrightwood Avenue flat with her sister for the duration of the latter's stay.

If Nannie had come to Chicago harboring doubts about Holmes, they soon disappeared, melted away by the force of his radiant charm. Within days of her arrival, she was already referring to him as "Brother Harry."

On July 3, 1893, Brother Harry took his "girls" to the fair. Though Minnie had already attended the Exposition with Holmes a few weeks before, she was giddy with excitement as she made her way around the White City again. Nannie, like virtually all first-time visitors, seemed overwhelmed by its sheer size and spectacle.

The trio spent a delightful day at the Exposition, squeezing in as many experiences as time would allow. They strolled along the spacious esplanades of the Court of Honor; wound their way through the seemingly endless galleries of the Art Palace; floated in a gondola along sparkling canals; marveled at the world's largest gold nugget and the life-size statue of Lot's wife, carved from an enormous block of salt; rode the Ferris wheel; visited the aquarium; viewed Thomas Edison's Tower of Light; dined on Bavarian cuisine; and in the evening watched a spectacular fireworks display from the roof of the Manufactures and Liberal Arts Building.

The next morning, at Holmes's prompting, Nannie wrote a letter to her uncle in Jackson, describing her trip to the fair and apprising him of another, even grander adventure upon which she was about to embark. "Sister, Brother Harry, and myself will go to Milwaukee," she wrote, "and will go to Old Orchard Beach, Maine, by way of the St. Lawrence River. We'll visit two weeks in Maine, then on to New York. Brother Harry thinks I am talented. He wants me to look around about studying art. Then we will sail for Germany by way of London and Paris. If I like it, I will stay and study art. Brother Harry says you need never trouble any more about me, financially or otherwise. He and sister will see to me."

Later that same day, Holmes proposed to Minnie that she remain behind at the flat, attending to some pressing household chores. Meanwhile, he would take Nannie—who had yet to set foot inside the Castle—over to Sixty-third and Wallace and give her a guided tour of his building.

After the fairyland splendors of the Exposition, Holmes's Castle must have appeared drab, even a bit dingy, to Nannie. Just three years after its construction, the building already gave off a vague air of decay.

Still, it was a substantial piece of property. Clearly, her brother-in-law-to-be had done well for himself.

That afternoon, Holmes's Castle would have seemed utterly lifeless and abandoned—the ground-floor shops closed for the holiday, the upstairs rooms vacant while their tenants were off at the fair, reveling in the July Fourth festivities. By the time Holmes finished leading Nannie around the dim, labyrinthine passageways, she must have felt slightly disoriented.

As they got ready to leave, Holmes paused abruptly, as though struck by a sudden realization. He needed to fetch something from his vault, he explained—an important business document that he kept stored inside a safe-deposit box. It would only take a moment.

Grasping Nannie by the hand, he led her toward the vault.

A short time later, Holmes reappeared at the flat. Nannie was not with him. He told Minnie that he had decided to treat both his girls to dinner at a restaurant on Stewart Avenue. Nannie was waiting at the Castle. They would pick her up on the way.

Minnie hurriedly changed her clothing, chattering excitedly all the while about their impending trip to Europe.

When she was ready, Holmes offered her his arm. Then he led her away to join her sister.

13

In the remarkable character of his achievements as an assassin we are apt to lose sight of Holmes' singular skill and daring as a bigamist.

—H. B. Irving, *A Book of Remarkable Criminals*
(1918)

H.H. Holmes was in love.

He had met Georgiana Yoke in March 1893, but during the months of his involvement with the Williams sisters, he'd been unable to pay her anything more than an occasional visit. As soon as Minnie and Nannie disappeared from his life, however, he began to pay her serious court.

A petite, twenty-three-year-old blonde, Georgiana was not conventionally pretty. She had a sharp nose and chin, and her blue eyes were so large that a few of her cattier acquaintances described them as "disfiguring." But a lively intelligence shone in those eyes, and the gaiety of her smile seemed to radiate from some deep core of well-being. She was one of those women whose vibrancy invests them with so much charm that even their imperfections seem appealing.

For a strictly raised young lady from a small Midwestern town, Georgiana possessed a bold and adventurous spirit. She had moved from her family home in Franklin, Indiana, two years earlier, determined to experience the glamour of the great metropolis before settling down to marriage. She was working as a salesgirl at Schlesinger & Meyer's department store when Holmes first saw her.

Little is known about their courtship, though it evidently proceeded at a rapid pace. Holmes was fervent in pursuit; she was beguiled by his ardor, smooth manners, and charm. A physiognomist, noting the dimension of her eyes, would have ascribed a high degree of perceptiveness to Georgiana—and for the most part his assessment would have been correct. But even so discerning a woman as she failed to see through Holmes's attractive facade.

By early fall, they were already engaged. Like all lovers, the two spent many tender moments together, learning all about each other's lives. In Holmes's case, of course, virtually everything he told Georgiana was a lie. Both his parents, he claimed, were dead—his mother of some unspecified disease, his father of a foot injury that had developed into lockjaw. His siblings, too, had all passed away at an early age, leaving Holmes "the last of his race."

His closest relative was his mother's brother, a childless bachelor named Henry Mansfield Howard, who had a special fondness for his one surviving nephew. He had promised to bequeath Holmes all his property, but only on one condition—that Holmes assume the name of his uncle, who (as Holmes put it) "had no son of his own to perpetuate the family appellation."

Georgiana seems to have accepted this story unquestioningly. She could never have guessed the actual reason for the elaborate lie—that her betrothed thought it best to commit polygamy under a new identity. As H. H. Holmes, he was already married to Myrta Belknap of Wilmette, while under his real name, Herman Mudgett, he was still legally wed to Clara Lovering of Tilton, New Hampshire.

The wedding was set for the winter. In the meantime, Holmes told Georgiana, he had some out-of-town business to attend to.

With his enemies closing in on him, the Castle had become not a stronghold but a trap. By the time of his engagement, Holmes was already plotting his escape. The building and all its contents would have to be abandoned.

But Holmes was not the sort of man to let so much valuable property go to waste. He was possessed of a monstrous audacity. Even as the victims of his financial deceit were uniting against him, he was busily contriving still another fraud.

Sometime close to midnight on a crisp Saturday in October—just a few weeks after Georgiana Yoke accepted Holmes's proposal of marriage—the top floor of the Castle burst into flames. Holmes was not present at the time, having left his confederate Pat Quinlan alone in the building with explicit directions, a bucket of coal oil, and a box of friction matches. By the time the fire company arrived and extinguished the blaze, the entire third floor had been destroyed, though the damage to the second story was minimal and the ground-level shops were essentially unharmed.

Holmes—who had taken out close to $25,000 worth of fire insurance with four separate companies—immediately tried to collect on his policies. An investigator named F. G. Cowie, however, had gotten wind of Holmes's increasingly dubious reputation. Inspecting the premises, he uncovered highly suspicious evidence, including signs that the fire had sprung up simultaneously in several different places—a strong indication that it had been deliberately set. For unexplained reasons, Holmes escaped criminal charges, though his claims were, of course, rejected.

But Holmes knew of more than one way to bilk an insurance company. Disappointed but undeterred, he immediately inaugurated another swindle. The plan he had in mind—considerably more complicated than his arson fraud—required a willing and trustworthy accomplice.

In his faithful lackey, Benjamin Pitezel, he had the perfect stooge.

Long before he decided to set his new plan into motion, Holmes had laid out its details to Pitezel. A large insurance policy would be taken out on Pitezel's life. After allowing a few months to pass, the two men would stage a violent accident. Pitezel would go into hiding while a badly disfigured corpse was substituted in his place and identified as his remains. The insurance company would make good on its policy and the two men would split the proceeds.

The plan was simple in concept but a good deal trickier to pull off. Among other things, its success depended on the acquisition of a substitute cadaver. But Holmes—who had long experience in such matters—insisted that he would have no trouble in that regard.

Indeed, he already knew exactly how and where to obtain the perfect corpse for his purposes. But this was a detail that he thought it prudent not to share with his accomplice.

And so the scheme was launched. On November 9, 1893, the Fidelity Mutual Life Association of Philadelphia, Pennsylvania, insured Benjamin F. Pitezel's life in the sum of $10,000.

Holmes's efforts to burn down his Castle finally lit a match under his creditors. In mid-November several dozen of them banded together and retained a lawyer, who presented Holmes with an ultimatum. If Holmes did not immediately come up with nearly $50,000 to settle his accounts, a warrant would be sworn out for his arrest.

The bill Holmes had been running up for over five years had finally come due. But of course, he had no intention of paying it.

On November 22, a physician named E. H. Robinson ran into Holmes on Van Buren Street and engaged him in a brief conversation. That same day, Pitezel dropped by a local jewelry shop and chatted with its owner.

It was the last time either Holmes or his minion was seen in Englewood.

From time to time over the next year, Holmes would show up in the Chicago area for a brief visit with his wife, Myrta, and their young daughter, Lucy.

Pitezel would never return again.

Part 3

Blood
Money

14

> It didn't take me long to make up my mind that these
> liars warn't no kings nor dukes at all, but just low-
> down humbugs and frauds.
>
> —Mark Twain, *Adventures of Huckleberry Finn*

Given his educational background, it is not surprising that
Dr. Holmes was a highly literate man who appreciated good
writing and possessed his own facile skill with a pen. Like
millions of Americans, he relished the books of Mark Twain
and bore a special affection for the character of Colonel
Beriah Sellers, the grandiose schemer of *The Gilded Age*.
Though he could chuckle at Sellers's extravagances, Holmes
nevertheless seemed to identify with Twain's creation, referring to him fondly on various occasions. In the wildly enterprising Sellers—symbol of the get-rich-quick spirit of the
day—Holmes evidently perceived a kindred soul.

In the months following his flight from Chicago, however,
Holmes's real kinship seemed to be not with Colonel Sellers
but with another of Twain's characters. Moving from state to
state, working increasingly desperate frauds, he and Pitezel
seemed like citified versions of the Duke and Dauphin—
those small-time scalawags from *Huckleberry Finn*, who rove
around the countryside, fleecing yokels, "skinning" orphans,
and staying just one step ahead of the law.

Sometime late in January 1894, the two of them showed
up in Texas. By then, Holmes had acquired another wife.

On January 9, under the name of Henry Mansfield Howard, he had married Georgiana Yoke in Denver, Colorado, the Reverend Mr. Wilcox officiating.

Nearly a year would pass before Georgiana was forced to confront the bitter truth about Holmes. Until then, she persisted in seeing him as a prosperous businessman whose interests required him to travel throughout the United States. When Holmes proposed that they combine business with pleasure by honeymooning down in Texas, Georgiana—who took tremendous pride in her new husband's success, as well as in her own role as helpmeet—agreed without hesitation.

Shortly thereafter, Holmes and his bride arrived in Fort Worth, accompanied by Benjamin Pitezel.

As far as Georgiana knew, Holmes had come to Texas to take possession of a valuable ranch bequeathed to him by his Denver uncle. In reality, he and Pitezel were there to milk as much money as possible from the property Holmes had finagled from his former mistress Minnie Williams.

Given his larcenous intentions, Holmes considered it prudent to adopt yet another identity. Checking into the fanciest hotel in Fort Worth, he registered himself and Georgiana as Mr. and Mrs. H. M. Pratt. Pitezel took the adjoining room under the name Benton T. Lyman. When Georgiana asked the reason for the ruse, her husband had a ready explanation.

Through business associates in Fort Worth, he had learned that a group of squatters had taken possession of his uncle's unoccupied ranch. Holmes was now faced with the unwelcome task of evicting them. Though squatters' rights received more serious recognition in the South than elsewhere, Holmes had no doubt that his efforts to reclaim his lawful property would ultimately succeed. Still, certain precautions were necessary. He was dealing with desperate men—and down here in Texas, a bullet was still a traditional means for settling such disputes. As a result, Holmes thought it best to proceed under the protective cloak of an alias.

Georgiana seems to have swallowed this story without blinking—as she would a hundred other lies her husband would feed her over the course of the next ten months. She was not an especially gullible woman, and her readiness to accept Holmes's most brazen fabrications says a great deal not only about his smooth plausibility but about the self-deluding nature of love.

Posing as Pratt and Lyman—two wealthy Northerners who had decided to resettle in Fort Worth—Holmes and Pitezel set about fleecing a score of local bankers and businessmen. Minnie Williams's property consisted of a large, vacant lot on the corner of Second and Russell streets, not far from the Tarrant County courthouse. Employing the scam that had succeeded so well in Chicago, Holmes commenced construction of an imposing three-story office building on the site, acquiring materials and furnishings on credit, issuing fraudulent notes for the labor, and using the deed as collateral for a string of substantial loans.

By the end of two months, the pair had managed to defraud an assortment of creditors—including a prominent attorney named Sidney L. Samuels and the Farmers and Mechanics' National Bank—out of more than $20,000.

Another embezzler, having made such a killing, might have taken the money and run. But it was in Fort Worth that a certain foolhardiness began to surface in Holmes. Like other psychopaths, he had always possessed a craving for risk and a brazen disregard of danger. Now, his characteristic audacity was turning into sheer, self-defeating recklessness. He began to commit serious mistakes.

Sometime in March, by means that remain obscure, he and his partner managed to purloin a freight-car load of blooded horses, which they shipped off to Chicago. This time, their larceny was discovered. Holmes and Pitezel found themselves facing a charge that Texans did not take lightly—horse theft.

With the law only a step behind, the pair—with Georgiana in tow—fled Fort Worth in the middle of the night. How Holmes explained this abrupt, nocturnal departure to his new bride is a matter of conjecture.

Her devotion to him never wavered—not even in St. Louis, where her faith in his fundamental rectitude was truly put to the test.

In the six months following their flight from Fort Worth,

Holmes and Pitezel remained constantly on the move, gradually migrating eastward by way of major cities: Denver, St. Louis, Memphis, Philadelphia, New York. By then, they had resolved to put their life-insurance scam into effect and were searching for the most convenient place to stage it. Along the way, they took whatever opportunities they could find to work the occasional fraud.

In St. Louis, Holmes's increasingly careless behavior finally caught up with him. There, he found himself in an unwonted situation—one that he had managed to avoid during all the years of his varied criminal career.

He landed in jail.

It happened in July. Settled briefly in St. Louis, Holmes—still going by the name of H. M. Howard—took advantage of the time by attempting one of his favorite swindles.

First, he located a tidy little pharmacy whose owner was eager to sell. Holmes purchased the store for a modest down payment, promising to come up with the balance in one month. As soon as the place was in his possession, he stocked it with supplies acquired on credit from the Merrill Drug Company.

Holmes then immediately turned around, sold off the entire inventory, and made out a phony bill of sale for the store itself to a fictitious party named Brown. When his creditors attempted to collect their money, Holmes coolly explained that the store no longer belonged to him and recommended that they get in touch with its new owner, Brown.

Apparently, Holmes believed that he could effect a leisurely escape from the city while his creditors blustered and threatened. If so, he made a serious miscalculation. On July 19, 1894, the Merrill Drug Company filed a charge with the St. Louis police, and Holmes was arrested and jailed for fraud.

Ten days later, Georgiana bailed him out. Holmes must have offered a convincing explanation for his arrest, since she seems to have regarded it as a gross miscarriage of justice.

As for Holmes, he saw the whole experience as a happy

twist of fate. Something had happened to him in jail that struck him as wonderfully fortuitous.

He had met and become acquainted with a fellow inmate, a train robber named Marion Hedgepeth.

That Holmes regarded this circumstance as such a fine piece of luck can only be interpreted as another sign of his increasingly clouded judgment. Certainly, no one who had crossed the path of Marion Hedgepeth ever counted himself lucky before.

For Marion Hedgepeth was an authentic desperado. No less an authority than William A. Pinkerton—son of the detective agency's legendary founder—described Hedgepeth as "one of the really bad men of the Old West. He was one of the worst characters I ever heard of. He was a bad man clear through."

15

A thief knows a thief as a wolf knows a wolf.

—Proverb

While other Western bandits continue to live on in story and song (or their modern-day equivalents, movies and miniseries), Marion Hedgepeth has faded into utter obscurity. Perhaps the problem is his name. Certainly it lacks the dashing, romantic ring of the outlaw names that have entered into legend: Jesse James, Billy the Kid, Butch Cassidy, Cole Younger, the Daltons. In his own day, however, Hedgepeth enjoyed a notoriety equal to that of the West's most fabled badmen.

Except for his birthplace—a small farm in Prairie Home, Missouri—nothing is known about his childhood. He left home in his teens and drifted out West. By the time he reached twenty, he was wanted by the law in Wyoming, Colorado, and Montana for crimes ranging from cattle rustling to bank robbery. He had also earned a reputation as the fastest gun in the Southwest—a killer so deadly that, on one occasion, he whipped out his Colt and shot down a foe who had him covered with a rifle.

Tall and straight, with black, wavy hair, dark eyes, and regular features, Hedgepeth cut a striking figure. He was vain about his appearance and dressed for his work with the fastidiousness of an Eastern dandy. His outfit of choice was a conservative blue suit, striped cravat, brown derby, and spit-polished shoes. But his pleasing appearance—the newspapers of the day dubbed him "The Handsome Bandit"—belied the ferocity of his character. In the ranks of Western outlaws, Hedgepeth was as ruthless as they came.

Sometime in 1882, Hedgepeth took up with a pair of burglars named Cody and Officer. Late that year, the trio knocked over a store in Tuscumbia, Missouri, and made off with $1,400 in cash. A posse followed their tracks to Bonner Springs, twenty miles west of Kansas City, but Hedgepeth and his cohorts managed to escape.

Several months later, Hedgepeth and Cody were cornered while attempting to blast open another safe in a small Kansas town. A ferocious gun battle ensued. Cody was killed, but once again, Hedgepeth got away.

He was finally caught in November 1883. Tried in Cooper County, Missouri, he was convicted of highway robbery and sentenced to a seven-year term in the state penitentiary. Awaiting his transfer, he broke out of the local jail and severely wounded a deputy sheriff in the process. He was quickly recaptured and bundled off to prison, narrowly escaping a mob of outraged citizens bent on a lynching.

Shortly after his arrival at the Jefferson Penitentiary, Hedgepeth met and befriended a train robber named Adelbert D. Sly, alias "Bertie." Released simultaneously in 1891, the two men immediately recruited another pair of hard cases—James "Illinois Jimmy" Francis and Lucius "Dink" Wilson—and launched into a series of bold, often brutal, robberies. Within a year, the outlaw quartet—known as "The Hedgepeth Four"—had gained a nationwide reputation. *The New York Times* described them as "the most desperate gang of train robbers that has operated in this country for many years."

Their first major crime was the robbery of a street-car company's offices in Kansas City. A few weeks later, the gang pulled off an identical job in Omaha, Nebraska. They also hit several post office branches in St. Louis and neighboring towns.

On November 4, 1891, they robbed their first train. Boarding the Missouri Pacific at Omaha, they rounded up the crew and held them at gunpoint while Hedgepeth blew open the express-car door, pistol-whipped the messenger, then emptied the safe of $1,000 in cash.

A week later, the gang struck again, this time hitting the Chicago, Milwaukee & St. Paul Express at Western Union Junction, Wisconsin, three miles outside of Milwaukee. Once again, Hedgepeth dynamited the express car, critically injuring the messenger. After cleaning out the safe, the bandits moved down the coach aisles, grain sacks in hand, relieving the passengers of their gold watches and jewelry. Altogether, the day's haul amounted to more than $5,000.

Two weeks later, on November 30, 1891, the Hedgepeth Four committed their biggest—and final—holdup at Glendale, Missouri, a tiny suburb of St. Louis. For the local citizenry, the crime produced a powerful sense of déjà vu, since, a dozen years earlier, Jesse James and his gang had pulled off a celebrated train robbery in the very same location.

At approximately nine-fifteen P.M., as the Frisco express chugged out of the Glendale station, Hedgepeth swung aboard the train. Six-shooter drawn, he stepped into the cab and commanded the engineer to "pull her up straight ahead." As the train braked to a halt, Sly, Francis, and Wilson came galloping up, raking the coaches with pistol fire.

Ordering the engineer down from the cab, Hedgepeth marched him back to the express car, put the six-gun to his head, and suggested that he hurry up and tell the messenger to unlock the door. The engineer complied but the messenger responded by firing a rifle shot through the window, whereupon Hedgepeth set a terrific charge of dynamite that blasted the entire side of the express car open. As the badly wounded messenger staggered out through the smoke, Hedgepeth coolly gunned him down. Then he cracked open the safe with another, smaller charge and scooped a stack of money envelopes, containing $25,000 in cash, into a burlap sack.

Sly, meanwhile, took the opportunity to remove the gold watch and chain from the dead messenger's vest pocket. Then—after peppering the coaches with a final round of gunfire—the four bandits leapt onto their mounts and disappeared into the woods.

The growing brazenness of the gang—and the magnitude

of the Glendale holdup—brought the law down on them hard. Within a week, a special train from Chicago arrived in St. Louis, carrying William A. Pinkerton and a team of the agency's top operatives. Along with the St. Louis police, they began scouring the city for the robbers. Plainclothes officers in squads of four roamed the streets day and night with orders to "kill Hedgepeth on sight." By then, however, the gang had dispersed.

James "Illinois Jimmy" Francis had taken his share of the loot and returned to his eighteen-year-old wife and infant son in Kansas City, Missouri. The Pinkertons located his home, but before they could arrest him, he and his brother-in-law were shot and killed by a posse following an attempted train robbery just outside of Lamar, Kansas.

Meanwhile, Hedgepeth, Sly, and Wilson had headed out for California. In December 1891, Robert Pinkerton, aided by Chief of Police Glass and a detective named Whitaker, managed to track down Adelbert Sly in Los Angeles, where he was apprehended on the twenty-sixth. At the time of his arrest, he was carrying the gold pocket watch he had lifted from the slain express messenger during the Glendale robbery.

Hedgepeth, however, continued to elude his pursuers. His capture finally came about through one of those strange bits of happenstance that occasionally help to crack a case wide open.

On Christmas morning, a man and his wife appeared at the St. Louis police headquarters to report that their little daughter had found a dime in a neighborhood shed. Chief of Detectives Desmond seemed distinctly unimpressed with this tidbit. But he sat up in his chair when the man continued with his tale.

Curious to see if he could turn up more money, the man had followed his daughter to the shed. Striking a match, he had discovered a spaded-up hole in a corner of the little outbuilding.

At that point in his recitation, the man reached into his coat pocket and produced a pair of objects that he had discovered in the hole. Detective Desmond could not suppress his excitement as he gazed at the two items—a Colt revolver and a torn money envelope of the type removed from the express company safe during the Glendale train robbery.

Law enforcement officials hastened out to the shed, where they immediately uncovered a supply of shells and several more empty express company envelopes. Before long, they had ascertained that the house to which the shed belonged had been rented to a man calling himself H. B. Swenson, who had abruptly departed for San Francisco a few days after the Glendale robbery.

On February 10, 1892, "Swenson"—one of Hedgepeth's several aliases—was surrounded at the general post office in San Francisco by a stakeout party. Hedgepeth was armed with a pair of Colt revolvers, but was overpowered before he could use them. He was returned to St. Louis under heavy guard.

His trial was a nationwide sensation. Hundreds of spectators—most of them women—flocked to the courthouse each morning for a glimpse of "The Handsome Bandit." Baskets of flowers from his female admirers were delivered to his jail cell every afternoon.

The jurors, however, proved resistant to his charms. In the spring of 1892, Hedgepeth was found guilty and sentenced to twenty-five years at hard labor in the Missouri state penitentiary. "Well," he said, shrugging after the verdict was read, "I guess that's the end of Marion Hedgepeth, who thought he was going to be a rich man."

That philosophic comment, however, was only a dodge. Hedgepeth had no intention of submitting meekly to his sentence. Held in the St. Louis jail while his attorneys appealed his conviction, he made a desperate breakout attempt but was quickly recaptured and thrown into solitary. When he emerged, he seemed more resigned to his situation. But in reality, he was only biding his time, waiting for fate to present him with a new chance for freedom.

That chance arrived—or so Hedgepeth quickly came to believe—in July 1894, when a swindler called H. M. Howard landed in the St. Louis jail on a charge of defrauding the Merrill Drug Company.

Why a man as cunning as Holmes chose to confide in a reprobate like Hedgepeth is an interesting question. Perhaps

DEPRAVED

Holmes was slightly starstruck by his cellmate—dazzled by Hedgepeth's celebrity and desirous of making a favorable impression on the notorious outlaw. Or perhaps the answer lies in something more prosaic: Holmes's need for a particular piece of information, which he believed—correctly—that Hedgepeth could provide.

Holmes's insurance scheme still lacked a crucial ingredient. In order to pull it off successfully, he required the services of a lawyer not averse to dirty dealings. So far, he had been unable to come up with a suitable man. And so, sometime during his stay in the St. Louis jail, Holmes broached the subject with Hedgepeth, detailing his plan and offering him $500 in return for the name of a "slick lawyer."

After listening attentively, Hedgepeth acknowledged that he knew exactly the man for the job—a St. Louis attorney named Jeptha D. Howe, who "had underworld connections."

Holmes promised to send Hedgepeth the money just as soon as he collected on the insurance. Shortly thereafter, he was bailed out of jail.

For both men, Holmes's brief incarceration had proved to be an unexpected boon—or so it seemed at the time.

Holmes had found his shyster. And Hedgepeth had ended up not only with the prospect of a $500 reward but with something even more potentially valuable—something the authorities might eventually give a good deal to know.

16

Trust that man in nothing who has not a conscience
in everything.

—Laurence Sterne, *Sermons*

At the time of Holmes's arrest, Pitezel and his family were
also living in St. Louis. Pitezel had sent for Carrie and the
children in the middle of May, shortly after arriving in the
city. With some money provided by Holmes, he had taken
a furnished, three-room flat in a wood-frame tenement on
Carondelet Street.

On the day Carrie's train was due in from Chicago, Pitezel
limited himself to a single shot of whiskey at the local saloon. Separated from his loved ones for nearly six months,
he had begun drinking heavily again. But now that Carrie
and the children were on their way to rejoin him, he was
determined to cut back.

When his wife stepped off the train at Union Depot, he
embraced her so fervently that a number of passersby
paused on the platform to stare. Pitezel kissed each of his
five children in turn—Dessie, Alice, Nellie, Howard, and
baby Wharton. Then, gathering up their luggage, he led his
family out to a cab and loaded them inside.

It was late afternoon when the carriage clattered up to
the weather-beaten tenement. The narrow street was overrun with children, housewives gossiped on their front stoops,
storekeepers lounged in the doorways of their meager shops.
Though a distinct air of seediness pervaded the place, the

street had a neighborly feel. But Carrie's face fell when she stepped inside the flat. The wallpaper was grimy and peeling, the furniture flimsy and sparse, and—even with the windows wide flung—the air was infused with the smell of old cooking.

Carrie was confused. Benny (her pet name for her husband) was a faithful correspondent, and she knew from his frequent letters that he and his employer had pulled off a big deal in Texas, which had netted them a substantial profit. What she didn't know, however, was that her husband had ended up with only a pittance. The vast bulk of his share had remained in the possession of Holmes, who had persuaded Pitezel to allow him to hang on to it. Holmes had a real estate venture in mind that would double their investment in a matter of months.

Pitezel, who continued to have perfect faith in Holmes's financial cunning, had gone along with the proposition. With the money he would realize from the deal, plus his cut of the pending insurance scam, he and his family would be set for life.

Sometime during the next two months—it is impossible to say precisely when—Pitezel took Carrie aside and laid out the details of the insurance fraud. She already knew about the $10,000 policy that named her as sole beneficiary. Benny had shown her the document the previous November, shortly after it had been issued. Now, he explained how he and Holmes intended to cash in on it.

They had decided to stage Pitezel's phony death in Philadelphia, where the Fidelity Mutual Life Association had its home office, calculating that Holmes could settle the matter most expeditiously that way. Pitezel would be traveling there soon under the name of Perry. He couldn't say exactly how long he'd be away. But the next time Carrie saw him, he would be a wealthy man.

To Pitezel's chagrin, his wife took a very dim view of the matter. She knew Holmes only slightly. Though her husband had been in his employ for nearly five years, she had seen the man only a few times. Since their move to St. Louis, Holmes had dropped by the house on two or three occasions, bearing treats for the children and doling out a little cash to help tide the family over. But in spite of these small generosities, she bore no special fondness for the man—and she did not care for his insurance scheme one bit. "I don't think much of it, Benny," she complained. "And I don't want to have anything to do with it."

It took some cajoling, but in the end—though she remained leery of the plan—Carrie agreed to go along with it. Seated on a kitchen chair, Pitezel drew her onto his lap and gestured at their shabby surroundings. Once this deal was over, he declared, they would never have to endure such conditions again. Their money troubles would be over. Raising his right hand to show that he was giving his solemn word, he promised that he would have nothing more to do with Holmes once this insurance business was settled. The Philadelphia job was the last dishonest thing he would ever do in his life.

In spite of Pitezel's resolve to stay sober, he had not been able to keep away from the neighborhood saloon. A few evenings following his conversation with Carrie, he left the flat after dinner and returned several hours later in a noticeably fuddled state.

Peering into the kitchen, he saw his seventeen-year-old daughter, Dessie, sewing at the table by lamplight. Pitezel made his way over to the table and lowered himself unsteadily into the opposite chair. After gazing at his daughter for a moment, he nodded decisively as though settling an inner debate. Then he cleared his throat and started to speak.

He knew he shouldn't say anything to her, he began. But he was afraid she would worry if she read something in the newspaper.

"Something about what?" asked Dessie.

"About my being dead."

Dessie looked at him in wonderment.

"Can't say anything more," her father mumbled. "Just remember—if you see it in the paper that I'm dead, don't you believe it. It's a fraud. That's all I can say."

Dessie couldn't make heads or tails of this speech. She told herself that her father, who was clearly under the influence, didn't know what he was saying—it was the liquor doing the talking, that was all.

By the next morning, she had put the incident out of her mind.

After a simple breakfast on Sunday morning, July 29, 1894, Benjamin Pitezel kissed his wife and children good-bye, grabbed his battered valise, and headed for the trolley. Forty minutes later, he arrived at Union Depot, where he caught the noon train for Philadelphia.

Just one day earlier, on July 28, Holmes had been released from the St. Louis prison. The previous ten days had been a terrible strain on Georgiana. Married for only six months, she had suddenly found herself in a desperately trying position, alone in a strange city, her husband suddenly carted off to jail. It had taken her over a week to arrange for his bail. Though she felt deeply indignant on behalf of Holmes, who had been victimized—so he led her to believe—by unscrupulous competitors, her main emotions were confusion and anxiety.

As soon as they arrived back in their flat, Holmes proposed that they leave St. Louis at once. Georgiana—the strain of the ordeal apparent on her pale, haggard face—was in urgent need of a rest. As for Holmes, he had some long-postponed business in Philadelphia related to his patented ABC copying device. That, at any rate, was the falsehood he fed to his young wife.

By the following afternoon, they had agreed on a plan. Georgiana would travel to Lake Bluff, Illinois, to spend a few days in the company of an old college friend, who had been urging her to visit for several years. In the meantime, Holmes would proceed to Philadelphia and find a place for them to stay. They would rendezvous there in a week.

Valise in hand, Pitezel strolled along the Philadelphia streets, looking for someplace to eat. He had built up a powerful hunger, not having consumed a bite since his arrival in the city that morning, Monday, July 30. Reaching the corner of Ninth and Cherry, he found a small neighborhood restaurant with the proprietor's name—Josiah Richman—painted in gold letters on the front window.

After treating himself to a substantial meal—broiled spring chicken, hashed browns, and asparagus, followed by apple pie and coffee—Pitezel leaned back contentedly and reached into his shirt pocket for a cigar. Then, catching the owner's attention, he beckoned him over.

Josiah Richman might have been forgiven for forming an unfavorable snap judgment of the stranger, based solely on appearance. Over the past dozen years, Pitezel had acquired an increasingly roughneck look—complete with broken nose and several missing front teeth—and his expression seemed fixed in a permanent scowl. His general air of disreputability, moreover, was intensified by his travel-rumpled clothing and by the scraggly goatee he had cultivated in recent months.

Still, when Pitezel began to address the proprietor, he spoke politely enough.

He was a stranger to the city, he explained, and was looking for a place to board temporarily until he found a house to rent for his wife and children, who would be joining him in several weeks. As it happened, Richman's sister ran a lodging house. Having decided that the well-spoken stranger was a perfectly respectable fellow after all, Richman provided him with the address.

Pitezel proceeded directly to Susan Harley's boarding-house at 1002 Race Street and rented a room for himself. Then he settled in to wait for Holmes.

The precise date of Holmes's appearance in Philadelphia remains uncertain, though by Sunday, August 5—the day Georgiana was scheduled to arrive from Illinois—he was already settled in a rooming house run by a widow named Adella Alcorn, who was a licensed physician, though she had long ago given up her practice.

When Georgiana's train pulled into the station, Holmes was waiting on the platform, a small bouquet in hand. He greeted her warmly. Then—exchanging the posy for her suitcase—he escorted her outside to a waiting coupé. Shortly after six P.M. the carriage drew up to the rooming house at 1905 North Eleventh Street.

Though Georgiana's visit with her friend had done wonders for her spirit, she was clearly in need of refreshment after her tiring, overnight trip. Mrs. Dr. Alcorn suggested to Holmes (whom she knew as Mr. H. M. Howard, the name he had inscribed in the register) that he and his wife join her for a cup of tea.

Seated in the parlor across from the couple, Adella Alcorn nibbled at a tea cake and questioned Mr. Howard about his business. He explained that he represented a firm marketing an ingenious device for copying business documents and had come to Philadelphia to see about leasing several of the machines to the Pennsylvania Railroad Company.

As he spoke, he reached out occasionally to squeeze the hand of his young wife, who had changed from her traveling suit into a blue skirt and matching shirtwaist. Sipping from her cup, the landlady smiled at the couple—the debonair businessman and his demure, soft-spoken wife. She herself had enjoyed thirty happy years of marriage, and it did her heart good to see these handsome young people, so obviously in love.

Over the next few days, Holmes left Georgiana at the rooming house while he went about his business, presumably the demonstration of his ABC Copier to officers of the Pennsylvania Railroad Company. In reality, he and Pitezel were meeting to work out the final details of their scheme.

They had already decided that Pitezel, under the name of B. F. Perry, would rent a house somewhere in the city and pose as a dealer in patents. This guise made sense since Pitezel did, in fact, possess some knowledge of the business. Several years earlier, he had tinkered together a cleverly constructed coal bin, designed to keep the lumps from being stolen and the dust from polluting the air. With Holmes's assistance, he had taken out a patent on his invention in 1891 and attempted to market it in Chicago. Nothing had come of the venture, but Pitezel had acquired enough first-hand experience to pass himself off convincingly as a patent broker.

Several important matters remained to be settled before they could execute their scheme: they had to locate a suitable place for Pitezel to set up shop, and Holmes had to come up with a substitute corpse to pass off as Pitezel's remains.

Still, things seemed to be going along nicely. But on Thursday, August 9, as they took their lunch at a small downtown eatery, they were shocked to discover that the entire plan—nurtured so lovingly for the better part of a year—had been jeopardized by the most outrageous of oversights.

For whatever reason—the number of details he was obliged to keep in mind, the brain-muddling effects of his boozing, or perhaps simple carelessness—Pitezel had neglected to send in the most recent premium on his life insurance.

For a moment, Holmes simply sat gaping at Pitezel, who stammered an apology and did his best to avoid his partner's eyes. Then, pounding the table so hard that the silverware flew, Holmes leapt from his chair and hurried from the restaurant, Pitezel following a few paces behind.

A short time later, a clerk at Fidelity's branch office in Chicago received a telegraphic money order for $157.50 as the semiannual payment on life insurance policy number 044145, registered under the name of B.F. Pitezel. As he recorded the transaction, the clerk noted that the money had arrived just in time. The payment was way overdue—indeed, August 9 was the last day of the grace period. A few hours later and the policy would have lapsed.

Mr. B. F. Pitezel, the clerk reflected, was a lucky man.

As soon as he and Pitezel laid eyes on the house, Holmes saw that it was just what he'd been looking for.

Even in the glare of that August afternoon, when the heat made the cobblestones shimmer, Callowhill Street had a dingy feel. A row of run-down, attached houses—two-and-a-half stories high with façades of faded brick—occupied one side of the block. Directly opposite stood the abandoned station of the Philadelphia and Reading Railroad, crumbling and desolate. It was important that Pitezel draw as little attention to himself as possible—and this was clearly a neighborhood where he could open up shop without worrying about attracting too much business.

The building at number 1316 had been vacant for some time—a testimony to its unfavorable location. The bottom floor had been converted into a little store, with a display window facing the street and a bare metal awning frame that stretched over the sidewalk, supported by a pair of iron stanchions planted close to the curb. The second floor of the building consisted of two small bedrooms—more than enough for Pitezel's needs.

Because the house had stood empty for so long, the rent had been reduced to $10 a week. And there was still another feature of the place that made it especially appealing to Holmes, a feature that had actively discouraged other potential tenants. But it suited Holmes's purpose to a tee.

Directly behind 1316 Callowhill Street—so close that only a narrow alleyway separated the two buildings—stood the city morgue.

17

From troublous sight and sounds set free;
In such a twilight hour of breath,
Shall one retrace his life, or see,
Through shadows, the true face of death?

—Ernest Dowson, "Extreme Unction" (1896)

It was one of Eugene Smith's neighbors who first spotted the sign—a plain muslin sheet painted with crude block letters of red and black—displayed in the ground-floor window of 1316 Callowhill Street: B. F. PERRY, PATENTS BOUGHT AND SOLD. The very next morning—Wednesday, August 22—Smith left his house on Rhodes Street and headed over to Callowhill to check out Mr. Perry's office for himself.

An unemployed carpenter and habitual tinkerer, Smith had recently devised an ingenious tool-sharpener that could put the edge back on a dull handsaw with a few strokes of the blade. Smith had assembled a model but had no idea how to go about peddling his invention. Mr. Perry might be just the man to help.

The bell above the doorway jangled as Smith stepped inside the office and glanced around. A more sophisticated man might have wondered at the shabbiness of the place, which had been fitted out with some cheap, secondhand furnishings: a couple of rickety chairs, a battered desk, an old wooden filing cabinet. The walls were barren except for a crude wooden shelf holding an assortment of chemicals—benzine, chloroform, ammonia—in brown, stoppered bottles.

The proprietor, who emerged a moment later from the gloom of the rear storeroom, looked more like a roustabout than a businessman. But Smith—a simple, unlettered individual, not liable to suspicion—was either unbothered by or oblivious to these details.

Putting out his right hand, he introduced himself to Mr. Perry and explained why he was there. The patent dealer listened attentively, stroking his wispy goatee. "Sounds interesting," he replied when Smith had finished talking. "Why don't you bring the thing around later today and let me have a look?"

Pumping Perry's hand again, Smith left the office and strode home excitedly, convinced that his hard luck had finally changed.

Shortly after lunch, he returned with his model. Mr. Perry carried it over to his desk and sat down to examine it. Hovering nearby, Smith—less out of curiosity than politeness—put a few friendly questions to Perry. How long he had been in the patent business? When had he opened up shop on Callowhill Street?

Perry, however, was disinclined to converse—indeed, his replies were so curt that Smith soon gave up the effort. He did, however, learn that Perry had recently moved to Philadelphia from St. Louis and had been operating in his present location for less than a week.

A few minutes later, Perry rose to his feet and—complimenting Smith on the cleverness of his device—said, yes, he believed he could do something with it. Smith was delighted. But when Perry explained that he would have to hold on to the model, Smith's expression suddenly changed. He couldn't see where Mr. Perry intended to keep his invention, he said. It certainly wouldn't fit inside the desk. And he was reluctant to leave it lying around in the open.

Nodding toward the rear of the office, Perry said that he would place it in the storeroom. It would be safe enough in there, though he would have to stow it on the floor. He intended to put up a counter any day now, but his tools were still in St. Louis and—

"I can build you a counter," Mr. Smith volunteered.

Perry mulled that over for a moment, then nodded okay. After agreeing on a day to do the job, Smith picked up his hat and made ready to leave.

Just then, the doorbell sounded, and as the two men glanced around, someone stepped inside the shop.

By the time Holmes realized that Pitezel had a visitor, it was too late. The man had already swiveled his head and seen him enter. Holmes was galled—he did not want any witnesses connecting him with Pitezel. For an instant, he considered turning on his heels and hurrying away, but decided against it.

Keeping his expression blank and his face slightly averted from the stranger, he strode directly to the rear staircase and nodded stiffly to Pitezel, who excused himself to the man, then followed Holmes upstairs.

On the dark second-story landing, Holmes grabbed Pitezel's arm. "Who is he?" he demanded, his voice a harsh whisper.

Pitezel quickly explained.

"Get rid of him," Holmes snapped.

Smith had reseated himself in one of the two straight-back chairs and was gazing idly around the office when the patent dealer reappeared, only moments after he had followed the nicely dressed gentleman up the stairs. "Well, I suppose my business is done with you," Smith said, rising. "There's no use in my detaining you any longer."

"Let me give you a receipt," replied Perry as he walked to his desk. Sliding open a drawer, he removed a little notebook, from which he tore a single sheet. He wrote out and signed the paper, then handed it to Smith, who glanced at it briefly and pocketed it. After shaking hands and promising to return in a few days to put up the counter, Smith departed.

As soon as he was gone, Pitezel hurried back up the narrow staircase.

He found Holmes waiting in the front bedroom, perched on the edge of the cot. Besides the office furnishings, Pitezel had purchased the cot and a cheap, three-drawer bureau from a dealer named Hughes, who operated out of a warehouse on Buttonwood Street. The bedroom window, which looked out over Callowhill Street, had been opened to its fullest extent, but even so, the little room was sweltering. Holmes, who had removed his derby and set it beside him on the mattress, was swabbing his brow with a big handkerchief.

Holmes had come with some important news. He had just received word from a certain physician he knew in New York City, a man he had done business with before, who was prepared to supply him with a male cadaver that sounded just right for their needs. Holmes would be traveling to New York City soon to secure the corpse and transport in back to Philadelphia. If things went smoothly, they would have the insurance money in a matter of weeks.

The two men spent a few more minutes talking, then Holmes rose from the cot. As he made ready to leave, Pitezel asked for some money to see him through the next week. Holmes removed a few bills from his wallet and handed them over, advising his partner not to drink up every penny.

On the appointed date—Thursday, August 30—Smith returned to the patent office with his toolbox. Then he and the man he knew as Perry headed over to a nearby lumberyard to pick up a board for the counter.

On the way back, Mr. Perry suggested that they stop for a drink at Fritz Richards's saloon, located just a few doors down from 1316 Callowhill. Smith ordered a beer, while Perry drank whiskey. Once again Smith tried to strike up a conversation with the patent dealer but met with as little success as before.

Returning to the office, Smith proceeded to put up a rough counter in the rear storeroom. Afterward, Perry offered him fifty cents for the job, which the out-of-work carpenter gratefully accepted. Perry assured Smith that things were progressing nicely with the saw-sharpener—he had already contacted several potential investors.

"Why don't you come round next week?" Perry suggested. "Maybe I'll have some news for you then."

Smith assured him he would, then gathered up his tools and left, pleased with his day's work.

Several days later, on Saturday, September 1, Pitezel strolled over to Fritz Richards's and stepped to the bar. Though he had been living in the neighborhood for only two weeks, he was already a regular customer. Indeed, this was his third visit to the saloon on that day alone, and it was not yet four o'clock.

After knocking back a few shots, he groped in his pocket for some cash and realized that he was down to his last few dollars. He was surprised at how fast his money was disappearing—virtually all of it down his throat.

Having been led to believe that Holmes would be departing for New York City the following morning, Pitezel decided to pay his partner a visit. He wasn't sure how long Holmes would be gone, and he did not want to risk running out of cash.

Holmes was sitting in an easy chair, reading that day's *Inquirer*, when someone knocked at his door, shortly after six P.M. It was the landlady, Mrs. Dr. Alcorn, who informed him that a gentleman was downstairs wishing to see him. Holmes thanked her and said that he would be down in a moment.

"And how is Mrs. Howard this evening?" the landlady inquired.

"Considerably improved," Holmes replied.

Georgiana, who had been feeling indisposed for the past few days, was sitting up in bed, reading a novel by lamplight, when Holmes walked into the bedroom. Donning his suit jacket, he explained that he had a visitor and would be back presently.

He returned about ten minutes later, smiling broadly. The caller, he told Georgiana, was an agent of the Pennsylvania Railroad. The company had decided to lease a dozen of his ABC copying machines. The deal had to be consummated immediately, however, since the official handling the matter was leaving on a business trip the following afternoon.

As a result, Holmes had arranged to travel to the official's home first thing next morning to sign the contracts. With his business completed, he and Georgiana could leave Philadelphia just as soon as she felt up to traveling.

With his pocketbook replenished, Pitezel was in a chipper mood. Stopping off for a little refreshment at Fritz Richards's, he struck up a conversation with the bartender, William Moebius. Pitezel explained that he was a newcomer to Philadelphia, where he hoped to establish himself in the patent business. As he polished off his fourth and final drink, he asked if the saloon would be open the following day.

Moebius shook his head. The city prohibited the sale of liquor on Sunday. If Pitezel wanted something to tide him over, he had better stock up now.

Pitezel placed four bits on the bar asked for a pint. Moebius handed him two half-pint flasks and Pitezel headed home.

A little while later, as he reclined on his cot in the second-floor bedroom, his lips pressed to the mouth of one of the flasks, he realized that he was low on another staple. Slipping his jacket back on, he walked to a nearby tobacco shop run by a woman named Pierce and purchased a handful of cigars.

Then, making his way back to Callowhill Street, he returned to his bedroom and his bottles and settled in for the night.

Early the next morning—Sunday, September 2—Holmes bid Georgiana good-bye, walked into the sunshine of that blazing Sabbath morn, and proceeded directly to 1316 Callowhill. The street was completely deserted as he strode briskly to the front door, unlocked it with his duplicate key, and slipped inside.

Moving stealthily across the floor, he paused at the foot of the rear staircase and listened intently. The liquid snore he could hear from above was precisely the sound he expected. Holmes was thoroughly familiar with Pitezel's habits and had been counting on his partner to drink himself into a stupor.

Even so, he kept as quiet as possible as he crept up to the second-floor landing. Peering into the front bedroom, he could see Pitezel, still fully clothed, sprawled faceup on the cot.

Reaching into the left pocket of his suit jacket, Holmes pulled out one of his oversize handkerchiefs and tied it around his head, so that it hung below his eyes like the bandannas worn by Marion Hedgepeth and other Western road agents. But the purpose of Holmes's mask was not to conceal his identity.

It was to protect him from the fumes.

From his opposite pocket, he withdrew another handkerchief, this one wrapped around a smooth, cylindrical object. He unrolled the object from the cloth. It was a small chemist's bottle filled with clear liquid.

Uncorking the bottle, he held his hands away from his body and saturated the handkerchief with the liquid.

Then, stealing into the shuttered room, he stepped to the bedside and bent to Benjamin Pitezel's face.

18

From that chamber, and from that mansion, I fled aghast.

—Edgar Allan Poe, "The Fall of the House of Usher"

Eager to learn if Mr. Perry had managed to drum up any interest in his invention, Eugene Smith returned to 1316 Callowhill on Monday afternoon, September 3. As he approached the building, he saw that the front door was closed, but when he climbed the concrete stoop and tried the knob, he found the office unlocked. He pushed open the door and stepped inside

A strange air of vacancy hung about the place. The room felt lifeless and musty, as though Perry had shut down his office for the weekend and had not yet gotten around to reopening it, though the time was already well past noon. The silence in the house seemed palpable. Mr. Perry was nowhere to be seen.

Smith stood in the center of the floor and, at the top of his voice, called out the patent dealer's name.

Receiving no reply, he decided that Perry must have stepped out for a moment—perhaps to the saloon where the two men had enjoyed a drink the previous week. Smith pulled up one of the chairs and seated himself.

Glancing around the room, he saw Perry's hat and a pair of cuffs hanging from a big nail in the rear hallway. Perry's chair had been moved away from his desk and stood, awkwardly angled, in a corner of the room. Otherwise there was nothing to notice about the office, except, perhaps, its complete lack of detail or character.

Smith crossed his legs, folded his hands in his lap, and waited.

About ten minutes later, a stranger entered—a sharp-featured man dressed in a black suit and carrying a black bag in one hand. The man had a full black beard and thick, black eyebrows that grew together above his nose. Smith decided that the man was a Jew.

"Is the boss in?" asked the stranger.

Smith shook his head. "I expect he'll be back promptly. Take a seat."

The black-suited man declined the offer. He glanced around the room for a moment, then, consulting his pocket watch, announced that he had no time to wait. He nodded to Smith and left.

Smith remained seated for a few more minutes, then rose with a sigh and walked to the door.

As he stepped into the sunlight, closing the door behind him, Smith—though in no way alarmed—felt the first inklings of concern. It seemed odd to him that Perry would simply walk away from his office in the middle of the day without even bothering to lock up.

Smith was back by nine the next morning. The front door was still closed, just as he had left it. He knocked and pressed an ear to the wood, listening intently.

Silence. He put his hand to the knob and turned. The door was still unlocked.

Inside, the office was exactly as it had been the previous afternoon. The chairs stood in precisely the same positions. Perry's hat and cuffs still hung from the nail. Smith didn't know what to think. He walked slowly to the chair he had occupied the day before and lowered himself onto the seat.

"Mr. Perry," he shouted.

In the unfinished office, his call echoed slightly, then faded into absolute silence.

Apprehension began to stir inside him. He halloed again, even louder. When his call went unanswered again he decided something was wrong.

Rising, he walked over to the foot of the stairwell.

He hesitated for a moment, peering upstairs. He listened hard for some living sound. But the house seemed completely deserted. An unpleasant smell drifted down from above. Slowly, Smith ascended the narrow staircase.

As he approached the top of the stairs, he could see a bedroom straight ahead. He paused on the landing and peered into the room. He could see an empty cot with some bedclothes on it. Otherwise the room seemed vacant.

The stench was much thicker up there, though Smith could not identify its source. He turned to look behind him.

And froze.

On the floor of the rear bedroom lay a body with its feet toward the unshuttered window and its head to the door. Its face was blackened and swollen. Smith needed only a single glance at the ghastly figure to realize that he was looking at a corpse.

Rushing from the building, he burst onto the street and ran for the Buttonwood stationhouse.

19

When death puts out your flame, the snuff will tell,
if we were wax or tallow by the smell.

—Benjamin Franklin, *Poor Richard's Almanack*

Dr. William Scott, who ran a little pharmacy on the ground floor of his residence at Thirteenth and Vine, had just opened shop for the day when Officer Billy Sauer strode into the store. A dead man had been discovered that morning at 1316 Callowhill Street, the policeman explained. From the evidence, it appeared that the victim had been killed in an explosion. Would Dr. Scott mind stepping over to the address and examining the remains?

Steeling himself for a grisly sight, the doctor followed Sauer a few blocks over to the faded little building, then up the narrow stairway and into the back room. Two men hovered over the prostrate corpse—a second police officer and a scrawny fellow in laborer's clothes, who stood with a handkerchief clamped over his nose. Dr. Scott fished out his hankie and held it to his face as he entered the room. Even so, he nearly gagged at the stench. But when he took a closer look at the corpse, a few things struck him as peculiar.

True, the face was in a putrid state—the skin dark and oozing, the thick tongue protruding, a noxious red fluid seeping out of the mouth. But instead of shattered limbs and mangled flesh—the mutilations one expected in a blast victim—the body was not only intact but stretched out neatly, almost ceremoniously, on the floor.

Stiff and straight, legs together, the dead man lay flat on his back, left arm extended at his side. His right arm, bent at the elbow, rested across his chest, the hand cupped over his rigid heart.

It almost seemed as though the man had passed away peacefully in his sleep. On the other hand, the body had clearly been charred by flames. The breast of his shirt was partly burned, as were his mustache and goatee, left eyebrow, and forelock. From the look of things, it seemed as though a sudden fire had flashed over his head and chest.

Other evidence, too, pointed to an explosion. Beside his head lay a burned wooden match, a corncob pipe packed with singed tobacco, and a broken bottle of red fluid. A row of identical bottles—all uncorked, all containing a pungent blend of liquid chemicals—was aligned on the fireplace mantel.

As Scott knelt beside the corpse for a closer examination, Officer Sauer proposed a theory. While lighting his pipe, the deceased had carelessly struck the match too close to the bottles, whose contents—judging by the smell—consisted of a volatile mix of benzine, chloroform, and ammonia. The flame had ignited the chemical fumes, touching off the fatal explosion.

It seemed feasible, but the closer Dr. Scott looked, the larger his doubts grew. If Sauer's scenario were correct, the corncob pipe would surely have been damaged by the blast. Almost certainly, it would have gone flying across the room. But in fact the pipe stood perfectly unscathed and upright a few inches from the corpse's head, as though it had been neatly placed there. Moreover, the broken chemical bottle looked as though it had been dropped, not shattered by an explosion.

Still, Scott did not have a better explanation at the moment. In any case, his attention was now fully focused on the corpse.

Death had blighted the features, though the scrawny working man—who introduced himself through his handkerchief as Eugene Smith, a business associate of B. F. Perry's and the one who had discovered the tragedy—confirmed that the clothing, hair color, and general stature of the corpse matched those of the patent dealer. Gazing down at the blackened face, with its singed wisp of goatee, Scott suddenly recollected that he himself had met Perry on a previous occasion. About a month earlier, a sullen-looking stranger who introduced himself as a new arrival to the neighborhood had come into Scott's pharmacy to make a small purchase. For some reason, one particular detail—the little tuft of hair sprouting from the man's chin—had stuck in Scott's mind.

Undoing the clothing of the dead man, Scott noted that, compared to the lower body, the upper torso and head were in a far more putrescent state. Here, too, Scott was struck by the arrangement of the corpse, which lay facing the open window. The shutters had been angled in such a way that, for much of the day, sunlight bathed the body from the waist up, accelerating the decay.

Sighing, Dr. Scott rose to his feet. There was nothing more he could do. It was time to transport the corpse to the coroner's lab for a formal autopsy—not much of a trip since, as Scott and the police officers knew very well, the city morgue was located only a few yards away. Indeed, the window of the room overlooked the morgue.

To Scott and the others, this seemed a grim coincidence. But the proximity of the morgue suggested something else, too. As foul as the stench from Perry's body was, the smell would not immediately have alerted the neighbors to his death. Wafting through the open window and up the chimney, the fetor was largely camouflaged by the death stink from the morgue.

If it hadn't been for Smith, the corpse might have lain there for a much longer period. Eventually it would undoubtedly have been discovered—but not until its features were thoroughly decomposed.

The autopsy took place that afternoon, the corpse having been stored for the interim in the cold house. Coroner's physician William Mattern conducted the postmortem, with two colleagues—morgue superintendent Benjamin and his assistant, Thomas Robinson—attending. Dr. Scott, who by now had developed a keen interest in the case, was also present as a witness (or "sight-seer," as he put it), jotting down notes of the proceedings in a book he had brought along for that purpose.

Mattern began by noting the disfiguration of the face through mortification. The teeth, which were in strikingly poor condition ("unkempt" was Mattern's description), were examined for irregularities. The corpse's hair was black and just starting to thin, with the front "combed pompadour" and a cowlick sticking out on the left. The only other distinguishing features were the small, "stumpy" mustache and the wispy goatee.

Opening the skull, Mattern found a normal brain, free of any congestion. Next, he removed the heart. It was empty of any blood. "Paralysis of the heart," Dr. Scott wrote to Mattern's dictation. "Indication—sudden death."

The lungs were highly congested and full of blood, the liver and spleen similarly engorged. A glance at the kidneys revealed that Perry had been a man who, as Dr. Scott noted, "never refused a drink when he had a chance to take it." The kidneys were nephritic or "pig-black," a condition characteristic of alcoholics.

Though the stomach was empty of food, it contained a significant quantity—perhaps an ounce or two—of a fluid that proved, through smell and taste, to be chloroform. The lungs, too, gave off the unmistakable odor of chloroform.

The involuntary muscles of the excretory organs had relaxed at the moment of death, causing a spontaneous evacuation of both bladder and bowels.

Mattern took note of one more detail. While flames had clearly singed Perry's right arm—the one found resting on his chest—there were no burn marks at all on the axilla or underside of the arm, the part lying against the body. To the coroner, this could only mean one thing—that (as Scott recorded in his notebook) "the burning had been done after the arm had been placed on the breast."

Mattern's conclusion—presented at the inquest that was held the following day—was that B. F. Perry had died of chloroform poisoning. The police, however, held firmly to their theory of death by explosion.

In the end, the jurymen rendered a verdict that covered

a range of possibilities—that Perry had died from "congestion of the lungs, caused by the inhalation of flame, or of chloroform, or other poisonous drug." The ultimate question—whether his death was due to accident, suicide, or foul play—was left open.

And that was how matters stood on Wednesday, September 5. News of the mysterious death of the equally mysterious B. F. Perry—whose body was returned to the cold house, where, according to local practice, it would be stored for eleven days, awaiting a claimant—appeared first in the *Philadelphia Inquirer*. The story was quickly picked up by the wire services, which sent out a squib to newspapers in all the major cities—including, of course, St. Louis.

20

A violent man enticeth his neighbor . . .
moving his lips he bringeth evil to pass.

—Proverbs 16: 29, 30

At first, she had prayed that the plan would be scuttled—
that Benny would come to his senses, or that Holmes, realizing the risks, would lose his stomach for the scheme. But as
the summer went by, she saw that they meant to go through
with it.

For weeks, she had been scanning the papers, expecting
the news any day. Even so, it came as a shock when the
story actually appeared—a single column in the September
6 issue of the *St. Louis Globe-Democrat,* reporting the death
of a Philadelphia patent dealer named B. F. Perry, killed
under peculiar circumstances.

It was not that she believed the article. Benny had assured
her that the news of his death would be false. What appalled
her was the enormity of the fraud and the terrible peril and
shame to which her husband had exposed them. If Benny
was caught, it was not only he who would suffer but she
and the children as well.

The weeks of strain and uncertainty had taken their toll
on her health. For days she had been suffering from blinding
migraines and bouts of nervous prostration. But she could
not afford to be sick. As it was, she and the children were
barely getting enough to eat.

Through the wall that separated the kitchen from the tiny

bedroom that all five children shared, she could hear a muffled, croupy cough. Little Wharton, less than a year old, had been ill for a week. But she had no money for a doctor. Before setting off for Philadelphia, Benny had provided her with some living expenses, but the meager funds had run out in mid-August. Since then, she had been forced to rely on whatever menial jobs she could find—laundry, mending, and the like.

In all her life, she could not remember ever feeling more frightened, alone, and confused.

Seated at the kitchen table, she started to read the story again, but her vision dissolved in a sudden blur of tears. Dropping the paper onto the table, she covered her face with her hands and surrendered herself to her misery.

The sound of her sobs brought the older children running. Huddling around her chair, they stroked her quaking shoulders and asked if she was sick. It was then that Alice glanced down at the newspaper and spotted B. F. Perry's name, which she recognized at once. She had seen it on the envelopes that her mama mailed off every week to Philadelphia. "It's Papa," she cried. "He's dead, he's dead!"

Her siblings stood dumbstruck for a moment, then broke into a tearful clamor. Even Dessie joined in the general outburst, having completely forgotten the evening, several months earlier, when her father had staggered into the kitchen and mumbled something cryptic about his death.

At that instant, someone pounded on the door. Composing herself as best she could, Carrie rose from her chair and made her way to the front of the flat.

Pulling open the door, she found herself face-to-face with H. H. Holmes.

When Holmes had returned to Mrs. Alcorn's boarding-house on Sunday afternoon—five or six hours after departing for his ostensible meeting in the suburban village of Nicetown—he seemed breathless and flushed. Entering the bedroom, he asked Georgiana if she was well enough to travel. Georgiana, who did in fact feel stronger than she had in days, looked curiously at her husband and nodded yes.

How had the meeting gone? she asked, eyeing him closely.

Perspiration dripped from his brow, and when he stripped off his suit jacket and shirt, she could see that his underclothes were soaked.

"As well as I could have hoped," he replied without elaborating.

"Is something wrong, Harry?" Georgiana asked. "You seem so hurried."

"Not at all, my dear. The day seemed so splendid that I decided to walk from the depot, and I'm simply a bit winded."

While Georgiana arose from the bed and began making preparations to leave, Holmes refreshed himself at the washstand, then donned a clean suit and went downstairs to inform Mrs. Dr. Alcorn of their imminent departure.

When the landlady asked where they were going, Holmes explained that they would be traveling to Harrisburg to close out the deal with the Pennsylvania Railroad Company. He instructed Georgiana to repeat the same tale.

That night, the two of them bid good-bye to Adella Alcorn, then climbed into a waiting carriage, which carried them to the depot, where they boarded the late train not to Harrisburg but to Indianapolis.

The overnight trip left Georgiana feeling drained. By the time they arrived in Indianapolis on Monday morning, September 3, she had suffered a setback. Holmes helped her to the nearest lodging, an unprepossessing little hostelry named Stubbins' European Hotel, located a block from Union Depot.

There Georgiana rested for the next two days. Holmes remained close to her side for much of the time, though he occasionally went out for an hour or two, presumably to check for messages and attend to unspecified business.

Late in the afternoon of Wednesday, September 5, he returned from one of these outings with some news. He had just received a telegram from a business associate in St. Louis, who required Holmes's presence at once.

Holmes assured Georgiana that he would be back in a few days. In the meantime, he had asked the hotelkeeper's wife to look in regularly and see to it that Georgiana received proper care.

Departing on Wednesday night, Holmes arrived in St. Louis the following day and headed directly for the law office of McDonald and Howe. Finding it closed, he proceeded to the Pitezels' flat, where he discovered the children in hysterics and Carrie at a point of near-collapse.

Though Carrie felt no fondness for Holmes, her misery and loneliness were such that, at the sight of his face, she threw herself against his chest and relapsed into helpless sobs. Patting her consolingly, Holmes led her to a chair, pulled an oversize handkerchief from his pocket, and pressed it into her hands. As Carrie wept into his hankie, Holmes noted that it was identical to the one he had used to asphyxiate her husband only a few days earlier. The thought seemed vaguely amusing.

Standing over her chair, he touched her shoulder again and assured her that Benny was fine. The dead body described in the papers was a substitute corpse that he had procured in New York City. This information, however, did little to soothe the distraught woman.

"Why do you carry on so?" Holmes asked, a slight note of impatience creeping into his voice. "You are making a terrible fuss about it, more so than if it were true."

"I am sick, the baby is sick," Carrie answered through her sobs. "Oh, how could Benny do this and get us all into trouble?"

"What is the case with the children?" Holmes inquired after a moment. "What do they believe?"

Her tears having somewhat subsided, Carrie wiped her face with Holmes's hankie and heaved a ragged sigh. "They believe their father is dead."

Holmes nodded. "Good. Do not relieve them of that notion. It will make matters easier."

Stepping to the kitchen doorway, Holmes beckoned to Dessie. Assuming an air of avuncular kindliness, he assured her that everything would be fine, that he had arrived to take care of them all. Then he instructed her to seek out the nearest doctor and fetch him to the house.

While Dessie was gone, Holmes crouched by Carrie's chair and spoke to her in low, urgent tones. She must get hold of herself. She had an important role to play over the next few days. The success of the plan depended on her participation.

Reaching into his coat pocket, he extracted a business card and placed it in her hands. Tomorrow morning, he explained, she must go to this address, bringing with her the $10,000 life insurance policy that Benny had left in her care. The office was located downtown in the Commercial Building.

Through her red, brimming eyes, Carrie stared down at the card. The name imprinted in its center was Jeptha D. Howe, Esq.

On that very day, a close acquaintance of Lawyer Howe's came upon the notice of B. F. Perry's death in the *St. Louis Globe-Democrat*. He, too, had been reading the papers regularly, searching for some indication that the swindler Howard had been telling the truth.

At the sight of the article, the man let out a wordless exclamation. In spite of Howe's assurances, he had never believed that Howard would really go through with the fraud. During the time they had spent as cellmates, Howard had struck him as a bag full of hot air.

A guard who was patrolling the corridor just outside the man's cell stopped short and peered through the bars. He had never heard Marion Hedgepeth make such a sound before and wondered what had provoked it.

The sound was something between a bark and a laugh—the sound of a man who has just received a surprise. A very pleasant surprise.

21

> In the domain of fabrication Herman Webster Mudgett, alias H. H. Holmes, is entitled to a very high place. With him, lying assumed the form of an art ... and to this, in large measure at least, his wonderful success in so long concealing his crimes must be attributed.
>
> —Matthew Worth Pinkerton, *Murder in All Ages* (1898)

George B. Stadden, manager of the St. Louis branch of Fidelity Mutual, was seated at his desk on Saturday morning, September 8, when the envelope arrived. Folded inside were a brief letter and a newspaper clipping about the death of a Philadelphia man named B. F. Perry. The letter—written in a neat, feminine hand, though peppered with misspellings—was from a Mrs. Carrie A. Pitezel, who wished to inform the company that the individual described in the article was her husband, Benjamin Freelon Pitezel, holder of life insurance policy number 044145.

Stadden read the article again, this time more slowly. Then he pushed his chair away from his desk and hurried from his office.

The president of Fidelity Mutual Life Association was a portly gentleman named Levi G. Fouse, who—seeking to set a good example for his subordinates—normally arrived for work no later than nine A.M., even on Saturdays. On this particular Saturday, however, personal matters had detained him at home, and it was almost eleven before he showed up at the company's Philadelphia headquarters on Walnut Street.

No sooner had he positioned himself behind his imposing mahogany desk than an office boy delivered a telegram from his St. Louis manager, George Stadden. The message read: "B. F. Perry, found dead in Philadelphia, is claimed to be B. F. Pitezel, who is insured on 044145. Investigate before remains leave there."

Fouse—a firm believer in Benjamin Franklin's injunctions against idleness—lost no time in notifying his claims manager, whose name, as it happened, was also Perry: O. LaForrest Perry. Locating file number 044145, Perry discovered that Benjamin F. Pitezel's life was indeed insured for $10,000—an impressive sum in 1894 currency. The policy had been issued on November 9, 1893, through the branch office in Chicago.

Several features of the case instantly struck Fouse and Perry as peculiar. The policy had been purchased less than a year before the man's sudden death—a circumstance that automatically provokes a certain leeriness in insurers. Moreover, the final payment had arrived by telegraphic money order on the very last day of the grace period. And then there was the matter of the man's alias. Why had he been going by the name Perry?

His suspicions aroused, Fouse immediately sent for another trusted aid, the company treasurer, Col. O. C. Bobyshell, and dispatched him to the city morgue, to see if the corpse matched the physical description of Pitezel as recorded on the policy application. Bobyshell returned after lunchtime to report that, though the dead man's face was badly disfigured, his general appearance did indeed tally with that of Pitezel. Bobyshell also brought back the basic facts of the case, which he had learned from the coroner.

Armed with this information, O. LaForrest Perry proceeded to 1316 Callowhill Street, where, in the company of an officer from the Buttonwood police station, he spent the better part of an hour examining the crime scene. Except for the removal of the corpse, the little room had been left untouched. The corncob pipe, burned match, and broken bottle lay exactly where they had been found on the previous Tuesday.

To Perry, the evidence suggested a setup, not an accidental explosion, as the police continued to claim. Thanking the officer for his assistance, Perry returned to company headquarters. Upon arrival he reported his findings to President Fouse, who immediately wired a message to Edwin H. Cass, manager of the Chicago branch office, instructing him to learn everything possible about Benjamin F. Pitezel and, in particular, to ascertain the names of his acquaintants.

Devoted as he was to the Fidelity Mutual Life Association, President Fouse was not the sort of man who permitted business to interfere with his domestic pleasures. By the time he returned home that Saturday evening, he had already managed to put the troublesome matter of the B. F. Perry case out of his mind.

When he arrived at his office on Monday morning, however, he found a message awaiting from a St. Louis lawyer named Jeptha D. Howe, attorney for Mrs. Carrie A. Pitezel. Lawyer Howe wished to inform President Fouse that, along with a member of the Pitezel family, he would soon be traveling to Philadelphia to identify the body and collect on the $10,000 policy.

From his experience with insurance companies, H. H. Holmes knew that a family member would be called upon to identify the remains, and he did not want that person to be Pitezel's widow. The woman simply could not be trusted to carry off the deception. She was already in a hopelessly overwrought state. Another shock—the sight of the decomposed corpse, for example, or even a few tough questions by insurance investigators—and she might break down completely and blurt out the truth.

Worse, she might recognize that the body laid out in the morgue really was her husband and not a substitute corpse at all. Foreseeing this possibility, Holmes had done what he could to obliterate Pitezel's features. But he would feel safer if Carrie did not have a chance to view the corpse at all. So he was prepared to take whatever tack was necessary—from heartfelt pleas to open threats—to persuade her to stay in St. Louis.

As it turned out, he did not have to bother, thanks to Carrie's ill health and the fortuitous sickness of her infant, Wharton. Carrie protested that she could not possibly travel such a distance. Nor could her oldest daughter, Dessie, who was needed at home to help tend to the young ones.

That left the next oldest child, Alice. As far as Holmes was concerned, the fifteen-year-old girl was the ideal choice—smart enough to follow instructions but not so clever that she might figure things out for herself and so jeopardize the plot.

Although Carrie had qualms about sending the girl off with Jeptha Howe, a more or less total stranger, Holmes assured her that Alice would be in good hands. Holmes had already arranged for a cousin of his to take charge of the girl as soon as she and Howe reached Philadelphia. This cousin, Holmes explained, was a lovely, highly responsible young woman who could be trusted implicitly.

Her name was Minnie Williams.

That evening—Sunday, September 9—Holmes and Howe met to make their final preparations. The following morning, Holmes departed from St. Louis, catching an early train to Wilmette, Illinois.

At roughly the same time that Holmes was boarding his Pullman, Edwin Cass—manager of the Chicago office of Fidelity Mutual—was mulling over the telegram he had just received from Philadelphia. After digging out the records on policy 044145 and identifying the agent who had sold it to Pitezel, he immediately sought out the man, whose name was Leon Fay.

Did Fay happen to know anyone acquainted with Pitezel? Cass inquired.

As it happened, Fay did. Several years earlier, before he entered the insurance business, Fay had been involved in various enterprises, one of which had brought him into contact with a well-to-do gentleman who made his home in Englewood. The previous September, this fellow had unexpectedly appeared in Fay's office to inquire about the cost of a $10,000 life insurance policy for himself. Fay had supplied him with the information but had heard nothing more from the man. Several months later, however, Benjamin Pitezel—explaining that he had been referred by Fay's acquaintance—showed up and applied for his own policy for precisely that amount.

In response to Cass's next question, Fay explained that the gentleman in question was the owner of a large office building at Sixty-third and Wallace, popularly known as the Castle. His name was H. H. Holmes.

The following day, Cass traveled out to Englewood, disembarking from the train into the bustle and din of Wallace Street. He had no trouble finding the Castle, which loomed like a great dark fortress on the corner across from the station. Approaching the building, Cass—with his trained, investigator's eye—immediately spotted the black signs of fire damage near the roofline. The top two stories of the structure seemed entirely vacant, the windows dark and empty. The street-level floor, however, was lined with shops, most of them open for business.

It didn't take long for Cass to discover that Holmes hadn't been seen in Englewood for nearly a year. One of the store owners, however—a jeweler named Davis—provided Cass with a promising lead. Though Holmes's rakish behavior suggested otherwise, rumor had it that he was a married man with a wife and baby daughter living somewhere out in Wilmette.

Urgent affairs kept Cass confined to his office the next day, but on Thursday, September 13, he journeyed out to Wilmette, having ascertained Holmes's suburban address— 38 North John Street, between Central and Lake avenues. The house turned out to be a tidy, red-frame affair, two stories high, with a pair of small wooden turrets flanking the porch roof. The front door was opened by a servant girl, who ushered Cass into the parlor, then bustled off to fetch her mistress.

Though Mrs. Myrta Holmes treated Cass politely, she seemed discomfited by his presence. Her husband, she explained, was rarely at home, his business affairs keeping him more or less constantly on the move. The two of them corresponded regularly, however, and she would be happy to transmit any messages that Mr. Cass cared to leave.

What Cass didn't know, of course, was that, only two days earlier, Myrta had received a sudden, unexpected visit from Holmes, who had stopped off at Wilmette on his way back to Indianapolis. Part of his motive was to see how his wife and daughter were getting along. In the years since Myrta had moved out to Wilmette, Holmes had continued to provide well for her and little Lucy, and to pay them periodic visits.

But, as was always the case with Holmes, he had an ulterior motive, too. Anticipating the very situation that Myrta now faced—a sudden call from an insurance investigator—he wanted to make sure that she knew what to say.

Cass wrote out a list of questions for Myrta to convey to her husband. He also handed her something else to pass along to Holmes—a news clipping about B. F. Perry's death, taken from a local paper, *The Chicago Report*.

The story had been copied from the wire service. But whoever had transcribed it had committed a single, significant error—an error that might have been Holmes's undoing, had the Pitezel family been blessed with better luck.

22

These letters ... exhibit the enormous capacity of Mr. Holmes for duplicity and deceit. In view of the subsequent developments of the case, they portray his many resources for meeting an occasion, and a sagacity which would have served him well, had he chosen to earn an honest living.

—Frank P. Geyer, *The Holmes-Pitezel Case* (1896)

Following his brief stopover in Wilmette, Holmes had traveled straight to Indianapolis, arriving at Stubbins' Hotel early Tuesday evening, September 11. He found Georgiana much improved in health, though disgruntled with the poor accommodations. Her spirits rose considerably when Holmes presented her with a gift he had brought back from his travels—a heart-shaped locket on a golden chain. Her mood brightened even more when, within an hour of his arrival, he packed up her belongings and conveyed her to the far more luxurious surroundings of the Grand Hotel.

For the next few days, Holmes acted the part of the attentive husband, treating Georgiana to a shopping spree, taking her to the fanciest restaurants in town, accompanying her on an overnight trip to her parents' home in Franklin. Returning to Indianapolis on Saturday afternoon, September 15, they checked into the Circle Park Hotel. Later that day, while Georgiana rested in bed, Holmes slipped out of their suite to check for messages. When he returned a half hour later, he told Georgiana that he had just received a telegram from the Pennsylvania Railroad Company, informing him that the cash payment for his copiers was ready and waiting in Philadelphia.

A communication had, in fact, arrived for Holmes, but it wasn't a message from the railroad company. It was an envelope from Myrta, containing the list of questions Edwin Cass had given her, along with the clipping from the *Chicago Report*.

Holmes was impressed at how quickly the insurance company had connected him with Pitezel, and he was ready with a reply. In spite of his busy schedule, he would be willing to come to Philadelphia to help identify the remains, etc., etc. But as he glanced over the newspaper clipping, his eye fell on a glaring mistake.

Though correct in other respects, the article reported that B. F. Perry's body had been placed in the morgue in *Chicago,* not Philadelphia.

Holmes had every reason to feel lucky. Had he failed to spot the error, he might have given the game away by revealing that he knew more—much more—about Pitezel's death than he was supposed to.

But how to deal with the erroneous information? It didn't take him long to decide. He would have to pretend that Pitezel's corpse was where the article claimed.

That evening, Holmes packed a bag and bid Georgiana good-bye, explaining that he was journeying to Philadelphia to collect the money for his copiers. Instead, he caught a late-night train to Columbus, Ohio. Taking a room in a hotel near the station, he sat down at once and composed a letter to Edwin Cass.

To Cass's first question—Who did Pitezel's dental work?—Holmes replied that he did "not think [Pitezel] took very good care of his teeth and may have had none done. I remember that seven or eight years ago when working for me, he had to give up work for some time on account of neuralgia in his teeth."

Turning next to the matter of identifying marks, Holmes wrote:

In a general way I should describe him a man nearly six feet high (at least five feet ten inches), always thin in flesh and weighing from one hundred

and forty-five to one hundred and fifty-five lbs.,
having very black and somewhat coarse hair, very
thick, with no tendency to baldness; his mustache
was a much lighter color and I think of a red tinge,
though I have seen him have it colored black at
times, which gave him quite a different appearance.
I remember also that he had some trouble with his
knees, causing them to become enlarged directly
below or in front of same, as a result of floor laying
when he was in the contracting business, but
whether this was a temporary or permanent affair,
I am unable to state. He also had some sort of
warty growth on the back or side of his neck, which
prevented him from wearing a collar when working.
Aside from these points, I can think of nothing to
distinguish him from other men, unless it be that
his forehead was lower than the average and crown
of head higher, causing one to notice same. I do
remember, however, that he had, or at least had
late in 1893, a boy about twelve years of age who
looked so much like him that if compared with
body supposed to be his father would show the
identity I should think.... If the identity is not
cleared up by the time you receive this letter and
you wish me to, I will go to Chicago any time after
Wednesday next, provided you will pay my transportation there and return.... I should be willing
to go without pay in ordinary times, but can hardly
afford to do so now.

Mr. Pitezel is owing me One hundred and eighty
Dollars, and if he is in reality dead, I should be
glad to have that amount detained from the sum
payable on his policy, as I very much need it ... I
have done a good deal for his family within the
past eight years and I think if need be, I could get
an order from his wife, authorizing you to retain
the amount due me.

The next morning, Monday, September 17, Holmes mailed
this letter off to Cass and continued on his journey, disem-

barking this time in Cincinnati, where—after checking into the Grand Hotel—he composed an extremely cunning follow-up:

Dear Sir:—

Since writing to you yesterday, I have seen from a file of Philadelphia papers, that the supposed body of Pitezel is in the hands of the coroner there instead of in Chicago, as per clipping you sent me. I shall be in Baltimore in a day or two, and I will take an afternoon train to Philadelphia and call on your office there, and if they wish me to do so, I will go with some representative of theirs to the coroner's, and I think I can tell if the man there is Pitezel:—from what I read here, I cannot see anything to lead me to think that the person killed was other than a man by the name of Perry.

Yours Respectfully,
H. H. Holmes

Satisfied at the way he had handled things, Holmes settled in for the night, leaving instructions with the desk clerk to awaken him at six A.M. He had an early train to catch and it was crucially important that he be on it.

That same night, Tuesday, September 18—around the time that Holmes was completing his second letter to Cass—Jeptha Howe knocked on the door of the Pitezels' shabby flat.

Alice—dressed in a patched calico shift and threadbare jacket—opened the door and admitted him. A cracked leather satchel, packed with the handful of garments that constituted her entire wardrobe, waited on the sitting-room floor.

Rising shakily from her sickbed, Carrie kissed her fifteen-year-old daughter good-bye and urged Howe to take good care of the girl. Alice's hand-me-down shoes were so old and worn-out that her stockinged toes poked through the tips. Howe promised that he would buy her a brand-new pair as soon as they reached Philadelphia.

Alice gave each of her siblings a hug, then followed Howe out to the landing. As she started down the stairwell, she turned for a final glimpse of her mother, who leaned against the doorframe, frightfully frail and pallid, her haggard cheeks slick with tears.

Carrying Alice's bag in one hand and his own suitcase in the other, Howe led the girl to the nearest streetcar stop. Moments later, a trolley turned the corner. After boarding, Howe asked if Alice had brought any spending money with her.

Alice nodded. "Mother give me a five-cents piece."

Digging into his pants pocket, Howe extracted a silver dollar, which he handed to the girl. Alice muttered a thank-you and stuck the coin into the satchel that rested between her feet. Not long afterward, they arrived at Union Depot, where they boarded an eastbound train.

The car was empty enough for Alice to occupy her own seat across the aisle from Howe. She curled her legs up onto the cushion and leaned against the window, gazing out into the darkness.

Though Alice was nervous about the trip—and particularly about the dreadful task that awaited her at the other end—her weariness finally got the better of her. As the night wore on, she fell into a solid sleep, lulled by the rhythmic rocking of the train.

Morning sunlight filled the car when she awoke hours later—just as the train was pulling into the Cincinnati depot.

23

Little girls, this seems to say,
Never stop upon your way,
Never trust a stranger-friend;
No one knows how it will end.

—Charles Perrault, "Little Red Riding Hood"

They changed trains in Cincinnati. The new coach was more crowded than the first, and Alice was forced to share a seat with Howe. He let her have the place by the window, and as the train pulled out of the station and picked up speed, she kept her eyes fixed on the passing scenery. The countryside was flat and featureless, but she liked to watch the landscape flow by.

After a while, she grew vaguely aware that Howe was talking to someone in the aisle. Suddenly, she realized that the person was addressing her. She glanced up and was startled to see Mr. Holmes, the man her papa had worked for, standing there smiling down at her.

"What a great surprise," Holmes said, reaching out for Alice's hand. "Hello, my child. I did not recognize your jacket at once, but when I saw your face, I knew it was my favorite girl."

Nodding to Howe—who arose and moved off to a different part of the car—Holmes sat down beside Alice.

"What a pleasure to see you, my dear," he said. "How are you feeling?"

Alice replied that she supposed she was fine.

"Very good. You are a brave child. You have been entrusted with a difficult errand. But Lawyer Howe and I are here to help to see you through it."

Keeping his voice low, Holmes proceeded to tell her precisely how she must behave in the presence of the insurance people if her family hoped to obtain the money from her poor father's policy. She and her family would be set up for life—but only if Alice followed Holmes's directions to the letter.

To begin with, she must never let on that she had seen and spoken to him on the train. Second, she must pretend that Holmes and her father were only casually acquainted. Finally, though the ravages of death might have marred her papa's face, she must state with absolute certainty that the body in the morgue was her father.

Beyond that, she should simply act in a natural manner. He and Lawyer Howe would take care of the rest.

Holmes asked the girl to repeat his instructions. Satisfied, he patted her hands, then got up and went off to find Howe.

As a precaution, Holmes and his confederate agreed to travel the last leg of the journey on separate trains. At Washington, D.C., Howe disembarked with Alice, while Holmes continued on to Philadelphia, where he took a carriage to Adella Alcorn's rooming house.

The landlady was delighted to see Mr. Howard (the name by which she knew him). What, she inquired, was the occasion for his visit?

Holmes replied that he had returned to conclude his deal with the Pennsylvania Railroad Company. Negotiations were taking longer than expected and might stretch out for an indefinite number of weeks.

He was interested in renting rooms not only for himself and his wife but also for his little sister, Alice, who was spending the winter in his care. As it happened, the three large bedrooms on the third floor of the house were presently available. Holmes agreed to take the entire floor.

The landlady could not have been more pleased. "And where are Mrs. Howard and your sister?" she asked.

Holmes explained that his wife and his little sister were

enjoying a holiday in Atlantic City. He planned to travel to the resort in a few days and bring Alice back with him. Mrs. Howard would probably remain there for another two or three weeks before joining them in Philadelphia.

Before repairing to his room, Holmes told the landlady that he was expecting a visitor—a gentleman who might call either that evening or the following day. Would Mrs. Alcorn kindly direct him upstairs the moment he arrived?

While Holmes was checking into Alcorn's, Howe and Alice were taking in the sights of Washington, D.C. Alice, who had seen nothing of the world beyond the small towns and city slums of the Midwest, was overwhelmed by the marble glories of the capital.

Late that night, they departed for Philadelphia, checking into separate rooms at the Imperial Hotel early the next morning, Thursday, September 20.

Alice had promised to write to her family, and she proved to be a faithful correspondent. In the coming weeks, she composed a series of letters that—for all their clumsiness of expression—possessed a terrible poignancy in the light of subsequent events. Though all were preserved, only a few ever reached their destination. Alice, of course, remained unaware of this fact. Nor could she have guessed at the critical role her simple letters were to play in the climax of the tragedy to come.

Alone in her hotel room that Thursday afternoon, with her guardian napping next door, Alice sat down to write to her mother:

Dear Mamma and the rest,

Just arrived in Philadelphia this morning. . . . Mr. Howe and I have each a room at the above address. I am going to the Morgue after awhile. We stopped off in Washington, Md. . . . Yesterday we got on the C. and O. Pullman and it was crowded so I had to sit with Mr. Howe we sit there quite awhile and pretty soon some one came and shook hands with me. I looked up and here it was Mr. H[olmes]. He did not know my jacket, but he said he thought it was his girl's face so he went to see and it was me. I don't like him to call me babe and child and dear and all such trash. When I got on the car Tuesday night Mr. Howe asked me if I had any money and I told him 5 cents and he give me a dollar. How I wish I could see you all and hug the baby. I hope you are better. Mr. H says that I will have a ride on the ocean. I wish you could see what I have seen. I have seen more scenery than I have seen since I was born I don't know what I saw before. This is all the paper I have so I will have to close & write again. You had better not write to me here for Mr. H. says that I may be off tomorrow. If you are worse wire me good-bye kisses to all and two big ones for you and babe. Love to all.

That same afternoon—while Howe relaxed and Alice sought distraction from her loneliness by writing to her loved ones—Holmes made his first visit to the Fidelity Mutual Assurance Building at 914 Walnut Street.

Claims manager Perry was conferring with President Fouse about an unrelated matter when Holmes appeared at the doorway of the latter's office. Introducing himself, Holmes explained that he had just arrived from Baltimore to assist in the B. F. Perry case. The claims manager gathered up his papers and exited the office, leaving Fouse and his visitor to talk in private.

Holmes, seated at the side of the president's big mahogany desk, began by asking Fouse about the precise circumstances of B. F. Perry's death. The clippings he had seen contained only incomplete details.

President Fouse reviewed all the known facts of the case, from the discovery of the corpse to the autopsy results.

"A most peculiar case," Holmes said, frowning. "And what was the verdict of the coroner's jury?"

"Congestion of the lungs," Fouse replied, "caused by flame inhalation or chloroform poisoning."

After soliciting a description of Benjamin Pitezel from

Holmes, Fouse asked why the fellow might have been using an alias.

Holmes stroked his mustache meditatively for a moment before replying. Pitezel, he believed, had run into some "financial difficulty" down South a few months earlier and might have thought it prudent to conceal his identity from his creditors.

Fouse went on to explain that he had received a communication from a St. Louis lawyer named Jeptha D. Howe, who was on his way to Philadelphia with a member of the Pitezel family. As soon as they arrived, the corpse would be exhumed for identification. Fouse asked Holmes to leave his Philadelphia address, so the company could contact him when the examination took place.

Holmes told Fouse that he had some pressing business that might require his immediate attention. If so, he would be sure to leave word of where he could be reached. Otherwise, he would stop by the office early Friday morning to see where matters stood.

Thanking Holmes for his help, Fouse saw him to the door, much impressed with the frank and forthright manner of the well-spoken gentleman.

Shortly after eight that evening, Jeptha Howe—refreshed after his full day of rest—knocked on the door of Alice's room to say that he was going off on an errand and would return in several hours. Outside, he headed straight for 1905 North Eleventh Street, arriving at Alcorn's boardinghouse just as its proprietress was stepping out the door on her way to her evening prayer meeting. By the light of the streetlamp, Adella Alcorn got a clear glimpse of the stranger, taking particular note of his boyish face and small, neatly trimmed mustache.

Upstairs, Holmes reported on his meeting with President Fouse. Then the two reviewed their strategy for the following day.

Their business concluded, the pair went off to sample the pleasures of a local whorehouse that Holmes had sometimes patronized during his previous stay in the city.

* * *

Late Friday morning, September 21, Alice sat down beside her open window and penned another letter to her family back home:

> Dear Mamma and Babe,
>
> I have to write all the time to pass away the time.
> Mr. Howe has been away all morning. Mamma have you ever seen or tasted a red banana? I have had three. They are so big that I can just reach around it and have my thumb and next finger just tutch. I have not got any shoes yet and I have to go a hobbling around all the time. . . . Are you sick in bed yet or are you up? I wish that I could hear from you but I don't know whether I would get it or not. . . . I have not got but two clean garments and that is a shirt and my white skirt. I saw some of the largest rocks that I bet you never saw. I crossed the Potomac River. I guess that I have told you all the news. So goodbye Kisses to you and babe.
>
> Your loving daughter.

Howe showed up at Alice's room in the early afternoon. After making sure that she remembered her instructions, he took her off to the Fidelity building, where they were immediately ushered into the office of President Fouse.

Howe had come equipped with various documents and credentials, including a letter of attorney from Carrie Pitezel. Carrie had also supplied him with some letters Benny had sent her during the summer. The return address on the envelopes read, "B.F. Perry, 1316 Callowhill Street, Philadelphia."

When Fouse asked Howe the question he had posed to Holmes—why had Pitezel adopted a pseudonym?—the lawyer gave essentially the same answer, explaining that, because of some "embarrassing financial transactions" in Tennessee, Pitezel had thought it "advisable to change his name and his location" for a while.

Fouse perused the letters, which left no doubt that Pitezel

had been passing himself off as Perry. Still, they did not prove that the dead man found at 1316 Callowhill Street was really Pitezel.

The lawyer (who had been tutored in this matter by Holmes) responded with a detailed description of Pitezel. Fouse was forced to concede that the man's appearance did indeed match the general attributes of the deceased.

Fouse then turned his attention to Alice, who had sat mutely during this exchange, her eyes downcast and her feet pulled up under her chair, as though to hide her wretched shoes from public view. Smiling down at the underfed girl in her ragtag clothes, Fouse asked if she could say what her father looked like. Alice mumbled a description that matched Howe's.

"And can you think of any special marks—scars, injuries, or the like—by which your father might be identified?" Fouse then inquired.

Alice chewed on her lower lip for a moment, then—in a voice so low and hesitant that Fouse had to lift himself off his seat and lean forward on his desktop—she stammered something about a permanently bruised thumbnail and "twisted" lower front teeth.

Just then, a clerk slipped into the office and whispered something to Fouse. "Very good," Fouse replied, then looked over at Howe and explained that a gentleman named Holmes—who had known Pitezel in Chicago and had kindly volunteered to help with the identification—had just arrived in the building. Would Howe care to meet him?

"Most assuredly," replied Howe.

Fouse greeted Holmes warmly when he entered the room, then introduced him to Howe. The two shook hands politely and exchanged the standard civilities.

Suddenly Holmes seemed to notice Alice for the first time. Stepping to her chair, he leaned down and smiled. "You are Alice, are you not? Don't you remember me, my dear? I knew your family in Chicago."

Alice shrugged, nodded, then allowed that she did recollect him.

Howe, who had been eyeing Holmes warily, suddenly addressed himself to Fouse. He did not mean to cast suspicions on a total stranger, he declared. Nevertheless, as the attorney for Mrs. Pitezel, he felt entitled to know the motives of Mr. Holmes. What precisely was his purpose in being there?

Holmes, acting slightly wounded, professed that he *had* no personal motives. He had been contacted by the insurance company and wished to do whatever he could to help resolve a matter that could only be a source of immeasurable pain to Mrs. Pitezel and her children.

Howe seemed mollified by this explanation and apologized if his words had offended Mr. Holmes. The latter graciously replied that no apology was necessary.

At that point, the three men turned to the matter that had brought them together—the identification of the body. Before long, they had agreed on a set of physical characteristics peculiar to Pitezel: a warty growth on the neck, a scar from an old injury on his right shin, the discolored thumbnail, and his jagged lower teeth.

The final arrangements were made. The next day, Saturday, September 22, all the parties would convene in Fouse's office and proceed from there to potter's field, where the three-week-old corpse would be disinterred for examination.

24

> He who shall teach the child to doubt
> The rotting grave shall ne'er get out.

—William Blake, *Auguries of Innocence*

When Holmes showed up at the Fidelity building on Saturday morning, Howe and Alice were already there, waiting upstairs with President Fouse, O. LaForrest Perry, and another man: the carpenter, Eugene Smith, who had been asked to come along to help identify the remains. It took Holmes a moment to recognize Smith as the fellow he had seen in Pitezel's office several weeks earlier. The realization gave him a start—Smith was the last person he wanted to see. Still, there was nothing to do but smile politely and pray that the man wouldn't recognize him.

At first, Smith appeared not to. But as Holmes turned his attention to the other people in the room, the carpenter eyed him closely. There was something strangely familiar about the new arrival, Smith thought. He could have sworn he had seen the dapper gentleman somewhere before, though for the life of him, he couldn't recollect where.

Leaving Fouse's office shortly before noon, the little party traveled to the city morgue, where they picked up Dr. William Mattern—the physician who had performed the autopsy—and Deputy Coroner Dugan. From there, they caught the first of the two streetcars that would carry them to potter's field on the outskirts of the city, where Benjamin

Pitezel's body had been buried on September 15, after lying in the coldhouse for the required eleven days.

As the horse-drawn trolley rattled over the cobblestones, Smith continued to scrutinize Holmes, who sat across the aisle from him, talking softly to President Fouse. When they changed cars forty minutes later, the carpenter made sure to seat himself next to Holmes.

By then, Smith had started to place him. Indeed, he was becoming more convinced by the minute that Holmes was the gentleman in the tan-colored suit who had entered the patent dealer's office on the afternoon of Smith's second visit and disappeared upstairs after signaling Perry to follow.

Clearing his throat, Smith asked Holmes how he came to be here now.

Holmes hesitated for a moment, as though considering how—or perhaps whether—to respond. Finally, he replied that Mr. Pitezel had been a business acquaintance of his in Chicago. Having been contacted by the insurance company, he had offered to come to Philadelphia to render whatever assistance he could.

"What line of business do you follow?" Smith asked.

"Patent agent," Holmes answered in a tone meant to discourage further inquiry.

Smith, however, was undeterred.

"That is interesting," he mused. "Mr. Perry was attempting to dispose of a patented invention of my own at the time of his death." Smith cast a hopeful look in Holmes's direction. "Perhaps you might be interested in handling the matter?"

Holmes uttered a noncommittal sound.

An awkward moment passed. "How did the insurance company get in touch with you?" Smith continued after a while.

Holmes sighed wearily. "I travel a good deal throughout the United States. The company telegraphed Mrs. Pitezel, who relayed the message to me."

Smith mulled this information over for a moment before asking, "If you travel about so much, how did she know just where to reach you?"

This time, Holmes answered with an icy stare. From that point on, the two men rode in silence.

As the streetcar approached its destination, Smith debated what to do. He believed that Holmes was the man he had seen at 1316 Callowhill Street several weeks earlier but couldn't be entirely sure. He felt the burden of his great responsibility. L. G. Fouse himself—president of the Fidelity Mutual Life Association Company—had asked for his assistance. He was petrified of committing a blunder and making a fool of himself.

After turning the matter over in his mind until it dizzied him, he settled on the safest course. He decided to say nothing.

Months would pass before Eugene Smith understood what a catastrophic choice he had made. And by then, of course, it was too late.

Arriving at the City Burial Ground around one P. M., the group was greeted by Dr. Lemuel Taylor, the official in charge of the cemetery. Having been notified that morning of the impending postmortem, Taylor and his assistant, Henry Sidebotham, had already exhumed the plain pine box and carried it to a wooden storage shed on the edge of the graveyard, not far from the crematory furnace.

Holmes and the others crowded into the shed, where the coffin had been placed on a makeshift table. Wedging the edge of a spade under the lid, Taylor pried open the coffin. Immediately, a foul miasma wafted into the room. Coughing and gagging, Fouse and Perry yanked out their hankies and clutched them to their faces, while Howe drew Alice away from the coffin, into the farthest corner of the shed.

Pitezel's body had been found in a fairly advanced state of decomposition on September 4. Now, nearly three weeks later, it was repulsive enough to make even Dr. Mattern wince.

Holmes, however, seemed unperturbed by its putrid condition. Peering into the open coffin at the black and bloated corpse, he coolly announced, "This is Benjamin Pitezel."

At that, Alice broke into cries so piteous that even Howe

was moved to tears. He placed an arm around the sobbing child and patted her shoulder.

"Perhaps I shall take the child outside until the examination is completed," Howe said, leading the girl toward the doorway. Fouse and Perry endorsed this idea and decided to join Howe and Alice outside.

As Mattern pulled on a pair of rubber gloves, Holmes, standing at his side, reminded him of the identifying marks that they were looking for—the bruised thumbnail, the scarred leg, and the warty growth. Eugene Smith, meanwhile, positioned himself on the opposite side of the table to observe the procedure. Taylor, Sidebotham, and Dugan waited nearby.

Reaching into the box, Mattern began his examination. He lifted up the corpse's hands and looked closely at the fingernails. It was difficult to detect any bruises, since all of the nails were discolored by putrefaction. Tearing open the seam of the right pants leg, he searched for a scar on the moldering flesh of the calf—but to no avail. Nor was the wart immediately visible.

Finally, he stepped away from the coffin. "I cannot find the marks," he muttered. The sight and stench of the cadaver seemed to have left him slightly shaken. Peeling off his gloves, he dropped them onto the table, stepped over to a bucketful of water that Taylor had set in a corner, splashed some on his face, and began scrubbing his hands.

As he did, Holmes stripped off his suit jacket, rolled up his sleeves, and picked up Mattern's gloves. Fitting them onto his hands, he reached into his vest pocket and removed a small lancet. Then, as Mattern came up beside him, he went to work on the corpse.

"Here," Holmes said. Using the point of the lancet, Holmes pried the darkened nail from the end of the right thumb and passed it over to Mattern. "Clean it with alcohol and see what you find."

From the inside of the right leg, about two and a half inches below the knee, he peeled away the skin, using only his fingers. The flesh of the leg was so rotten that Holmes did not need the lancet. Beneath the skin, the cicatrix of an old wound, which had fused itself to the bone, was clearly visible.

"We must turn him over," Holmes announced. Taylor, who was reluctant to have any contact with the corpse, stuck his spade into the coffin and used it to work the body around. Holmes and Mattern assisted by reaching in and pulling on the clothing.

With the corpse lying facedown, Holmes pointed to a growth on the back of its neck. "Look," he said to Mattern, using the lancet to etch a circle around the spot.

Asking Holmes to step aside, Mattern took the lancet from his hand, excised the wart, wrapped it in a sheet of paper, and placed it carefully in his shirt pocket.

The body was restored to its original position in the wooden box. Mattern found an old cloth lying about and draped it over the corpse's face, leaving only the gaping mouth exposed. Then the lid was arranged on the coffin top so that the body was concealed from the neck down.

Stepping out of the shed, Holmes returned a few moments later with Alice and Howe. Fouse and Perry remained outside. Leading Alice by the hand to the tableside, Holmes gently asked her to look at the teeth and say if they resembled her papa's. Sobbing, Alice forced herself to look at the ghastly sight, then nodded yes and quickly buried her face in her hands.

As Taylor and his assistant began to replace the coffin lid, Holmes declared solemnly that he would pay whatever it cost to have the body cremated. Howe, his arm around the hysterical child, replied that he would ask the widow how she wished to dispose of the remains, though he concurred that cremation sounded like the wisest choice.

Some of them, such as Howe and Perry, sat silently during the return trip, too sobered by the experience to engage in casual talk. Others, relieved that the ordeal was over, chattered away.

Holmes took the opportunity to tell President Fouse that because of pressing business affairs, he would only be able to remain in Philadelphia for one more day. Though Fouse was unhappy about disrupting his Sabbath, he agreed to come to the office early the next morning.

Back in the city, Holmes accompanied Alice and Howe to the Imperial Hotel, conferring with the latter in his room while the girl packed up her meager belongings. When she was ready, Holmes took her to Adella Alcorn's place. The landlady had gone off to the shore for the weekend, leaving a longtime tenant, an old man named John Grammer, in charge. Holmes introduced Alice as his little sister, just arrived from Atlantic City.

Grammer looked curiously at the girl, who seemed frightfully pale and shaky, as though she'd just suffered a terrible shock. Without elaborating, Holmes explained that his sister was slightly indisposed, though he was certain she would be fine by the morning. Bidding the old man good evening, Holmes showed Alice to her quarters, then retired to his own room for the night.

Shortly after ten the next morning—Sunday, September 23—Holmes and Alice returned to Fouse's office. Lawyer Howe and O. LaForrest Perry were already present, along with Coroner Samuel H. Ashbridge, who proceeded to take the following statement from Alice:

"I am in the fifteenth year of my age. Benjamin F. Pitezel was my father. He was thirty-seven years old this year. My mother is living. There are five children. My father came East on July 29th. He left St. Louis.... We learned of his death through the papers. I came on with Mr. Howe to see the body. On Saturday, September 22d, I saw a body at the City Burial Ground and fully recognized the body as that of my father by his teeth. I am fully satisfied that it is he."

As soon as she was done, Holmes gave his own sworn affidavit:

"I knew Benjamin Pitezel for eight years in Chicago. I had business with him during that time.... I received a letter from E.H. Cass, Agent of Fidelity Company, about B.F. Pitezel, he sending a clipping to me. I came to Philadelphia and saw the body on Saturday, September 22d, at the City Burial Ground. I recollected a mole on the back of the neck; a low growth of head on the forehead; the general shape of the head and teeth. His daughter Alice had described a scar on the right leg below the knee in front. I found those on the body as described to me by Alice. I have no doubt whatsoever but that it is the body of Benjamin F. Pitezel, who was buried as B.F. Perry. I last saw him alive in November, 1893, in Chicago. 1 heard he used an assumed name recently, but I never knew him to use any other name than his own before. I found him an honest, honorable man, in all his dealings."

The business concluded, Holmes shook hands all around and received a $10 check from President Fouse to cover his traveling expenses. Howe arranged to return the following morning.

Holmes, Howe, and Alice left the Fidelity building together. A few blocks away, they paused on a street corner. Howe explained to Alice that he would have to remain in Philadelphia to receive the insurance money. In the meantime, he was turning her over to the care of Mr. Holmes, who would escort her back to St. Louis. He thanked her for her help and her courage. She had done a splendid job.

That evening, Holmes and Alice boarded a westbound train. At that point, the girl had every reason to believe that she was on her way back home.

But she was wrong.

25

Truth is stranger than fiction, and if Mrs. Pitezel's story is true, it is the most wonderful exhibition of the power of mind over mind I have ever seen, and stranger than any novel I have ever read.

—The Honorable Michael Arnold

In her husband's absence, Georgiana had filled her days with assorted activities—needlework, reading, window-shopping, sight-seeing strolls, and another brief visit to her parents' home in Franklin. Even so, she had ample time to develop a friendship with Mrs. Rodius, the hotel owner's ruddy-faced wife.

Mrs. Rodius was very curious about Georgiana's husband. She had caught only a fleeting glimpse of him when he had signed the hotel register. He had gone off again just a few hours later, leaving his wife to occupy herself as best she could.

But as the two women became better acquainted, it became clear that Georgiana doted on her husband. She spoke with particular pride about his self-made success. Through hard work and shrewd dealings, her Henry had become a wealthy man, with considerable property holdings in Chicago and Texas. He also owned a substantial estate overseas, in Berlin, Germany. Indeed, they would soon be traveling to Europe and might move there permanently once her husband had settled his affairs in the States.

Mrs. Rodius was suitably impressed and looked forward

to being properly introduced to Mr. Howard, who was due back in Indianapolis any day. But as it happened, she never got the chance.

Late Monday afternoon, September 24—the day after he and Alice Pitezel departed from Philadelphia—Holmes appeared suddenly at the door of the hotel room. Georgiana flew into his arms. But no sooner had he finished embracing her and filling her in on the ostensible progress of his railroad deal than he announced, in a voice full of regret, that he would have to leave again almost immediately.

Understandably, Georgiana was dismayed, though Holmes managed to placate her with some small gifts and a promise to return within the week.

And where, asked Georgiana, was he off to this time?

To St. Louis, he replied. To meet with his lawyer, a gentleman named Mr. Harvey, in regard to settling the unfortunate matter that had landed him in jail several months earlier.

The first part of this statement, at least, was true. Holmes was indeed on his way to St. Louis—though for a very different reason than the one he presented to his wife. As usual, Georgiana had not the slightest conception of her husband's true activities. Among the myriad facts she did not know was that he had actually arrived in Indianapolis much earlier that day.

With him was Alice Pitezel—who was at that moment sitting in a shabby hotel room not far from the train station, wondering when she would see her mother again.

As their train crossed the border into Ohio, Holmes—talking in the way she hated, as though she were his favorite little girl—had broken the news to Alice. They were not going back to St. Louis after all. Though he hadn't said anything about it in Philadelphia, he had been corresponding with her mother, who was feeling much better and was back on her feet. For reasons too complicated to explain, they had decided that Alice's family should move away from St. Louis—perhaps to Indianapolis or Detroit or a place farther east.

Before making this move, Carrie wanted to pay a visit to her folks in Galva. Since it didn't make sense for Alice to travel all the way to St. Louis and then back again, the arrangement they had worked out was this: Holmes was to put Alice up in a hotel in Indianapolis, then continue on to St. Louis to fetch two of her siblings, Nellie and Howard. Holmes would bring them back to Indianapolis to keep Alice company, while her mother, Dessie, and baby Wharton made the trip to Galva. Afterward, they would all be reunited and decide on a place to live. With the money they had inherited from Alice's poor, dead papa, they would buy their own house and live comfortably forever.

Simple and naïve, Alice swallowed this story without question. She was disappointed that she would not see her mama for a while. But it was a comfort to know that she would soon have Nellie and Howard for company. And the thought of living in a big house with Mama and Dessie and the little ones made her happy.

When the train pulled into Union Depot, Holmes led her straight to Stubbins' European Hotel and rented her a room. Explaining that he would be gone for a few days, he asked if she would like him to carry a letter to her family. While Holmes returned to the front desk to leave instructions with the hotelkeeper, Alice sat down and wrote the following:

Dear Ones at Home:

I am glad to hear that you are all well and that you are up. I guess you will not have any trouble getting the money. [Mr. Holmes] is going to get two of you and fetch you here with me and then I won't be so lonesome.... I have a pair of shoes now if I could see you I would have a nough to talk to you all day but I cannot very well write it I will see you all before long though don't you worry. This is a cool day. Mr. Perry said that if you did not get the insurance all right through the lawyers to rite to Mr. Foust or Mr. Perry. I wish I had a silk dress. I have seen more since I have been away than I ever saw before in my life. I have another picture for your album. I will have to close for this time now so good bye love and kisses and squeeses to all.

Holmes returned to the room just as Alice was signing her letter. Folding it carefully in fourths, he tucked it away in his jacket pocket. Then he took his leave of Alice and repaired to the Circle Park Hotel for his brief reunion with Georgiana.

Jeptha Howe, meanwhile, was on a train headed back to St. Louis. He, too, was bearing something for Mrs. Pitezel— a check for nearly $10,000 from the Fidelity Mutual Life Association Company.

Though the cause of Benjamin Pitezel's death remained unclear, the officers of the company had decided to halt their investigation and honor his policy without further delay. Their motives were partly humanitarian and partly a matter of public relations. The sufferings of young Alice— a child so poor that she did not even own a decent pair of shoes—had affected Fouse deeply. Her pitiable situation reflected the plight of her whole family—penniless, unprotected, bereft of their only provider. Fouse did not want to be perceived as the head of a company that dealt cold-bloodedly with a destitute widow and her poor, fatherless children.

Moreover, though Lawyer Howe had struck him as a sharpie, Fouse had been highly impressed by the manly demeanor of H. H. Holmes. Since the true circumstances of Pitezel's death would probably never be known, Fouse was obliged to base his decision on other factors. That a gentleman as fine and upstanding as Dr. Holmes had vouched for Pitezel's integrity left little doubt that the claim was legitimate. In the absence of hard evidence to the contrary, the death must be ruled accidental.

And so, on Monday morning, September 24, Howe had presented himself at President Fouse's office, where he was handed a check for $9,715.85—the policy value minus the expenses that the company had incurred in conducting its investigation. Howe had made some noises about the deduction, but decided not to press the point. Shaking hands with

President Fouse and Mr. Perry, he had gone straight back to his hotel room, thrown his things into his bag, and lost no time in getting out of Philadelphia.

On Tuesday, September 25—the morning after his sudden appearance at Georgiana's doorsill—Holmes kissed his wife good-bye and took a train to St. Louis. After catching a few hours of sleep in a downtown hotel, he cabbed over to the Pitezels' flat early the next day.

Carrie invited him in. Though no longer bedridden, she looked terribly careworn and gaunt. Shooing the children out of the kitchen, she seated herself beside Holmes at the table and immediately asked about Alice.

Gazing earnestly into her eyes, he assured her that her daughter was fine. He had provided Alice with lodging in the finest hotel in Indianapolis and had paid the proprietor extra money to look after the girl. All her needs were being taken care of. Holmes had even bought her a book to read while he was gone—Mrs. Stowe's *Uncle Tom's Cabin.*

Carrie was startled and confused. Why hadn't he brought Alice home? And where was Benny?

Holmes's tone grew confidential. Benny was alive and well. The scheme had worked to perfection. But certain precautions still had to be taken, and Carrie must listen very closely to what Holmes had to say.

Though the insurance people had fallen for the scheme, they might well continue to investigate the case, at least for a while. Benny was going to have to disappear for a time. He had decided to move down South until the "clouds rolled by." At the moment, he was lying low in Cincinnati where he wanted to see Carrie before he headed south.

It wasn't safe, however, for Carrie to travel with all the children. If the insurance company did have detectives on the case, they would be on the lookout for a lone woman accompanied by five children. Therefore, Holmes and Benny had worked out a plan. Holmes would take Nellie and Howard to Indianapolis, where they would pick up Alice and then continue on to Cincinnati. Holmes had already rented a house there for the winter. He would leave the three children in the care of his cousin Minnie Williams, who had agreed to watch them until Carrie arrived.

In the meantime, Carrie would go back home to Galva with Dessie and Wharton for a visit with her parents. After a few weeks, the three of them would travel to Cincinnati to join the others. Then, Carrie could see Benny before he went into hiding.

By the time Holmes finished laying out this plan, Carrie's head was spinning. Frightened and alone, caught up in a plot even more devious than she knew, she was defenseless against the suave duplicity of Holmes. Besides, what choice did she have but to trust him? She was desperate to see Benny again and would do whatever was required of her. The idea that detectives might be on her husband's trail made her shudder. She did not think she could bear the shame that his arrest would bring down on them all.

In the end, she assented completely to the proposal. On Friday morning, she would bring Nellie and Howard to the train depot and turn her little ones over to Holmes.

When she arrived at the station on Friday, September 28, with Nellie and Howard in tow, Carrie was surprised to see Lawyer Howe waiting on the platform with Holmes. The two men were deep in conversation.

As Carrie approached, Howe turned to her and smiled. He shook her hand and congratulated her. The insurance money had been paid, he declared. He had the check waiting back in his office.

Holmes glanced at him and said, "You had better give her some money."

Nodding, Howe pulled a roll of greenbacks from his pocket and peeled off a $5 bill.

"Thank you," Carrie said softly, accepting the bill. Then she knelt on the platform and hugged both of her little ones, embracing her ten-year-old boy for so long that Holmes grew impatient.

"We do not have time to fool around," he said to her. "The train is about ready to leave."

After loading the children's trunk on board, Holmes took

each of them by the hand and led them to their seats in the car.

Carrie remained on the platform until the train was out of sight. Then, heavy-hearted, she trudged from the depot. Lawyer Howe walked by her side, explaining that they must arrange a time for her to come to his office and sign the final papers.

She barely heard him, so absorbed was she in thoughts of her children. Three of them were now in the care of Holmes. She could never have imagined that—even before he had left Philadelphia—he had already decided to kill them all.

26

There is a method in man's wickedness.

—Beaumont and Fletcher, *A King and No King*

Except for his sojourns in Fort Worth and St. Louis, Holmes had been leading a nomad's existence since his flight from Chicago. But that life seemed almost settled compared to the wanderings to come. On Friday, September 28—the day he took Howard and Nellie Pitezel away to join their older sister—he embarked on a journey so apparently bizarre that, to some later observers, it seemed driven by madness.

But if Holmes was a madman, he was the type who fulfills his compulsions in a frighteningly methodical way. And behind the tortuous odyssey he conducted in the fall of 1894, there lay a devious design. Moving constantly from city to city, dragging his young victims from pillar to post, he was attempting to trace a course so dizzyingly complex that no one would ever be able to follow it.

Early Friday morning, Holmes had wired a message to Robert Sweeney, clerk at the Stubbins' Hotel, requesting him to bring Alice Pitezel to the depot to meet the St. Louis train. Arriving in Indianapolis, Holmes found Alice and Sweeney waiting on the platform. Thanking the clerk, he led Alice onto the Pullman, where she broke into delighted squeals at the sight of her siblings. The three chattered excitedly all the way to Cincinnati.

By the time they arrived it was late and the children were

exhausted. Holmes took rooms in a cheap hotel called the Atlantic House, close to the depot, signing the register as "Alexander E. Cook and three children." The following morning—Saturday, September 29—he transferred them to a different hotel, the Bristol, at the corner of Sixth and Vine streets. Still using the name Cook, he rented a single room with two beds for himself and the children.

No sooner had they settled into the room than Holmes announced that he was taking Howard out on an errand. He told Alice and Nellie to stay put. Then, leading Howard by the hand, he went off in search of a vacant house.

Clerk George Rumsey was seated at his desk in J. C. Thomas's real estate agency when a well-dressed gentleman entered with a small boy at his side. Looking up from his papers, Rumsey greeted the man, who explained that he was there to see about renting a house. Rumsey pointed to Mr. Thomas's door and told the gentleman to go right in. As the man and boy made their way past his desk, Rumsey gazed after them. He assumed that they were father and son and was struck by how shabbily clothed the child was in comparison to his handsomely dressed father.

Shaking hands with Mr. Thomas, Holmes introduced himself as A. C. Hayes. He was looking for a small house to rent in a quiet neighborhood for himself and his family. Shuffling through his files, Mr. Thomas came up with just the thing—a nice, tidy place at 305 Poplar Street. Holmes, who explained that he was in something of a hurry, agreed to take the house sight unseen. Paying fifteen dollars in advance, he received the keys from Mr. Thomas, then grasped the boy by the hand and headed for the front doorway, pausing at George Rumsey's desk to ask the name of the nearest used-furniture dealer.

A few hours later, Miss Henrietta Hill, who resided at 303 Poplar Street, heard an unaccustomed noise coming from the vacant house next door. Stepping out onto her porch, she was surprised to see a horse-drawn furniture wagon pulled up in front of number 305. As she watched, a neatly groomed man in a brown coat and derby removed a key from his pocket and unlocked the front door, while two laborers hauled a stove out of the rear of the wagon and maneuvered it into the house. Standing in the front yard, his hands stuck deep in the pockets of his gray coat, a raggedy little boy looked on in silence.

Two things struck Miss Hill as curious. The first was the size of the stove. It was an enormous, cylindrical thing, more suitable for a barroom than a modest-sized house. The second was the contents of the wagon—or more properly, the lack thereof. Besides that single object, the wagon held nothing—no fixtures, no furnishings. Just the huge, iron stove, big enough to heat a beer hall.

With the moving men gone and the boy amusing himself outside in the yard, Holmes paced back and forth in the vacant living room, trying to cool his fury. So much time and money gone to waste. The house was not nearly as isolated as he had been led to believe. He had spotted the neighbor woman watching him from her front porch. Holmes knew the type. Before long, every busybody in the neighborhood would know all about the mysterious new tenant who had rented the empty house at 305 Poplar Street and brought in nothing but a big stove and a little boy. It took him a good twenty minutes to calm down enough to make a measured decision. There was nothing to do but switch plans.

Next time, he would be more careful.

Early Sunday morning, Miss Hill's doorbell rang. The caller was her new neighbor, Mr. Hayes, who proceeded to explain that, because of a sudden change in his business affairs, he would not be renting the house next door after all. He had already purchased a perfectly good stove, however, and was wondering if Miss Hill would care to have it. She was welcome to it, free of charge.

Then, tipping his hat to the puzzled spinster, he turned and disappeared down the street, never to be seen in the neighborhood again.

Later that day, Holmes took Alice, Nellie, and Howard to the Cincinnati Zoo—the only time in their lives that the children had visited such a magical place. They petted the ostriches, gawked at the giraffes, exclaimed over the bison, and had an altogether wonderful afternoon.

Holmes's motives for treating the young ones to such a pleasant time were, of course, purely sinister. For as long as they were in his keeping, it served his purpose to beguile both the children and the world at large into seeing him as a loving guardian. A casual observer, spying Holmes with his three ragtag charges, might have taken them for a kindly uncle on a Sunday outing with his visiting nieces and nephew. Such a person could never have conceived the truth—that what he had seen was really a trio of tiny prisoners and a keeper who had already condemned them to death.

Back at the hotel after their trip to the zoo, Holmes told the children to get ready to leave. That evening, the foursome traveled to Indianapolis. From the depot, Holmes took them to a place called the Hotel English, registering the children under their mother's maiden name, Canning.

They remained there only overnight. Early the next morning—Monday, October 1—he moved them to a hotel called the Circle House, a short distance from the Circle Park Hotel, where Georgiana was still whiling away her time, awaiting her husband's return.

As soon as the children were settled in, Holmes informed them that he would be leaving for St. Louis that evening to fetch the rest of the family. Alice, Nellie, and Howard were to remain in their room—reading, drawing, playing with their few simple toys. Holmes would arrange for their meals to be brought to them.

When he asked if they would like to send messages home, the two girls sat down at once and penned letters to their mother. Alice described the wonders of the zoo ("The ostrich is about a head taller than I am so you know about how high it is. And the giraffe you have to look up in the sky to see it"). Thirteen-year-old Nellie, an erratic speller, offered random observations on the weather and the accommodations ("It is quite worm here and I have to wear this worm dress becaus my close an't ironet. It is awful nice place where we are staying").

The letters completed, Holmes folded them carefully away, promising to deliver them personally to the girls' mama. He was lying, of course. None of the notes the children composed ever reached their destination. But Holmes did not destroy the letters. Instead, he stored them neatly away in a small metal box.

Clearly, he foresaw a time when this correspondence might come in handy—a time when he might be called upon to prove that, during the weeks the Pitezel children were in his care, he had treated them with a father's kindness.

Later that day, Holmes made a surprise appearance at the Circle Park Hotel. But before Georgiana could get overly excited about seeing him, he announced that he had to leave again at once. He had only returned because he missed her so desperately—he needed to gaze upon her dear face if only for a moment, and to feel the touch of her lips upon his own. Urgent business, however, required his immediate return to St. Louis, though he swore to rejoin Georgiana in a matter of days.

Georgiana's disappointment was somewhat allayed by the splendid news Holmes had brought back from St. Louis. He had found a purchaser for his building in Fort Worth, a businessman willing to pay $35,000 for the property. This gentleman was expected to arrive in St. Louis the following day with $10,000 cash advance.

Georgiana was delighted—for herself as well as for Henry. With the Fort Worth business out of the way, their European trip was a step closer to reality.

The pair spent a few tender hours together. Then Holmes took leave of his wife, satisfied with his stratagem. Of course, the Fort Worth businessman had been a complete fabrication, but when Holmes returned from St. Louis, he expected to be a substantially richer man, and the real estate sale would account for his sudden increase in wealth.

By Tuesday morning, October 2, Holmes was back in St. Louis. Shortly before noon, he picked up Carrie at her flat and escorted her to the offices of McDonald and Howe.

By the time the lawyers got through with her, Carrie felt so battered and distraught that she wanted nothing more to do with the whole sordid affair. "I don't care about the money anymore," she said through her tears. "I just want to go home."

Holmes, ever the kindly family counselor, advised her to sign the papers and have done with it. Carrie finally relented. After endorsing the insurance check and paying Howe's fee—a hefty $2,500 plus a few hundred more for various expenses—she received several piles of greenbacks, which she stuffed into a shopping bag she had brought along for that purpose. Then Holmes shook hands with the lawyers and led Carrie off to the First National Bank.

She had already been fleeced by the lawyers. Now it was Holmes's turn to skin her completely.

Inside the bank, he took her aside to apprise her of her husband's financial situation. Holmes began by reminding her that, along with himself, Benny was half-owner of a valuable piece of real estate that the two of them had purchased in Fort Worth. To finance the deal, they had taken out a $16,000 loan. Benny still owed $5,000 on the note and would lose his share of the property unless that sum was paid immediately.

Carrie peered inside her bag. It was crammed with $100 bills. Never in her life had she seen—let alone held—so much money. But it wasn't in her possession for long.

Taking the bag from her hands, Holmes reached inside and counted out $5,000. Then he carried the money to a cashier's window on the far side of the lobby, while Carrie waited at the customer's service counter, her back to Holmes.

When Holmes returned a few minutes later, he handed her a canceled promissory note for $16,000 drawn against the Fort Worth National Bank. The note was signed "Benton T. Lyman"—the alias Pitezel had been using down in Texas. The matter was now taken care of, Holmes said with a grin. She had done well. Benny would be proud of her.

Holmes, it need hardly be said, had not turned the money over to the bank. Standing by the cashier's window, he had simply shoved the bills into his own pocket. He hadn't entirely lied to Carrie. He and her husband did indeed owe $16,000 to a Fort Worth businessman named Samuels. But Holmes had as much intention of repaying it as he had of confessing to Pitezel's murder. The promissory note he had given Carrie was a worthless scrap.

Before they left the bank, Holmes relieved Carrie of an additional $1,600—$1,500 for his own services, plus an extra $100 to cover her children's living expenses.

"I believe that makes us about even," Holmes said, tucking away the money.

Carrie, so dazed by this time that she barely knew up from down, simply nodded wearily. Out of the nearly $10,000 realized from her husband's life insurance policy, she had ended up with $500.

Before taking leave of her, Holmes asked if she would like to send a message to the children. Carrie scribbled a greeting, which Holmes pocketed, intending to destroy it as soon as she was out of sight.

Outside the bank, Holmes impressed upon her the importance of leaving St. Louis at once. It was Benny's desire that she take Dessie and the baby to her parents' home in Galva and remain there until she received further word. "Go tomorrow," Holmes commanded. "And then when I write to you in Galva, do as I say. These are your husband's instructions, remember."

Then, promising her that she would be reunited with Benny and the children soon, he headed for the train station, his pocket bulging with cash.

As Holmes traveled back to Indianapolis, he must have felt suffused with satisfaction. The venture had worked out well for everyone. His cut had been the healthiest of all—over $6,500 all told. That was only fair, of course. After all, he had devoted nearly a year of his life to the project. Howe had come away with $2,500 for what amounted to only a few days' of work. Even Carrie had ended up with a few hundred bucks.

Given Holmes's plans for her and her family, that was certainly an adequate amount. He doubted that she would be able to spend it in the time she had remaining to her.

But another party was also expecting to share in the profits—to the tune of $500. And Holmes had failed to take this individual into account. Whether this failure was accidental or deliberate, Holmes would live to regret it—like every other man who had made the mistake of crossing Marion Hedgepeth.

27

The nerve, the calculation and the audacity of the man were unparalleled. Murder was his natural bent. Sometimes, he killed from sheer greed of gain; oftener, as he himself confessed, to gratify an inhuman thirst for blood. Not one of his crimes was the outcome of a sudden burst of fury—"hot blood," as the codes say. All were deliberate; planned and concluded with consummate skill.

—*Chicago Journal,* May 9, 1896

Holmes returned to Georgiana in a jubilant mood, sweeping her up in his arms and spinning her around the hotel room. Everything had gone smoothly in St. Louis, he said happily—"slick as a whistle." Reaching into his jacket, he extracted a fat pack of $100 bills, held it up, and gave it a smug little shake.

Georgiana's saucer eyes grew even bigger. "Is that ten thousand dollars, Harry?" She had never seen so much money before.

"Five thousand, my dear. I forwarded the other five to my broker, Mr. Blackman, in Chicago."

He tossed the money onto a side table, then knelt by his valise. "I have some gifts for you," he said. "For being so patient with me." Undoing the clasp, he reached inside the bag and brought out a leather-bound Bible, plus two velvet jewelry boxes, one containing a locket set with pearls, the other a pair of diamond earrings.

Georgiana threw her arms around Holmes and declared herself the luckiest woman in the world.

They lingered in bed until late the following morning, then spent the afternoon out on the town, shopping, dining, strolling in the park. The fall was at its peak and the trees flamed with color.

It was early evening by the time they returned to their hotel room. Georgiana had just untied her bonnet when Holmes suddenly remarked that he had forgotten to check at the front desk for messages. He would run downstairs and be back in a moment.

When he entered the room again a few minutes later, Georgiana could see at once that he bore disappointing news. She struggled, with only partial success, to keep reproach from her voice. "Don't say that you must leave again, Harry," she protested. "Not so soon."

"It is a most urgent matter. It cannot be postponed."

She expelled a sigh. "Where must you travel to this time?"

"Cincinnati."

Georgiana dropped onto the edge of the mattress and sat silently for a moment before announcing that she would not remain another day in the Circle Park Hotel. She was beginning to feel like a prisoner. Even the company of her new friend, Mrs. Rodius, had begun to feel oppressive.

Seating himself at her side, Holmes placed an arm about her. He was all sympathy. Perhaps she should go back to Franklin again for a few days, he suggested. He would wire her there as soon as he had a better idea of his situation. Georgiana, her shoulders slumped, blew out another sigh and nodded.

The next day—Thursday, October 4—Holmes accompanied her to the station, waiting on the platform until her train disappeared from sight.

Then, with his wife out of the way, he turned his steps toward the Circle House, where the Pitezel children waited, alone and unsuspecting.

They were crestfallen when he broke the news to them: he had not brought their mother back with him after all.

She had decided to pay one last visit to her folks in Galva before journeying east. The children would have to wait a little while longer to see her—maybe a week at the most.

Alice and Nellie tried not to let their disappointment get the best of them. But Howard was inconsolable. Being stuck in a hotel room with nothing to do but draw pictures and read about the life of General Sheridan was hard on the high-spirited ten-year-old. His sisters, too, were growing unhappier by the day.

Telling them to throw on their jackets, Holmes took them on a shopping spree, buying dresses and hair ribbons for the girls, wooden toys and a box of crayons for Howard, and new "crystal" pens for all three, so that they could write to their mama and report how much fun they were having with "Uncle Howard" (as Holmes insisted they call him). He bought them a fine meal at a restaurant—chicken, mashed potatoes, milk, and lemon pie.

Afterward, they strolled along Washington Street, pausing before a shoe store to watch an oil painter turn out landscapes at the rate of one every minute and a half. Each customer who purchased a pair of shoes for a dollar received a painting for free (plus a small charge for the picture frame). Alice wished she could afford one of the paintings, they were all so pretty and colorful.

Holmes had assumed that the little expedition would keep the children satisfied for a while. But no sooner had they entered the Circle House front doors than Howard began throwing a fit—kicking, screaming, shouting that he did not want to be cooped up in the room again. Holmes had to drag the boy across the lobby by the hand.

The proprietor of the hotel, Herman Ackelow, looked on from behind the front desk, shaking his head. He felt sorry for the children. His eldest son, who sometimes brought them their meals, had returned from their room on several occasions and reported that he had found all three of them in tears. They missed their mama terribly and couldn't imagine why she had not written to them.

Back in the room, Alice and Nellie did their best to comfort their brother. It wasn't until Holmes threatened to give him a hiding, however, that the boy finally calmed down.

Ordering them all to stay put, Holmes promised to return the following day.

On his way out of the hotel, he stopped to talk to Mr. Ackelow, who had been led to believe Holmes was the children's uncle.

What was the trouble with the little fellow? the hotelkeeper inquired.

Holmes's expression turned somber. The boy was a bad one, he said sadly. Trouble from the day he was born.

"I do not know how my sister will be able to manage," he continued, his voice heavy with concern. She was a sickly widow whose good-hearted but improvident husband had left her without a red cent.

Holmes was considering various alternatives on her behalf—maybe binding the boy out to a farmer or placing him in an institution. He hadn't figured out the best course of action yet. But something was going to have to be done about the boy.

And soon.

It was almost five that same afternoon when the bell over the door of Schiffling's Repair Shop jingled. The owner, Albert Schiffling, glanced up from his workbench as a well-dressed gentleman stepped into the shop, a pair of slender black cases cradled in his arms.

Introducing himself as a physician, the gentleman placed his cases on the counter, undid their latches, and swung open the lids.

"I would like to have these sharpened," the gentleman said. "How long will you need?"

Schiffling looked down. The cases were full of gleaming surgical tools—scalpels, knives, saws.

Schiffling replied that he could have the job done by the following Monday.

The gentleman stroked his mustache thoughtfully for a moment, then said, "That will do."

Schiffling wrote out a receipt and handed it to the doctor, who thanked him and left.

Outside, in the thinning daylight, Holmes consulted his

pocket watch. It was too late to start looking for a suitable house now. He would commence his search tomorrow.

Samuel Brown—who operated a small real estate agency out of his house in Irvington, a picture-pretty village about six miles from downtown Indianapolis—was just settling back to read his daily newspaper on the afternoon of Friday, October 5, when the stranger entered. Brown, a genial-looking sixty-year-old with a personality that matched his appearance, removed his reading glasses and greeted the gentleman cheerfully.

The stranger, however, seemed in no mood for pleasant-ries. Without so much as a "good afternoon," he explained that he had just rented a house from Dr. Thompson and had been told that Mr. Brown was holding the key. He would like to have it. At once.

Though somewhat taken aback by the fellow's brusqueness, the good-natured old man complied without delay. Sliding open the center drawer of his desk, he rummaged among its contents until he came up with the key. Without a word, the stranger plucked it from his hand, then swiveled and hurried from the office.

For a few moments, Brown simply sat there, clucking his tongue. He was unaccustomed to being treated so rudely. Finally, he replaced his glasses on his nose and returned to his paper, wondering what the world was coming to.

Several hours later, Holmes showed up at the children's room in the Circle House and announced that he had de-cided to take Howard away. The boy was going to stay with Holmes's cousin, Minnie Williams, a wealthy lady with no children of her own who would take wonderful care of him. Miss Williams owned a big house in Terre Haute, and How-ard would get all the fresh air and exercise he wanted. The girls, meanwhile, would remain in Indianapolis until the rest of the family—Mama, Dessie, and baby Wharton—arrived.

Holmes instructed Alice to pack her brother's belongings in his small wooden trunk. He would be back for the boy early the next day.

When Holmes arrived on Saturday morning, however, Howard was nowhere to be seen.

"Where is he?" Holmes demanded.

"He snuck out," Alice said sheepishly. "Me and Nellie were busy packing his things, and when we turned back around, he was gone." She made an exasperated sound. "He just won't mind me at all no more."

Holmes was furious, but he had pressing matters to attend to and no time to hunt for the boy. He told Alice that he would be back in a day or so. And this time, Howard had better be ready and waiting.

When Holmes returned to the Circle House on Monday, Howard was seated cross-legged on the floor, playing with a little wooden top. Ordering the boy into his coat, Holmes told Alice and Nellie to bid their brother good-bye. Both girls broke into tears as they covered Howard's cheeks with kisses.

"Do not take on so," Holmes admonished. "You will all be together again soon."

Then, directing Howard to grab one end of the small wooden trunk, Holmes took hold of the other and led the boy from the room, leaving the heartsick girls to comfort each other as best they could.

The house Holmes had rented from Dr. Thompson was far more secluded than the one he had been forced to abandon in Cincinnati. A one-and-a-half-story cottage with an attached barn, it stood a short distance from Union Avenue on the outskirts of Irvington. No other houses were in the immediate neighborhood—only the Methodist church, located directly across the street. The west side of the cottage was sheltered by a grove of catalpa trees. To the east stretched a large, grassy common. The tracks of the Pennsylvania Railroad lay two hundred yards to the south. All in all, Holmes could not have asked for a more isolated site.

Even so, he had an unexpected visitor on Tuesday, October 9. Strolling past the property that morning, Elvet Moorman—a rawboned, flap-eared sixteen-year-old who did odd jobs for Dr. Thompson—paused to watch a pair of men unload some furniture from a horse-drawn wagon and carry it into the house. Assisting the movers were a gentleman in rolled-up shirtsleeves and a little boy in a gray coat, who helped with some of the lighter objects.

Later that afternoon, Dr. Thompson asked Moorman to return to the house to milk the cow that was kept in the attached barn. Moorman had just hunkered down on his stool when the gentleman he had seen earlier entered and asked if Moorman would lend a hand. The man, who did not introduce himself by name, needed help putting up a large coal stove that he had moved into the barn.

As they set to work, Moorman asked the man why he did not make a connection for natural gas and use a gas stove instead of a coal-burner.

"Because I do not think gas is healthy for children," the man replied in an odd, almost smirking tone.

Moorman left as soon as the job was completed. As he lugged his milk can past the house, he called out a greeting to the little boy in the gray coat, who stood by himself on the front porch and gave Moorman a forlorn little wave in return.

The following morning—Wednesday, October 10—a well-dressed gentleman, carrying a child's gray coat rolled up into a bundle, entered a little grocery store in Irvington. The gentleman explained that he had been called away on an urgent business matter and wanted to make sure that the owner of the coat, a ten-year-old boy who had accidentally left it at his house, got it back. Could he leave the coat with the grocer?

The grocer agreed. Taking the coat from the man, he tucked it away beneath his counter.

The boy would come by to pick up the coat very soon, the gentleman said as he headed for the doorway. Probably no later than Thursday morning.

But the little boy never appeared.

28

The case of Holmes illustrates the practical as well as
the purely ethical value of "honor among thieves,"
and shows how a comparatively insignificant misdeed
may ruin a great and comprehensive plan of crime.

—H. B. Irving, *A Book of Remarkable Criminals*

As far as the officers of Fidelity Mutual were concerned, the
Pitezel case was closed. But one person in the company remained suspicious. That was part of his job. His name was William Gary, and he was Fidelity's chief investigator and
adjuster.

From the start, Gary had questioned the theory that Pitezel had been killed in an accidental explosion. To his eyes,
the physical evidence at the death scene—the burned match,
broken bottle, and corncob pipe—had all the earmarks of a
setup. Fouse and his fellow executives had settled the policy
against Gary's advice, then turned their attention elsewhere.
But Gary—an experienced sleuth who had begun his career
as a member of the Philadelphia police force—had continued to brood over the affair.

As a result, when a business matter entirely unrelated to
the Pitezel case brought him to St. Louis in early October,
Gary did a little poking around on his own. The day after
his arrival, he paid a visit to Jeptha D. Howe.

Seated in the young attorney's office, Gary chatted about
the Pitezels for a while. Then, putting a match to a cigar

and leaning back in his chair, he casually asked, "I suppose you received a good fee for your work?"

Howe hesitated a moment, then replied, "Twenty-five hundred."

Gary whistled at the impressive sum.

"I earned every penny," Howe grumbled. "It should have been a third."

Gary left the lawyer's office more certain than ever that his company's assumptions were wrong, but he had no solid proof to back up his doubts.

And then on the morning of Tuesday, October 9, fate placed that proof quite literally into his hands.

Gary was seated in the office of branch manager George Stadden when a message arrived from St. Louis police chief Lawrence Harrigan, requesting that an agent of the company call on him at once. Harrigan had just received a communication that bore on a case involving Fidelity Mutual.

Gary proceeded immediately to police headquarters, where Major Harrigan handed him a letter that had arrived earlier that day. The letter, Gary learned, was from a prisoner in the city jail who had shared a cell some months earlier with an accused swindler named H. M. Howard.

The prisoner's name was Marion Hedgepeth, and this is what his letter said:

DEAR SIR:—

When H. M. Howard was in here some two months ago, he came to me and told me he would like to talk to me, as he had read a great deal of me, etc.: also after we got well acquainted, he told me he had a scheme by which he could make $10,000, and he needed some lawyer who could be trusted, and said if I could, he would see I got $500 for it. I then told him that J. D. Howe could be trusted, and he then went on and told me that B. F. Pitezel's life was insured for $10,000, and that Pitezel and him were going to work the insurance company for the $10,000, and just how they were going to do it; even going into minute details; that he was an expert at it, as he had worked it before, and that being a druggist, he could easily deceive the insurance company by having Pitezel fix himself up according to his directions and appear that he was mortally wounded by an explosion, and then put a corpse in place of Pitezel's body, etc., and then have it identified as that of Pitezel. I did not take much stock in what he told me, until after he went out on bond, which was in a few days, when J. D. Howe came to me and told me that that man Howard, that I had recommended him to, had come and told him that I had recommended Howe to him and had laid the whole plot open to him, and Howe told me that he never heard of a finer or smoother piece of work, and that it was sure to work, and that Howard was one of the smoothest and slickest men that he ever heard tell of, etc., and Howe told me that he would see that I got $500 if it worked, and that Howard was going East to attend to it at once. (At this time I did not know what insurance company was to be worked, and am not sure yet as to which one it is, but Howe told me that it was the Fidelity Mutual of Philadelphia, whose office is, according to the city directory, at No. 520 Oliver Street.) Howe came down and told me every two or three days that everything was working smoothly and when notice appeared in the *Globe Democrat* and *Chronicle* of the death of B. F. Pitezel, Howe came down at once and told me that it was a matter of a few days until we would have the money, and that the only thing that might keep the company from paying it at once, was the fact that Howard and Pitezel were so hard up for money that they could not pay the dues on the policy until a day or two before it was due, and then had to send it by telegram, and that the company might claim that they did not get the money until after the lapse of the policy; but they did not, and so Howe and a little girl (I think Pitezel's daughter) went back to Philadelphia and succeeded in identifying and having the body recognized as that of B. F. Pitezel. Howard told me that Pitezel's wife was privy to the whole thing. Howe tells me now that Howard would not let Mrs. Pitezel go back to identify the supposed body of her husband, and that he feels almost positive and certain that Howard deceived Pitezel and that Pitezel in following out Howard's instructions, was killed and that it was really the body of Pitezel.

The policy was made out to the wife and when the money was put in the bank, then Howard stepped out and left the wife to settle with Howe for his services. She was willing to pay him $1,000 but he wanted $2,500. Howard is now on his way to Germany, and Pitezel's wife is here in the city yet, and where Pitezel is or whether that is Pitezel's body I can't tell, but I don't believe it is Pitezel's body, but believe that he is alive and well and probably in Germany, where Howard is now on his way. It is hardly worth while to say that I never got the $500 that Howard held out to me for me to introduce him to Mr. Howe. Please excuse this poor writing as I have written this in a hurry and have to write on a book placed on my knee. This and a lot more I am willing to swear to. I wish you would see the Fidelity Mutual Life Insurance Company and see if they are the ones who have been made the victim of this swindle, and if so, tell them that I want to see them. I never asked what company it was until today, and it was after we had some words about the matter, and so Howe may not have told the proper company but you can find out what company it is by asking or telephoning to the different companies. . . . Please send an agent of the company to see me if you please.

Yours Resp., etc.
MARION C. HEDGEPETH

In the company of a police stenographer, Gary promptly set off for the city prison, where he took a sworn statement from Hedgepeth that was essentially a recapitulation of the letter.

Armed with both documents, plus a rogues'-gallery portrait of the swindler H. M. Howard, Inspector Gary returned to Philadelphia that night. The following morning he met with the officers of Fidelity Mutual in President Fouse's office and reported his findings. Unwilling to admit that they had been suckered, Fouse and his colleagues scoffed at Hedgepeth's accusations. The outlaw, they argued, was obviously trying to pass off phony information in a cunning bid to have his sentence reduced.

Gary acknowledged that—in addition to striking back at Howard for cheating him of his fee—Hedgepeth was undoubtedly looking to curry favor with the authorities. But Gary insisted that the story must be true. The letter contained information that Hedgepeth could only have learned from one of the conspirators—the bit about the tardy insurance payment, for example.

Fouse found the latter point hard to refute. Frowning, he asked to see the picture of H. M. Howard. As soon as he laid eyes on it, the color drained from his face.

Looking back at him from the photograph was the personable physician whose decency and kindness had impressed Fouse so favorably several weeks before.

Early the next morning, Inspector Gary and a colleague set off from Philadelphia, having been authorized by the officers of Fidelity Mutual to use every means at their disposal to track down and apprehend Dr. H. H. Holmes.

29

Here comes a candle to light you to bed,
Here comes a chopper to chop off your head.

—Nursery rhyme

By the time Gary and his partner embarked on their man-hunt, Holmes was already gone from Indiana.

He had returned for the girls on the evening of Wednesday, October 10. Alice and Nellie had filled the days since Howard's departure with their usual pastimes—drawing pictures, reading *Uncle Tom's Cabin,* playing with their few simple toys. Sometimes, they would do nothing but sit and stare through the window at the life that flowed along the busy street outside. At other times, worn down by the tedium and isolation, they would lie in each other's arms and weep.

Finding them in tears, the hotel chambermaid, a middle-aged German woman named Caroline Klausmann, assumed that they were orphans, grieving for their lost parents. Her heart went out to the stricken children and she yearned to offer words of comfort. But speaking no English, she could only gaze at them with compassionate eyes.

When Holmes checked Alice and Nellie out of the Circle House that night and brought them to the train station, they must have felt like prisoners sprung from solitary. They had no way of knowing that they were simply being transferred to another cell.

*   *   *

The following day, Georgiana received a long-awaited telegram from her husband, in which he asked her to meet him immediately in Detroit. On Friday morning, she left her parents' home in Franklin and boarded a train. The ride lasted all day and by that evening, she was in the grip of one of her "sick headaches." Shutting her eyes, she tried to sleep but was disturbed by the sudden sensation of another passenger sliding onto the vacant seat beside her. When she turned her head to look, she was startled to see her husband.

He pulled her close and kissed her brow. What a wonderful surprise! he said, laughing. Evidently, they had been riding in separate cars all day without realizing that they were sharing the same train. He would never have spotted her if he hadn't decided to get up and stretch his legs.

When they arrived in Detroit an hour later, Holmes secured a suite at the Hotel Normandie, registering as "G. Howell and wife, Adrian." Georgiana, still suffering from her migraine, took to bed immediately. She was lying in the dark with her eyes shut tight when she heard the door creak open and her husband slip out of the suite.

He had ridden beside the two girls until the train was an hour away from its destination. Then—inventing some cock-and-bull story to explain why he couldn't be seen arriving with them—he had taken his bag and moved to a different car. The girls were to get off at Detroit and wait until he came to fetch them.

Alice and Nellie had followed his orders and were sitting slumped on a bench inside the station, satchels at their feet, when he showed up just before midnight.

Transporting them by cab to a hotel called the New Western, Holmes rented a room for the girls, signing them in under the names "Etta and Nellie Canning." Then he hurried back to the Hotel Normandie, changed into his nightshirt, and quietly slipped into bed beside his sleeping wife.

Georgiana felt much better in the morning. Explaining that his affairs might keep them in Detroit for a while, Holmes checked them out of the hotel and into a boardinghouse on Park Place. When the proprietor inquired as to his profession, Holmes—evidently enjoying a sly joke—replied that he was an actor.

Holmes hauled their luggage to their room and helped Georgiana settle in. Then—following his usual modus operandi—he went off in search of a secluded house.

At roughly the same time in Galva, Illinois, Carrie Pitezel was packing a trunk for herself, Dessie, and the baby in preparation for their imminent trip to Detroit.

In obedience to Holmes, she had journeyed to her parents' place on Friday, October 5. For six days she had waited with mounting anxiety for word of her husband's whereabouts. Holmes's letter had finally arrived on the eleventh. Ben was in Detroit, it said. She should plan on traveling there in the middle of the following week.

Desperately lonely for her husband—and pining for Alice, Nellie, and Howard—Carrie had decided to defy this directive, wiring Holmes to expect her on Sunday the fourteenth. She did, however, comply with another of his orders—to destroy his letter as soon as she finished reading it.

When Carrie's train arrived in Detroit on Sunday afternoon, Holmes was waiting on the platform. Had he been capable of the emotion, Holmes might have been shocked by Carrie's appearance. As it was, he experienced a sense of mild surprise at how pinched and feeble she looked, as if the strains of the preceding months had propelled her into old age. Dessie, who cradled baby Wharton in her arms, followed her mother off the train. Gathering up their luggage, Holmes led them to a carriage.

During the ride to the hotel, Carrie grilled him about the other children. How were they getting on? And why hadn't she received any letters from them?

"They are in Indianapolis, in the care of a very nice widow lady," Holmes assured her. "They are probably too busy with their school duties to write to you, but I am certain you will hear from them soon."

"What is the name of this widow?" Carrie demanded. "I am not in the habit of letting my children stay with strangers without knowing who they are."

Holmes took his bottom lip between his teeth and furrowed his brow. "It is a peculiar name," he said after moment. "I cannot think of it just now."

"Cannot think of her name?" Carrie exclaimed. "How did you find this woman?"

"My wife's parents intend to move to Indianapolis from their current home in Franklin. I agreed to help them find a house. One of the real estate agents I consulted provided me with the widow's name."

"But when will I see my children?" Carrie cried.

Holmes patted her hands. "Very soon. Once you have finished visiting with Benny, I will take you to Indianapolis. My wife's parents will not be ready to move into their new house for several months. In the meanwhile, you and the children are free to live there without paying rent."

Somewhat mollified, Carrie closed her eyes and leaned her head against her daughter's shoulder until the carriage arrived at Geis's European Hotel.

When Holmes registered them as "Mrs. C. A. Adams and daughter," Carrie pulled him aside and asked why he had given a false name.

"It is safer this way," he answered. "You need not be so proud to keep your own name."

Then—leaving Carrie and the children in the care of the housekeeper, Miss Minnie Mulholland—Holmes hastened away.

Miss Mulholland showed the new arrivals to their room. As she headed back to the front of the hotel, the housekeeper wondered what in the world could be troubling the poor woman. She had never seen a human being who looked more bowed down with care.

Not long afterward, Holmes checked Alice and Nellie out of the New Western Hotel and transferred them to a boardinghouse at 91 Congress Street run by a woman named Lucinda Burns.

There, on that same afternoon, Alice sat down and composed a letter to her loved ones in Galva. It was the last letter she would write.

DEPRAVED

Dear Grandma and Grandpa,

Hope you are all well Nell and I have both got colds and chapped hands but that is all. We have not had any nice weather at all I guess it is coming winter now. Tell mama that I have to have a coat. I nearly freeze in that thin jacket. We have to stay in all the time. Howard is not with us now. We are right near the Detroit River. We was going on a boat ride yesterday but it was too cold. All that Nell and I can do is draw and I get so tired of siting that I could get up and fly almost. I wish I could see you all. I am getting so homesick that I don't know what to do. I suppose Wharton walks by this time don't he I would like to have him hear he would pass away the time a goodeal.

Everything about this letter is almost unbearably heartbreaking. There is, to begin with, Alice's simple reference to her brother—"Howard is not with us now"—whose ominous significance she could not possibly have known. There are the small cries of loneliness and boredom—the only complaints she had ever permitted herself in her letters—that so poignantly convey the misery of her physical confinement and long separation from her family. There is the terrible fact that, at that very moment, her mother, her older sister, and the baby brother she ached to see were lodged in a rooming house only a few blocks away, though Alice would never know of their proximity.

And then—perhaps most distressing of all—there are the remarks about her jacket.

For days, Alice and her sister had been begging for warmer clothes. Holmes kept promising to buy them a new winter wardrobe. He was lying, of course. From his point of view, such a purchase would be a complete waste of cash.

In another few days—if everything went according to his plan—Alice and Nellie would no longer be bothered by the cold.

*   *   *

By Monday, October 15, Holmes was ready.

He had located and rented a house—a small, secluded place at 241 E. Forest Avenue on the outskirts of the city.

He had dug a hole in the rear of the cellar—four feet long, three and a half feet wide, three and a half feet deep.

But on Wednesday the seventeenth, before he had a chance to consummate his scheme, a wire arrived from a Chicago associate named Frank Blackman. Holmes did not like what it said. Once again—as in Cincinnati—he was forced to abort his plan at the eleventh hour and find a different place to do the job.

When Holmes got back to his room that evening, he surprised Georgiana by announcing that—as a way of expressing his gratitude for her unfailing devotion—he had decided to take her to Niagara Falls. They would travel by way of Toronto, where he had a little business to take care of—a matter of renewing some contracts on his copying machines.

Early the next morning, while Georgiana packed their things, Holmes excused himself to run an errand. Outside, he headed straight for Geis's hotel, where he found Carrie and her children installed in a gloomy back room that faced an alleyway. Carrie's face brightened with expectation when she saw Holmes at the door. But her hopeful look faded as soon as he opened his mouth.

It pained him to say it, but she would have to wait a little longer to see Benny. "I have searched all over Detroit for a vacant house where the two of you can meet," he grumbled. "But I cannot find a suitable place. Benny cannot take a chance on being seen. By now, there might be people looking for him."

"What am I to do?" Carrie cried despairingly.

Holmes filled her in on the latest plan, which he and her husband had worked out last evening. Carrie and Ben would have their rendezvous outside the United States. Ben was already on his way to Canada. Carrie, Dessie, and Wharton were to follow on the eleven-thirty A.M. train to Toronto. Holmes already had their tickets. When they arrived that night, they were to wait at the depot until Holmes came to fetch them. He himself was leaving for Toronto at nine A.M.

Carrie's whole body sagged with dejection and fatigue, and Dessie let out a dispirited groan. Giving her daughter a little rub between the shoulder blades, Carrie asked Holmes if it was necessary for Dessie to come along. "She is so tired," Carrie said. "Perhaps she can go down to Indianapolis and stay with the others while I travel up to meet Benny."

Holmes took a moment to consider this before shaking his head. "You will need her to take care of the baby while you go and see Ben."

Nodding resignedly, Carrie accepted the tickets that Holmes pressed into her hand.

Holmes's next stop was Lucinda Burns's boardinghouse. Alice and Nellie listened despondently as Holmes told them what they must do. Before leaving, he pulled another pair of train tickets from his pocket—these for the following morning—and turned them over to the girls.

Then he rushed back to his room, where he found his wife ready and waiting.

Arriving in Toronto around suppertime that night, Holmes took Georgiana to a hotel called the Walker House, registering again under the name Howell. A few hours later, he left Georgiana in their room and returned to the Grand Trunk Station, where he found Carrie Pitezel occupying a bench alongside her eldest daughter, who cradled the dozing infant in her arms. Both mother and daughter looked thoroughly drained and distraught.

"Where have you been?" Carrie cried as Holmes approached. "We have been waiting here nearly an hour and a half!"

"I have only been in Toronto a half hour myself," said Holmes. "My train was late."

"I don't see how it could be three hours late," Carrie replied bitterly. "You told me you were leaving at nine." By then, however, she felt too fatigued to argue. "Where is Benny?"

"He is hiding out in Montreal. I am to rent a house here in Toronto where the two of you can be together. As soon as I have found a place, I will send word to Ben and he will come down at night to meet you."

Carrie, who had expected to find her husband waiting in Toronto, looked as if she were about to cry.

"You will be happy to hear," Holmes said quickly, reaching into his jacket and extracting a folded sheet, "that I have received a letter from the children."

Carrie snatched the paper from his hand and scanned it eagerly. Almost at once, however, her mouth formed itself into a deep frown. "I cannot read this," she exclaimed.

"Of course not," Holmes said, chuckling softly. "It is written in cipher. As a precaution." Plucking the letter from her fingers, he began to read it aloud. " 'Dear Mamma, we are well and going to school. We have plenty to eat, and the woman is real good to us.' " Holmes looked up from the letter, smiling.

"Is that all?" Carrie asked.

Nodding, Holmes folded the note back into quarters and returned it to his pocket. Then he grabbed up their luggage and led them to the Union Hotel, not far from the place where he and Georgiana were staying. Checking them in as "Mrs. C. Adams and daughter," Holmes promised to call on them the next day with more news of Benny.

Holmes, however, did not keep his promise. Instead, he spent the day sight-seeing and shopping with Georgiana. At eight that night, after dinner at a fashionable restaurant, he escorted her back to their room. As his wife slipped out of her overcoat, Holmes said he felt too "full of pep" to retire and thought he might go for a short, postprandial walk.

Outside, he made directly for the depot, arriving just in time to meet the train from Detroit. After greeting Alice and Nellie, he turned them over to a porter from the Albion Hotel, handing the man a four-bit tip for himself and enough money to cover a day's lodging for the girls.

At this point, Holmes was performing a feat worthy of a master marionetteer: maneuvering three sets of human puppets—his wife; Carrie and two of her children; and Alice and Nellie—from one city to the next and lodging them within a short distance of each other, while keeping them completely unaware of each other's presence.

Holmes showed up at the Albion first thing Saturday morning and took Alice and Nellie out for a stroll. Before long, both girls were shivering in the sharp Canadian air. After seeing them back to their room, he paid their board for another day, explaining to the chief hotel clerk, Herbert Jones, that the girls were his nieces. They were awaiting the arrival of their mother, who was due in from Detroit later in the week.

Then, he hurried off in search of a real estate office. He had promised to take Georgiana to Niagara Falls that afternoon, and he had a critical matter to take care of first.

On Wednesday, October 24, Thomas William Ryves—a seventy-year-old semi-invalid who still spoke with a distinct burr, though nearly fifty years had passed since he'd left his native Scotland—shuffled to the front of his home at number 18 St. Vincent Street in response to a persistent knocking on his door. Ryves had never set eyes on the caller before—a handsomely dressed gentleman who explained that he had just rented the neighboring house for his sister.

Standing in the doorway, Ryves cupped his free hand behind one ear and tilted his head toward the stranger.

"My sister will be arriving from Hamilton, Ontario, in a few days," the latter continued, raising his voice to a near-shout. "I wonder if I might borrow a shovel from you. I would like to arrange a place in the cellar where my sister can keep potatoes."

"You are welcome to it," Ryves replied. "You'll find it in the shed out back."

Thanking Ryves, the stranger walked around to the rear of the house. A few moments later, he reappeared with the spade in his hand.

Later that day, as Ryves sat rocking by the window, he saw a wagon pull up at number 16. Perched on the front seat were the driver—a squat-looking fellow in a slouch hat—and the same gentleman who had borrowed the spade. As Ryves watched, the two men unloaded an old bed, a mattress, and a trunk from the wagon and carried them into the house.

The old man was surprised at the sparseness of the load and assumed that additional furnishings would follow.

But none ever did.

*　　*　　*

On Thursday, October 25, Herbert Jones was at his post behind the front desk of the Albion when the uncle of the two little girls arrived, as he had every morning for the past six days, with the exception of Sunday. A few moments later, after settling the daily bill, he called for his nieces in their room and led them away. This, too, was his standard procedure. He had taken the girls sight-seeing virtually every day since their arrival.

Sometimes, the girls stayed away until suppertime, though they were usually back in a few hours.

This day, however, was different.

This day, the two girls didn't return at all.

Later that same afternoon, Carrie took Dessie shopping at Eaton's department store on Yonge Street. They remained there for several hours, passing slowly from floor to floor, marveling at the dazzling profusion of dress goods, jewelry, toiletries, and sundries.

By four the baby was getting fussy. Carrie declared it was time to head back to the hotel.

They were almost to the exit when Carrie suddenly found herself face-to-face with Holmes. For an instant, both of them simply froze. Then Holmes did something so peculiar that Carrie could not make sense of it.

He turned deathly pale.

A moment later, however, he appeared to have recovered himself. "I have been hunting all over for you," he said, keeping his voice low.

"What is the matter?"

"Wheelmen," said Holmes, using the slang term for bicycle-mounted policemen. "Two of them—in citizen's clothes. They are watching the house I rented."

"How—?"

"I do not know. It is possible that they are looking for someone else. Perhaps a previous tenant who is wanted by the law. In any event, we cannot take the risk of bringing Ben here."

"What are we to do?" Carried cried. The distress in her voice brought stares from several nearby shoppers.

Gesturing emphatically, Holmes signaled Carrie to lower her voice.

"If you have made any purchases," he whispered, "have them sent immediately to your hotel. I want you to leave here tonight." Glancing around, he saw that he and Carrie were continuing to draw curious looks. "Wait here," he said. "I will be back in a moment. I need to pick up something at the other end of the store." Turning, he disappeared into the crowd of shoppers.

Carrie and Dessie waited for nearly ten minutes with mounting confusion. Finally, Carrie asked her daughter to go look for Holmes. When the girl returned without having found him, Carrie handed her the baby and went off on her own fruitless search. Bewildered and dismayed, they returned to the hotel and began to pack.

At around five, Holmes showed up at their room. He said nothing about his sudden disappearance, and Carrie was too distraught by then to ask. Handing her some train tickets, Holmes instructed her to leave immediately for Prescott, Ontario, then cross down to Ogdensburg, New York. He would meet them in Ogdensburg tomorrow.

A few moments later, after making sure that Carrie had the directions straight, Holmes rushed off.

Back in his own hotel room, Holmes informed Georgiana that they must leave Toronto at once. He had decided that it was time for them to make their long-delayed trip to Germany. They would take a steamship from Boston. On their way down to Massachusetts, he had several brief stops to make—a few loose ends to tie up involving his copier business.

Georgiana was delighted, though she was also puzzled by the urgency in her husband's manner. By now she was used to these abrupt departures. But there was something different about Harry's behavior this time. Generally, he seemed like a man in a hurry.

Suddenly, he seemed like a man on the run.

30

> Vice may triumph for a time, crime may flaunt its
> victories in the face of honest toilers, but in the end
> the law will follow the wrong-doer to a bitter fate,
> and dishonor and punishment will be the portion of
> those who sin.
>
> —Allan Pinkerton

William Gary had decided that St. Louis was the logical
place to start searching for Holmes. Arriving with O. LaForrest Perry on Friday, October 12, Gary immediately sought
out Carrie Pitezel, only to discover from a neighbor named
Becker that the newly widowed woman had abruptly left
town the week before, along with her infant son and oldest
daughter. From the rogues'-gallery portrait that Gary
showed him, Becker was able to identify Holmes as the man
who had called on the Pitezels several times during the late
summer and early fall.

Thanks to the report put together by Edwin Cass, Fidelity's Chicago branch manager, Gary and his colleague knew
that Holmes kept a domicile in Wilmette, Illinois. The following day, the pair showed up at the trim, red-frame house
on North John Street.

Myrta Holmes was no more forthcoming with the two
investigators than she had been with Cass. But once again,
a neighbor proffered some useful information. Dr. Holmes,
this individual revealed, was rarely seen in the neighborhood. According to rumor, however, he was well-known in

Englewood, where he had run into some trouble with the law.

That same afternoon, the two men traveled down to Englewood. They spent the remainder of that day and most of the next interrogating Holmes's neighbors and acquaintances—including his broker and business associate, Frank Blackman, who grabbed the first opportunity to contact Holmes with the news that insurance men were on his trail. It was this wire that caused Holmes to abandon his plan in Detroit.

Checking in with the Chicago police, Gary and his partner conducted an interview with two detectives named Norton and Fitzpatrick. As the insurance men listened, a picture emerged of Holmes that confirmed Gary's strongest suspicions. Gary learned all about the druggist's financial misdeeds and manifold frauds, including the failed fire-insurance scam at his "Castle." He also discovered that both Holmes and Pitezel were wanted down in Texas on charges of swindling and horse theft.

It had become increasingly clear to the insurance men that they were chasing a bold and wily criminal whose trail extended over a wide geographical area—from Philadelphia to Fort Worth, St. Louis to Englewood. At this point, Holmes might be anywhere in the country. Two men working on their own—even ones as capable as Gary and his colleague—were simply inadequate for the job. What they needed was the aid of a detective service with the manpower and know-how to conduct a nationwide hunt.

The next morning, Gary wired his recommendation to L. G. Fouse. It was time to call in the Pinkertons.

Instead of disembarking at Prescott, Holmes did something that struck Georgiana as peculiar. He escorted her off the train at the previous station and hired a carriage to drive them the rest of the way. When Georgiana asked the reason for this expedient, Holmes mumbled something about the need to conceal his movements from unprincipled competitors, who would stop at nothing to sabotage his business.

The carriage dropped them off at the ferry landing. Not

long afterward, they docked in Ogdensburg, New York, after a choppy trip across the St. Lawrence River.

Accompanied by her two children, Carrie arrived in Ogdensburg one day later, Sunday, October 26. Taking a room at the National Hotel, she settled in to await further instructions. Holmes—who had left Georgiana resting in a nearby rooming house—showed up early that evening and laid out his latest plan.

He would be leaving for Burlington, Vermont, on Tuesday, he explained. Carrie and her children were to remain in Ogdensburg until November 1, then follow on the early train. Holmes would meet them at the depot. In the meantime, he would arrange for Benny to journey down to Burlington, where Carrie and her husband would have their long-deferred reunion.

Holmes and Georgiana made the trip to Burlington on October 30. Once again, he insisted on detraining at the preceding stop and finishing the journey by carriage. After an overnight stay at the Burlington Hotel, they transferred to Ahern's boardinghouse where Holmes registered as "Mr. Hall and Wife."

That same afternoon, using the alias "J. A. Judson," Holmes rented a furnished house at 26 Winooski Avenue, explaining to the agent that he was taking it for his widowed sister, whose name he gave as Mrs. Cook.

Much to Holmes's annoyance, Carrie and the children did not arrive the following morning, as planned. Holmes returned to the station to meet the afternoon train. The moment Carrie climbed down with her children, he began berating her. "Why didn't you come on the train I told you to?"

"They told me it was a local train," Carrie replied in an unapologetic tone. "It's bad enough traveling with the baby on a fast train."

"Whenever I tell you to do anything," Holmes growled, "you do it."

Carrie, however, was rapidly reaching the end of her tether. She was through being browbeaten. Meeting his anger with a defiant glare, she maintained an icy silence during the carriage ride to Winooski Avenue.

Inside the house, Carrie sank into a chair while Dessie, baby in arms, went off to explore the rooms. "I would have taken you for supper," Holmes said coolly, "if you had come on the earlier train."

"I don't care about supper," Carrie shot back. "I only care about one thing—seeing my husband and children. Where is Benny now?"

"Still in Montreal," Holmes replied. Carrie need not worry. She and her husband would soon be together.

The following morning, Holmes returned to Winooski Avenue and asked Dessie if she would like to go out and see a little of the city. With Carrie's permission, Dessie agreed. As Holmes led the seventeen-year-old girl toward the streetcar, he casually asked if her father had ever mentioned anything to her about a plan involving life insurance.

Sometime during the preceding week, Dessie had, in fact, remembered the puzzling remarks that her papa had made back in St. Louis. Now, she repeated his words to Holmes.

"Have you mentioned this to anyone else?" Holmes asked quickly.

Dessie shook her head.

"Good," replied Holmes, more persuaded than ever that he must act at once.

A few hours later, he dropped Dessie back at the furnished house. Before leaving, he asked Carrie how she was fixed for money.

"I am strapped," Carrie answered bitterly. All the moving around Holmes had put her through had drained her meager funds.

Pulling some loose bills from his vest pocket, Holmes handed them to Carrie and told her to go shopping tomorrow for food.

Holmes did some shopping himself the next morning. Shortly after noon, he returned to the rented house on Winooski Avenue with a purchase wrapped in cloth.

As he'd expected, Carrie and her children were not at home. Letting himself in with his duplicate key, he snuck down to the basement, taking each of the wooden stairs slowly and carefully, as though fearful of making a misstep. Crouching by the coal bin, he gently unwound the cloth from the object it protected—a bottleful of thick, colorless fluid—which he gingerly secreted behind some decayed boards in the bin.

Carrie did not see or hear from Holmes again for nearly a week and assumed that he had gone to fetch Benny. But when Holmes showed up unexpectedly on the evening of November 7, he was alone. When Carrie realized that he had not brought her husband back with her, her long-simmering frustrations finally reached a boil.

"You have been lying to me all along," she shouted. "Nothing comes of what you say!"

"I have never lied to you," Holmes said calmly.

"I won't stand it any longer," she yelled. "I'm going to Indianapolis to see my babies!"

"They are not in Indianapolis anymore." Holmes said he had moved them to a house in Toronto, which he had rented from an "old maid." That's where he had been for the past week. "You said you liked Toronto."

"Yes, I like Toronto," snapped Carrie. "But I don't give a care where I am so long as I have the children with me."

"Well, you will have them soon."

"How are my babies?" Carrie cried.

"Perfectly happy," Holmes said with a smile. They were excited about the new house. They had gone running all around it, exploring every corner and closet.

Holmes had bought Howard and the two girls new heavy coats so that they "wouldn't take cold." Alice had grown into "a real little woman." Why, just a few evenings ago, she had fixed him a wonderful dinner.

Carrie was somewhat mollified. She even chose to believe him when he promised her that he would leave the next morning to bring Benny down from Montreal.

That evening, Holmes told Georgiana that he was setting off the next day on a brief business trip to close out his contracts on his copying machines. She was to meet him in Lowell, Massachusetts, in one week. From there, they would travel to Boston and board a steamship for Europe.

As usual, Holmes was deceiving both women. He had no intention of traveling back to Canada. Nor did his trip have anything to do with the ABC Copier.

His actual destination was Gilmanton, New Hampshire.
Herman Webster Mudgett was going home.

The Pinkerton company logo—a staring eye above the
motto "We Never Sleep"—had given the agency its nickname among criminals. "The Eye," they called it. (Eventually, the term would filter into general usage as the slang
name for all private detectives or "private eyes.")

Within a week of being called onto the case, "The Eye"
had spotted the elusive Dr. Holmes.

A team of Pinkerton agents had picked up his trail in
Prescott and followed him to Ogdensburg and from there
to Vermont. It would have been a simple matter to arrest
him in Burlington. But—hoping that he might lead them to
other conspirators in the insurance swindle—the detectives
decided to put him under surveillance for a time.

They were shadowing him when he showed up at his parents' doorstep on November 8.

At the sight of their child, whom they had not laid eyes
on for over seven years, Levi and Theodate Mudgett—
churchgoing people, well-versed in scripture—must have
been reminded of the parable of the Prodigal Son. Holmes
himself—who later wrote of the reunion in the most tear-
jerking terms—preferred a different biblical analogy, com-
paring himself to Lazarus returned from the dead.

Holmes passed the following week revisiting his childhood
haunts. To his parents and siblings he dished out extravagant
lies about his life. Sometime during this period, he also made
a trip to Tilton to see his abandoned wife and thirteen-year-
old son.

The reunion with Clara Lovering Mudgett—who had remained faithful to her husband, never doubting that he
would return to her someday—was an emotional experience
for Holmes. Touched by her devotion, he swore that—
though he must leave again soon on an urgent business
trip—he would return for good in April. There was, however, one small matter that he felt honor-bound to disclose.
He was embarrassed to admit it, but a little less than a year
ago he had accidentally married another woman.

The story he told Clara was outrageous even by Holmes's mythomaniac standards. A year earlier, he claimed, he had been severely injured in a train wreck out West and had been transported, unconscious, to the nearest hospital. Upon awakening, he was amazed to discover that all recollection of his former self had been blotted out. "Who I was, my name, occupation, home, parents, friends—the memory of all had fled. On the night of the accident, a curtain had dropped between myself and the past, and all knowledge of my former self had been swept into oblivion."

While lying in this amnesiac state, he was visited by the patroness of the hospital—a "beautiful, wealthy woman, who brought flowers to the sick and read to us from books, and with her gentle voice sought to bring cheer into the dull hospital wards." This good woman—whose name was Georgiana Yoke—had fallen in love with him, and he with her. Upon his convalescence, they were married.

Deeply moved by her new husband's constant suffering as he "endeavored in vain to regain the threads of memory" of his past, Georgianna had finally secured the services of a "great surgeon," who performed a "wonderful operation" on his brain. When he came out of the ether, he discovered that his "memory had like a flood come back upon me, and to my unspeakable horror I realized what a wrong I had committed in marrying this sweet woman who had administered to me as I lay helpless and sick in the hospital. For it was only then that I remembered that I was a married man, and that my real wife was you, dear Clara."

It is yet another mark of Holmes's extraordinary persuasiveness that Clara evidently swallowed this whopper whole, though her reaction could hardly have been of much relevance to Holmes, since he had no intention of ever seeing her—or any other member of his family—again.

In one respect, Holmes's enormous lie to Clara contained a symbolic truth about his connection to the past. A grotesque caricature of American traits, he had become the frightening realization of the culture's most pathological possibilities: Holmes had reinvented himself so many times that even he could no longer remember all of his identities. After a week at his family home, he was ready to leave his earliest life behind forever.

On November 15, he hired a carriage to convey him to Boston and bid a tearless farewell to the past.

His immediate past, however, was quickly catching up to him. Indeed, by the time he reached Boston, he knew he was being followed.

Taking a room at the Adams House, he immediately sat down and composed a letter to Carrie, instructing her to meet him in Lowell in a week. Before she left Burlington, however, there was a small task he wanted her to perform.

For reasons too complicated to explain in a letter, he had stashed a bottle of expensive chemicals behind the coal bin in her house. He had since decided that the bottle might get damaged in its present location. As soon as Carrie finished reading—and then destroying—this letter, she was to remove the bottle from the basement, bring it up to the attic, and conceal it in a safe place until Holmes could come and fetch it

As he was waiting for the ink on the letter to dry, Holmes remembered how nervous he had felt transporting the cloth-wrapped bottle to the house on Winooski Avenue and his relief at finally getting shed of it.

Then—regretting that he would not be present to witness the fireworks when Carrie climbed three flights of rickety stairs with the ten-ounce bottle of nitroglycerin—he hurried out to mail the letter and to begin making the rounds of steamship offices.

On Friday, November 16, John Cornish, head of the Pinkerton office in Boston, held an urgent meeting with Orinton M. Hanscom, deputy superintendent of police and himself a former Pinkerton man. Holmes was getting ready to leave the country. It was time for the law to move in.

At approximately three o'clock the following afternoon, Holmes—who had transferred to a room at 40 Hancock Street—found himself surrounded by four police officers as he stepped from the lodging house. He surrendered without a struggle

Though the apprehension of Holmes was a source of great satisfaction to the Pinkertons—another feather in the agency's cap—they had no way of knowing what a coup his arrest really was. At the time, they regarded Holmes as the mastermind of a uniquely insidious plot. Only later would the full enormity of his crimes become apparent.

To their other accomplishments—the recovery of a stolen Gainsborough masterpiece after a relentless twenty-year hunt, the thwarting of an early assassination plot against Abraham Lincoln, the smashing of the Confederacy's most active spy ring, and much more—the Pinkertons would add another celebrated feat: the capture of the man soon to gain nationwide infamy as "the most dastardly criminal of the age."

31

It was ordained at the beginning of the world that certain signs should prefigure certain events.

—Cicero, *De Divinatione*

The telegraph wire strung above the roof of his house hadn't bothered Linford Biles much. But when the telephone company added a second wire only a few inches away from the first, he began to get nervous. And with good reason. Whenever a stiff wind blew and caused the two wires to touch, sparks would go shooting onto the shingles.

Still, Biles was not the sort of man to cause a fuss. At sixty-four, he'd spent the better part of his life as a loyal, uncomplaining worker for the Atlantic Oil Refining Company of Philadelphia, where he held the position of paymaster. Though his two grown children—who lived with their widowed father in his modest house on Tasker Street—repeatedly urged him to notify the city, Biles wouldn't hear of it. Not even after the accident.

It happened on Saturday, November 17—the very day of H. H. Holmes's arrest in Boston. As a half dozen laborers made their way home from the oil works at Point Breeze during that gusty afternoon, they spotted a tongue of flame licking up from one of the houses lining Tasker between Tenth and Eleventh streets. Hurrying in the direction of the fire, they saw that the two live wires running over the roof at number 1031 had become entangled, showering sparks onto the ivy vine that grew along the south side of the house.

The sparks had ignited the vine. By the time the workers arrived, the fire was climbing rapidly toward the roof.

While one of the workmen ran for the nearest fire alarm, the others put up a shout. Within moments, the street was filled with people. The fire department responded with admirable speed. Before any real damage could be done to the house, the flames were extinguished and the sparking wires uncrossed. Linford Biles lost most of his ivy plant, but otherwise his property was unscathed.

Among the crowd watching the barely averted tragedy was an old woman named Crowell. As she gazed up at the wires "spitting about like devils" in the air, a strange conviction overtook her. To her eyes, the fire looked less like an accident than a portent—a "dark message," an "evil warning."

Something bad was on the way, Mrs. Crowell felt sure. And it was coming for Linford Biles.

Part 4

Hyde
and Seek

32

Truth exists, only falsehood has to be invented.

—Georges Braque

Right from the start, the Holmes case was front-page news, not only in the cities where his major crimes took place— Philadelphia and Chicago—but throughout the country. To be sure, the initial coverage was skimpy compared to the media circus still to come. But in an age obsessed with get-rich-quick schemers, Holmes became an overnight sensation—"an adventurer" (as one newspaper described him only days after his arrest) "whose deeds make him a most formidable rival to the most villainous characters ever depicted in fiction."

From New York City to San Francisco, the whole nation seemed gripped by a powerful fascination with the devious Dr. Holmes. And in the beginning—before horror and outrage overwhelmed it—this fascination was flavored with a grudging admiration for the sheer audacity of the man.

That boldness was on full display from the first day of his capture. Taken directly to Boston police headquarters, Holmes was led into the office of Deputy Superintendent Hanscom, who informed him that he had been picked up on a warrant from Fort Worth, Texas. The charge was horse theft. For a moment, Holmes had to struggle to maintain his sangfroid, since the prospect of doing time in a Texas prison filled him with dread. But he recovered his coolness a moment later, when O. LaForrest Perry strode into the room.

Even after calling in the Pinkertons, Fidelity's main investigators, including Perry, had continued their own detective work. Assisted by Major James E. Stuart of the U.S. Postal Inspector's Department, they had traced several of Holmes's letters to Burlington. Perry immediately caught a train for Vermont. Along the way, he received word that a man and woman resembling Holmes and Mrs. Pitezel had been spotted in New York City, where they had checked into a fashionable midtown hotel.

Making a quick change in his travel plans, Perry proceeded to Manhattan, arriving at the hotel around dusk. Informed by the clerk that the couple in question had gone out to the theater, Perry took a seat in the lobby. When the suspects returned a few hours later, however, he saw at once that he had been following a false lead.

Drained and disheartened, he had headed back to Philadelphia for some badly needed rest. No sooner had he arrived home than he received a dispatch from the Pinkertons' Boston office, informing him that Holmes had been shadowed to that city. Instantly reinvigorated, Perry reboarded a train. He reached Boston not long after the police closed in on Holmes and hauled him down to headquarters.

As soon as Holmes saw Perry, he half-rose from his chair and, extending his right hand, greeted the insurance man cordially. "I guess I know what I'm *really* wanted for," he said in a tone of almost palpable relief. Infinitely preferring the hospitality of the Pennsylvania prison system to a stint in a Texas penitentiary ("I dislike fearfully to go to Fort Worth to serve a term," he confided to an acquaintance. "I had rather be here in Philadelphia five years than there one"), Holmes was not just ready but positively eager to admit to the insurance fraud. With Perry looking on and Hanscom and John Cornish asking the questions, he proceeded to offer his first complete—if largely fabricated—confession.

Under the stern gaze of his captors, Holmes assumed a guise of heartfelt sincerity and cooperation. Looking his interrogators straight in the eye, he replied in a bluff, manly fashion that gave the impression of absolute frankness. When the circumstances warranted it, he could also call up a ready tear of sorrow, pity, or remorse.

His style was nicely described by an individual who would have ample opportunity to watch Holmes in action over the coming months. "In talking," this observer wrote, "he has the appearance of candor, becomes quite pathetic at times when pathos will serve him best, uttering his words with a quaver in his voice, often accompanied by a moistened eye, then turning quickly with a determined and forceful method of speech, as if indignation or resolution had sprung out of tender memories that had touched his heart."

Holmes readily admitted that he and Pitezel had connived to cheat Fidelity Mutual out of $10,000. He insisted, however, that the corpse found at 1316 Callowhill was not Pitezel's but a body provided by a New York City physician—an old medical school chum who had conspired with Holmes on previous insurance scams.

Holmes had packed the cadaver in a trunk, arranged to have the trunk shipped to Callowhill Street, then hurried back to Philadelphia. After turning the claim ticket over to Pitezel, Holmes had immediately departed the city again, leaving his partner with explicit instructions on how to fake the accidental explosion as soon as the express company delivered the corpse.

Pitezel, in short, was very much alive. Holmes had seen him on several occasions since that time—in Cincinnati and Detroit—though he was a little fuzzy on the dates.

Holmes's interrogators were, of course, very eager to know the name of the physician who had supplied the body, but Holmes steadfastly refused to betray his accomplice, even at the risk of incurring their anger. "I don't mean to antagonize you in the least," he apologized. "But for the time being I'd rather not answer that."

His motives, he let his captors understand, were largely selfless. His friend, after all, had an untarnished reputation, and such a scandal would be the end of his career. At the same time, Holmes admitted, "he is a man now well enough to do that if my wife becomes penniless, if I am shut up for a term of years, I think I can call upon him for help."

Seeing that they were not going to discover the doctor's identity—and suspecting the true reason for Holmes's reluctance to reveal it (namely, that no such individual existed)—Hanscom and Cornish turned to another, even more pressing matter: the whereabouts of Alice, Nellie, and Howard Pitezel.

To account for the missing children, Holmes spun a tale every bit as convoluted as the route he had followed during the weeks when he had the little ones in his clutches. According to this story, Pitezel—after using the substitute corpse to fake his own death—had fled to Cincinnati and holed up in a room. Holmes, meanwhile, had traveled back to St. Louis, taken charge of Nellie and Howard from their mother, then picked up Alice in Indianapolis and brought all three children to Cincinnati, where he had installed them in a hotel. Carrie and her remaining children were to follow along a few days later. In the interim, Holmes was to rent a house where she and her husband could have a private reunion before Ben went into hiding for the winter down South.

Compliant as she was, Carrie had been adamant on one point. For the time being at least, the children—who truly believed that their father was dead—must remain in the dark. She was terrified that if they discovered the truth, they might let it slip out and give away the game. Carrie was emphatic about this: if the little ones found out that Ben was alive, the deal was off. She would pull out of the plot—"throw it over," as Holmes put it.

Holmes respected Carrie's position. After all, as he told Hanscom, "you could not depend on ten- or eleven-year-old children to keep the fact—keep them from speaking among themselves or before strangers." But shortly after his arrival in Cincinnati, a most unfortunate incident occurred. The problem resulted from Ben Pitezel's terrible loneliness, compounded by his predilection for drink.

As soon as Holmes finished checking Alice and her siblings into a hotel, he had paid a visit to Pitezel, who had obviously spent the preceding twenty-four hours in the warming company of a whiskey bottle. Under Ben's persistent—if slightly fuddled—questioning, Holmes had foolishly revealed the whereabouts of the three little ones.

The very next day, while Holmes was visiting the children, the door had suddenly flown open. As the children gaped in wonder, their teary-eyed father—apparently resurrected from the grave (where, judging by his smell, he had been preserved in rotgut)—stumbled into the hotel room, blubbering about how much he missed them. And completely blowing the plan.

As soon as Pitezel sobered up, Holmes—as vexed with himself as with his dipsomaniac partner—spelled out their predicament. Carrie's proviso—that the children remain ignorant of their papa's existence—had been violated. The only solution, as far as the two men could see, was to keep Carrie apart from the children so that she could not find out what had happened.

That very day, Pitezel had set out for Detroit with little Howard in tow. Holmes followed shortly afterward with Alice and Nellie. To confound anyone who might be following them, he disguised the younger girl as a boy.

Not long after arriving in Detroit, Holmes received an alarming message from an associate in Chicago. A pair of police officers from Fort Worth had been nosing around town, asking questions about Holmes and Pitezel. Clearly, the law was hot on their trail and might trace them to Detroit any day. With no time to lose, Holmes turned the two girls over to their father, who immediately lit out for New York City, planning to hop a steamer to South America. If he couldn't book passage right away, he intended to take the children by train to Key West.

"Then you believe that he and the children are alive and well?" asked Hanscom.

"Yes, sir," Holmes replied.

"You have every reason to believe that?"

"Yes, sir." Holmes could not say precisely where they were—either South America or Florida—but he knew for a fact that all four of them were, even at that moment, residing in some sunny clime.

Cornish and the others exchanged a look of open skepticism. After clarifying a few points about the extent of Carrie

Pitezel's complicity in the fraud—and making a final, futile effort to extract the name of the corpse dealer—Cornish made their doubts explicit. "I must tell you," he warned, "that unless Pitezel is produced alive, we must consider him dead."

"I understand," said Holmes, "and that is why I say that I don't care how soon Pitezel is brought to the front now. I have almost got to do it to protect myself. It is not that I wish to go back on him by any means."

"You expect in any event that there will be imprisonment to go with it?" asked Deputy Superintendent Hanscom.

"I certainly do. I told my wife—I begged her—to go away and drop it because I expected a term at the penitentiary."

"Of course," Hanscom said with a smirk, "it is desirable for you not to be held for the greater offense."

"I certainly don't want to be held for murder. While I am bad enough on smaller things, I am not guilty of that."

Perhaps the most striking aspect of this confession is the reaction of Hanscom and Cornish. In spite of Holmes's disarmingly forthright manner, his explanation for the children's whereabouts clearly had the quality of desperate improvisation. Nevertheless, his questioners appeared less concerned with the ultimate fate of Alice, Nellie, and Howard than with that of Pitezel. Hanscom and his associates continued to believe that Holmes—for all his protestations of innocence—had done away with his partner. But the idea that terrible harm had befallen the little ones seems not to have crossed their minds, undoubtedly because the notion was simply too outrageous to conceive. After all, only a creature hopelessly lost to sanity or feeling would slaughter helpless children. And Holmes, though a self-confessed scoundrel, was clearly not a madman or a fiend.

Or so they thought at the time.

Holmes, of course, was not the only one the police wanted to question. Even as the interrogation was taking place, a Pinkerton man named Lane—masquerading as a messenger from Holmes—was in Burlington, delivering a decoy letter for Carrie Pitezel. The letter, penned by Holmes at Hanscom's dictation, directed Carrie to bring Dessie and Wharton to Boston at once.

Had Holmes's plot against the remaining Pitezels been successful, Lane would have found nothing at 26 Winooski Avenue but smoldering debris. But Carrie's suspicions had been aroused by the fluid-filled jar hidden away in her basement, and—instead of transferring it up to the attic, as Holmes had instructed—she had carefully brought it out back and buried it in the yard.

Accompanied by Lane, Carrie and the children traveled to Boston, where they were met at the depot by another of Holmes's ostensible accomplices—in reality, Inspector Whitman of the Boston police. The two men loaded Carrie and her children into a cab for the trip to police headquarters. When the truth of her situation finally became apparent, she swooned from the shock. She revived a few moments later, only to break into such hysterical sobbing that she seemed on the verge of a nervous collapse. Arrest and imprisonment—and their attendant disgrace—were the fulfillment of her most dreaded fears. At the time, she could not imagine that even worse nightmares awaited.

Carrie's first confession, given on Monday, November 19, contained a number of fabrications. Her interrogators suspected as much. But they understood that her lying was the product of her panic and fear—not (as in Holmes's case) a function of inveterate dishonesty.

Asked about her participation in the insurance fraud, Carrie steadfastly denied any foreknowledge of the scheme. As far as she knew, her husband had gone off to Philadelphia to conduct some legitimate business under the name Perry. When she read that Perry's corpse had been discovered at 1316 Callowhill Street, she had naturally assumed that Benny was really dead.

"Before the time that you got this news from the press," asked Hanscom, "had you known anything about this scheme?"

"No, they did not tell me anything about it."

"Nothing had been said to you about it?"

"No."

"Never had been talked over with you?"

"No."

"Had you no intimation, not the slightest sign that it had been talked over?"

Carrie was emphatic. "I had no knowledge of what was to be done."

The news of Benny's death had been a devastating blow to Carrie. She was still prostrate with grief when Holmes—or Howard, as he was calling himself at the time—showed up in St. Louis a week later with an amazing announcement.

"What did he say to you?" asked Hanscom.

"Why, I told him that I saw something in the paper in regard to my husband, and I wanted to know if it was my husband and if it was true, and he said, 'You need not worry about it.'"

"Did he ease your mind regarding the death of your husband before he went away, telling you that your husband was not dead?"

"Yes."

Carrie, however, remained completely in the dark about the insurance scheme. It was not until later, when Holmes brought her to the office of Lawyer Howe to collect the payment on her husband's life insurance policy, that Carrie first became suspicious. Even then, however, she was only obeying Holmes's instructions and—as she believed—the wishes of her husband. At no point was she herself an active conspirator in the plot.

If Carrie's desperate denials rang false to Hanscom and his colleagues, her dismay and bewilderment over her husband's present whereabouts were unmistakably real. Even her harshest inquisitors—those least disposed to excuse her evident lies—were moved to pity by the cruel manipulations to which Holmes had subjected her.

"He has kept you moving, hasn't he?" Hanscom asked in the soft, sympathetic tone of an understanding friend.

Blinking to keep back the tears, Carrie lowered her head and nodded. "Yes," she answered, her voice barely above a whisper.

"I wish to ask you one question direct," Hanscom went on. "Do you believe now that your husband is alive?"

Carrie glanced up at him quickly. "Well, there must be

Herman Webster Mudgett, alias H. H. Holmes.
(Illinois State Historical Library)

A rare photograph of Benjamin Freelon Pitezel, taken when he was twenty-eight. (Courtesy of Mildred Vooris Kerr)

Dessie and Nellie Pitezel. (Courtesy of Mildred Vooris Kerr)

Alice and Howard Pitezel. (Courtesy of Mildred Vooris Kerr)

Dessie Pitezel holding her infant brother, Wharton. (Courtesy of Mildred Vooris Kerr)

A rare photograph of Holmes's Castle. (Chicago Historical Society)

Ned Conner. (Illinois State Historical Library)

Julia Conner. (Illinois State Historical Library)

Minnie Williams. (Illinois State Historical Library)

Marion Hedgepeth, "The Handsome Bandit."
(UPI/BETTMANN)

DETECTIVE FRANK GEYER.
[Who Is Searching for Howard Pitzel's Body.]

Detective Frank Geyer.
(Illinois State Historical Library)

Pat Quinlan, the janitor of the Castle and suspected accomplice of H. H. Holmes.
(Illinois State Historical Library)

QUINLAN, THE JANITOR.

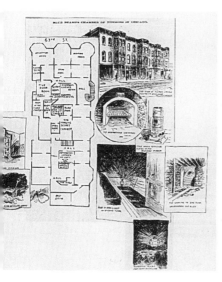

"Bluebeard's Chamber of Horrors" is the headline of this newspaper illustration, which shows the labyrinthine second floor of the Castle, along with some of the building's sinister features. (Illinois State Historical Library)

Curiosity-seekers gather around the Castle.
(Illinois State Historical Library)

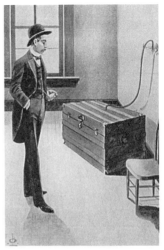

Holmes forces the Pitezel girls into his oversized trunk, then feeds a rubber tube, connected to a gas jet, into the pre-drilled hole.

Holmes stands by coolly while Alice and Nellie asphyxiate inside the trunk.

Holmes strangles Howard Pitezel.

DEPRAVED

something in it," she said in a tone more expressive of hope than conviction. An instant later, her shoulders sagged. "I am sure I could not swear to it, for I don't know for a fact that he is alive. All I know is what you have been telling me and what he has been telling me, and that is all I know."

"But he has kept you moving from point to point," Hanscom said again. "I would like to have you tell it in your own way."

Carrie exhaled a tremulous sigh. "Well, I have been moving from one point to another. I have been just heartbroken, that is all there is about it."

"Yes, I know," Hanscom commiserated. "We are sorry for you." He paused for a moment before continuing. "Can you tell me the points in the order of them, how you have been moving about since you left home?"

Carrie squeezed her eyes tight, as though trying to retrace the tortuous route in her mind. "I went from my parents, from there to Chicago, from Chicago to Detroit, and from there to Toronto, from there to Ogdensburg, from there to Burlington."

"Have you had confidence in Howard all the way through, that he would finally take you to your husband?"

"I thought so."

"Has your confidence ever been shaken?"

Carrie's voice became as fragile as a frightened child's. "Well, sometimes, I thought maybe he was fooling me or something."

Her greatest concern at the moment was the current location of her three children. Carrie explained that she had not set eyes on Alice since September, when the girl had gone off to Philadelphia in the company of Lawyer Howe.

"Who is he?" Hanscom interrupted.

"He is the lawyer, the attorney."

Hanscom shot a look at Cornish, who flipped open a notepad and scribbled down the name.

"A St. Louis man?" asked Hanscom.

"Yes, sir."

"Do you know where his office is in St. Louis?"

"Well, it is in the Commercial Building."

Hanscom glanced at Cornish to make sure that he had

copied the information, then returned to the subject of Carrie's missing children. "Into whose custody did you place the other two?"

"He took the other two. That is, Holmes took them from St. Louis to where Alice was."

"What was his reason for taking them? What reason did he give?"

"He said he would take them there and I could go home and make my parents a visit, and not be bothered with them, because my parents were getting along in years, and he would take the children, and then I could go over there when I got through visiting."

"He was going to take them to meet Alice?"

"Yes, sir."

"And that they would all be stopping with some widow lady?"

"Yes."

"Did he give her name?"

"No, sir, I told you he did not."

Hanscom pursed his lips in frustration. "Has he ever told you since then that they were with the father?" he continued after a moment.

"No, sir, he told me he took them to Toronto, that is all I know about it."

"You understood from him that they are there?"

Carrie nodded. "At Toronto."

"With friends of his, or whom do you believe them to be with? Your husband?"

"No. He said he would give them to some friends there. I don't know whether he has."

Hanscom stared at Carrie. Her answers seemed so evasive that he felt sure she must be withholding information. It was inconceivable to him that a mother would send three of her children off with anyone—let alone a person like Holmes—without knowing such elementary facts as where they were going, how long they would be staying, and who would be taking care of them.

"We believe this man to be a very bad man," Hanscom said grimly after a moment, "and we want to get at the truth."

"Well, that is as far as I know," Carrie cried out. "I can't tell you any more because I don't know!"

"You did not understand then that these children were going to join their father?"

"No, sir," Carrie replied miserably.

"There is a boy and two girls?"

"Whoever told you that?" Carrie asked, her lower lip trembling.

"We have been talking with him," Hanscom said softly. "We are not doing anything to undertake to make you feel bad. We are trying to get at the matter and sift it. He has kept you moving about the country from point to point, and you look as though you have been through a good deal. We want to get all the light we can. We don't believe this man very much. That is why we are asking you these questions."

Suddenly Carrie's right hand shot out and clutched at Hanscom's sleeve. "Do you know where the children are?" she asked desperately.

Hanscom shook his head sadly. "No. That is one of the things we want to find out. We want to find them as much for your sake as for any other reason in the world. In fact, we may say that all these questions that are being asked now regarding these children are in your behalf."

But Carrie was no longer paying attention. Bowing her head, she gazed blankly at the floor and said, in a hollow, hopeless voice, "I thought maybe I would see the children here."

The interview ended soon afterward. Carrie was informed that she was being held on a charge of conspiracy after the fact. Terrified and friendless, she begged that her children be permitted to remain with her overnight. Since the police had made no provisions for Dessie and the infant, they agreed.

When Carrie got to her feet, she found that she could barely stand, let alone walk. Hanscom beckoned to one of his subordinates.

Then—supported by a burly policeman and accompanied by her teenage daughter and infant son—the stricken woman was led off to the Tombs.

33

Barring that natural expression of villainy which we all have, the man looked honest enough.

—Mark Twain, "A Mysterious Visit"

Though it would be months before the world discovered the true extent of Holmes's depravity, his arrest was already regarded as a triumph of the law. In the days immediately following his capture, the press lavished praise on all the parties involved, from the insurance company investigators to the Boston police to what *The Philadelphia Inquirer* described as "the octopus-like system of the Pinkerton Detective Agency."

Other parties, meanwhile, were eager to share in the credit. Among those busily patting themselves on the back was the president of Fidelity Mutual, L. G. Fouse, who lost no time in revising his role in the drama from rather bumbling bit player to star. Interviewed by reporters on November 18, Fouse declared that—far from having been hoodwinked by Holmes—he had "scented something wrong from the start" and had been "determined to throw every legitimate obstacle in the way of the settlement of the policy."

According to Fouse's revisionist version, he had seen through Holmes's imposture immediately. It was Jeptha Howe who had beguiled him by playing on Fouse's inordinately good nature. "If there was anybody in the world calculated to throw a man off his guard, it was Howe," Fouse proclaimed. "He was an innocent, boyish-looking fellow, with a frank, honest face. When I began to question him, he appealed to my soft side. He told me I was a man of experience in these things, and he was only a novice at the bar, and he begged me not to hinder him in his efforts to win success."

Even so, Fouse, with his keen nose for deception, had ordered his men to investigate Howe and Holmes, and "before long my suspicions were confirmed." From that point on, it was only a matter of time before the conspirators were brought to justice, thanks largely to the efforts of President L. G. Fouse.

In point of fact, Howe was still at large at the time of Fouse's interview. But on Monday morning, November 19, a contingent of law officers—acting on an urgent dispatch from Philadelphia police superintendent Linden—showed up at Howe's office in the Commercial Building and arrested him on a charge of conspiracy. Hauled down to headquarters, Howe was interrogated by St. Louis police chief Harrigan and William E. Gary for several hours before being released on a $3,000 bond.

Outside the building, Howe was accosted by several reporters, who pressed for a statement. "I will say the same to you that I have said to Mr. Gary and the chief," Howe declared. "I do not, in the first place, believe a fraud has been committed. I believe the body identified by Pitezel's fifteen-year-old daughter was that of her father. The marks of identification were perfect. As to how Pitezel met his death, I cannot say. But as I said to Mr. Gary, if a fraud has been committed, I am as anxious to have it investigated as anyone and will do all in my power to bring the guilty to punishment. I took the case in good faith and acted as any attorney would have done. Mr. Gary asked me if I would be willing to return to the company my fee if this were proved a fraud. I told him I would be not only willing but would not under any circumstances keep any part of it."

Outraged at the injustice of the accusations and the injury to his name, Howe intended to leave at once for Philadelphia to prove his innocence and redeem his reputation.

Howe's righteous indignation, not to mention his credibility, was somewhat undercut by Chief Harrigan, who—shortly after the young attorney's release—publicly disclosed the content of Marion Hedgepeth's letter, which had cracked the case open in the first place. Harrigan also revealed that, according to the bandit, Howe had attempted "to smuggle him keys and to aid him on various occasions to escape"— a charge confirmed by jail guard J. C. Armstrong, who, in a sworn statement to the St. Louis authorities, declared "that he was approached by Jeptha D. Howe for the purpose of getting his assistance in Hedgepeth's escape."

That same afternoon, the grand jury convened in Philadelphia to hear the testimony of President Fouse and Coroner Ashbridge. At two P.M., after concluding its deliberations, the jury issued true bills of indictment against Herman Mudgett, alias H. H. Holmes, Mrs. Carrie Pitezel, and Jeptha D. Howe, charging them with "conspiracy to cheat and defraud" the Fidelity Mutual Life Association Company of $10,000.

Significantly, one name was missing from the indictment— Benjamin F. Pitezel. The omission reflected the widespread belief that—in spite of Holmes's insistence that his partner was still alive—Pitezel had, in fact, been murdered.

From the moment the story broke, Pitezel's fate was a matter of heated debate among the authorities and intense fascination in the press—a dark, spellbinding mystery that baffled the law and kept newsreaders guessing. PITEZEL MYSTERY STILL UNSOLVED, proclaimed *The Philadelphia Inquirer*. DID HOLMES KILL PITEZEL? asked *The New York Times*. POLICE PUZZLED OVER THE PITEZEL INSURANCE SWINDLE, trumpeted *The Chicago Tribune*. Papers throughout the country played up the melodrama for all it was worth, treating the Holmes-Pitezel case less as an unfolding news story than a serialized suspense novel, with each day's installment dished up on page one.

At first, the consensus among insiders was that the double-crossing Holmes had slain his unsuspecting partner. L. G. Fouse, for example, insisted that the Callowhill remains were unquestionably those of Pitezel.

According to the theory Fouse advanced to reporters, "it was the original intention of Holmes to bring Pitezel to this city [Philadelphia] and have him rent the rooms at number 1316 Callowhill Street. He was to assume the name of B. F. Perry. Then Holmes, being a chemist, was to disfigure Pitezel's cheek so that it would have the appearance of being burned, give him a drug to make him unconscious, and lay him on the floor. A broken pipe and other articles that would give indications of an explosion were placed about the room. Then the physician was to be called in. The doctor would, of course, think the man the victim of an accident. After the doctor had taken his departure, Pitezel was to be revived, washed up, and smuggled out.

"But I think that the latter part of the plot was never carried out," Fouse continued, "and that instead of sharing in the spoils, Pitezel was murdered. I have every reason to think that the body interred in potter's field is really that of B. F. Pitezel." Holmes's eager confession to fraud, Fouse concluded, was simply a ploy to "ward off the still greater charge of murder."

Coroner Ashbridge likewise scoffed at Holmes's contention that the corpse had been procured from a New York City physician and smuggled to Philadelphia in a trunk. According to Holmes's confession, he had forced the cadaver into the trunk by bending it at the waist. "But a body once bent does not become rigid again," Ashbridge pointed out—and the corpse found at the Callowhill address "was stretched flat upon the floor and perfectly rigid." Moreover, "if the body *had* been in the trunk, it would have shown marks of where it had been doubled up. But no such marks were found upon the body."

There was also the matter of the dried blood staining the floor near the corpse. As Ashbridge asserted, "blood could not have been extracted from the vein of a corpse such as Holmes described except with a force pump." Finally, the coroner explained, "had the cadaver been obtained from a doctor in New York, it would have been preserved in alcohol. The body found in the Callowhill Street house was not preserved in this way."

The inescapable conclusion was that someone had been

killed on Callowhill Street, and the likeliest candidate was Pitezel, though whether his death was deliberate or not, Ashbridge was unable to say. It was conceivable, the coroner opined, that Pitezel had died from an accidental overdose of chloroform, administered "so that his cheek might painlessly be marked with burns which could be shown to a physician." On the other hand, it was equally plausible that, after knocking Pitezel out with the anesthetic, Holmes had made sure that his accomplice would never waken again, thus obviating the need to split the insurance money two ways.

There was, of course, a third possibility, too, initially advanced by the Boston police—that the dead man was not Pitezel at all but rather another person entirely, who had been lured to the Callowhill Street house under some pretext and there done away with by the two conspirators. Pitezel, as one officer revealed to reporters, "was a drinking man, and it would have been an easy matter for him to secure a victim from some of his barroom acquaintances."

This theory was given a boost on Monday afternoon, when L. G. Fouse received a wire from William E. Gary, informing him that Pitezel had been known in Forth Worth as Benton T. Lyman and might still be at large under that alias.

Of course all this was pure speculation. Only one person knew the truth of what had happened at 1316 Callowhill Street on the morning of September 2. And he wasn't telling it.

Detective Thomas Crawford of the Philadelphia Bureau of Police arrived in Boston early Monday morning, bearing warrants for the arrest of both Holmes and Mrs. Pitezel, who agreed to forgo formal extradition proceedings. At seven-thirty that evening, the prisoners boarded a train for Philadelphia in the company of Crawford, O. LaForrest Perry, and a pair of Pinkerton detectives. Also included in the party were Dessie Pitezel, who hugged her infant brother to her chest, and Georgiana Yoke Howard, who continued to keep up an appearance of wifely loyalty, though her taut face and anguished eyes spoke plainly of her mortification. After ten months of marriage, Georgiana was finally confronting the bitter truth—that her life with Holmes had been a complete lie from the beginning. The police, who did not regard her as a suspect, understood this. From the start, they perceived that the pretty young woman was not Holmes's accomplice but rather another of his many victims.

In contrast to his wife's grim demeanor, Holmes—even with one hand cuffed to Crawford's wrist—seemed the very picture of relaxed unconcern. Impeccably dressed in a handsome wool cutaway, matching vest, black four-in-hand tie, and stylish gray trousers, he spent the better part of the trip regaling Crawford with the ostensible history of his criminal career.

He had been born, raised, and educated in Burlington, Vermont, Holmes claimed. After graduating from the University of Vermont, he taught school for a while in Burlington, then went off to study medicine at the University of Michigan, where he first made the acquaintance of the individual—then a fellow med student, now a prominent New York physician—who had supplied him with the substitute corpse used in the recent swindle. Fidelity Mutual, however, was not the first insurance company Holmes had defrauded. Far from it. He and his physician friend—whose identity he still refused to divulge—had first worked the scheme twelve years before. Short of funds, they had taken out a $12,500 policy on the friend's life, obtained a "bogus body" in Chicago, transported it east, and successfully "palmed it off" on the insurance company.

Since that time, Holmes claimed, he had repeated the fraud on a number of occasions. One of these he related to Crawford in detail.

After insuring his life for $20,000, Holmes illegally procured a cadaver from a medical college in Chicago, then traveled to Rhode Island, where he took a room in a seaside hotel. At the time, he was sporting a full, bushy beard, which he had been cultivating for the preceding six months.

Toward sunset, Holmes left the hotel, announcing to the desk clerk that he was going for an evening swim. Once out of sight, he hurried to an isolated spot several miles from the resort, where, in the underbrush fringing the beach, he had stashed the cadaver. Dragging the body down to the shore, he cut off its head and arranged the mutilated corpse so that, in his words, it "looked as though it had been washed up by the waves."

The following afternoon, after shaving off his beard, Holmes returned to the hotel in disguise and registered under a different name, inquiring of the desk clerk if he knew of a gentleman named Holmes. Yes, said the clerk. Mr. Holmes had checked in the day before but hadn't been seen since the previous evening, when he had gone out for a swim. When Holmes failed to return by nightfall, a search was made and the mutilated body—presumably that of the unfortunate Mr. Holmes, who had evidently drowned and been feasted on by sharks—was located on the beach.

Unfortunately, Holmes sighed, bringing his account to a close, "this particular scheme fell through" and he was unable to collect on the policy.

All this was extremely interesting to Crawford and his colleagues, though they already knew enough about Holmes to view virtually everything he said with intense skepticism. The story, in any event, seemed wildly improbable—though no more so than the next part of Holmes's recitation. Clearly anticipating that he would soon be suspected of even greater crimes, Holmes had an extraordinary tale to relate.

While living in Chicago with his second wife, he had fallen in love with a pretty young woman in his employ—a "typewriter girl." Before long, the two had become intimate and were sharing a furnished apartment on the outskirts of town.

A few weeks later, the elder sister of Holmes's mistress arrived for a visit. Insanely jealous, his mistress soon began accusing her sibling of flirting with Holmes. One day while Holmes was away, the two women had a violent argument in his office. In the heat of the quarrel, his mistress grabbed a wooden stool, brought it down on her sister's skull, and killed her.

"When I came back," Holmes continued, "I found the dead body in the room. I took the corpse, put it in a trunk, weighed it down with rocks, and sank it in Lake Michigan in the dead of night. This was a year and a half ago. The younger sister, in danger of arrest for murder, was anxious to escape. She owned some property in Fort Worth, amounting to forty thousand dollars. Pitezel and I took this property off her hands and gave her the money to fly the country.

"We then bought horses, getting credit on the strength of the Fort Worth property. But the deeds were not straight, and we needed money to keep things going. So the two of us agreed to work the insurance scheme, and that's how this trouble began."

Crawford chewed over this information for a moment, then asked if Holmes had been involved in any other crimes.

The prisoner suddenly turned coy. "Oh," he replied with a casual wave of his free hand, "I have done enough things in my life to be hung a dozen times."

The little party rode in silence for a while. As the train passed through Providence, Holmes leaned toward his custodian.

"See here, Crawford," he whispered. "I think my wife can raise five hundred dollars. I'm a hypnotizer—learned how to do it from a fellow doctor. I can hypnotize people very easily. If you let me hypnotize you so that I can escape, I'll give you the five hundred dollars."

"Sorry," replied the detective. "Hypnotism always spoils my appetite. I'm afraid five hundred dollars is no inducement when weighed against possible dyspepsia."

This episode, widely reported in the press, was taken as still another sign of Holmes's colossal brazenness, and his claim to mesmeric power dismissed as sheer nonsense. At this point, he was not yet the demon he would later become in the popular imagination—a creature of almost supernatural evil, possessed of a Dracula-like ability to hypnotize his victims at a glance.

The train pulled into Philadelphia's Broad Street Station at precisely six-ten P.M. on Tuesday, November 20. Still handcuffed to Crawford, Holmes—whose handsome attire, as one reporter noted, "bespoke the prosperous man of business, [though] his face seemed to set forth the fact that he was cool and calculating, a man to be feared"—was led directly to the City Hall police station. Carrie's nervous condition was such that she was unable to walk without the support of one of the Pinkertons.

Inside the station, Holmes was led directly to a darkened cell on the second tier. After being grilled for several hours by Superintendent Linden, President Fouse, and O. LaForrest Perry, he was brought down to the identification department, where he was photographed and measured according to the system pioneered by the French criminologist Alphonse Bertillon.

Carrie, meanwhile, was locked in the upper cell of the first tier. Dessie and the baby remained outside in the corridor under the sympathetic gaze of a police matron named Kalboch.

The sight of the two children playing just beyond the bars of her cell offered little comfort to their wretched mother, who wept continuously from the moment the iron door clanged shut behind her. The pitiable situation of Mrs. Pitezel was becoming a matter of increasing concern both to the authorities and the public at large. Even the officials of Fidelity Mutual, who regarded her, at the very least, as an accessory after the fact, were moved by Carrie's plight. Naïve and (as the newspapers put it) of "no more than ordinary intelligence," she had clearly been an easy subject for the ruthless manipulations of Holmes, who had—so Coroner Ashbridge and many others continued to believe—widowed her into the bargain.

Even more worrisome was the unresolved mystery of her three missing children. For the first time, a dreadful possibility was being not only entertained but openly discussed by the police—that Holmes had done away with Alice, Nellie, and Howard.

As *The Philadelphia Public Ledger* revealed in a front-page story on Wednesday, November 21, "the question of the disposition of Pietzel's three children, who were taken by Holmes to be placed in the care of their father, is agitating the authorities. An effort is being made to find them, but as yet it has resulted unsuccessfully. The police think that if the charge of Pietzel's murder can be substantiated against Holmes, there will be little doubt that he has added the killing of the children to his long list of crimes, for which he himself admits he should be hanged."

34

I like that fellow, even if he *is* a rascal.

—Prison guard, quoted in *The Chicago Tribune*,
November 25, 1895

While Holmes sat brooding in his dark Philadelphia cell, his crimes were rapidly coming to light in Chicago. Less than twenty-four hours after his arrest, nearly fifty victims of his various frauds showed up at the Englewood police station to put in claims against his property.

Every day brought a fresh spate of revelations about his seemingly endless swindles, from his worthless elixir to his phony gas-generating machine to his sharp dealings with building contractors and furniture suppliers. Dozens of former acquaintances, associates, and employees stepped forward to recount tales of his deceits—often with a kind of appreciative chuckle for the sheer daring and ingenuity of the man. As one newspaper put it, Holmes "swindled with a dash and vim that won the admiration even of those he tricked."

Typical of such gossip was an interview given by a gentleman named C. E. Davis, owner of a jewelry shop on the ground floor of Holmes's Castle. "I'll give you a sample of the man," Davis told a reporter for *The Chicago Times-Herald*. "Nearly every particle of material in this building and its fixtures was got on credit and very little of it was ever paid for.... Holmes used to tell me he had a lawyer paid to keep him out of trouble, but it always seemed to

219

me it was the courteous, audacious rascality of the man that pulled him through. One day he bought some furniture for his restaurant and moved it in, and that very evening the dealer came around to collect the bill or remove the goods. Holmes set up the drinks, took him to supper, bought him a cigar, and sent the man off laughing at a joke, with a promise to call the next week for his money. In thirty minutes after the man took his car, Holmes had wagons in front loading up that furniture, and the dealer never got a cent. He was the only man in the United States that could do what he did. I believe he was an English crook who had found the old country too hot for him."

Davis's remarks show how quickly Holmes's notoriety grew. Within days of his arrest, the legend was already taking shape: Holmes "the archconspirator," "boss crook of the century," "swindler of men and betrayer of women, who has left behind him a wake of ruin and tears that not all the courts of America can wash away."

Noting his proficiency "at half-a-dozen lines of crooked work," *The Chicago Tribune* proclaimed him "about the smoothest and best all-around swindler that ever struck this town." It was Holmes's "astonishing versatility" that raised him "above the run of ordinary criminals"—that and his remarkable power over women. According to the paper, Holmes had ruined at least two hundred "pretty young girls" and had six wives and twenty-five children scattered around the country.

But there were growing indications of an even darker side to his career—of crimes far worse than swindling and seduction, or even the murderous betrayal of a faithful confederate. By Wednesday, November 21, two names had been connected to Holmes's bizarre tale of rivalry and bloodshed between a jealous mistress and her older sister—the names of Minnie and Nannie Williams.

Assisted by their counterparts in Fort Worth, the Chicago police had already uncovered a great deal of information about Minnie Williams—her background, upbringing, relationship to Holmes, and—not incidentally—considerable inheritance. "Those people in Englewood who knew Holmes and the Williams girl can tell enough stories to fill a book," averred *The Chicago Tribune.* Among those with especially intriguing stories to tell was the former caretaker of the Castle, Pat Quinlan, who would soon fall under official scrutiny himself, suspected of assisting in Holmes's foulest crimes. Interviewed by detectives on the evening of Tuesday, November 20, Quinlan offered vivid recollections of Minnie Williams and confirmed certain details that seemed to support Holmes's version of events—including the fact that Holmes kept a small wooden stool in his office, of the kind Minnie had presumably used to bash in the skull of her sister.

Most people, however, continued to dismiss Holmes's account as a complete fabrication. Some maintained that, from the first, Minnie had been an active accomplice, who had "stuck by Holmes through all his peculiar career." But others—including the girls' uncle, the Reverend C. W. Black of Jackson, Mississippi, who had not heard from either of his nieces since July 1893—remained firmly convinced that Holmes, perhaps assisted by Pitezel, had done away with both sisters in order to get his hands on the Forth Worth property.

The Williams sisters were not the only young women widely believed to have been murdered by Holmes. In a front-page story on November 21, *The New York Times* revealed that "H. H. Holmes, the life-insurance swindler now under arrest in Philadelphia, is charged with being the cause of the mysterious disappearance of a third woman during his operations in Chicago. That person is Miss Kate Durkee, and she is said to have had considerable property."

One year before, the article went on to say, "creditors of Holmes had made a desperate effort to find out who and where Miss Durkee was. It was supposed that she was an accomplice of Holmes's and that property illegally obtained was being transferred to her name. Suddenly, Miss Durkee dropped from sight and, like the Williams sisters, has left no trace behind."

George B. Chamberlain, proprietor of a Chicago mercantile agency and one of Holmes's many creditors, harbored no doubts about the poor woman's fate. Interviewed by reporters on November 22, he stated his absolute belief that "Miss Durkee was murdered."

With evidence of Holmes's villainy mounting daily, reporters began digging into every aspect of his life, from his New Hampshire boyhood to his medical-school career in Ann Arbor to the frenzied entrepreneurialism of his Englewood years. Accounts of his illicit activities began pouring in from every part of the country, from Kankakee to Omaha, Terre Haute to New Orleans.

One of the most striking reports came from Providence, Rhode Island. According to authorities there, a corpse had been removed from the graveyard of the State Mental Institution several years earlier—at precisely the time of Holmes's professed insurance scam at the seaside resort. The decapitated body of the dead man—an inmate named Caleb R. Browne—had subsequently been recovered, though the head was never found. This report lent considerable credence to the story Holmes had told to Detective Crawford. And it added another outrage to the growing list of Holmes's crimes. In addition to swindling, bigamy, and murder, Holmes now stood accused of grave-robbing.

Given the zeal of the press to probe every corner of Holmes's shadowy life, what happened next was inevitable. On November 25, a small but significant passage appeared on page one of *The Chicago Tribune*—the first printed description of Holmes's property at Wallace and Sixty-third streets in Englewood.

"In America's whole domains," declared the writer, who had evidently snuck into the building and made a hurried tour, "there is not a house like unto that one, and there probably never will be. Its chimneys stick out where chimneys never stuck out before, its staircases do not end anywhere in particular, it has winding passages that bring the rash intruder back to where he started with a jerk and altogether it is a very mysterious sort of a building."

For the first time, the newspapers, the public—and the police—were beginning to take note of the bizarre and mysterious building that would soon be known throughout the country as Dr. Holmes's Horror Castle.

Though Holmes possessed a real flair for self-pity, he put up a stoic front during his early days of captivity, assuming the guise of the repentant sinner: a man who knew he had done wrong and was prepared to swallow his medicine—two years of jail time, the maximum sentence for conspiracy in Philadelphia. Carrie Pitezel, on the other hand, continued to be overwhelmed with horror and shame. During her first long night in the Philadelphia cell, she gave herself over to such uncontrolled grief that Police Surgeon Andrews had to be summoned first thing in the morning. He managed to soothe her with the aid of a sedative, and she remained prostrate on her cot for most of the day. Once or twice, she got unsteadily to her feet, shuffled to the cell door, and peered through the iron grate at her infant boy, who toddled up and down the corridor, clasping a tin cup provided by Matron Kalboch.

The third member of the conspiracy, Jeptha D. Howe, was due in Philadelphia on the evening of Wednesday, November 21, but failed to appear. Instead, his employer, Marshal McDonald—the former district attorney of St. Louis and law partner of Howe's older brother, Alphonso—slipped quietly into the city. After checking into the Lafayette Hotel, McDonald sought out his old friend Police Superintendent Linden. The two men conferred for several hours, then met with the reporters.

"I believe Mr. McDonald to be a perfectly honorable man," Captain Linden declared, "and entirely innocent of any illegal connection with the Pitezel conspiracy. He tells me that Jeptha D. Howe is only a beginner with the firm and says he was unwittingly led astray by the scoundrel Holmes."

Elaborating on the police chief's statement, McDonald asserted that "whatever indiscretions Howe may have committed were due to the influence exerted on him by Holmes. Howe is only twenty-two years of age. He is a graduate of the law school of Washington University and is married to a most estimable young lady of a very good family in St. Louis. This was his first case, and he went into it with all the ardor of a beginner. At the time Holmes approached Mr. Howe, both myself and my partner, Alphonso Howe— the young man's elder brother—were in Colorado. If we had

223

been at home at the time, he never would have become mixed up in the case."

When asked about Howe's present whereabouts, McDonald explained that the young man had stopped off in Washington, D.C., to seek the advice of Senator Cockrell of Missouri, an old family friend. Howe was expected in Philadelphia the following morning and would immediately turn himself over to authorities.

In spite of the assurances of his old friend, Captain Linden detailed two of his men to search for Howe, suspecting that the young lawyer might have been smuggled into the city and stashed in a hotel, so that he could surrender himself in the morning when bail could be arranged, thus avoiding a night in jail. The two men assigned this task were Thomas Crawford and a second detective who would soon play a celebrated role in the Holmes-Pitezel affair, Frank P. Geyer.

McDonald, however, was telling the truth. The following morning at around ten, Howe arrived at the train station, where he was met by McDonald, who immediately escorted him to City Hall. Before entering Superindendent Linden's office, the young lawyer agreed to meet the press. Taken to the reporters' room on the eighth floor of the building, Howe—invariably described as "boyish" and "innocent looking," with "a face as smooth as a baby's"—proceeded to provide such a detailed account of his dealings with Mrs. Pitezel that McDonald felt compelled to cut him off. Howe wrapped up his statement quickly, declining to say anything about his connection with Holmes or his involvement with Marion Hedgepeth.

At that point, he was brought into the superintendent's office, where he formally surrendered himself and spent some time answering questions. Halfway through his interrogation, L. G. Fouse showed up.

"Well, Mr. Fouse," Howe said cordially, rising to shake hands with the insurance executive. "You treated me with such kindness and courtesy I am sorry that you think I am a criminal."

"So am I," Fouse answered coldly. "But it will take a good deal to convince me of your innocence."

Howe protested that Fouse was only prejudiced against him because of the false accusations leveled by Holmes.

Fouse replied with a snort. "You knew Holmes, and, in fact, you met him on your way to this city. In the office of our company, you both met as strangers. You exclaimed, when told that he was in this city, 'Who is this man? What does he mean? What is he here for?' And when you were introduced, you acted in a way that led us to believe that you had seen him for the first time. When you can explain to me why you did this, I will believe you innocent."

Howe was taken to the sixth-floor office of District Attorney George S. Graham, who set bail at $2,500: the money was put up later that afternoon by a saloonkeeper named William McGonegal, a friend of McDonald's. After his release, Howe told reporters that he would remain in Philadelphia for a day or so to consult with his attorney, A. S. L. Shields, before returning to St. Louis to await his trial.

That night, Howe and McDonald attended the South Broad Street Theatre, where they watched a performance by the St. Louis actress Della Fox. Afterward, Howe appeared perfectly relaxed and carefree, chatting and laughing with McDonald as they strolled up Broad Street toward the Lafayette Hotel, shadowed by a pair of reporters.

While Jeptha Howe was doing the town, Holmes and Carrie Pitezel continued to languish in jail. By Friday, November 23, arrangements were being made to transfer them to the county prison, commonly known as Moyamensing.

Early that morning, Detectives Crawford and Geyer escorted the prisoners from their City Hall cells to the Court of Quarter Sessions. There, Assistant District Attorney Kinsey, Police Surgeon Andrews, and Mr. Benjamin Crew, secretary of the Society to Protect Children from Cruelty, consulted over the advisability of allowing Dessie and the baby to remain with their mother. Crew urged that the children be placed in the care of his organization. Overhearing his proposal, Carrie broke into hysterics. "You will not take my baby from me, will you?" she wailed.

Immediately, Police Surgeon Andrews placed his arm around the overwrought woman, assuring her that she would not be separated from the infant. "Send the girl, too," he said to Kinsey. "The woman is in no condition to take care of the baby by herself."

The matter settled, Carrie and her children were helped into a closed carriage for their trip to the county prison. Holmes, meanwhile, was unceremoniously loaded into a van full of drunks ("a crowded conveyance filled with a filthy lot of humanity" as he later described it) and driven to Moyamensing, where he was locked in a nine-by-fourteen-foot whitewashed cell.

Meanwhile, speculation about Pitezel's fate continued to rage. Rumors circulated at such a dizzying pace that, as a reporter for *The Philadelphia Inquirer* put it, they were enough to "exhaust anyone attempting to keep up with them." Certain people close to the case, including Coroner Ashbridge and Jeptha Howe, held firm to their conviction that Pitezel was dead. Others, however, were beginning to revise their opinion, including L. G. Fouse, who had received tips from his investigators that Pitezel had been spotted in Chicago as recently as early November, in Detroit a few weeks before that, and was currently rumored to be in New York City.

To further confuse matters, a man named E. A. Curtis—who owned a furniture warehouse in Englewood where Pitezel had apparently stored some of his belongings before clearing out of Chicago the previous year—claimed that he knew the latter's precise whereabouts and could locate him within thirty-six hours, for a suitable reward.

From his cell in Moyamensing, Holmes did his best to muddy the waters even more by making a most remarkable retraction. Through a lawyer named Harry Hawkins—who had agreed to defend him in the conspiracy case—Holmes let it be known that his melodramatic account of the two Williams sisters and their murderous rivalry had been nothing but a hoax.

Speaking to reporters on Saturday, November 24, Hawkins described a conversation he had held with his client earlier in the day. "Holmes told me with tears in his eyes that he was absolutely innocent of the murder of Pitezel and that the man was alive and well. Holmes told me that the story he told Detective Crawford about one of the Williams sisters having murdered the other, and he having thrown the body in the lake, was a fake, pure and simple. He declared that both of the girls are alive. He said that Pitezel met Nannie Williams in New York and gave her a thousand dollars after the insurance money was collected. This money was to take her and her sister south."

What had motivated Holmes to concoct such an elaborate lie in the first place? the newspapermen demanded.

"Holmes said that Crawford was such a gullible-looking fellow," Hawkins replied, "that he thought he would have some fun with him."

It had already occurred to the authorities that there was one sure way to determine whether Pitezel was alive or not, and that was by disinterring the Callowhill corpse a second time and having Carrie Pitezel view the remains. This measure had been discussed as early as November 21, when O. LaForrest Perry declared that "it was not improbable that the body will be re-exhumed." As the police and insurance officials were debating the desirability of such an act, Holmes settled into his new accommodations at Moyamensing.

In the memoirs he would publish during his imprisonment, Holmes described his cell as "virtually a place of solitary confinement," lighted only by a narrow, grated window and secured by double doors—an inner one of latticed iron and a second one of solid wood, "which, when closed, excludes nearly all sound." Even so, he was by no means cut off from the world, since he was allowed to read the newspapers every day. As a result, he knew all about the proposal to reinspect Pitezel's body.

On Friday, December 7, he also learned something else—that Carrie Pitezel had broken down and revealed everything she knew about the insurance scheme. By that point, Dessie and Wharton had been removed from Carrie's cell and placed in the care of the Society to Protect Children from Cruelty.

Holmes understood that if the police went ahead and dug up the corpse, he would stand revealed as a barefaced liar, since he had continued to maintain that Pitezel was in hiding down South. Even worse, he would undoubtedly be charged with murder. And so he resorted to a typically brazen ploy. Summoning R. J. Linden to his cell, he made a great show of remorse and announced that he had decided to come clean.

He had been lying all along, he confessed. The dead man interred in potter's field really was Pitezel. But Holmes hadn't killed him.

The truth, Holmes solemnly declared, was that Benjamin Pitezel had committed suicide.

35

I have commenced to write a careful and truthful account of all matters pertaining to my case, including the fact that Pitezel is dead and that the children are with Miss Williams.

—From the prison diary of H. H. Holmes

Linden summoned a stenographer to the cell, and Holmes began dictating his formal statement. The date was December 26, 1894. The timing was no coincidence, Holmes having deliberately waited until the day after Christmas to confess, as though the holiness of the season had moved him to unburden his soul.

According to Holmes, he had visited the house on Callowhill Street perhaps four or five times after Pitezel set up his phony patent dealer's business. Sometime around the "last of August," Holmes dropped by and found Pitezel in a deeply despondent mood. He had clearly been hitting the bottle. When Holmes "took him to task for it," Pitezel replied "that he guessed he had better drink enough to kill him[self] and have done with it." After loaning Pitezel $15, Holmes left, having "stayed five or six hours."

The following Saturday, September 1, "quite late [in the] evening," Pitezel turned up at Adella Alcorn's boardinghouse on North Eleventh Street "and said he had received a telegram that his baby was sick and he had to go home. . . . I raised no objection to his going. When we got the arrangements all made, he said, 'You will have to let me have some money to go with.' "

Holmes asked what had happened to the $15 Pitezel had borrowed only a day or two before. "Well, I haven't got it," Pitezel replied. Holmes refused to fork over any more money, and Pitezel retreated into the night.

"The next morning about ten-thirty," Holmes continued, "I went to his house. I had been provided with a key to go in with. I found no one there either on the first or the second floor, where his sleeping apartment was. He had a cot up there which I do not think he ever made up."

Holmes repaired to the Mercantile Library and whiled away an hour, then strolled over to Broad Street "where I had a private mailbox." After checking for letters, he bought a morning paper and returned to 1316 Callowhill Street. Finding the place still empty, Holmes "went upstairs and laid down on the cot and read the paper." This was around noon.

A half hour later, Holmes went downstairs, intending "to write some letters" at Pitezel's desk. As he crossed the vacant office, he spotted something lying on the desktop: "a scrap of paper with a . . . cipher on it that we used." Holmes quickly decoded the cipher. The message read, "Get letter out of bottle in cupboard."

Puzzled, Holmes fetched the letter from the cupboard and was shocked to find that it was a suicide note. "It told me that he was going to get out of it, and that I should find him upstairs, if he could manage to kill himself."

Dashing up to the third story, Holmes flung open the door "and saw him lying on the floor apparently dead. I felt his pulse and laid my hand on his and found it was cold." Pitezel was stretched on his back with a towel muffling his face. On a chair beside the body sat a gallon bottle of chloroform, rigged up with a four-foot length of rubber tubing that fed the deadly fluid directly into his mouth.

The fumes were so overpowering that Holmes was forced to flee the room. "I went and opened the windows in the other room and came back and started to go in again, but had to give it up, and went to the second floor again. As soon as I could, I did go in again." Looking more closely at

Pitezel, Holmes saw that he was lying "with his left hand folded over his abdomen and his right hand lying at his side."

At this point, Linden interrupted and asked what had become of the suicide note.

"I did not keep the letter which was in the bottle," Holmes replied, "but destroyed it with the other papers the next day on the train going from Philadelphia to St. Louis."

Linden told Holmes to continue.

Gazing down at his lifeless partner, Holmes quickly realized that—regrettable though it was—Pitezel's suicide provided him with a golden opportunity, obviating the need for a substitute corpse. Within minutes he had swung into action. "I removed the furniture from the third-story room and took it to the second story, leaving the body until the last. Then I brought the body down into the second story and arranged it in the way it was found. This was about three o'clock."

The next step was to stage the phony accident. "I had arranged with Pitezel that when he placed the substitute body, a bottle should be broken and . . . the fragments scattered around the room. I held the bottle up and broke it with a blow of the hammer upon the side. That bottle contained benzine, chloroform, and ammonia, which was to be used for burning the floor to indicate that an explosion had occurred. I took some of this fluid and put it on his right hand and side and on the right side of his face and set fire to it . . . I gathered together the rubber tube, towel, and the bottle of chloroform and left the house as soon as I could, about a quarter of four."

Holmes concluded his statement by describing his hasty departure from Philadelphia that evening and his trip to St. Louis late the following Wednesday. Arriving on Thursday morning, he had purchased a newspaper and saw "a report that the body had been found. . . . I went to Mrs. Pitezel's and found that they had also seen the report. The children were greatly worried, but Mrs. Pitezel was not, as she believed the scheme had been carried out. We talked the matter over a couple of hours, and I came back that night and saw Howe and explained what had been done, not telling him that it was Pitezel but leaving him to believe that the plan of placing a substitute had been carried out, and retained him on behalf of Mrs. Pitezel to procure the money from the company."

When Holmes reached the end of his confession, Linden looked at him sternly. Perhaps the story was true, he said. Or perhaps Holmes had found Pitezel in a drunken state and then forced him to swallow the chloroform.

Holmes indignantly denied this accusation, insisting that his partner was already dead by his own hand when Holmes had discovered him.

"If Pitezel is dead," Linden demanded, "then where are the three children?"

Holmes replied without hesitation, "In safe hands." He had brought them to Detroit and turned them over to his former mistress.

Alice, Nellie, and Howard were in the care of Minnie Williams.

36

There is not the slightest doubt that Holmes, in his many stories, has not confined himself strictly to the truth.

Philadelphia Public Ledger, November 24, 1894

Holmes's revised statement—"Confession No. 2," as the authorities labeled it—inspired even greater skepticism than his first. The police scoffed at the claim that Pitezel had committed suicide—particularly by the outlandish method Holmes described. The notion that anyone would lie flat on the floor with a towel over his face, like a man in a barber's chair, and suck chloroform through a long rubber tube seemed completely preposterous. The whole story seemed like a flagrant fabrication, concocted to explain away the incontrovertible evidence—a dead man on a bedroom floor with a stomachful of chloroform.

The identity of that dead man, however, remained a matter of debate. Dismissing Holmes's latest story, Inspector Gary and his colleagues continued to press their search for Pitezel and the missing children in various parts of the country. Coroner Ashbridge, on the other hand, would not be swayed from his conviction that Pitezel had been murdered. Anyone hunting for Holmes's partner need look no further than potter's field, he maintained, and re-exhuming the body would corroborate this. But as the winter came on, authorities continued to dither over the issue.

In the meantime, Holmes kept busy in his cell, monitoring

the daily news reports on his case, scheming with his lawyers, and doing his manipulative best to impede the investigation. Georgiana, who continued to stick by her husband, paid him periodic visits. Perceiving that his highly presentable wife was a boon to his public image, Holmes did everything he could to remain in her good graces, professing his undying love and tearfully repenting the pain he had caused her.

Locked in his solitary cell, he resolved on a strict, daily regimen. In the prison diary he would append to his published memoirs, he described his self-improving schedule in terms that would have done Benjamin Franklin proud:

> *January 1, 1895—The New Year. I have been busy nearly all day in prison formulating a methodical plan for my daily life while in prison, to which I shall hereafter rigidly adhere, for the terrible solitude of these dark winter days will otherwise soon break me down. I shall rise at 6:30, and after taking my usual sponge bath shall clean my room and arrange it for the day. My meal hours shall be 7:30 A.M., 12, and 5 and 9 P.M. I shall eat no more meat of any kind while I am so closely confined. Until 10 A.M. all the time not otherwise disposed of shall be devoted to exercise and reading the morning papers. From 10 to 12 and 2 to 4, six days in the week, I shall confine myself to my old medical works and other college studies, including stenography, French and German, the balance of my day shall be taken up with reading the periodicals and library books with which——keeps me well supplied. I shall retire at 9 P.M. and shall as soon as possible force myself into the habit of sleeping throughout the entire night.*

Holmes's insistence that the dead man found at 1316 Callowhill Street really was Benjamin Pitezel created a legal complication, since the conspirators had been charged with using a substitute corpse to pull off the swindle. Shortly after Holmes offered his second confession, the officers of Fidelity Mutual retained a respected Philadelphia lawyer, Thomas Barlow, to represent the company in the case. By early May, a new indictment had been found, charging Holmes and Howe, as well as Marion Hedgepeth, "with having conspired to cheat the Fidelity Mutual Life Assurance Company by alleging that one B. F. Pitezel ... had died as the result of an accident." Designed to cover every possibility, this indictment was valid whether Pitezel was dead or alive—a suicide, murder victim, or fugitive.

On May 27, 1895, Holmes was brought to trial under this second indictment in Philadelphia's Quarter Sessions Court, Judge Hare presiding.

Led to the dock shortly before eleven A.M., the prisoner exchanged a few words with his counsel—R. O. Moon and Samuel P. Rotan—then gazed around at the courtroom, casually twirling one waxed tip of his handlebar mustache. Observing Holmes closely from the packed spectator gallery was Detective Frank P. Geyer, who had come at the request of District Attorney Graham.

In spite of Holmes's New Year's resolution to exercise daily and watch his diet, he had gained weight during his months of imprisonment. Dressed in a handsome black suit, with a sack coat, black tie, and heavy gold watch-chain strung across his paunch, he looked more like a bank manager than America's most infamous criminal.

The proceedings began with the empaneling of the jury. District Attorney Graham offered no objections to the first twelve men who were seated. But Defense Attorney Moon was less easily satisfied. Noting the extraordinary publicity attending the case, he asked leave of the Court "to question the jurors if they have formed or expressed any opinions as to the guilt or innocence of the prisoner." In the end, several of the jurors were rejected on Moon's challenges. Another, who suffered from heart disease, begged to be excused because he feared that a lengthy trial might endanger his health.

He needn't have worried. As it turned out, the trial lasted only one day. Graham began by clarifying the nature of the conspiracy charge, recapping the facts of the case, and reviewing the contents of Holmes's two confessions. "No matter which statement of the prisoner you choose to believe," Graham told the jurors, "it makes no difference to

235

the Commonwealth's case, since both of them show the intent to cheat and defraud the insurance company."

He pointed out that the dead man found at 1316 Callowhill Street could not possibly have been killed as the result of an accidental explosion. "Everybody knows," he said, "that where a person is burned, the forces of nature respond and rush to repel the injury, and the result is the forming of a blister. Whereas, if a *dead* body is burned, the flesh simply sizzles and roasts like a steak. That was the case with this body. There were no blisters upon it, and there can be no other conclusion but that the burns had been made after death took place."

Without ever raising the charge of homicide, Graham made it clear that, in his opinion, Pitezel had been murdered. He referred repeatedly to Carrie (who occupied a prominent seat in the courtroom) as "the widow" and stated explicitly that he "did not believe the suicide story."

Graham ended his statement on an ominous note, referring to "Pitezel's three little children," who had been "under Holmes's care." "Whatever has become of them," the district attorney intoned, "only God and the prisoner know."

L. G. Fouse, the first witness called to the stand, offered a detailed account of his dealings with Holmes, dwelling at some length on the latter's cool, if not cold-blooded, behavior during the postmortem inspection of the disinterred corpse. The jurors looked grim as Fouse described the perfect nonchalance with which Holmes had wielded his surgeon's knife, breezily slicing the identifying marks from the putrified body of his former partner. Two more witnesses—Police Superintendent Linden and Col. O. C. Bobyshell, former president and current treasurer of Fidelity Mutual—testified briefly before Judge Hare adjourned for the day.

Conferring with Moon and Rotan at the end of the day, Holmes—perceiving that his position was hopeless—instructed the attorneys to cut a deal with the DA. In return for a reduced sentence, Holmes would change his plea—"thereby saving at least a week's valuable time to the Court," as he explained.

The following morning, in obedience to their client's wishes, Holmes's lawyers entered a plea of guilty, and the trial came to an abrupt end. Judge Hare announced that he would defer sentencing until after the trial of Jeptha D. Howe.

In the company of his lawyers, Holmes was removed to the "cell room" in City Hall to await the conveyance that would carry him back to Moyamensing. Holmes was in a celebratory mood. Assuming that Judge Hare sentenced him to only half the maximum term and allowed the six months he had already spent in prison, he would be a free man by October.

He had just leaned back in his chair, legs outstretched, fingers laced behind his neck—the very picture of a man without a worry in the world—when word arrived that District Attorney Graham wished to see him in his office immediately.

37

Knowing me as you do, can you imagine me killing little and innocent children, especially without any motive?

—H. H. Holmes, in a letter to Carrie Pitezel

A long conference table occupied the center of the DA's private office. On one side sat Holmes and his attorneys. Facing them were Graham and Thomas Barlow, who had been named special assistant district attorney earlier that day.

Graham was about to speak when the door swung open and two more men stepped into the room—Detective Frank Geyer and Police Captain Miller. In the hallway just outside the office, a crowd of reporters clamored for news. As Miller slipped through the doorway, one of the reporters—a writer for *The Philadelphia Inquirer*—poked his head into the room and shouted, "What's up?" Miller waved the man back—"I can't say anything!"—then slammed the door shut and took a seat beside his fellow officials.

Turning back to Holmes, Graham wasted no time in getting to the point. He had decided to drop the case against Carrie Pitezel, he explained, and set her free without delay. The poor woman had "suffered quite enough. The uncertainty of the fate of Alice, Nellie, and Howard, coupled with the death of her husband, has almost dethroned her reason." He fixed Holmes with a hard stare. "It is strongly sus-

238

pected," said Graham, "that you have not only murdered Pitezel but that you have killed the children."

Holmes opened his mouth to protest, but the DA hushed him with an upraised hand.

"The best way to remove this suspicion is to produce the children at once," Graham declared. "Now where are they? Where can I find them? Tell me and I will use every means in my power to secure their early recovery. It is due to Mrs. Pitezel—and to yourself—that the children should be found. When you were arrested in November, you said the children were in South America with their father. It is now May, and we have heard nothing from them. You subsequently said that you gave the children to Miss Williams." Graham let out a sigh. "I am almost persuaded that your word cannot be trusted, Holmes."

Holmes looked injured but chose not to reply.

Hands folded on the table, Graham leaned forward in his seat, his eyes locked on Holmes's. "Even so, I am not averse to giving you an opportunity to assist me in clearing up the mystery which surrounds their disappearance and their present abode. I now ask you to answer frankly and truthfully—Where are the children?"

Meeting Graham's stare without a blink, Holmes replied that he was "glad of the opportunity thus afforded me to assist in the restoration of the children to their mother." Suddenly, his eyes seemed to moisten with tears. Speaking with a slight quaver in his voice, he vehemently denied that he had killed Pitezel or done harm to the little ones. "Why should I kill innocent children?" he cried.

"Then tell us what has become of them," Graham said again.

Holmes took a moment to collect himself. Then, speaking "with every appearance of candor" (as one of the witnesses later reported), he launched into the story he had been privately rehearsing for the past several weeks.

"The last time I saw Howard," he began, "was in Detroit, Michigan. There, I gave him to Miss Williams, who took him to Buffalo, New York, from which point she proceeded to Niagara Falls. After the departure of Howard in Miss Williams's care, I took Alice and Nellie to Toronto, Canada, where they remained for several days. At Toronto, I purchased railroad tickets for them for Niagara Falls, put them on the train, and rode out of Toronto with them a few miles, so that they would be assured that they were on the right train. Before their departure, I prepared a telegram, which they should send me from the Falls if they failed to meet Miss Williams and Howard. I also carefully pinned inside Alice's dress four hundred dollars in large bills, so Miss Williams would have funds to defray their expenses.

"They joined Miss Williams and Howard at Niagara Falls, from which point they went to New York City. At the latter place, Miss Williams dressed Nellie as a boy and took a steamer for Liverpool, whence they went to London. If you search among the steamship offices in New York, you must look for a woman and a girl and two boys and not a woman and two girls and a boy. This was all done to throw the detectives off the track, who were after me for the insurance fraud. Miss Williams opened a massage establishment at Number Eighty Veder or Vadar Street, London. I have no doubt the children are with her now, and very likely at that place."

There was a momentary silence as Graham and his colleague absorbed this unlikely tale. Attorney Barlow—whose face clearly registered the depth of his skepticism—was the first to break it. "Can you give me the name of a single respectable person to whom I can go," he demanded, "either in Detroit, Buffalo, Toronto, Niagara Falls, or New York, who will say that they saw Miss Williams and the three children together?"

Holmes looked stung. "Your question seems to imply a disbelief in my statement."

"It certainly does," answered Barlow. "Indeed, I believe your entire story to be a lie from beginning to end."

Holmes heatedly insisted that his story was true—and that he had a way to verify it. He and Miss Williams had worked out a means by which they could communicate in an emergency, he explained. This involved placing a coded advertisement in the personal column of *The New York Herald*. To prove his veracity, Holmes offered to furnish the code to Graham, who could then plant a decoy message that would flush Minnie Williams out of hiding.

DEPRAVED

Agreeing to give Holmes one final chance to vindicate himself, Graham told him to supply the cipher by the following afternoon. Shortly thereafter, the conference was ended and Holmes transported back to Moyamensing.

The next day—Wednesday, May 29—Graham received the following letter from Holmes:

Dear Sir:—

The adv. should appear in the *New York Sunday Herald* and if some comment upon the case can also be put in body of paper stating the absence of children and that adv. concerning appears in this paper, etc., it would be an advantage. Any words you may see fit to use in adv. will do ... only one sentence need be in cipher as she will know by this that it *must* come from me as no one else, unless I told them, could have same. ...

The *New York Herald* is (or was a year ago) to be found at only a few places regularly in London.

Very respectfully,
H. H. Holmes

The code Holmes appended to the letter was a simple cipher based on the word *republican*. Spelled out in capitals, the word corresponded to the first ten letters of the alphabet; in lower-case, the word represented the next ten letters; and the final six letters of the alphabet remained uncoded. This was the cipher as Holmes wrote it out:

REPUBLICANrepublican
abcdefghijklmnopqrstuvwxyz.

To show how the cipher worked, Holmes spelled out his own name in code:

CbepBa
Holmes.

241

Following Holmes's suggestion, Graham immediately contacted the Philadelphia correspondent for the *New York Herald,* who prepared an article about the case, which was published on Sunday, June 2, 1895. In the same edition, the following advertisement appeared in the newspaper's personal column (the names Adele Covelle and Gereldine Wanda were, according to Holmes, pseudonyms occasionally employed by Minnie Williams):

> MINNIE WILLIAMS, ADELE COVELLE, GER-
> ELDINE WANDA—
> AplbcnRun nb CBRc EBLbcB 10th PREeB
> cBnucu PCAeUcBu
> Rn buPB. . . . CbepBa. Address George S. Graham,
> Philadelphia, Penn., U.S.A.

The coded part of this message translated as follows: "Important to hear before 10th Cable. Return children at once. . . . Holmes."

In the meantime, Graham had contacted Scotland Yard, supplying them with a detailed summary of the case and requesting their assistance in tracking down Miss Minnie Williams, currently the proprietress of a massage establishment at 80 Veder or Vadar Street. Graham received a reply by return post.

The letter informed him that there was no street by either of those names in the city of London.

In spite of Holmes's avowals that Minnie Williams would respond to the coded message "without delay," two weeks passed without an answer—a fact that surprised no one in the district attorney's office. On June 17, Holmes took pen in hand again, this time to compose a lengthy letter to Carrie Pitezel, in which he reiterated the lies he had told to Graham and the others. He began with a graphic account of Ben's increasingly erratic and suicidal behavior during the months preceding his death.

"Facts you should know are as follows," Holmes wrote. "Ben lived out West, and while drunk in Fort Worth, Texas, married a disreputable woman by the name of Mrs. Martin. . . . When he became sober and found what he had done, he threatened to kill himself and her, and I had him watched by one of the other men until he went home. When we straightened up the bank account, he had fooled away or been robbed by her of over $850 of the money we needed so much. Later, he wanted to carry out the insurance work in Mississippi, where he was acquainted, and I went there with him, and when I found out what kind of a place it was, would not go any further with it there and told him so, and he said if I did not, he would kill himself and get the money for you, etc. To get him out of the notion, I told him I would go to Mobile and if I could get what was wanted [i.e., a substitute corpse] would do so, if not, I would go to St. Louis and write for him to come. . . . When I reached St. Louis I wrote him, and in the letter he left me after he died, he said he tried to kill himself with laudanum there, and later I found out this was so."

Pleading as an old family friend who had always had her best interests at heart, Holmes urged Carrie to trust in her own common sense, not the cruel accusations of strangers. "I was as careful of the children as if they were my own," he wrote, "and you know me well enough to judge me better than strangers here can do. Ben would not have done anything against me, or I against him, any quicker than brothers. We *never* quarreled. Again, he was worth too much to me for me to have killed him, if for no other reason not to. As to the children, I never will believe, until you tell me so yourself, that you think they are dead or that I did anything to put them out of the way. Knowing me as you do, can you imagine me killing little and innocent children, especially without any motive?"

He continued to maintain that Alice, Nellie, and Howard were in the care of Minnie Williams. "So far as the children's bodily health is concerned, I feel sure I can say to you that they are as well today as though with you, also that they will not be turned adrift among strangers, for two reasons. First, Miss W., though quick tempered, is too soft hearted to do so; second, if among others where their letters could not be looked over and detained, they would write to their grandparents."

Insisting that his most immediate concern was to see her set free, Holmes concluded with the fervent hope that "your suffering here is nearly ended."

Carrie Pitezel's suffering was far from ended; indeed, the coming weeks had unspeakable anguish in store. But her confinement, at any rate, was over. On the very day she received Holmes's letter—Wednesday, June 19—Graham, making good on his promise, arranged for her immediate discharge from Moyamensing.

Blinking in the summer sunlight, Carrie was escorted down the steps by her two oldest friends, who had made the trip from Illinois to lend their support. After a brief stop at City Hall, where she climbed to the rooftop for a sweeping view of the city, she proceeded to the office of her lawyer, Thomas A. Fahy.

Dessie and the baby—who had spent the past six months as the wards of the Society to Protect Children from Cruelty—were waiting for her there. After an emotional reunion, Carrie and her children spent several tender hours sequestered in Fahy's chambers.

Before setting off for the hotel room Fahy had reserved for her, Carrie agreed to speak to a reporter for *The Inquirer*. It was the first interview she had granted since her arrest.

Sitting across from her, the reporter was struck by how haggard she appeared. In spite of her black hair, she looked as wizened as a crone. He found it hard to believe that the infant cradled in her arms was her own child and not the baby of the blooming eighteen-year-old seated beside her.

The reporter began by asking her opinion of Holmes. Did Mrs. Pitezel think he was telling the truth about her missing children?

"Holmes would do anything," Carrie replied bitterly. "He is a smooth-tongued scoundrel. He has lied to me and cheated me and I would not put it past him to make away with the children if it would do him any good."

Next, the newspaperman asked about her husband. Did Mrs. Pitezel harbor any hope that he was still alive?

"I believe the body was that of my husband, for if Mr.

Pitezel was alive, he would certainly come back here and make Holmes take back some of the things he said."

And the children . . . ? the reporter asked softly.

"What has become of them I don't know," she said with anguish. "I feel like tramping all over the world to see if I can find any trace of them." Her lower lip shook, and tears spilled down her furrowed cheeks. A full minute passed before she was able to speak again.

"Even knowing they were dead," she said, "would be a relief."

Finding Alice, Nellie, and Howard had become a matter of paramount importance for the district attorney, too. His motives were partly humanitarian. His heart went out to Mrs. Pitezel, who—until the fate of her little ones became known—was condemned to a life of torturous uncertainty.

But he was determined to locate the children for another, perhaps even more pressing reason. Graham knew perfectly well that, in capturing Holmes, the police had hooked something much bigger than an insurance swindler. And he had no intention of letting his catch wriggle free.

By the time Carrie was released from prison, Graham, along with his assistant, Thomas Barlow, and Police Superintendent Linden, had decided to launch one final, painstaking search for the missing children. Many of Linden's subordinates viewed this undertaking as hopeless—a waste of the department's time and money. William Gary and his fellow insurance detectives, they pointed out, had been hunting futilely for the children since the preceding November.

The consensus among police officials was that Holmes had killed his little captives. It did not seem possible, as one of them put it, "that such an astute and wily criminal [would leave] a trace behind him." Most probably, Holmes had sunk the bodies in a lake or a river, as he claimed to have done with the corpse of Nannie Williams.

Graham, Barlow, and Linden, however, were undeterred by these arguments. That the insurance men had been unable to locate the children simply meant that their investigation, in Graham's words, "had been unskillfully made." The district attorney was not persuaded that the children were dead. But if they were, he believed that a "careful and patient search" would inevitably uncover "the blunder which a criminal always makes between the inception and consummation of his crime." It was simply impossible, Graham insisted, that "in this day and age, a man could kill three children and escape discovery."

True, it was a daunting task that would require the skills of an extraordinarily resourceful detective.

Fortunately, the district attorney had the very man near at hand.

38

"If he shall be Mr. Hyde," he had thought, "I shall be Mr. Seek."

—Robert Louis Stevenson, *The Strange Case of Dr. Jekyll and Mr. Hyde*

In a policeman's uniform, Frank Geyer looked like a character in a Mack Sennett comedy—beefy frame, balding dome, bushy mustache, and black, slanted eyebrows, so thick and dark that they might have been smeared on with greasepaint. Twenty years after the Holmes affair, Sennett would have all of America roaring with his silent two-reelers. Watch one of them now and you will see a dozen dead ringers for Geyer, clinging by their fingernails to a runaway trolley or crashing their paddy wagon through the nearest brick wall.

But Geyer was no Keystone Kop. Quite the contrary. He was a formidable individual—a twenty-year veteran of the Philadelphia Bureau of Police with a well-earned reputation as the city's top detective.

But along with his great professional acclaim, Frank Geyer had experienced enormous personal tragedy. In March 1895—just three months before District Attorney Graham decided to mount an all-out search for the missing Pitezel children—a fire had consumed Geyer's home, killing his beloved wife, Martha, and their only child, a blossoming twelve-year-old girl named Esther.

Detective Geyer, who thrived on such challenges, would

have been eager to undertake Graham's mission in any event. But the loss of his loved ones infused him with even greater zeal for the search. Partly, this was simply a matter of distracting himself from his grief—he hoped to lose himself in his hunt for Alice and her siblings. But something else was at work, too.

Life had taught Geyer a terrible lesson—that no horror compares to the death of one's child. That one human being would deliberately inflict this horror on another seemed inconceivably wicked to him—nothing short of demonic. And Geyer would not rest until he saw the malefactor pay.

And so, on Wednesday, June 26, 1895, Detective Frank Geyer carried his gripsack to the railway depot and set out on his quest.

Geyer didn't have much to go on, but he wasn't traveling entirely in the dark. The dozen or so letters written by Alice and Nellie—which Holmes had preserved for his own devious purposes—had been found in a tin box among his possessions at the time of his arrest. For all their crude spelling and grammar, the letters were scrupulously correct in one regard: following the conventional format, each was headed with both the date and place of origin.

As a result—though the insurance detectives had been stymied in their efforts to turn up the missing children—they had managed to map out the route Holmes had followed the previous fall, from Cincinnati to Indianapolis, Detroit, Toronto, and finally Burlington.

Geyer knew that the answers he was seeking lay somewhere along this circuitous trail. To find them, he would have to start from the beginning.

Armed with mug shots of Holmes and photographs of the children—taken in 1893 when they were pupils at the D. S. Wentworth School in Chicago—Geyer arrived in Cincinnati on the evening of June 27. He checked into the Palace Hotel, downed a quick dinner, and then proceeded to police headquarters, where he ran into an old friend, Detective John Schnooks. The two men reminisced for a while before Geyer explained the reason for his visit. Schnooks advised

Geyer to return the next day and confer with his chief, Superintendent Philip Dietsch.

A firm believer in the benefits of a hearty breakfast, Geyer took the time to fortify himself with a platter of flannel cakes, bacon, and eggs before setting off for City Hall the following morning. Dietsch greeted him cordially and—after hearing the facts of the case—buzzed in Schnooks and directed him to "render Detective Geyer all the assistance in your power."

With that, the two men headed out into the city. The Great Search (as Geyer later came to think of it) had commenced in earnest.

Geyer and his colleague began by checking the hostelries around the train depots. By morning's end, they had located the two hotels—the Atlantic House and the Bristol—where Holmes had taken rooms for himself and the children under the name Cook—the same alias (as Geyer knew) that he had made Carrie Pitezel use in Burlington. W. L. Bain, clerk at the Bristol, positively identified Holmes and the children from Geyer's photographs.

Knowing that his nemesis had habitually rented houses in the cities he had passed through, Geyer decided to switch tactics and concentrate on real estate agencies instead of hotels. He and Schnooks traipsed throughout the city, fruitlessly questioning scores of agents, before finally coming upon the office of J. C. Thomas, whose clerk, George Rumsey, had no trouble recognizing the photographs of Holmes and Howard, whom he had taken for father and son. Rumsey recalled being struck by the disparity between the older man's slick, well-to-do appearance and the ragtag apparel of the boy.

Unfortunately, Rumsey could offer no further information about the house Holmes had rented since the records were locked up in the office of Mr. Thomas, who had gone home for the day. The clerk did not know his boss's home address, only that Thomas had recently moved out to Cumminsville, a suburban town about five miles from Cincinnati.

Believing that time was of the essence, Geyer and Schnooks immediately headed out to Cumminsville but were unable to locate Thomas, whose name was not yet listed in the local directory. Disappointed, the two detectives decided to call it a day.

They were back at the real estate office first thing the following morning. The owner arrived a few minutes later and, like his clerk, instantly recognized the photographs of Holmes and Howard.

Thomas had no need to consult his records for the information the detectives were seeking. He clearly remembered the handsomely dressed gentleman who had paid a $15 advance for a vacant house at 305 Poplar Street and then disappeared abruptly only two days after renting it. What had become of the fellow, Thomas could not say. He suggested the Geyer and Schnooks call on Miss Henrietta Hill, who lived directly next door to the rental property and might have additional facts to offer.

Miss Hill did indeed have a vivid recollection of the mysterious tenant who had abandoned the neighboring house within days of moving in. What had puzzled her most, she explained, was the enormous cylindrical stove he had brought with him. Not only was the stove far too large for such a modest-sized house, but—even more baffling—it was the only item in the moving wagon.

Thanking Miss Hill for her assistance, Geyer and Schnooks departed, well pleased. Having tracked down the places Holmes had stayed during his brief sojourn in Cincinnati and discovered the two aliases he had gone under— Cook and Hayes—Geyer felt confident that he "had taken firm hold of the end of the string that would lead me ultimately to the consummation of my mission." At that point, Miss Hill's information about the immense iron stove seemed like an intriguing but not especially relevant detail.

Weeks would pass before Geyer discovered its terrible significance.

39

Detective Geyer called on me, and, in a long conversation with him, I made a most honest endeavor to place him in possession of all the facts that would be instrumental in facilitating the proposed search.

—From the prison diary of H. H. Holmes

Knowing from their letters that the children had been taken from Cincinnati to Indianapolis, Geyer left immediately for the Indiana capital, arriving around seven-thirty P.M. on Saturday evening, June 29. After registering and supping at the Spencer house, he repaired to police headquarters, where he introduced himself to Captain Splann, head of the detective corps.

Before Geyer had a chance to explain his situation, the captain was called away to investigate a reported murder in the northern part of the city. It wasn't until much later that night that Geyer had an opportunity to talk to Splann's superior, Police Superintendent Powell. Like his counterpart in Cincinnati, Powell offered his full cooperation, assigning a detective named David Richards to assist Geyer in his search.

During the next few days, Geyer followed the same routine that had served him so well in Cincinnati. Beginning with the hostelries around Union Depot and moving on to the neighborhood known as the Circle, the two detectives quickly turned up an entry for the children in the registry of the Hotel English. From Geyer's photographs, the clerk identified Holmes as the man who had rented a room for the children on the evening of September 30 and then checked them out the following morning.

At that point, Geyer and Richards ran into a dead end. They were unable to turn up any trace of the children after October 1. Undeterred, the two detectives proceeded to make a methodical search of every hotel and lodging house in the city—without success. Only then did Richards remember a small hotel called the Circle House, which had been operating on Meridian Street in September 1894 but had since gone out of business.

By Monday morning, Geyer and Richards had managed to track down the former proprietor of the Circle House, Herman Ackelow, who was currently running a beer saloon in West Indianapolis.

Ackelow—who had no trouble remembering Alice and her siblings—painted a grim picture of the three forlorn children, shut up in their room for days on end. He talked of the times that his teenaged son had brought the children their meals and found them weeping miserably, overwhelmed by the loneliness and unrelieved tedium.

Particularly disturbing was Ackelow's recollection of little Howard's hysterical outburst after returning from a rare, midday outing with Holmes. The saloonkeeper described his subsequent conversation with the smooth-talking gentleman who had represented himself as the boy's uncle.

"He told me the boy was a bad one from the day he was born," Ackelow recalled. "Said he didn't know how his poor widowed sister could handle him no more, and he was thinking of maybe binding him out to a farmer or putting him in an institution. Just wanted to be shed of him, that's all."

Ackelow's words chilled Geyer. The detective came away from the interview feeling sure that Howard had not left Indianapolis alive. This belief, however, was contradicted by the findings of Fidelity Mutual's own investigators, who had turned up "positive information that Holmes and the boy were seen in Detroit."

Back in his hotel room that night, Geyer carefully considered his options. He knew that Detroit had been the next stop on Holmes's diabolical journey. But there was a loose end Geyer hoped to tie up.

Before embarking on his search, he had visited Carrie
Pitezel, who had supplied him with a detailed description
of the children's trunk—the one she had sent off with
Nellie and Howard when they had departed from St. Louis
with Holmes. The trunk had since disappeared. Geyer had
also interviewed Holmes, who maintained that he had left
the trunk in Chicago—in a hotel situated on West Madison Street, close to the corner of Ashland Avenue. Geyer
was eager to find the trunk, believing that it might offer an
important clue to the whereabouts of the missing children.

And so, shortly before noon on Monday, July 1, Geyer
left Indianapolis on a train headed north to Chicago.

Beginning early Tuesday—the morning after his arrival in
Chicago—Geyer spent two days in a fruitless effort to locate
the trunk. Indeed, he never managed to find the hotel
Holmes had supposedly left it in—for the very good reason
that no such hotel existed. The information Holmes had volunteered, Geyer quickly realized, was simply another flagrant attempt to throw the detective off the trail.

The trip to Chicago was not a total waste, however. Accompanied by Detective Sergeant John C. McGlinn, who
had been detailed to help him, Geyer made a painstaking
search of West Madison Street. About fifty feet from the
corner of Ashland Avenue, they happened upon a boardinghouse run by a woman named Jennie Irons. While Miss
Irons didn't recognize the photographs of the Pitezel children, she immediately identified Holmes as the gentleman
she had known as Harry Gordon. According to the landlady,
Gordon had occupied rooms in her lodging house for several
months in 1892 with a pretty young woman he had introduced as his new bride.

Only later did Geyer learn that the lovely "Mrs. Gordon"
was actually a former mistress of Holmes's—Emeline Cigrand—who had mysteriously disappeared from Chicago in
late 1892, never to be seen again.

Geyer also learned from Herman Ackelow that a German
immigrant named Caroline Klausmann was the chambermaid of the Circle House during the time that Holmes and

the children stayed there. Ackelow was not sure how helpful she would be since she didn't speak English very well, but he knew she was now living in Chicago. Geyer found her working at the Swiss Hotel on Wells Street.

Miss Klausmann's English was no better than it had been a year earlier, but Geyer knew enough German to communicate the reason for his visit. The moment he showed her the photographs of Alice, Nellie, and Howard, the good woman's eyes filled with tears. It still grieved her to remember the three heartsick children and her inability to offer them comforting words.

Geyer was no nearer to finding the children. But each day was bringing dismaying new evidence of the misery they had endured under the heartless custodianship of Holmes.

Before leaving Chicago, Geyer was eager to talk to one other person. And so, immediately after breakfast on Wednesday, July 3, he and McGlinn boarded a cable car for Englewood.

They were on their way to Sixty-third and Wallace to interview Pat Quinlan—the janitor of Holmes's Castle.

The morning sunlight did nothing to dispel the dismal, vaguely derelict air that hung about the massive building, with its decaying facade and blank upper windows. Climbing a dark, winding staircase to the second floor, the detectives found Quinlan's apartment. Geyer rapped on the door. "Detectives Geyer and McGlinn," he called out, his words resounding in the utter silence of the Castle. Through the wood, a muffled voice requested them to enter.

Inside, the detectives found themselves facing a pale, slim man of medium height with light, curly hair and a sandy mustache. Geyer judged his age to be about thirty-eight. Geyer presented his card. Quinlan perused it, then invited the two lawmen to take seats.

Geyer got right to the point, grilling Quinlan hard about Holmes and the children. Though he stopped short of accusing the janitor of collusion, the detective made it clear that he believed Quinlan could tell him all about the missing children. But Quinlan remained staunch in his denials. He admitted that he knew the Pitezel family "very well" but insisted that he had not laid eyes on any of them for almost a year. He was more than willing to help in any way he could. But as to the whereabouts of Alice, Nellie, and Howard, he just didn't have a clue.

Geyer was inclined to believe Quinlan, partly because the janitor was a father himself and therefore unlikely—in the detective's view—to have schemed against innocent children. Even more to the point, it was clear from Quinlan's comments that he harbored little affection for Holmes.

His employer was a "dirty lying scoundrel," Quinlan snarled. He had been following all the newspaper stories about Holmes's crimes, and nothing he had read surprised him in the least. The man was capable of anything.

"If that corpse they found in Philadelphia really was Ben Pitezel," Quinlan said, "you can wager good money that Holmes was the one who done it. And if he done for Pitezel, then he's murdered the children, too."

A few moments later, Geyer and McGlinn rose from their chairs, thanking Quinlan for his time. The janitor followed them to the door.

Geyer was halfway across the threshold when Quinlan reached out and grabbed him by the coat sleeve. "If you find out those little ones is dead, I hope Holmes swings for it," he said fervently. "And when that day comes, I'd be glad to be the man that springs the trap."

40

Time shall unfold what plighted cunning hides.

          —Shakespeare, *King Lear*

Frank Geyer was a man on a mission, and he had no intention of resting until the children were found. And so on Thursday, July 4—while his compatriots laid aside their summer labors for the flag-waving festivities of Independence Day—Geyer traveled to Detroit, where several eyewitnesses had reportedly seen Holmes with Howard Pitezel.

Arriving around six P.M., Geyer checked into the Hotel Normandie, then proceeded immediately to police headquarters. There he met an old friend, Detective Thomas Meyler, who introduced him to the captain in charge. Early the following morning, Geyer was back at headquarters to confer with Superintendent Starkweather, who assigned a detective named Tuttle to assist him in his search.

Geyer and Tuttle headed first for the local office of the Fidelity Mutual Life Association, whose investigators had turned up an important lead—the name of the real estate agent who had rented Holmes a house the previous October. The two detectives immediately called on the agent, a man named Bonninghausen, who informed them that Holmes had come by his office looking to rent a place "on the outskirts of the city" and had put down a $5 advance for a vacant house on East Forest Avenue. Bonninghausen seemed to recall that Holmes had a little boy with him, about nine or ten years old. His clerk, a fellow named Moore, was under the same impression.

Over the years, Geyer had learned to trust his hunches. Intuitively, he continued to believe that Howard had been murdered in Indianapolis. But he couldn't discount the testimony of Bonninghausen and Moore, which contradicted that theory. He decided to make a search of the city's hotels and lodging houses, to see if he could turn up any proof of Howard's presence in Detroit.

Beginning in the neighborhood of the train depot, he and Tuttle visited half a dozen hostelries before coming upon an entry for "Etta and Nellie Canning" in the registry of the New Western Hotel. The proprietor, P. W. Cotter, needed only one look at Geyer's photographs to identify the girls as the Pitezel sisters and Holmes as the man who had checked them into the hotel. But Cotter had seen no sign of the little boy.

From Alice's last, pathetic letter to her grandparents, Geyer knew that the girls had been taken next to Lucinda Burns's boardinghouse at 91 Congress Street. The landlady had a vivid memory of Alice and Nellie, recalling them as unusually "quiet and reserved" children, who never left their room and seemed to spend the entire time reading and drawing.

Like P. W. Cotter, however, Mrs. Burns testified that the girls had been alone. She had never laid eyes on the dark-eyed little boy in the photograph Geyer showed her.

It was possible, of course, that—for his own diabolical reasons—Holmes had wanted to keep Howard close by his side. Shifting his focus away from the girls, Geyer decided to see if he could discover where Holmes had stayed in Detroit and whether he had been accompanied by a little boy. In the register of the Hotel Normandie, the detective came upon an entry for "G. Howell and wife" and immediately recognized both the handwriting and the alias as Holmes's.

After that, however, Geyer and his partner ran into a dead end. Searching through the records of all the hotels in the city, they failed to turn up any further trace of Holmes. They decided to try the boardinghouses.

The following day, the pair spent hour after tedious hour tramping through the sweltering streets, ringing dozens of doorbells and questioning countless landlords and ladies, none of whom recognized the photograph of Howard Pitezel or of Holmes.

Finally, as evening came on, they happened upon Ralston's rooming house at 54 Park Place, where Holmes—posing as "a member of the theatrical profession"—had stayed briefly with Georgiana. The proprietress, Mrs. May Ralston, clearly recollected the handsome couple. When Geyer questioned her about Howard, however, she declared absolutely that Holmes and his wife did not have a child with them.

Within two days of his arrival in Detroit, Geyer had managed to reconstruct the movements of the Pitezel girls and Holmes. But—except for the statements of Bonninghausen and Moore—he had failed to turn up any leads on Howard. His trip out to East Forest Avenue to check out the house Holmes had rented proved equally fruitless.

Admitted by the current tenant, Geyer and Tuttle made a thorough examination of the house. They scrutinized the cellar, inspected the furnace, and (in Geyer's words) "searched every spot of ground adjacent to the premises to see if the earth had been disturbed." Nothing seemed to be amiss.

The tenant, however, revealed that, shortly after moving in, he had discovered a peculiar excavation in the basement, which he had since refilled. Measuring about four feet long, three feet wide, and three and a half feet deep, the hole had evidently been dug by his predecessor—the mysterious gentleman who had occupied the house for a few days the previous fall.

Perhaps, the tenant speculated, the gentleman had been digging a place to store turnips and potatoes for the winter.

Geyer, however, guessed that it had been dug for a far more sinister purpose—and he wondered what unexpected turn had kept Holmes from carrying out his dark design.

The mystery of the children's missing trunk continued to vex Geyer. Before leaving Detroit, he did his best to find it, questioning scores of liverymen and hackmen and visiting virtually every freight depot, omnibus company, and express office in the city. But—much to his annoyance—he could turn up no clue to its whereabouts.

Geyer was troubled by another matter, too. The records of the Circle House in Indianapolis indicated that the Pitezel children had checked out on Saturday, October 6. According to the registry of the New Western Hotel, the girls had arrived in Detroit on Friday, October 12. It disturbed Geyer that he was not able to account for the six-day gap between locations.

In spite of these unresolved questions, Geyer believed that he had accomplished as much as he could in Detroit. There was only one more visit he wanted to make before setting off on the next leg of his journey.

During his interview with Carrie Pitezel, Geyer had learned that, upon her arrival in Detroit with Dessie and the baby, Holmes had checked them into Geis's European Hotel. Early Sunday morning, July 7, Geyer walked to the hotel and interviewed the housekeeper, Miss Minnie Mulholland, who took one look at Carrie's photograph and immediately identified her as the anguished woman she had known as Mrs. Adams. Geyer pressed her for information, but the housekeeper had no revelations to offer—only a heartbreaking description of the desolate Mrs. Adams, a woman so ravaged by care that she moved like an invalid.

Geyer's route back to his hotel led him past Lucinda Burns's place at 91 Congress Street. The rooming house, where Holmes had boarded the two Pitezel sisters for five days, was located only a few blocks away from Geis's Hotel, where Carrie had been lodged during the same period with Dessie and Wharton.

Pausing before the little wood-frame building, Geyer thought of Alice's terrible longing for her mother, older sister, and infant brother, all of whom—at the very moment she was writing her last, wrenching letter to them—were less than a five-minute walk away. Even for Geyer, a man accustomed to tragedy, it was a circumstance almost too painful to dwell on.

As he turned his steps back toward the hotel, he was struck anew by Holmes's monstrous nature—the heartless cunning of a man who had contrived to keep two desperately homesick children apart from their mother while coolly plotting their utter destruction.

41

> Thus it was proved that little children cannot be murdered in this day and generation beyond the possibility of discovery.
>
> —Frank P. Geyer, *The Holmes-Pitezel Case*

Geyer left Detroit on Sunday evening, July 7. At around nine-thirty the next morning, he stepped off the train in Toronto.

Geyer had visited the city before and had several acquaintances on the police force, among them Detective Alf Cuddy, who was promptly detailed to assist him.

The two men got off to a promising start. Within a few hours of commencing their search, they had traced Holmes first to the Walker House, then to the Palmer; Carrie, Dessie, and Wharton to the Union Hotel; and Alice and Nellie to the Albion.

At the last of these, Geyer learned an ominous fact from the chief clerk, Herbert Jones. After examining the photograph of Holmes, Jones identified him as the gentleman who had taken the two girls out sight-seeing every morning during their stay. The girls had generally returned alone in the late afternoon, well in time for supper.

On the morning of October 25, after paying their daily board bill, Holmes had gone off with the girls as usual. This time, however, the children had never returned. "It was the last time they were seen by me or anyone in the hotel," Jones said.

Having retraced Holmes's steps from city to city, Geyer was thoroughly familiar with the man's *modus operandi*. He also knew that Holmes had abruptly departed Toronto on October 26. Putting all the facts together—including what he'd found out from Jones—Geyer drew a grim conclusion. The following morning, he conveyed it in a letter to his superior, Police Superintendent Linden:

"It is my impression that Holmes rented a house in Toronto, the same as he did in Cincinnati, Ohio, and Detroit, Michigan, and that on the 25th of October he murdered the girls and disposed of their bodies by either burying them in the cellar, or some convenient place, or burning them in the heater. I intend to go to all the real estate agents and see if they can recollect having rented a house about that time to a man who only occupied it for a few days and who represented that he wanted it for a widowed sister."

Even as he penned the final line, Geyer realized that he faced a daunting task. But the detective was imbued with the can-do spirit of a confident era. He never doubted for a moment that (as he later put it) "perseverance and energy would bring forth some good result."

Early Wednesday morning, July 10, he armed himself with a city directory and proceeded to police headquarters to meet with his partner. Over the next few hours—while Cuddy read and Geyer copied—the two detectives compiled a list of every real estate agent in Toronto. Then they headed out into the city.

They began in the business district. It quickly became clear to Geyer that the job was going to take much longer than he'd expected. At every office on their list, he and Cuddy had to start from scratch, patiently explaining the nature of their investigation and waiting while the agent checked his books. Before they knew it, night was upon them and the agencies had shut down for the day.

Clearly, the detectives needed a different approach. One of Geyer's great strengths as a police officer was his bulldog tenacity. Now, mulling over the problem, he displayed another, far less common, gift, too—a sophisticated sense of the media's power. Long before the era of press agents and

PR specialists, Geyer was astute enough to recognize the uses of publicity. He decided to call a news conference.

That night, Geyer's room at the Rossin House was crammed with reporters, who were quick to perceive the story's dramatic appeal: an intrepid detective on the trail of three missing children who had fallen victim to a fiend. Geyer provided complete details of the case, passed around the children's photographs, and made a plea to "all the good citizens" of Toronto for their full cooperation.

The tactic worked. The next morning, every newspaper in the city carried at least two front-page columns on the case. This time, when Geyer and Cuddy made the rounds of the real estate offices, their job was much easier, since they were relieved of the need to repeat the story at every stop. Most of the agents had already checked their records before the detectives appeared.

Still, the day was disappointing. Once again, the two men came up empty-handed. When they returned to police head-quarters that evening, however, they found a message from a local real estate agent who had read about Geyer's investigation. The man wished to report that, the previous fall, he had rented a house on the outskirts of the city to an individual named Holmes. The house, situated at Perth and Bloor streets, stood in the middle of a field and was surrounded by a six-foot-high fence.

Reluctant to wait until morning, the two detectives hastened to the address. They found the house occupied by an elderly couple and their twenty-year-old son. Geyer ran through his story yet again, concluding with his opinion that Holmes had killed the children and buried them somewhere under the house.

The old man listened attentively. "That would account for that pile of loose dirt under the main building," he said to his son.

Cuddy and Geyer exchanged a significant look. Then Cuddy turned to the son and said, "Get a shovel."

While the young man hurried away, his father led the detectives to a hatch leading down to the crawl space. Pulling off their coats, the two men squeezed under the floor and quickly came upon the mound of loosened dirt. It was fully dark by then and the detectives called for some light. The son, who had returned with a shovel, went off to fetch some coal lamps, which he passed down the hatchway to the detectives. Taking turns, Geyer and Cuddy dug a hole about four-feet square and several feet deep—without turning up anything. Sopping and breathless in the suffocating space, they decided to call it a day.

Early the next morning, they sought out the real estate man who had contacted the police. The agent studied Holmes's mug shot for a few moments, then shook his head emphatically. The face in the photograph was completely unknown to him, he declared. It certainly did *not* belong to the man who had rented the house at Perth and Bloor.

Deeply frustrated by this development, Geyer switched tacks and spent the remainder of the day interviewing railway ticket agents in an effort to determine where Holmes had gone after leaving Toronto. By evening, he felt sure that Holmes had traveled to Prescott. Writing to his chief, Geyer announced his decision to make that city his "next stopping place . . . in the event of my not meeting with success in Toronto."

Still, Geyer wrote, he remained so firmly convinced "that Holmes disposed of the children in Toronto that I cannot think of leaving until I have made a more extended search."

On Saturday morning, Geyer took a quick trip to Niagara Falls, where Holmes had gone sight-seeing with Georgiana. Geyer located their names in the registry of the King's Imperial Hotel. The chief clerk verified that the couple had been there by themselves, without any children—confirming Geyer's belief that Georgiana had known nothing about the Pitezel girls. Though the bigamous Holmes had betrayed Georgiana's trust from the start, he had, at least, shielded her from the knowledge of his most reprehensible crimes. It was the single redeeming feature Geyer was willing to concede to the man.

Returning to Toronto in the early afternoon, Geyer spent the rest of the day searching through the newspaper morgues, checking the classifieds for all the private renters who had advertised houses the previous fall. Beginning Monday, he intended to call upon every one of them.

Meanwhile, the papers continued to run daily updates on the case.

When Geyer called for Cuddy on Monday morning, his partner was in a chipper mood. The police had just received word from a man named Thomas Ryves, who had been following Geyer's progress in the papers. Ryves recollected that, toward the tail end of the previous October, a man matching Holmes's description had rented the house next door to his own. The fellow had been accompanied by two young girls. But when he left abruptly about one week later, the children were not with him. The house in question was located at 16 St. Vincent Street.

Consulting the classified ads he had culled from the newspaper files, Geyer discovered one for the St. Vincent Street place. The ad stated that interested parties should contact Mrs. Frank Nudel at 54 Henry Street.

As it happened, Cuddy was acquainted with Frank Nudel, who held a job as a clerk for the Educational Department of Toronto. Cuddy suggested to Geyer that the two of them pay a visit to Nudel before proceeding to St. Vincent Street.

Geyer didn't allow himself the luxury of exaggerated hope. He had already been involved in too many wild-goose chases. Still, Ryves's recollection seemed the strongest lead to date. The two detectives set off at once for the Educational Department.

Nudel's eyes widened when the detectives told him the reason for their visit. He confirmed that the house had been rented the previous fall, then abruptly abandoned only a week or so later. But that was as much as he knew. The house belonged to his wife, who took care of the rentals. She was the one to talk to.

The two detectives decided to first pay a visit to Thomas Ryves—the elderly gentleman who had notified the police. When Geyer showed Ryves the photographs of Holmes and the Pitezel girls, Alice was the only one he had no trouble identifying. But his story left little doubt that the mysterious stranger who had briefly been his neighbor was Holmes.

As Ryves told it, the fellow had dropped by one morning, explaining that he had rented the house next door for his widowed sister, who would be arriving in a few days. He wanted to dig a place in the cellar where his sister could store potatoes and asked if he might borrow a shovel. Ryves had obliged.

That afternoon, the old man had watched through a window as the stranger moved a mattress, an old bed, and a large trunk into the house. Several days later, Ryves had observed him hauling away the trunk.

That was the last Ryves had seen of him.

By now, Geyer felt certain that he and Cuddy were on the right track. Telling Ryves that they would return within the hour, they quickly repaired to the Nudels' home at 54 Henry Street.

Mrs. Nudel seemed in the mood to chat, but Geyer had no time for pleasantries. Pulling out his photographs, he asked if she had ever seen the man in the picture.

"Why, yes," she replied after studying Holmes's mug shots for a moment. "This is the man who rented the St. Vincent Street house last October and only occupied it for a few days." He had given her a month's rent in advance—$10—promising to pay the balance the next time he saw her. Then he had disappeared without a trace.

Leaving Mrs. Nudel with a hurried thanks, the two detectives rushed back to St. Vincent Street where Ryves was seated on his front porch, anxiously awaiting their return. Geyer asked for a shovel, and the old man disappeared around the rear of his house, returning a few moments later with the same implement he had loaned to Holmes nine months before.

Then the two detectives walked next door to number 16.

It was a quaint, two-story cottage with a single gabled window in front and a covered veranda festooned with flowered vines. Stepping onto the porch was like entering a garden bower. Geyer paused at the front door, taking in the scene and wondering if the two Pitezel girls had truly met their deaths in this place. It was hard to conceive of this peaceful cottage as the site of such an atrocity.

The current tenant, a Mrs. J. Armbrust, clucked her tongue with amazement when Geyer explained why he and Cuddy were there. Leading them into the kitchen, she lifted a large piece of oilcloth from the center of the floor, revealing a small trapdoor, about two feet square. Geyer raised the door and peered down into the blackness. Mrs. Armbrust bustled away, returning moments later with an oil lamp, which she handed to Cuddy.

Then, with Cuddy leading the way, the two men descended a steep, narrow staircase into the pitch-dark cellar.

Cuddy held the light while Geyer moved around the little cellar, poking the shovel blade into the ground, searching for signs of disturbance. Suddenly, he found what he was looking for—a soft spot in the southwest corner. Cuddy directed his light into the corner while Geyer commenced to dig. The loose-packed soil came up easily.

Geyer had gone about a foot down when the earth gave off a carrion stench.

Two feet more and he turned up a human armbone, black with rotting flesh.

Cuddy gagged. Geyer, breathing through his mouth, shoveled dirt back into the hole to keep down the stink. Then the two men climbed out of the reeking cellar and into the kitchen.

Cuddy, looking ashen, stood near an open window and inhaled great drafts of garden air.

"We must get to a telephone," Geyer said, his voice tense with a mixture of triumph and horror.

They found one in a telegraph office on Yonge Street. Cuddy called Inspector Stark, who congratulated the men on their discovery, then recommended that they seek out B. D. Humphrey, an undertaker who resided nearby.

Minutes later, Geyer and Cuddy were at Humphrey's establishment. The undertaker agreed to accompany the detectives back to St. Vincent Street to assist with the exhumation. Geyer described the condition of the bodies and suggested that Humphrey bring three pairs of rubber gloves.

Back at the house on St. Vincent Street, the men took a moment to steel themselves, then descended into the cellar. It took only a few moments for Geyer to uncover the bodies. Humphrey shouted up to Mrs. Armbrust, telling her to send her teenaged son back to his establishment and have his assistant dispatch two coffins to the house.

In the shallow, noisome pit, Alice lay on her side, with her head to the west. Nellie lay on her face, crossways to her sister, her legs resting on Alice's body. Both girls were naked.

The three men bent down and gently grasped Nellie's body. Her flesh was so putrefied that, as they lifted the little corpse from the makeshift grave, her scalp—pulled free by the weight of her plaited hair—slithered wetly from her skull.

By then, a wagon had arrived with the coffins. Laying Nellie's body on a sheet, the three men carried it upstairs, laid it inside one of the coffins, then returned to the cellar and removed Alice's corpse. The bodies were taken directly to Humphrey's establishment and from there to the city morgue.

"By this time," Geyer later recalled, "Toronto was wild with excitement. The news had spread to every part of the city. The St. Vincent Street house was besieged with newspaper men, sketch artists, and others. Everybody seemed to be pleased with our success, and congratulations, mingled with expressions of horror over the discovery, were heard everywhere."

The fetor of death was still thick in Geyer's nostrils that night, the images of corruption still sharp in his mind. The thought of the slaughtered children filled him with outrage and sorrow. But as he lay in the dark of his hotel room, a profound restfulness began to overtake him.

True, his job was not over—Howard Pitezel remained to be found. But in less than three weeks of searching, Geyer had managed to solve a major part of the mystery. And in doing so, he had not only accomplished a notable feat of detection. He had done something that gave him a far deeper sense of satisfaction.

He had sealed the fate of H. H. Holmes.

42

What greater pain could mortals have than this:
To see their children dead before their eyes?

—Euripides, *The Suppliant Women*

The newspapers were full of sensational stories during the third week of July 1895—tragic mishaps, extraordinary sightings, and terrible crimes. In Baltimore, a young carpenter named George List met a dreadful end when a stack of lumber standing directly behind him tottered and fell, knocking him headfirst into the spinning blade of a large circular saw. A twenty-four-year-old Philadelphia woman named Rose Gearhart, abandoned by her brutish husband, committed suicide by swallowing strychnine after administering a fatal dose to her four-year-old daughter, who died after three hours of agonized convulsions.

New Yorkers were startled by accounts of a horned, hundred-foot sea serpent spotted in Long Island Sound and a monstrous, reptilian creature with a thunderous voice inhabiting a pond on Staten Island. (The former turned out to be a dead, bloated python discarded from a steamer out of Singapore, while the pond monster proved to be an overgrown bullfrog.) In Manhattan, a middle-aged widow named Elizabeth Lachmann plunged to her death while attempting to retrieve her false teeth from the first-story ledge of her apartment building, where they had landed after slipping from her mouth as she leaned out of her bedroom window.

And from Ashland, Kentucky, came reports of an appallingly savage act: a pretty seventeen-year-old named Carrie Jordan was abducted by three male acquaintances, who carried her off to an abandoned cabin, brutally assaulted her, then nailed her by the hands to a wall and left her for dead.

But all of these horrors and prodigies were quickly overshadowed by the news from Toronto: that the highly publicized quest of Philadelphia's intrepid detective Frank P. Geyer had climaxed in the uncovering of Alice and Nellie Pitezel's remains.

MURDERED THE CHILDREN! trumpeted *The Philadelphia Inquirer*. INFANTS' BLOOD SHED! blared *The Chicago Tribune*. GIRLS BODIES FOUND! proclaimed *The New York Herald*. Throughout the country, Geyer's grim discovery was front-page news.

In Philadelphia, District Attorney Graham had been the first to get the word, having received a telegram from Geyer on Monday evening, July 15, the date of the discovery. Graham planned to keep the news from Holmes, intending to spring it on him during a private conference the following day. The attorney general hoped that Holmes would be so rattled that he would break down and confess. Around eleven Tuesday morning, Graham telephoned the authorities at Moyamensing, instructing them to withhold all newspapers from the prisoner.

The call came too late. Earlier that morning, a crowd of reporters had appeared at the prison, clamoring for an interview with Holmes. Suspecting that a major break had occurred, Holmes sent out for the papers. By the time court officers Gentner and Alexander arrived to transport him to City Hall, he had seen the headlines and was braced for a brutal grilling.

Taken in shackles to the district attorney's office, he maintained a stubborn silence while Graham and Thomas Barlow bombarded him with questions for nearly two hours. Holmes later claimed that had been speechless with grief over the killings (which he would try to pin on Minnie Williams and a mysterious accomplice named "Hatch").

Led back to his cell, however, he did mutter a comment to one of his guards: "I guess I'll hang for this."

* * *

Even as Holmes was uttering this prediction, Detective Geyer was doing everything possible to make sure it came true. Early Tuesday morning, he and Cuddy set out to find evidence that would confirm the identities of the two murdered girls, whose corpses were decomposed beyond recognition.

Before lunchtime, they had succeeded in locating the tenants who had moved into the St. Vincent Street house immediately after Holmes absconded from it—a family named McDonald, now residing at 17 Russell Street. Mrs. McDonald testified that, except for an old bedstead and mattress, the house had been completely vacant. Her sixteen-year-old son, however, produced a simple toy that he had found in a second-floor closet: a painted egg concealing a little snake that sprang out like a jack-in-the-box when the wooden shell was parted.

Geyer reached into his coat pocket and produced a folded sheet of paper. It was an inventory he had gotten from Mrs. Pitezel, detailing all the possessions her children had carried with them on their fateful journey with Holmes. Scanning the sheet now, Geyer let out a small exultant cry.

Included on the list was a toy egg containing a spring-loaded snake. It had been Howard Pitezel's favorite plaything.

Though Geyer still believed that Howard had been slain in either Indianapolis or Detroit, he knew from Thomas Ryves that Holmes had moved an oversize trunk into 16 St. Vincent Street. Perhaps, Geyer speculated, Holmes had killed the boy in the States, stuffed him in the trunk, then transported the corpse to Canada for disposal.

Returning to 16 St. Vincent Street, Geyer—assisted by Cuddy and several other officers—spent the next several hours digging up the fetid basement and making a thorough examination of the barn and outbuildings. But all they found were some skeletal scraps that turned out to be chicken bones.

Geyer, however, did obtain some key corroboration from the current tenant, Mrs. Armbrust. Shortly after moving in, she had gone to use the fireplace in the north front room and discovered that the chimney was blocked. Reaching a hand up the flue, she had pulled out a mass of charred straw and singed rags.

The rags were unmistakably the remnants of female clothing—a scrap of blue dress, a piece of gray blouse, some reddish brown material from a girl's woolen garment. Someone had apparently tried to incinerate the clothing but had packed it too tightly inside the chimney, choking off the burning straw.

In the woodbox by the hearth, Mrs. Armbrust had discovered something else, too—a pair of girl's black button-boots.

None of this evidence existed anymore—Mrs. Armbrust had discarded it long ago. But her description was completely consistent with Carrie Pitezel's inventory of Alice and Nellie's belongings.

The children's bodies, meanwhile, had been transferred from B. D. Humphrey's undertaking establishment to the city morgue, where Coroner Johnston and a trio of doctors performed a postmortem early Tuesday morning. Though the extreme putrefaction of the corpses made it hard for the physicians to reach a definitive conclusion, they believed that the girls had died of suffocation before being interred in the basement—a finding that led to further speculation about the sinister function of Holmes's large trunk.

At the time of Holmes's arrest, the trunk had been recovered from his hotel room. The Boston police had subjected it to a thorough examination and had discovered a small hole neatly drilled below the lid. Geyer now surmised that Holmes had somehow lured the two girls into the trunk, closed and locked the lid, then inserted one end of a long rubber tube into the hole. The opposite end he attached to a gas jet. Then, opening the valve, he had calmly stood by while the children asphyxiated.

Though their findings were necessarily tentative, given the condition of the bodies, Johnston and his associates felt fairly confident about their conclusions. They were puzzled, however, by one anomaly: the feet of the smaller child were missing.

At first, they supposed that the feet had been accidentally severed by a shovel blade when the corpses were exhumed.

But no trace of the feet had been found during the subsequent search of the cellar.

Geyer, however, provided the solution to this mystery. Having questioned Carrie closely about her daughter's distinctive traits, he knew that little Nellie was slightly clubfooted.

The conclusion was inescapable: Holmes had sought to obscure the identity of the child's corpse by amputating its misshapen feet.

At seven-thirty that night, the coroner's jury convened at the morgue to examine the bodies as part of the preliminary inquest. Geyer was there, too, having been asked to attend by Coroner Johnston.

By that time, the citizens of Toronto were in such an uproar over the gruesome discovery that Geyer (as he later wrote) "felt sure they would have made short shrift of Holmes" had they "been furnished with the opportunity." Indeed, the public had already begun clamoring for Holmes's extradition. Meeting with reporters shortly before the opening of the inquest, Geyer assured them that Holmes would certainly stand trial in Canada for the killing of the Pitezel children should he somehow escape the noose in Philadelphia for the murder of their father.

Then, while Geyer remained in the waiting area, Coroner Johnston led the jury members—all of them respected city merchants—in to view the girls' bodies. Moments later, the jurors came hurrying out again, overwhelmed by the ghastly sight—and unbearable stench—of the rotting remains.

The following evening, the inquest resumed at the Police Court in City Hall. Called as a witness, Thomas Ryves testified that the girls in Detective Geyer's photographs were the same children who had briefly lived next door to him the previous fall. Then Geyer took the stand and spent nearly two and a half hours narrating the history of the Holmes-Pitezel affair, concluding with a detailed account of his own dogged search for the missing children.

At that point, the inquest was adjourned. Though no one doubted that the decomposed corpses lying in the morgue were those of Alice and Nellie Pitezel, there was no positive proof of their identities. Only one person could provide that proof.

The inquest would have to wait until Carrie Pitezel arrived in Toronto to view what was left of her two youngest daughters.

Like Holmes, Carrie had learned the devastating news from the papers. The previous week, she had traveled to Chicago from her parents' home in Galva in order to pursue her own inquiries into the children's whereabouts. She was staying with her old friends, the Haywards, when the newspaper arrived.

At the sight of the headline, she succumbed to such hysterical grief that her hosts sent their eldest child running for Dr. Hubbert, the family physician. With the help of "quieting mixtures," Hubbert temporarily tranquilized the stricken woman, but had to return twice more during the day to administer additional opiates. Finally, the drugs lulled her into a troubled sleep.

When she awoke later that night, she found a telegram from District Attorney Graham, informing her that the coroner's jury could not proceed without positive means of identifying the bodies.

Early Thursday morning, July 18, Carrie set off by herself for Toronto.

No one recognized her during the long train ride, though her black mourning clothes and ravaged look drew curious stares. In Toronto, however, a crowd of several hundred gawkers had gathered at the Union Depot. Fortunately, Geyer was there, too. The moment Carrie alighted from the train at around nine P.M., he took her by the arm and led her briskly through the jostling mob to a waiting carriage, which drove them to the Rossin House.

By the time Geyer got her to her room—directly across the hallway from his own—Carrie was on the verge of collapse. Heartsick and exhausted, she swooned as he led her toward her bedroom. Geyer, who had arranged to have smelling salts brought to the room, immediately applied the restoratives. Gradually, Carrie's eyes fluttered open and focused on the detective.

"Oh, Mr. Geyer," she moaned. "Is it true that you have found Alice and Nellie buried in a cellar?"

Geyer took her by the hand and, in the gentlest tones he could manage, told her that she must prepare herself for the worst.

Through her tears, Carrie replied that she would do her best.

With that, Geyer confirmed that her daughters were dead—though he stopped short of revealing the condition of their bodies or the precise circumstances of the discovery. After arranging for a chambermaid to look after her, Geyer returned to his room for the night.

Carrie seemed slightly better the next morning when Geyer stopped by to see her. He was on his way out, he explained, to make arrangements for her to view the children. Geyer picked up Cuddy at police headquarters, then the two men proceeded to the home of Coroner Johnston, who informed them that the bodies would be ready for inspection at four that afternoon.

Returning to the hotel, Geyer and his partner tried to steel Carrie for the coming ordeal. Geyer marshaled all the tact at his disposal but could no longer conceal the dreadful truth about the state of her children's remains. When he told her "that it would be absolutely impossible for her to see anything but Alice's teeth and hair, and only the hair belonging to Nellie," Carrie came close to passing out.

The two men stayed by her side until the carriage arrived at four. Then—arming themselves with brandy and smelling salts—they escorted the trembling woman to the waiting cab.

As a small, morbid crowd milled outside the city morgue, Geyer and Cuddy hurried Carrie inside. Leaving her in the waiting area, they passed inside the deadhouse to make certain that everything was in readiness.

Later, Geyer gave a graphic account of the harrowing scene that followed:

"I found that Coroner Johnston, Dr. Caven and several of his assistants, had removed the putrid flesh from the skull of Alice. The teeth had been nicely cleaned and the bodies covered with canvas. The head of Alice was covered with paper, and a hole sufficiently large had been cut in it, so that Mrs. Pitezel could see the teeth. The hair of both children had been carefully washed and laid on the canvas sheet which was covering Alice.

"Coroner Johnston said that we could now bring Mrs. Pitezel in. I entered the waiting room and told her we were ready, and with Cuddy on one side of her and I on the other, we entered and led her up to the slab, upon which was lying all that remained of poor Alice. In an instant she recognized the teeth and hair as that of her daughter, Alice. Then, turning around to me she said, 'Where is Nellie?' About this time she noticed the long black plait of hair belonging to Nellie lying on the canvas. She could stand it no longer, and the shrieks of that poor forlorn creature are still ringing in my ears. Tears were trickling down the cheeks of strong men who stood about us. The sufferings of the stricken mother were beyond description.

"We gently led her out of the room and into the carriage. She returned to the Rossin House completely overcome with grief and despair and had one fainting spell after another. The ladies in the hotel visited her in her room and spoke kindly to her and expressed their sympathy with her in her sad bereavement, and this seemed in a measure to ease her mind."

Later that afternoon, Geyer received word from Coroner Johnston, who wanted Carrie to testify that very evening at the inquest. Though somewhat taken aback by this request, Geyer put it to Carrie, who replied that she wished "to go and get through with it."

She remained on the stand for over two hours, answering questions in a tremulous, barely audible voice. When the Crown's Attorney dismissed her around ten, the strain of that unendurable day finally broke her, and she gave way to her grief, shrieking wildly for Alice, Nellie, and Howard. Several doctors in attendance helped calm her. She was returned to the Rossin House in the care of a professional nurse, who remained at her bedside throughout the night.

The remains of Alice and Nellie Pitezel were buried in St. James Cemetery the following afternoon, Saturday, July 20, 1895, the funeral expenses being borne by the City of Toronto.

*   *   *

Her daughters were gone. But Carrie still held out hope that Howard was alive. Geyer did not share her optimism, though he kept his opinion to himself. In any case, he was resolved to discover the little boy's fate.

On Sunday morning, July 21, the pair boarded a train for the States. Carrie traveled to Chicago, where the good women of the Christian Endeavor Society helped take care of her.

Geyer got off at Detroit.

43

To parallel such a career one must go back to past ages and to the time of the Borgias or Brinvilliers, and even these were not such human monsters as Holmes seems to have been. He is a prodigy of wickedness, a human demon, a being so unthinkable that no novelist would dare to invent such a character. The story, too, tends to illustrate the end of the century.

—*The Chicago Times-Herald*, May 8, 1896

In the meantime, Holmes continued to protest that he was "as innocent as a newborn babe of murdering the Pitezel children"—and on Thursday, July 18, a mysterious stranger came forward to lend weight to that claim.

His name was Francis Winshoff, and he appeared that morning at the office of Holmes's attorney, William A. Shoemaker, to announce that he was an "old pal" of the accused. He had been with Holmes in Toronto, "knew the Pitezel children well," and was willing to swear that "Holmes had no hand in the murder."

Newsmen covering the case were openly dubious of Winshoff, partly because he was such an odd-looking character—squat and shaggy-browed, with dark, piercing eyes, a headful of bushy black hair, and a mouth concealed beneath a matted clump of grizzled whiskers. He had an excitable manner, gesticulating wildly with his hands (one of which was bereft of all but a single finger). He identified himself as a Canadian, which led his listeners to conclude that his thick foreign accent was French.

The papers reported his story in tones ranging from polite skepticism to outright scorn, *The Philadelphia Inquirer* deriding it as "one of the most beautiful and picturesque romances yet spun" in the case. Lawyer Shoemaker, however, confidently declared that Winshoff was a "living witness" who knew "just who killed the children" and would positively "clear Holmes of complicity" in the crime.

The newspapers turned out to be right.

By Friday afternoon, Winshoff was revealed to be a fifty-year-old Russian émigré and "spiritualistic crank" who resided on Brown Street, where he made his living by conducting séances for a small but devoted following. In his spare time, he bottled and sold his own patented "nerve medicine" and attempted, through the application of his occult powers, to transform clay balls into diamonds by rolling them around in his one good hand.

Though Winshoff subsequently confessed that he had never actually met Holmes, he stuck to his story, insisting that he had received his information from unimpeachable sources in the spirit world.

That a crackpot like Winshoff could attract so much attention was a sign of the public's continuing fascination with the Holmes case. But for all its intensity, that fascination was still comparatively mild. Fueled by the excesses of the yellow press, it was about to explode into something like frenzy.

The story of the Holmes-Pitezel affair first broke at a particularly bitter moment in the nation's life. The country's economy was (as one contemporary observer put it) "in the throes of an unprecedented fiasco," brought about by the devastating panic of 1893. It was a time of widespread industrial collapse, massive unemployment, and violent labor disputes. Chicago—scene of the dramatic Pullman strike of 1894—was especially hard hit by the depression.

The public's obsessive interest in Holmes derived in part from these grim economic conditions (which persisted until 1896). To many, Holmes personified everything that had gone wrong with the country. He symbolized all the hollowness and corruption at the heart of the American "success ethic"—what the poet Walt Whitman decried as "the depravity of the business classes." He was the living incarnation of "money lust," of the evils to which the unbridled pursuit of individual wealth could lead.

In the third week of July 1895, however, the public's perception of Holmes underwent a dramatic shift. Suddenly, he was seen as something infinitely more diabolical than a bold, ruthless schemer who had killed his accomplice for money. Partly, this change resulted from the discovery of the murdered Pitezel girls, whose deaths could not be attributed to simple greed.

But something else occurred, too, that caused Holmes to be seen not simply as "the boss crook of the century" but as a being of monstrous, indeed mythical, proportions—a creature on the order of Bluebeard, Dr. Jekyll, even the Devil himself.

This transformation—from "archswindler" to "archfiend"—took place literally overnight. For on Friday evening, July 19, 1895, the Chicago police finally entered and began exploring Holmes's Castle.

From the moment of Holmes's arrest, rumors had been circulating that the bodies of the missing Williams sisters were buried in the cellar of his Englewood building. The police had been planning to investigate the stories for weeks but were deterred by the protests of the Castle's shopkeeps, who were reluctant to have an army of officers digging up the basement—presumably because it would be bad for business. When the buried corpses of the Pitezel girls were uncovered in Toronto, however, Inspector Fitzpatrick of Chicago's Central Detective Detail immediately resolved to go ahead with the excavation.

Investigators began on Friday night, but the size of the cellar, which measured more than fifty by one hundred sixtyfive feet, made the dig a daunting task. After poking around by lamplight for a few hours, the men retired for the night.

They were back early Saturday morning, supplemented by a crew of city construction workers. Armed with picks and shovels, they set about their work, searching for a likely spot—perhaps a hidden well—where Holmes might have deposited his victims.

In the meantime, Inspectors Fitzpatrick and Norton, accompanied by reporters from the city's major newspapers, ascended to the second story of the building. They were dumbfounded by what they encountered—a dizzying maze of unmistakably sinister design. Groping their way around the twisting passages, they came upon secret rooms and hidden stairwells, blind hallways and mysterious sliding walls, trapdoors opening onto tightly sealed chambers and camouflaged chutes feeding into the cellar.

Stunned and bewildered, the explorers struggled to make sense of what they were seeing. But there was simply too much to take in. Indeed, it would be several more weeks before the second-floor labyrinth was fully surveyed and charted—and even then, the precise function of some of its more bizarre architectural features would defy explanation.

But one thing seemed immediately clear: in the midst of America's most booming metropolis, Dr. Holmes had built himself a dwelling place that brought to mind a castle of horrors from a gothic romance.

Proceeding to the top floor, the searchers found several other grim surprises, including Holmes's enormous walk-in vault, its walls heavily padded with asbestos—presumably (so the police quickly theorized) to deaden any sounds from within. Adjacent to the vault was Holmes's private office, which contained an immense iron stove, fully eight feet tall and three feet in circumference. Opening the door (which, as one witness noted, was "sufficiently large to admit a human body"), Inspector Fitzpatrick began poking through the debris with his cane. Suddenly, he frowned, reached in a hand, and pulled out a charred object that bore a striking resemblance to a human rib bone.

Tearing off his jacket and rolling up a shirtsleeve, Fitzpatrick stuck his arm into the stove and scooped the remaining contents onto the floor. Scattered among the ashes were more burned, bonelike fragments. There were also several small buttons that had evidently come from a woman's dress and the remains of what appeared to be a lady's gold watch chain.

Later that day, the police showed the six-inch piece of chain to C. E. Davis, who ran the jewelry shop on the Castle's ground floor. Though the links were partially melted, Davis identified the chain at once.

He had made it himself, he told the police. It had been purchased by H. H. Holmes as a gift for his lady friend, Minnie Williams.

As Fitzpatrick knelt on the floor, carefully wrapping the evidence in a handkerchief, one of the newspaper reporters took down the stovepipe and peered into the chimney. All at once, he let out a cry, reached into the opening, and came out with a clump of charred human hair whose length made it plain that it had come from a woman.

By that time, the crew excavating the cellar had made some discoveries of their own, including a singed woman's slipper and a charred scrap of grosgrain silk from a woman's garment, both sifted from an ash heap in a dark corner of the cellar. Still, there was no sign of a buried well.

As they made their way along the south wall, however, rapping it at regular intervals with their implements, they discovered a hollow spot about twenty-five feet from the Wallace Street side. Applying their picks, the workmen quickly broke through the wall. Peering into the opening, they were astonished to see a mysterious wooden tank, bristling with pipes.

One of the men squeezed through the opening and gave the tank a sharp, exploratory rap with his pick. The pick-point pierced the wood, releasing such a foul vapor that the entire crew dropped their tools and fled.

A plumber was summoned, but before he could arrive, three of the men returned to the basement to see if the fumes had evaporated. As they made their way through the dark murk of the cellar, one struck a match against a wall.

The basement exploded.

The blast shook the Castle to its foundations and sent the terrified ground-floor storekeepers fleeing into the street. A policeman patrolling nearby hurriedly put in an alarm, and

within minutes, Fire Chief Joseph Kenyon was on the scene
with Engine No. 51 and Truck No. 20. By then, several of
the workmen had dashed down to the basement and pulled
out their critically injured comrades.

Before the firemen could set up their equipment, the
flames had burned themselves out. Chief Kenyon decided to
open the tank and let the noxious gas dissipate. He and
several of his men made their way down to the cellar but
were so overcome by the vapor that they barely managed
to stagger back up to the street. Kenyon was delirious for
over two hours and, at one point, seemed close to death.
But he was sufficiently recovered by late afternoon to over-
see the cleaning out and boarding up of the deadly chemical tank.

By Sunday morning, the basement air was breathable
again and the investigators were back on the job. Their work
was somewhat hampered by the crowds of curiosity seekers
who swarmed through the building, drawn by the lurid headlines about H. H. Holmes's "murder factory." The police
finally managed to clear out the Castle, though not before
the intruders had helped themselves to assorted souvenirs,
including personal letters and financial records from
Holmes's office.

Apart from a bloodstained woman's undergarment, which
Inspector Fitzpatrick turned up in an ash heap in the north-
east corner of the cellar, the police made no significant discoveries on Sunday. They did, however, make a sensational
revelation to the press, announcing that the Williams sisters
were not the only objects of their search.

For several weeks they had been investigating the mysterious disappearance of Mrs. Julia Conner, who was known to
have fallen under the baneful influence of Holmes. Mr. and
Mrs. L. G. Smythe of Davenport, Iowa, parents of the missing woman, had been pressing the Chicago authorities to
step up their search.

In light of recent developments, the police were now persuaded that both Mrs. Conner and her four-year-old daughter, Pearl, had been killed by the "fiend of Sixty-third
Street."

The diggers redoubled their efforts on Monday, though they unearthed nothing besides the sole of a woman's shoe (size four), the broken lid of an opera-glass case, and some skeletal fragments that appeared to be chicken bones.

At the west end of the cellar, however, they came upon a padlocked storage chamber, which they promptly broke open. The floor of the chamber was littered with rubbish, and at the bottom of the rubbish the police discovered a length of stout rope. One end of the rope had been made into a plaited loop.

The opposite end—darkly stained with what looked like dried blood—had been tied into a hangman's noose.

"The length of the rope is such," wrote a reporter for *The Philadelphia Inquirer,* "that were the plaited loop attached to the upstairs wall of the secret dumb-waiter shaft, a body hanging from the noose would just clear the floor at the bottom of the shaft. This coincidence convinced some of the detectives that Holmes' alleged victims had been pushed through the upstairs door in the dumb-waiter and strangled to death in the shaft below."

Meanwhile, Detective Sergeant Norton, reading through the papers in Holmes's third-floor office, came upon a poignant letter from Julia Conner's mother, mailed from Davenport and dated October 1, 1892. The contents suggested that Mrs. Smythe had made at least one attempt to contact her daughter at the Castle and had received a reply in which Holmes denied any knowledge of Julia's whereabouts.

"[Your letter] surprised us very much," Mrs. Smythe had written back, "as we supposed our daughter Julia in your company. We are very anxious to know her whereabouts, and her daughter also, and by answering this letter and telling us where she is you will greatly relieve her poor old gray-haired father and mother."

The police felt certain that Holmes—"the Modern Bluebeard," as the newspapers had taken to calling him—had dispatched his former mistress, as he had Minnie and Nannie Williams, though to date they had no hard proof to back up their suspicions. On the afternoon of Tuesday, July 23, however, one mystery appeared to be solved: the fate of Julia's little daughter, Pearl.

Sifting through a mass of quicklime they had found in the cellar, the searchers turned up part of a decomposed skeleton. Examining the bones by lamplight, Dr. C. P. Stringfield pronounced that they were almost certainly the rib cage and pelvis of a human being and that—judging by their size—they could only have come from a child between the ages of four and eight.

Apprised of this grisly discovery, Holmes vehemently denied any part in the killing of Julia Conner or her daughter, though he finally admitted that his former mistress was, in fact, dead—the tragic consequence, he claimed, of a botched abortion. "Mrs. Conner got into trouble," he told reporters, resorting to the euphemisms of the day, "and a Chicago doctor performed an operation. The job was such a bungling one that the woman died."

As for the Williams sisters, he reverted to his original story, the one he had told at the time of his arrest to Detective Thomas Crawford. "Soon after Nannie Williams arrived in Chicago," Holmes told the newsmen, "Minnie began to get jealous of her. One day in a fit of anger, Minnie hit her sister with a chair and killed her. I put the body in a trunk and dropped it into Lake Michigan. Then at my advice, Minnie transferred her property to me and fled to Europe."

But no one—not the public, the police, or the press—believed a word of it. "The man is an infernal liar," growled Superintendent Linden of the Philadelphia Bureau of Police.

As the excavation of the Castle continued, the authorities realized that they were dealing with a frightening new phenomenon—so unique in their experience that they couldn't put a name to it. A Chicago journalist came up with the term *multimurderer*. Nearly a hundred years would pass before criminologists coined the phrase *serial killers* to describe creatures like Holmes.

Each day now, the names of new alleged victims appeared in the papers: Emeline Cigrand, the lovely twenty-year-old stenographer who had gone to work for Holmes in the summer of 1892 and abruptly disappeared the following December. Emily Van Tassel, a pretty grocer's cashier who vanished shortly after striking up an acquaintance with Holmes in 1893. Wilfred Cole, a wealthy lumberman from

Baltimore who traveled to Chicago for some unspecified business dealings with Holmes and was never heard from again. A physician named Russler, reportedly an intimate acquaintance of Holmes's, who hadn't been seen since 1892. Harry Walker, a young man who had gone to work as Holmes's private secretary in 1893 and disappeared a few months later after taking out a $15,000 life insurance policy. A handsome—and wealthy—widow named Mrs. Lee who had kept company with Holmes, then dropped out of sight "as completely and mysteriously as though she had fallen off the earth" (in the words of one witness).

There were the three missing members of the Gorky family: a middle-aged widow named Kate, who ran a restaurant on the first floor of Holmes's Castle during the time of the Chicago World's Fair; her comely sister, Liz; and her pretty teenaged daughter, Anna. There were also an indeterminate number of female clerical workers who had supposedly vanished after taking jobs at the Castle, including a beautiful Boston girl named Mabel Barrett, a sixteen-year-old stenographer named Miss Wild, and a bookkeeper named Kelly. (According to one report, Holmes had "employed more than one hundred young women during his years in Englewood.")

In addition, Holmes was now suspected of having killed Mary Cron—a middle-aged woman brutally attacked in the bedroom of her Wilmette home in November 1893—and of masterminding the sensational 1892 abduction of little Annie Redmond, the daughter of a Chicago blacksmith.

On July 29, Detective Geyer publicly accused Holmes of having plotted to kill his wife, Georgiana, presumably to get his hands on her estate. Two days later, *The New York Times* leveled an equally sensational charge, claiming that, at the very start of his criminal career—while still going under his real name, Herman Mudgett—Holmes had done away with a little boy.

According to this story, Holmes had appeared one day in the small upstate town of Mooers, New York, and "created such a good impression that he was engaged to teach the village school. This occupation he found uncongenial. He left Mooers and went to Massachusetts, but returned in a

286

short time, accompanied by a small boy, who disappeared shortly after arrival, Holmes saying he had gone home.

"It is now believed that the boy was the murderer's first victim."

Several witnesses swore that they had narrowly escaped death at Holmes's hands. Jonathan Belknap—grand uncle of Holmes's Wilmette wife, Myrta—sent a letter to the Chicago police, describing a nerve-racking night at the Castle. Belknap had traveled to Chicago in 1891 after discovering that Holmes had forged his signature on a $2,500 bank note.

"I knew Holmes was a scoundrel," Belknap wrote. "On my going to his house with him, he showed me all through it and insisted that I should go up on the roof with him. But I was very suspicious of the man and refused to go with him. I did not want to remain in the house that night but he would not let me go. When I went to bed, I carefully locked the door.

"I was awakened sometime after midnight by stealthy steps along the hall. Presently, I heard my door tried and then a key was slipped into the lock. I asked who was there and heard the sound of feet shuffling down the hallway. Evidently two men had been there, for Pat Quinlan's voice answered that he was there and that he wanted to get in and sleep with me—that there was no other place there. I refused to open the door. He insisted for a time and then went away.

"I am confident now that if I had gone on the roof of the house with Holmes that day, or if I had allowed Quinlan to come into the room that night, I would have been a dead man."

Another person now convinced that the archfiend had been plotting her murder was a washerwoman named Strowers, who lived on Sixty-third and Morgan and often laundered Holmes's clothing. According to Mrs. Strowers, Holmes had approached her in 1891 and tried to persuade her to take out a $10,000 insurance policy on her life.

"You take out the policy," Holmes had reportedly told her, "and I will give you six thousand dollars cash for it at once."

Mrs. Strowers acknowledged that she had been tempted by the offer. But as she stood there mulling it over, Holmes had leaned toward her, fixed her with his hypnotic gaze, and whispered, "Don't be afraid of me." There was something so unsettling in his look that Mrs. Strowers refused to consider the proposition and never spoke to Holmes about it again.

Among the countless crimes ascribed to Holmes during the first, frenzied days of the search was the killing of Mrs. Pat Quinlan, wife of the building's janitor. "Are more murders to be added to the list of Holmes' atrocities?" began the front-page story in the July 25 edition of *The Chicago Inter Ocean*. "Is the wife of Pat Quinlan alive? Did Holmes the arch-fiend make away with her, and are her bones rotting in some cellar buried in quick lime?"

Less than twenty-four hours after these feverish questions were posed, however, Mrs. Quinlan showed up at Chicago police headquarters and was promptly taken into custody, along with her husband, a wiry little man with a walrus mustache and nervous eyes. Held on charges of complicity, both of the Quinlans were subjected to relentless grillings. After countless hours "in the sweatbox," Mrs. Quinlan finally broke down and confessed to her knowledge of Holmes's fire insurance scam.

Her husband, however, refused to budge. "I am innocent," he sobbed to reporters after yet another brutal interrogation. "I knew Holmes and worked for him. All these people you say were murdered I knew, and when they went away, as Holmes claimed, I thought it funny. You say I helped him to commit murder, but I did not. I am innocent and I cannot tell you what you claim I know. Let me alone. I am innocent!"

Chief Badenoch, however, scoffed at Quinlan's disclaimer, stating flatly that the man "was a murderer." At the time of his arrest, the janitor had been carrying a big iron ring containing more than three dozen keys to all the doors in the Castle.

No one with that sort of access to the innermost recesses of the building could have stayed ignorant of its grisly secrets: the acid vats and quicklime tanks. The death shafts and asphyxiation chambers. The stained wooden dissecting table and chests full of blood-caked surgical tools. The underground furnace, converted to a private crematorium. The heaps of human bones.

Informed in his prison cell that the police had turned up a skeleton pile in a corner of the basement, Holmes indignantly declared that these remains were nothing but "butcher-shop refuse." Forensic analysis confirmed that some of the bones did indeed come from animals. But others were held to be human.

Apparently, Holmes had sought to conceal the evidence of his butchery by mixing human remains with old soup bones.

In spite of these finds—the "ghastly treasures" dug up daily from the damp earthen floor of the cellar—the police had yet to turn up any definitive proof linking Holmes to the disappearance of Minnie and Nannie Williams, Julia Conner, or Emeline Cigrand (who, according to Holmes's latest story, had been so guilt-stricken over her illicit relations with him that she had run off and entered a convent).

And then, on Friday, July 26, Lt. William Thomas of the Cottage Grove station tracked down Holmes's former employee and freelance anatomist, Charles M. Chappell. Within forty-eight hours, the police announced that they had recovered the articulated skeletons of two adult women—one from the home of a West Side physician, the other from the LaSalle Medical School—plus a Saratoga trunk containing an assortment of "human relics," including an armbone, a hand, and a skull.

The newspaper headlines, already given to shrill allegations, reached a new pitch of hysterics: A CHAMBER OF HORRORS! screamed *The New York World*. CASTLE IS A TOMB! thundered *The Chicago Tribune*. SKELETONS TAKEN FROM HOLMES CHARNEL HOUSE! cried *The Philadelphia Inquirer*.

Unsurprisingly, the sensational press indulged in the wildest excesses, publishing the most extravagant rumors as unvarnished fact. Among the lurid stories that appeared in these papers were reports that Holmes's tidy dwelling in

Wilmette was a second "house of horrors," complete with "secret chambers, hidden apartments, subterranean vaults, concealed doors, and false partitions." The papers cited neighbors who swore that they had spied "mysterious beings" hauling suspicious objects out of the house "in the dead hours of night." Other witnesses testified that they had seen Holmes digging a "private graveyard" behind his house.

On the afternoon of July 27, a newsman from *The Chicago Inter Ocean* trekked out to Wilmette to investigate these rumors. His report appeared the following day. "Here is a simple statement of the truth. That house does not contain a single mysterious feature. The articles which have been 'secretly removed' during the past two weeks were vegetables, a child's hat, two boxes of glass, and an old stove. The 'grave' in the garden is a cess-pool, and the statement is authorized that anybody can explore it who wishes to."

Admitted to the house by Myrta, the reporter was seated in the front parlor, while six-year-old Lucy—the Holmes's "fair-haired, sweet-faced" daughter—was sent off to play with her "dollies."

The reporter was moved by Myrta's agonizing situation. A courteous and obviously well-bred person who attended daily services at the local Episcopal church, she had been—in his view—"more cruelly persecuted and misrepresented" than any other woman alive. "She has been hounded by would-be detectives, reporters, and vulgar curiosity-seekers. At all hours of the day and night, they have gone to her home. Because they were refused admittance, many of them hurled oaths at her and made all kinds of threats."

The reporter was struck by her devotion to Holmes. Though she frankly confessed that he was capable of "dishonorable financial transactions," she insisted that he could not possibly be guilty of murder. "In his home life," she testified, "I do not think there was ever a better man than my husband. He never spoke an unkind word to me or our little girl. He was never vexed or irritable but was always happy and free from care. In times of financial trouble or when we were worried . . . his presence was like oil on troubled waters."

The proof of his essential goodness could be seen in his feelings for children and animals. "It is said that babies are better judges of people than grown-up persons," she declared. "And I never saw a baby that would not go to Mr. Holmes and stay with him contentedly. He was remarkably fond of children. Often when we were traveling and there happened to be a baby in the car he would say, 'Go and see if they won't lend you that baby a little while,' and when I brought it to him, he would play with it, forgetting everything else, until its mother called for it or I could see she wanted it. . . . He was a lover of pets and always had a dog or cat and usually a horse, and he would play with them by the hour, teaching them little tricks or romping with them. Is such a man without a heart?"

As she spoke, tears rose in her eyes, though her tone made it clear that they sprang as much from frustration as sorrow. "Ambition has been the curse of my husband's life," she said. "He wanted to attain a position where he would be honored and respected. He wanted wealth. He worked hard, but his efforts failed. He was involved. Temptation to get money dishonestly came and he yielded. He fell. He did defraud people, I fear—but he did not commit murder! He has been accused of crimes which happened on the same date in Chicago, Canada and Texas. Will not people see the absurdity of charging to him all crimes that cannot otherwise be accounted for?"

By then, her voice had risen to a desperate cry. "Mr. Holmes is a human being," she exclaimed through her tears. "He is not supernatural!"

By then, in fact, some of the more responsible papers had begun to print certain retractions. The "charred human ribs" discovered in Holmes's office stove, for example, had been found to be fragments of fireclay, while assorted "blood-stained" articles proved to be discolored with rust. The testimony of the self-confessed skeleton mounter, Charles Chappell, had been called into question, his own family dismissing it as the ranting of a hopeless drunk. And supposed victims such as Kate Durkee and her sister Mary turned out to be alive and well and very much astonished by reports of their murder.

On July 29, *The Chicago Tribune* printed a cartoon that acknowledged the truth of Myrta Holmes's accusation—that the charges against her husband had reached the point of "absurdity."

Two days earlier, newspapers throughout the country had published sensational accounts of a massacre in Jackson Hole, Wyoming. Reportedly, a tribe of "hostile Bannocks" had butchered every white settler in the area.

The stories turned out be totally spurious. In fact, the tension in the area had been stirred up by local cattle ranchers who coveted the Bannocks' land and were attempting to drive them from their reservation. Before the truth was uncovered, the *Tribune* ran its self-mocking cartoon.

In the drawing, Holmes is shown standing in his jail cell, holding up a newspaper whose front page reads, "BANNOCK INDIANS ON WARPATH—SETTLERS MASSACRED."

Holmes looks profoundly dismayed—not because of the deaths but because he knows he's about to be blamed for them. Staring straight at the reader, he cries out in protest, "I AM INNOCENT!"

Even so—and in spite of Myrta's insistence that her husband was "not supernatural"—the papers continued to characterize Holmes in precisely those terms, describing him as a "human monster," "bloodthirsty fiend," "murder-demon," "ghoul," and "ogre." On the very day that the *Tribune* ran its satiric cartoon, it printed a story captioned NO JEKYLL, ALL HYDE—a headline that summed up a common perception of the double-faced Dr. Holmes, who struck many observers as the flesh-and-blood incarnation of Robert Louis Stevenson's fictional monster. *The New York World*, meanwhile, printed a floor plan of the Castle under the title BLUEBEARD'S CHAMBER OF HORROR.

And indeed, as the exploration of the building entered its second week, the police continued to uncover enough gruesome evidence to justify such lurid characterizations.

Sections of a human skull. A hip socket, a shoulder blade, and several pieces of collarbone. Blood-clotted clothing in the chamber once occupied by Julia Conner.

The police made one of their most unsettling discoveries during their inspection of Holmes's walk-in vault—a discovery that left little doubt that at least some of his victims had suffered the agonies of slow asphyxiation.

Locked inside the suffocating vault, one of these poor souls had clearly made a frantic effort to break free. The sign of her struggle was still visible on the inside of the massive iron door.

There—a few feet off the floor, as though she had braced her back against one wall, placed her foot against the door, and shoved with all her might—was the imprint of a woman's naked sole.

Convinced that the Castle had divulged its darkest secrets, the police decided to halt their search on Monday, August 5. One question remained: What was to become of Holmes's "nightmare house"?

Some voices called for its immediate demolition. The place, they argued, was a death trap—and not only because of the numberless victims who had already perished within its walls. On July 23, E. F. Laughlin, an inspector for the Chicago Department of Buildings, had made a tour of the Castle and been appalled by its shoddy construction. "The structural parts of the inside are all weak and dangerous," he wrote in his report to Commissioner Joseph Downey. "Built of poorest and cheapest kind of material . . . All dividing partitions between flats are combustible. . . . The sanitary condition of the building is horrible."

His final recommendation: "The building should be condemned."

To others, however, tearing down the Castle seemed a terrible waste. True, the place might not be fit for habitation. But there were other uses to which it might be put. On Sunday, July 28, nearly five thousand people had swarmed to Sixty-third and Wallace, hoping for a glimpse of the Castle's ghastly interior—its "torture dungeon" and "suffocation vault" and "corpse chambers." The following week, *The*

New York Times published a story headlined KNOWS HOW IT FEELS TO SMOTHER, about a Chicago man named William Barnes who locked himself inside a jeweler's vault because he wanted to "learn the sensations of some of Holmes's victims."

Clearly, the archfiend continued to exert a powerful grip on the public imagination. There was good money to be made from such morbid fascination, as an enterprising ex-policeman named A. M. Clark was quick to perceive. Even before Detective Norton called a halt to the investigation, Clark had arranged to lease the building from its court-appointed receiver. On Sunday, August 11, he made his announcement to the press.

Beginning that week, the Castle would be turned into a tourist attraction—a "murder museum" with an admission charge of fifteen cents per person and guided tours conducted by Detective Norton himself.

44

Truth will come to light; murder cannot be hid long.

   —Shakespeare, *The Merchant of Venice*

Along with their exhaustive coverage of the Castle investigation, the newspapers had been publishing regular updates on Detective Geyer's progress. By the first week of August, the public knew that Geyer had headed back to Indianapolis after failing to turn up any trace of Howard Pitezel in Detroit.

What no one knew but Geyer himself was that—for the first time since he set out on his arduous quest—he was beginning to doubt whether the mystery of the missing boy would ever be solved.

Geyer had arrived in Detroit shortly before suppertime on July 21—too late to do anything more than drop in on his old friend Thomas Meyler, who insisted on springing for steaks at a local chophouse to celebrate Geyer's success in Toronto.

The next morning—accompanied once again by Detective Tuttle—Geyer sought out the two witnesses who claimed to have seen Holmes in the company of Howard Pitezel. Questioned more closely this time, both men admitted that they might have been mistaken. Mr. Bonninghausen—the real estate agent who had rented Holmes the house on East Forest Avenue—declared that he had "no absolutely positive recollection of the matter," though he was certain that his clerk, Mr. Moore, "had noticed a little boy with Holmes."

Moore, however, explained that there had been "several persons with children in the real estate office that day." He *thought* one of the youngsters—a small, brown-haired boy—had been with Holmes. But now he "was not sure."

Repairing again to the house at 241 East Forest Avenue, Geyer and Tuttle made another thorough search of the premises, including the cellar, barn, outhouses, and yard. They found nothing to suggest that Howard had been murdered there. The cellar did contain an enormous furnace—a convenient place to dispose of a child's body, Geyer believed. But there was nothing "which indicated that a body had been consumed therein."

The only truly sinister clue was the mysterious hole—four feet long, three feet wide, and three and a half feet deep—which the current tenant had discovered in the cellar shortly after moving in. But that, too, had been empty.

Back in his hotel room that night, Geyer reviewed all the facts. Now that Bonninghausen and Moore had revised their testimony, there wasn't a single piece of evidence to prove that Holmes and Howard had been together in Detroit. Geyer knew, moreover, that—in her letter of October 14, 1894—Alice had written that "Howard is not with us now."

He knew something else, too: that the cellar hole Holmes had dug in the Forest Avenue house was precisely the same size as the Pitezel girls' makeshift grave in Toronto. Under the circumstances, it seemed plausible that the hole had been intended for Alice and Nellie, not Howard. When some unexpected turn forced Holmes to abandon the house, he had spirited the girls off to Canada and consummated his monstrous plan there.

Putting all these considerations together, Geyer was convinced that by the time Alice and Nellie checked into the New Western Hotel on October 12, they were alone; Howard had never reached Detroit.

The next morning, Geyer sent a wire to his superiors in Philadelphia, informing them of his decision to return to Indianapolis.

*　　*　　*

He arrived on the morning of July 24. Twenty minutes later he was at police headquarters, conferring with Superintendent Powell, who detailed Detective Richards to assist him again. Geyer knew exactly what he was searching for: a house that had been rented in early October 1894 by a man who claimed that he was taking it for his "widowed sister"—the same falsehood Holmes had used in Cincinnati, Detroit, and Toronto.

Procuring a city directory, Geyer and Richards compiled a list of every real estate agent in Indianapolis and set about visiting each one. In the meantime, the newspapers ran front-page stories on Geyer's search, complete with pictures of Holmes and Howard Pitezel. As in Toronto, the headlines galvanized the public. "It seemed," Geyer would later remark, "as if every man, woman, and child in Indiana was alert and watchful and aiding me in the work of finding the missing child"—though, in fact, the countless leads that began pouring in all proved to be worthless.

Day after day, in the swelter of one of the hottest Midwestern summers in memory, the two men tramped and trolleyed through the city—to no avail. By month's end, even Geyer—for all his resolve—couldn't keep from feeling disheartened. "It began to look," he confessed, "as though the bold and clever criminal had outwitted the detectives, both professional and amateur, and that the disappearance of Howard Pitezel would pass into history as an unsolved mystery."

Just when Geyer's faith began to falter, his spirits were buoyed by a letter from Assistant District Attorney Thomas Barlow, who continued to feel certain that "skill and patience would yet win." After analyzing the letters written by Alice and Nellie Pitezel, Barlow had concluded that the children could not possibly have checked out of the Circle House on October 6, as the proprietor, Herman Ackelow, had claimed.

Proceeding to the hotel, Geyer rechecked the registry and discovered that Barlow was right—the last payment on the Pitezel children's board had been made on October 10. Since Geyer had already "ascertained to a certainty" that Alice and Nellie had arrived in Detroit on the evening of October

12, he now felt sure that he "was hot on the track, with only forty-eight hours to be accounted for," not six days as he had previously believed.

Sometime during those forty-eight hours, Howard Pitezel had disappeared—"either in Indianapolis or between that city and Detroit."

On Thursday evening, August 1, Geyer received a telegram from District Attorney Graham informing him that a child's skeleton had been uncovered in the cellar of Holmes's Castle. Geyer was in Chicago before breakfast the next morning, conferring with Chief Badenoch and Inspector Fitzpatrick. It quickly became clear to him, however, that the remains could not possibly be those of a little boy.

He was preparing to travel back to Indianapolis when another telegram arrived from Graham, requesting his immediate return to Philadelphia. Stepping off the train on the afternoon of August 3, he was mobbed by reporters, clamoring for an interview with the hometown hero. Geyer had become a celebrity.

Appreciating the value of publicity, which had proved to be such an important tool in his search, Geyer was always glad to oblige the press. But he was too travel-worn at the moment to offer more than a few weary words. Indeed, Geyer was so clearly exhausted by his efforts that his superiors insisted that he remain in Philadelphia for a few days until he had a chance to recover.

By Wednesday evening, August 7, he was ready to resume his quest. This time, however, he would be accompanied by another skilled detective—W. E. Gary, chief investigator for the Fidelity Mutual Life Assurance Company, who had been involved with the Holmes case even longer than Geyer.

The two men headed first to Chicago, where they interviewed Pat Quinlan and his wife, both of whom "stoutly maintained their ignorance of the children." Geyer was inclined to believe that they were telling the truth.

Next, he and Gary traveled to Logansport, and from there to Peru, Indiana, Montpelier Junction, Ohio, and Adrian, Michigan. In each of these towns, they spent several days searching among hotels and boardinghouses and interviewing real estate agents—"all to no purpose." The two detectives finally decided to return to Indianapolis and (in Geyer's words) "settle there until District Attorney Graham told us to stop or until we had found the boy."

By this time—his third trip to Indianapolis—Geyer was growing discouraged again. "The large stock of hope I had gathered up in the district attorney's office in the Philadelphia City Hall was fast dwindling away," he admitted. "The mystery seemed to be impenetrable."

Once more the papers printed headline stories about the resumption of his search. Once more he was inundated with tips about "mysterious people who had rented houses for a short time and then disappeared." Geyer and Gary ran down each of these leads. They also made a list of all the newspaper classifieds from October 1894 offering private houses for rent. Altogether, the two men checked out no less than nine hundred clues without coming any closer to a solution.

Having exhausted every possibility in Indianapolis itself, they turned their attention to the nearby towns. Two weeks later, they had investigated virtually all of them without turning up any sign of the boy.

There was only one place left to look—the little town of Irvington, six miles outside the city.

On Friday, August 23, Geyer composed a letter to District Attorney Graham. "By Monday," he wrote, "we will have searched every outlying town except Irvington, and another day will conclude that. After Irvington, I scarcely know where we shall go."

Geyer and Gary took the trolley to Irvington early Tuesday morning, August 27. There were no hotels in town for the detectives to check, so they turned their attention instead to the real estate agents.

Not far from the trolley stop, Geyer spotted a sign for a real estate office run by a Mr. Brown. Inside, they discovered a pleasant-faced old man seated behind his desk. After making his introductions, Geyer asked Brown if he "knew of a house in this town which had been rented in October of 1894 by a man who said he wanted it for a widowed sister." Removing a well-worn photograph of Holmes from the package he carried, Geyer handed it to Brown, who adjusted his spectacles and studied the face for a long moment.

Finally the old man looked up from the picture and nodded. "Yes," he said. "I remember a man who rented a house under such circumstances in October of 1894, and this picture looks like him very much. I did not have the renting of the house, but I had the keys, and one day last fall, this man came into my office and in a very abrupt way said, 'I want the keys for that house.' I remember the man very well because I did not like his manner. I felt that he should have had more respect for my gray hairs."

For a few moments, Geyer and Gary simply stood there, frozen in place. Finally they turned, exchanged a look, and sank down into the two chairs facing Brown's desk.

"All the toil," Geyer later wrote, recalling the emotions of that moment, "all the weary days and weeks of travel—toil and travel in the hottest months of the year, alternating between faith and hope, and discouragement and despair—all were recompensed in that one instant, when I saw the veil about to lift and realized that we were soon to learn where the little boy had gone."

The detectives were out of their seats in an instant. Seeing the urgency in their faces, Brown volunteered to escort them to Dr. Thompson's home.

The physician, who lived only a short distance away, was seated in his office when the three men arrived. One look at Geyer's photographs was all Thompson needed to identify Holmes as the man who had rented his house the previous fall. He also told Geyer that a boy in his employ—a youngster named Elvet Moorman—had seen and spoken to Holmes.

At Geyer's request, Dr. Thompson sent his little daughter running for Moorman, who arrived a few minutes later. "Why, that is the man who lived in your house," the teenager exclaimed after studying Holmes's photograph. "The one who had the small boy with him." When Geyer showed him Howard Pitezel's picture, Moorman nodded emphatically. There was no doubt about it—that was the child he had seen at the house with the man.

By then, Geyer and Gary could scarcely contain their excitement. With Thompson leading the way, they hurried to the house, which stood a little distance from Union Avenue in the extreme eastern part of town.

The detectives made directly for the cellar, which was divided into two parts. In the rear compartment, which was evidently intended as a washroom, the floor was made of cement; in the front, hard clay. The detectives could see at a glance that both areas of the cellar floor were undisturbed. They decided to search the outside of the house.

A small wooden porch, its sides enclosed by latticework, extended from the right wing of the house. As Geyer peered through the latticework, something caught his eye.

Prying off the porch steps, he squeezed himself underneath and brought out the broken remnant of a wooden trunk.

For weeks, Geyer had been troubled by the mystery of the children's missing trunk. Now he felt certain that he had solved it. Taking a moment to examine this critical piece of evidence, he noticed a strip of blue calico, about two inches wide and printed with the figure of a white flower, which had been pasted along an inside seam, evidently as a patch.

Sticking his head back under the porch, Geyer detected a place where the earth looked disturbed. Procuring a shovel, he crawled back under the porch and dug up the spot to see if a body was buried there. But he found nothing.

Geyer and Gary spent the next few hours searching the premises without turning up anything incriminating. By then, a crowd of several hundred people had gathered around the house, milling about the property and seriously impeding the investigation. Evening was coming on, too, and—as Geyer was eager to interview the real estate agent who had rented the property to Holmes—he and Gary decided to suspend their search until the following day.

Taking the trolley back to Indianapolis, they sought out the agent, J. S. Crouse, who readily identified Holmes from Geyer's photograph. According to Crouse, Holmes had rented the house "for a widowed sister by the name of Mrs.

A. E. Cook." Crouse had received one month's rent in advance and had never seen the man again.

If the detectives still had any doubt that they had finally located the house, Crouse's testimony dispelled it. Geyer knew that Holmes had registered under the alias A. E. Cook during his trip to Cincinnati with the three Pitezel children.

The two men headed next to the Western Union office, where Geyer wired a message to Carrie Pitezel in Galva: "Did missing trunk have a strip of blue calico over seam, white figure on bottom?"

They were waiting for a reply when a telephone call came in from the *Indianapolis Evening News,* requesting that Geyer come immediately to the newspaper office. There, the city editor informed Geyer that an urgent message had just arrived from a physician named Barnhill—Dr. Thompson's partner. Barnhill was on his way from Irvington with "something important to communicate" and wanted Geyer to meet him at the news office.

A short time later, Barnhill hurried in, carrying a little bundle, which he immediately unwrapped on the city editor's desk.

Inside were several charred fragments of human bone—part of a femur and a chunk of skull, its sutures showing plainly. Barnhill was convinced that the remains were those of a child between the ages of eight and twelve.

In response to Geyer's questions, Barnhill explained that—after the detectives had departed—he and Dr. Thompson had continued to search the premises. In the meantime, a pair of neighborhood boys named Walter Jenny and Oscar Kettenbach had decided to "play detective" in the cellar.

A chimney stood in the rear part of the cellar against the farthermost wall. Sticking his hand into the pipe hole, young Walter pulled out a big handful of ashes. Among the ashes was a burnt chunk of bone. Reaching in again, he brought out more bones and ashes. At that point, the boys had run to call the doctors.

In spite of the lateness of the hour, Geyer and his partner hurried back to Irvington, where they found the house overrun with neighborhood curiosity seekers. The marshal of police was there, too, attempting to maintain order, and the three men finally cleared everyone out of the place except Drs. Thompson and Barnhill and several members of the press.

Proceeding to the cellar, Geyer used a hammer and chisel to take down the lower part of the chimney. Using an old fly screen as a sieve, he began sifting the ashes and soot from the chimney.

Almost at once he found a complete set of teeth and part of a lower jaw.

A few minutes later, he pulled a large, charred mass from the bottom of the chimney. It was baked so hard that Dr. Thompson had some difficulty cutting it open.

Inside were the blackened remains of a stomach, liver, spleen, and intestines.

After two grueling months, Frank Geyer had found Howard Pitezel.

The discoveries of that day were the stuff of nightmare. Yet back in his hotel room, Geyer enjoyed a sweet and dreamless sleep.

He did not bask in self-satisfaction for long, however. The success of his quest had brought him personal fame. But as an agent of justice, he knew that his mission wasn't completed. As Geyer put it, "all that had been unearthed would count but for little if Holmes were permitted to elude the firm grasp of the law or to avoid punishment."

The most important task still remained: "The greatest of criminals had yet to be brought to answer for his deeds."

Part 5

The Devil to Pay

45

> I have commenced to write a careful and truthful account of all matters pertaining to my case.
>
> —From the prison diary of H. H. Holmes

Two weeks after it was vacated by the Chicago police, H. H. Holmes's "Horror Castle"—newly remodeled as a tourist attraction under the management of A. M. Clark—was almost ready to receive its first paying customers. But shortly after midnight on Monday, August 19, Clark's get-rich-quick dreams went up, quite literally, in smoke.

No one ever found out how the fire started. Some saw it as an act of divine retribution—God's furious purging of Holmes's iniquitous den. The police, on the other hand, took a more down-to-earth view, suspecting that one or more of Holmes's confederates had started the blaze to conceal incriminating evidence that the investigators had overlooked.

Whatever its source, the fire made short shrift of the building, confirming Inspector Laughlin's assessment of the Castle's "combustibility." At precisely 12:13 A.M., George J. Myler—a night watchman at the Western Indiana railroad crossing—spotted flames shooting from the Castle's roof. Before he could turn in an alarm, a series of explosions rocked the building, blowing out the windows of Fred Barton's ground-floor candy shop. By the time the first engines arrived, the fire was already out of control.

A half hour later the roof collapsed, taking down part of

the building's rear wall. Under the direction of Chief Kenyon, the firefighters managed to keep the conflagration from spreading to the flat frame houses in the rear. Nevertheless, by the time the blaze was extinguished, at around one-thirty A.M., much of the Castle had been consumed.

Though the ground-floor shops sustained only minimal damage, the two upper stories were completely gutted. Altogether the losses amounted to approximately $25,000. The "murder museum" was a blackened shell, and A. M. Clark—former cop and would-be impresario—was out of show business for good.

Others, however, had better luck in exploiting the public's obsession with Holmes. In Philadelphia, for example, C. A. Bradenburgh—whose Dime Museum on Ninth and Arch streets specialized in such topflight attractions as "The Fat Ladies' Wood-Sawing Contest," "Professor Catulli's Naiads of the Phosphorescent Fountain," and "Count Ivan Orloff, The Living Transparent Man"—drew in large crowds during the summer months by converting his establishment into a "Holmes Museum." Included in the exhibit were a scale-model replica of the Castle, phrenological charts illustrating the archfiend's cranial abnormalities, and a human skull whose measurements were purportedly identical to those of Benjamin Pitezel.

For readers whose interest had not been slaked by weeks of front-page news coverage, the bookshops were full of pulp, true-crime paperbacks on the case. Most of these were simple rehashes, cobbled together from previously published accounts. Others—like *Sold to Satan: A Poor Wife's Sad Story*—offered new (and wholly fabricated) revelations about the archfiend's murderous career.

The appearance of these shoddy "instant" books, which proliferated in the months of Holmes's imprisonment, further ratified his status as a genuine cultural phenomenon. For Holmes was not merely America's original serial killer. He was its first celebrity psycho.

Psychopath or not, Holmes was no fool, and he quickly perceived the commercial potential of his infamy. Clearly, there was a booming market for books on his case. Even unalloyed hackwork was selling briskly—cut-and-paste jobs like Robert L. Corbitt's *The Holmes Castle* and the anonymous *Holmes, the Arch Fiend, or: A Carnival of Crime. Sold to Satan*, the trashiest of the lot, was such an immediate success that it was quickly translated into several languages, including German (*Dem Teufel verkauft Holmes!*) and Swedish (*Massemorderen Holmes, alias Mudgett*). Frank Geyer himself would ultimately cash in on the craze, publishing his own bestselling account, *The Holmes-Pitezel Case: A History of the Greatest Crime of the Century.*

Seeing a prime opportunity to profit from his crimes, Holmes decided to produce his own book.

He had another motive besides simple avarice for undertaking the project. If the newspapers had been reckless in their accusations against Holmes, some of the new books were completely unbridled. The anonymous author of *Sold to Satan*, for example, went so far as to blame him for the notorious 1879 killing of a New York City socialite, Mrs. Jane Lawrence DeForrest Hull, who had been strangled in her bedroom by a vagrant named Chastain Cox. According to this writer, Cox had committed the crime while under the hypnotic influence of Holmes, who had mesmerized the "mulatto brute" and sent him off to slay the "splendid woman" for no other motive than "pure deviltry." Cox was "but the ignorant puppet in the hands of the hideous creature who, by his diabolical power, caused him to do as he did."

Holmes saw his book as a way of countering such charges. In its pages, readers would discover a personality very different from the Holmes of popular myth—not a blood-crazed monster but a common (and not especially successful) crook. With his trial date nearing, it is easy to see why he was eager to present himself in the most innocuous light—as "a swindler, yes, but innocent of murder." Though cast as an autobiography, the book was actually intended as Holmes's personal public-relations campaign.

After enlisting a freelance journalist named John King to assist him with every phase of the project, from copyediting to promotion, Holmes commenced his handwritten account in midsummer 1895. By early fall, *Holmes' Own Story* was already on the stands, published by the Philadelphia firm of Burk & McFethridge.

A fat, paperbound volume priced at twenty-five cents, the book follows Holmes's criminal career from his boyhood to imprisonment. An engraved likeness of its infamous author adorns the cover. Holmes's efforts to humanize himself in the eyes of the world are immediately apparent in this picture. It is hard to conceive of a less menacing figure than the portly, bearded gentleman who stares gravely at the viewer like a bank president posing for a company portrait.

Though Holmes had a taste for good fiction (he whiled away his time in prison reading Victor Hugo's *Les Misérables*), his own book is more or less completely devoid of literary merit, veering wildly between mawkish sentimentality and lurid melodrama. What unifies the work is its overwritten style—prose, as one commentator put it, "of the most vibrant purple"—and its shamelessly self-serving intent. For all his attempts to project an air of candor and sincerity, his deeply manipulative nature comes through in every line.

Even before the story proper begins, Holmes starts pulling out the emotional stops, making a flagrantly flag-waving appeal to his readers' patriotic feelings. "My sole object in this publication," he intones in a brief preface, "is to vindicate my name from the horrible aspersions cast upon it, and to appeal to a fair-minded American public for a suspension of judgment, and for that free and fair trial which is the birthright of every American citizen, and the pride and bulwark of our American constitution."

The story opens with a cloying evocation of Holmes's childhood world. "Come with me, if you will, to a tiny, quiet New England village, nestling among the picturesquely rugged hills of New Hampshire.... Here, in the year 1861, I, Herman Mudgett, the author of these pages, was born. That the first years of my life were different from those of any other ordinary country-bred boy, I have no reason to think. That I was well-trained by loving and religious parents, I know, and any deviations in my after life from the straight and narrow way of rectitude are not attributable to the want of a tender mother's prayers or a father's control."

Despite his insistence on the normalcy of his background, however, an unsettling, even sinister, note immediately intrudes. In place of the pleasant recollections one might expect from such an idyllic introduction, Holmes describes a number of disturbing, if not traumatic, childhood events. He recalls the time his sadistic schoolmates dragged him through the "awful portals" of the village doctor's office and brought him "face to face" with the "grinning skeleton" dangling from its wooden display stand. He recounts an incident in which an itinerant photographer, who had set up shop in the village, removed his wooden leg in front of the eight-year-old boy, providing little Herman with his first, horrified view of an amputated limb. And he lingers over an episode in which he mailed away his "entire wealth" for a treasured watch and chain that turned out to be dross. Within days of its arrival, its "wheels had ceased to turn, its gold had lost its lustre, and the whole affair had turned into an occasion of ridicule for my companions and of self-reproach to myself."

A common theme informs these memories—a sense of the world's duplicitous nature, of the underlying foulness and corruption concealed beneath the bright, innocent surface of things. That Holmes selects these particular experiences to represent his earliest life reveals more, perhaps, about the fundamental darkness of his vision than he intended.

If *Holmes' Own Story* has any claim to distinction, it lies in the work's stunningly self-justifying quality. The book is a tour de force of rationalization, the printed equivalent of one of Harry Houdini's escape acts. For two hundred pages, the reader cannot help but be amazed as Holmes performs the most painful contortions to wriggle free of blame. And when the irrefutable facts make it impossible for him to do so, he resorts to a simple expedient—he refuses to acknowledge their existence. Thus, he makes no mention at all of his New Hampshire wife, Clara Lovering (or, for that matter, of his second, bigamous marriage to Myrta Belknap).

After briefly attending the University of Vermont at Burlington, Holmes moved to Ann Arbor to complete his medical education. Beyond a titillating allusion to "some ghastly experiences" in the dissection room, he provides no details about those years. He is at pains, however, to deny one of the more sensational charges leveled against him—that he paid his way through college by robbing graves and peddling the cadavers to his fellow students as anatomical specimens. To bolster his assertion, Holmes points to the "well-known fact that in the State of Michigan, all the material necessary for dissection work is supplied by the state."

Holmes describes his first, aborted venture as a swindler at some length, though—characteristically—he glosses over its more repellent details. After a stint teaching school in Mooers Fork, New York, he opened a doctor's office in the village, providing "good and conscientious service" in return for "plenty of gratitude but little or no money." With "starvation . . . staring me in the face," Holmes (so he implies) had no other choice but to swindle an insurance company, deploying a plan he had worked out with a Canadian friend, a former fellow student at Ann Arbor.

The convolutions of this scheme defy paraphrase. As Holmes explains it:

> At some future date a man whom my friend knew and could trust, who then carried considerable life insurance, was to increase the same so that the total amount carried should be $40,000; and as he was a man of moderate circumstances, he was to have it understood that some sudden danger he had escaped (a runaway accident) had impelled him to more fully protect his family in the future. Later, he should become addicted to drink, and while temporarily insane from its use should, as it would appear, kill his wife and child.
>
> In reality, they were to go the extreme West and await his arrival there at a later date. Suddenly, the husband was to disappear, and some months later a body badly decomposed and dressed in the clothing he was known to wear was to be found, and with it a statement to the effect that while in a drunken rage he had killed his family and had shipped their dismembered bodies to two separate and distant warehouses to conceal the crime, first

having partially preserved the remains by placing them in strong brine. That he did not care to live longer, and that his property and insurance should pass to a relative whom he was to designate in this letter.

At the proper time, he was to join his family in the West and remain there permanently, the relative collecting the insurance, a part of which was to be sent to him, a part to be retained by the relative, and the remainder to be divided between us [i.e., Holmes and his Canadian friend].

As Holmes diplomatically puts it, this scheme called for "a considerable amount of material"—namely three dead bodies to pass off as the remains of the husband, wife, and child. Holmes and his Canadian accomplice agreed "that they should both contribute to the necessary supply."

The conspirators did not have a chance to put their scheme into motion until 1886, when Holmes was living in Chicago. After securing two corpses—"my portion of the material," as he puts it—from an unnamed source, Holmes was suddenly called away to New York City. For reasons he chooses not to explain, he "decided to take a part of the material there and leave the balance in a Chicago warehouse. This necessitated repacking the same."

One of the most chilling aspects of Holmes's autobiography is his consistent reference to dead bodies as "material," as though decomposed corpses were simply the stuff of his trade—the equivalent of a seamstress's cloth or a cobbler's leather.

Registering in a downtown hotel, Holmes "divided the material into two packages," placed one in the Fidelity Storage Warehouse and shipped the second to New York City.

The plan, however, was never realized. Shortly after his return to Chicago, Holmes came across several newspaper accounts "of the detection of crime connected with this class of work" and realized "for the first time how well organized and well prepared the leading insurance companies were to detect and punish this kind of fraud." "This," he writes, "together with the sudden death of my friend, caused all to be abandoned."

The abrupt cancellation of his scheme left Holmes with two dead bodies to dispose of—a problem he solved by burning part of the "material" in the furnace of his Castle and burying the remainder in a remote corner of the cellar. Holmes describes this operation in the most matter-of-fact tone, as though the household incineration of human corpses were a routine domestic chore. He concludes by insisting that the skeletal remains "lately found" in the Castle by police investigators were nothing but the burned and buried scraps of these discarded cadavers.

In recounting this episode—and another, similar adventure that turned into a kind of ghastly comedy of errors when Holmes's custom-designed, corpse-smuggling trunk sprang a leak—Holmes clearly intends to create an impression of disarming frankness. Indeed, judging by the self-satisfied tone that occasionally creeps into his narrative, he apparently feels that he deserves credit for the ingenuity of his schemes and the energy with which he pursued them. Once again, he appears completely oblivious of the true picture he projects—of a life steeped in the stench of decomposed corpses, and a sensibility so warped that it regards a dead child's body as a financial resource.

At this point in the story, Benjamin Pitezel first appears on the scene. Since Pitezel's murder was the immediate charge confronting Holmes, he spends much of the book exonerating himself of the crime by depicting his late accomplice as a hopeless, embittered failure who neglected his children, abused his wife, and ultimately took his own life in a fit of drunken despair.

This portrait of Pitezel is consistent with Holmes's strategy throughout the book. To counter the "horrible aspersions cast upon" his name, he relies on the clever device of casting horrible aspersions upon others. At the same time, he presents himself as a model of affection and fidelity—a devoted friend and patron who did everything in his power to assist Pitezel and his family, but, in the end, could not save his wayward associate from those "pernicious habits" that finally drove him to suicide.

Even more egregious in this regard is Holmes's portrait of Minnie Williams—a woman, by all accounts, of such extreme naïveté that she sometimes appeared to possess as little worldly sense as a newborn. In Holmes's version, she emerges as a hardened sophisticate with a highly checkered past—a woman who had been seduced and betrayed by various lovers; suffered a nervous collapse after aborting an illegitimate child; been committed to a mental institution; slaughtered her own sister in a jealous rage; and ultimately absconded to London to open a "massage establishment" with her current lover, a shadowy character named "Edward Hatch."

Of the countless fabrications in the book, perhaps the most fascinating is Hatch, the mysterious being on whom Holmes pins the deaths of the three Pitezel children. There is no doubt that Hatch was pure invention. At the time of Holmes's trial, thirty-five witnesses—from Cincinnati, Indianapolis, Detroit, Toronto, and Burlington—traveled to Philadelphia to offer their testimony. None had ever seen the children in the company of anyone but Holmes.

In Holmes's telling, however, Hatch "accompanied us" everywhere. It was Hatch who took Howard away on the day the boy was murdered; Hatch into whose care Holmes placed Alice and Nellie; Hatch who was with the girls in Toronto the last time Holmes saw the two sisters alive.

And yet, Hatch remains a completely amorphous figure in the book—Holmes supplies him with no dialogue, no distinguishing features, no psychological motivation. As the story progresses, the reader comes to see Hatch less as a separate human being than as a dark alter ego: the name Holmes gives to his own most malevolent tendencies. Indeed the name itself—with its suggestions of subterfuge (as in "to hatch a plot") and concealment (as in "to keep under hatches")—points in this direction. It is as if Holmes were unconsciously confirming the popular comparison of himself with Dr. Henry Jekyll, and creating, in the sinister figure of Edward Hatch, his own version of Robert Louis Stevenson's Edward Hyde.

In recounting his journey back to Gilmanton just before his arrest, Holmes goes straight for the reader's heartstrings:

"My pen cannot adequately portray the meeting with my aged parents, nor, were it possible, would I allow it to do so for publication. Suffice it to say that I came to them as one dead, they for years having considered me as such.... That after embracing them, as I looked into their dear faces once more, my eyes grew dim with the tears kindly sent to shut out for the moment the signs of added years I knew my uncalled-for silence of the past seven years had done much to unnecessarily increase." Holmes's self-described ability to "let loose the font of emotions" is nowhere more apparent than in the trumped-up pathos of this episode.

Shameless to the end, Holmes concludes his book by insisting that his own fate is a matter of indifference to him, and that his single concern is to see justice served: "And here I cannot say finis—it is not the end—for besides doing this there is also the work of bringing to justice those for whose wrong-doings I am today suffering; and this is not to prolong or even save my own life, for since the day I heard of the Toronto horror I have not cared to live."

For a man who had given up on life, Holmes took an exceptionally active interest in the success of his book. Shortly after the manuscript had been transcribed by a professional typist and was ready to be sent to the printer, Holmes composed a letter to his associate, John King:

Dear Sir:

My ideas are that you should get from the New York *Herald* and the Philadelphia *Press* all the cuts they have and turn those we want over to the printer, to have them electroplated at his expense. Use the large cut with full beard published August 25 in the *Herald* for my picture on page opposite the opening chapter, having the autographs of my two names (Holmes and Mudgett) engraved and electroplated at the same time, to go under the picture....

As soon as the book is published, get it onto the Philadelphia and New York newsstands. Then get reliable canvassers who will work afternoons here in Philadelphia. Take one good street at a time, leave the book, then return about a half hour later for the money. No use to do this in the forenoon, when people are busy. I canvassed when a student this way, and found the method successful.

Then, if you have any liking for the road, go over the ground covered by the book, spending a few days in Chicago, Detroit, and Indianapolis. Give copies to the newspapers in these cities to comment upon, it will assist the sale.

Holmes's eagerness to see the book distributed was a function, in part, of his business acumen—his desire to exploit his notoriety while public interest in the case was at its peak. But there was another reason for his urgency. On September 23, 1895, he was arraigned at the Philadelphia Court of Oyer and Terminer, and his trial date set for October 28.

If he hoped (as he wrote in his preface) to "appeal to a fair-minded American public for a suspension of judgment" and a "free and fair trial," he was rapidly running out of time.

46

The Holmes case, whose shocking details have had
world-wide notoriety, has from the time of the discovery of Benjamin F. Pitezel's corpse in the old house
on Callowhill Street been conspicuous for one feature. In the unfolding of its mysteries, in the exploration of its dark windings and turnings from city to
city, it has always been the unexpected, the sensational, or the dramatic that has happened. The opening of the trial was no exception.

—*The Chicago Tribune,* October 29, 1895

"The Trial of the Century," as it was touted by the press,
opened on a brilliant fall morning, Monday, October 28,
1895. For the six days of its duration, it held the nation in
thrall. Only the murder trial of Lizzie Borden, two years
earlier, had generated comparable excitement. America
would not see the like again until 1924, when Clarence Dar-
row defended a pair of pampered, teenaged "thrill killers"
named Leopold and Loeb.

With Holmes's notoriety having spread overseas, newspapermen from every corner of the country were joined in
Philadelphia by a contingent of European correspondents.
Local dignitaries, including Mayor Warwick himself, occupied front-row seats or—in the case of such "guest jurists"
as ex–Chief Justice Paxson—places of honor beside the presiding judge. A number of Philadelphia's most prominent
clergymen were also in attendance, drawn, perhaps, by the

unprecedented opportunity to get a firsthand glimpse of the
Adversary in his most up-to-date guise.

A crowd of onlookers—large enough (as one newsman
observed) to "pack the Academy of Music"—began gathering outside the courthouse at daybreak, hoping for seats in
the gallery. But the trial was the hottest ticket in town.
Those without some political pull found it almost impossible
to gain admission. A squad of police officers under the command of Sergeant Newman was stationed at the entranceway
to maintain order and screen aspiring spectators.

For the most part, ordinary citizens had to content them-
selves with the newspaper accounts. Day after day, the front
page of *The Philadelphia Inquirer* read like the program
for a popular melodrama: HOLMES PLACED ON TRIAL:
PROCEEDINGS ARE FILLED WITH INTERESTING
INCIDENTS AND UNUSUAL SCENES! HOLMES
FIGHTS FOR HIS LIFE: QUICK AND STARTLING
CHANGES MARK THE SECOND DAY OF THE RE-
MARKABLE TRIAL! MRS. PITEZEL'S SAD STORY: A
SCENE OF DRAMATIC INTEREST!

And indeed, the Holmes case would offer the public a full
range of theatrical experience, from tragedy to farce, with a
star performance "that kept the onlookers spellbound" (as
the *Inquirer* reported). The opening-day audience was prepared for a sensation—and no one went home disappointed.

Even before the first witness was called, the histrionics
began.

With his silky white hair, bushy black brows, and grave
demeanor, the Honorable Michael Arnold was the very picture of judicial solemnity as he entered the courtroom—an
impression heightened by his new, flowing black gown, a
ritual vestment that the Philadelphia judiciary had only recently adopted. (Indeed, the proceedings were a minor mile-
stone in this regard, marking the first time in the city's
history that a gowned judge presided at a murder trial.)

No sooner had Judge Arnold seated himself than another,
equally compelling figure appeared in the room, led in
through a side door by a pair of grim-faced bailiffs. All eyes
turned to Holmes as he took his place in the prisoner's dock,

a waist-high enclosure of heavy wire mesh positioned beside the defense table.

In the six months since he last stood in the courtroom to answer the charge of conspiracy, Holmes had undergone a striking transformation. Now thin to the point of frailness, he wore a black double-breasted suit that emphasized his jailhouse pallor. His fierce, heavy mustache had been carefully trimmed and the squareness of his jawline softened by a neat Vandyke beard. With his fine features and wan complexion, he projected an air of almost feminine delicacy—though one reporter remarked on the distinctive shape of his nose, "sharp and marked with those peculiar indentations that Dickens always ascribed to characters with cruel natures."

As to Holmes's frame of mind, opinions varied. After placing his derby on the floor beside his chair and lowering himself onto the seat, he cast a sweeping glance around the crowded courtroom. Some observers perceived in that look a flash of his old audacity and defiance. Others took note of the heavy volume he kept clutched in one hand. Believing it a Bible, they speculated that perhaps Holmes had found religion during the dark days of his imprisonment. (In fact, the book was a copy of Stephen's *Digest of the Laws of Evidence*.)

And some detected uncharacteristic signs of agitation in the notoriously unflappable archcriminal. His tapered fingers twitched, his eyes shifted nervously about, and he could not seem to position himself comfortably in his seat. Fidgeting with the chair, he accidentally set one of its legs onto his derby, hopelessly crushing the hat out of shape.

But if Holmes was feeling anxious, he quickly recovered his sangfroid. Indeed, he was about to put on one of the most remarkable displays of self-assurance his audience had ever witnessed.

Jury selection was the first order of business. Before the first talesman could be questioned, however, one of Holmes's lawyers, William A. Shoemaker—who had come rushing into the courtroom only moments before, having somehow contrived to be fifteen minutes late for the most important occasion of his career—sprang to his feet. Speaking in a thin, reedy voice that barely carried to the bench, Shoemaker requested a continuance, arguing that "the time allowed for the preparation of the defense in this case, commencing with the indictment, has been hopelessly short and inadequate."

Judge Arnold turned his gaze toward the prosecutor's table and addressed District Attorney George Graham. "Do you agree to this postponement?"

Graham rose from his seat. "I do not," he answered emphatically. With his black frock coat and abundant mustache, Graham—a tall, clean-favored forty-five-year-old—was an imposing figure. He was also an extraordinarily popular one, currently serving his fifth three-year term as Philadelphia's district attorney. "This motion comes within no rule of the court, except that it may be an appeal to Your Honor's discretion, and I strenuously oppose the motion for a continuance."

Unlike Shoemaker—who had been told repeatedly by the judge to "speak louder"—Graham required no such admonition. His sonorous voice carried to every corner of the room. "Witnesses have been gathered from states far distant from here who are voluntarily in attendance and have come simply because of their duty to the cause of justice," he argued. "I cannot compel their attendance, and I am quite sure I will never be able to get these witnesses here again. If a continuance is granted, it means absolute destruction of the Commonwealth's case."

His voice took on even more dramatic shadings. "There is one person who has been subjected to an unusual—nay, an awful!—strain, and that is Mrs. Pitezel, the widow of the deceased. Her condition is such that it is absolutely perilous to the Commonwealth's case to permit it to go over again. These gentlemen have had full and complete time for preparation. No legal grounds have been laid, and therefore I object to the continuance."

No sooner had he finished speaking than Holmes's other attorney, Samuel Rotan—a moon-faced young man with a florid complexion made even rosier by the flush of emotion now spreading across it—leapt to his feet. "May it please this honorable court," he began. "This man is charged with a crime which is the highest known to the law! It is the purpose of the district attorney, as stated in the newspapers—"

"I beg your pardon," interrupted Graham. "My purpose has not been stated in the newspapers. On the other hand, the statements of the defense have been numerously and copiously quoted."

"I have only to say," Rotan retorted, "that I will leave it to those who read the newspapers to say where those purposes come from."

Judge Arnold's gavel came down sharply, cutting short this dispute. "We are not trying the newspapers," he snapped. "The motion to continue the case is overruled. Let the jury be called."

With that, Lawyer Shoemaker cleared his throat and addressed the bench. His voice was still so soft that many of the spectators had to strain to hear him. But in the quiet of the courtroom, his words exploded like a bomb:

"The step we are about to take fills us with the greatest pain and regret. We are profoundly sensible of its seriousness, of its unusual occurrence. But with respect to this court, in justice to our client, and in consideration of the duty we owe to ourselves, we must ask Your Honor to permit us to withdraw from this case, however painful it may be. We cannot continue in it."

At this extraordinary pronouncement, the audience broke into an astonished buzz. Banging his gavel for silence, Judge Arnold looked sternly at Shoemaker. "Counsel in a case like this have no right to withdraw. Your duty is to remain. Of course, I cannot force you to stay and do your duty. The remedy of the Court is—if counsel withdraw upon the eve of a murder trial without consent—to enter a rule on them to show cause why they should not be disbarred."

Standing beside his senior colleague, Lawyer Rotan took up the argument. Without a "reasonable" delay to permit them to gather the necessary witnesses, the trial, he insisted, would be "a farce."

"It will be no farce," Judge Arnold replied grimly. "Call a jury!"

Barely thirty minutes had elapsed since the trial had

started. But the atmosphere was already so charged that even District Attorney Graham seemed unsettled by the tension. Uncharacteristically, he allowed his impatience to flare during his examination of the first prospective juror, a streetcar conductor named Enoch Turner.

In response to Graham's lead question, Turner acknowledged that, based on his newspaper reading, he had already formed an opinion as to Holmes's guilt.

"Could you, notwithstanding that opinion, enter the jury box, and under your oath as a juror, try this case upon the evidence as you hear it in the courtroom, aside from what you might have read in the papers?" inquired Graham.

"Well, I might," offered Turner.

"Don't you know whether you could or not?"

"I don't know that I could."

"You are called as a juror in this case to try it according to the evidence," Graham continued, sounding more exasperated by the moment. "What I want to know is this: Can you not take your place under the obligation of your oath and try this man fairly and impartially according to the evidence as you hear it in the courtroom?"

Turner thought this over for a moment before replying, "Well, I hardly know."

"Haven't you strength of mind enough," Graham snapped, "to try this case according to the evidence as you hear it in court and lay aside these outside objections?"

"Yes, sir," Turner said sheepishly.

Having finally managed to say the right thing, Turner was approved by the Commonwealth.

All during this interrogation, Holmes had been huddling with his attorneys. Now, Rotan turned to the bench and announced that his client wished to make a statement.

Standing in the dock, Holmes addressed the judge in a tone of humble entreaty—the voice of a man who has no thought for himself, only the welfare of others. "May it please the Court, I have no intention to ask Mr. Rotan and Mr. Shoemaker to continue in this case when I can see that it is against their own interests. Bearing that fact in mind, I ask to discharge them from the case. These gentlemen have stood by me during the last year, and I cannot ask them at this time to stay when it is against their interest—"

"We do not want the Court to receive the impression we are deserting this man," Rotan interrupted. "He now states that he would rather go on with the case himself."

Ignoring the rotund attorney, Judge Arnold spoke directly to Holmes. "You cannot discharge them, Mr. Holmes. That is for the Court, and if they decide to withdraw from this case, they will be punished."

"If Your Honor will only give me until tomorrow to secure additional counsel," implored Holmes in a tremulous voice.

"We will have no more debate, Mr. Holmes," the judge replied, then turned to Shoemaker and Rotan, who were holding a hurried, whispered parlay with their client. "Are you going to examine this juror?" Arnold asked with some asperity. "If not, he goes into the jury box."

Rotan glanced up at the judge. "May it please the Court, the defendant says that he intends to examine these talesmen himself, that he does not want us to interfere with the examination of them, and that is what he is going to do."

Judge Arnold looked at Holmes. "If you wish to do your own examining, you may do so. It is your constitutional right to try your own case."

While Rotan and Shoemaker reseated themselves at the defense table, Holmes placed his hands on the dock rail and leaned toward the witness stand. After putting a few questions to talesman Turner—who reaffirmed that he had "formed an opinion as to the probable guilt or innocence of the defendant"—Holmes used one of his twenty peremptory challenges to have the man dismissed.

At that point, Rotan spoke up again. "May it please Your Honor, there is no use at all for Mr. Shoemaker and me to stay here. The defendant is going on and will not allow us to do anything. We ask leave to withdraw. We do so reluctantly, and at the same time, it is with full appreciation of what we are doing."

The judge gave a sigh of resignation. "Very well. But you will have to bear the consequences—and you know what they are."

Then, while the spectators gasped in amazement, Holmes's attorney's picked up their briefcases, put on their hats, and marched from the room.

It took a moment for Judge Arnold to restore the court to order. When the audience finally settled down, he turned to the prisoner and said, "Mr. Holmes, you have discharged your attorneys. We intend to go on with this case, and you may as well cease your efforts to force a continuance. You are now your own lawyer."

With that, Holmes armed himself with pencil and paper and proceeded to put on a show. The audience sat spellbound as he underwent an amazing transformation. From the emotion-choked supplicant of a few moments before, he turned into a "cool, collected" figure (as one eyewitness reported), "handling his own case with a readiness that would have done credit to the most experienced lawyer at the bar." Examining each of the talesmen in turn, he displayed a canniness and skill that brought grunts of grudging admiration even from a few representatives of the Commonwealth.

His questions focused largely on the publicity surrounding the case. Each prospect was asked if he had visited the "sensational display" at the Dime Museum on Ninth and Arch streets or arrived at a conviction based on his newspaper reading. Judge Arnold was obliged to point out to Holmes that "an opinion formed on the basis of what appears in the public print is no longer a sufficient cause for challenge. It was at one time. It was found impossible to enforce it as a reason for excluding jurors. Newspapers are so numerous that everybody now reads them, and, of course, they obtain impressions from them. Therefore, unless his opinion is so fixed as to be immovable, the juror is competent."

"Is it my privilege to take an exception to that rule?" Holmes inquired.

"Yes," said the judge. "You are entitled to that."

"Then I wish one noted," the defendant replied. Describing Holmes's demeanor at that moment, one commentator observed that "Blackstone himself could not have handled the situation with more aplomb."

In another instance, Holmes challenged a prospect for the

opposite reason—not because the juror, a railroad watchman named James Collins, had been influenced by the newspapers but because he strained credulity by insisting that he had never read a single word about the case. After the man was dismissed, Holmes turned to the audience with an expression of exaggerated disbelief that brought appreciative chuckles from the gallery.

The Commonwealth, meanwhile, reserved most of its challenges for those with a bias against capital punishment. A paper-bag manufacturer named Harry S. Coles, for example, was denied a place on the jury after admitting to "scruples on the subject of capital punishment"—a position he himself clearly regarded as a somewhat embarrassing character flaw.

"You are now called upon to act here as a juror," District Attorney Graham reminded him, "where you have nothing to do with the question of punishment, but simply the guilt or innocence of this prisoner. Can you not enter the jury box and discharge your duty according to the evidence?"

"No, sir," Coles replied. "Not if it was murder in the first degree. I could not conscientiously do it." A self-reproachful note entered his voice. "It is a weak point of mine."

"When did you first form that opinion?"

"That has been a fault of mine ever since I have been married, for the last fifteen years."

Graham's eyebrows rose. "Surely your being married has nothing to do with it."

"Well, I know," Coles acknowledged with an apologetic shrug. "It has always been my fault."

Having admitted to such a shameful weakness, Coles was challenged for cause and dismissed.

By two o'clock, the jury had been impaneled and sworn. It consisted of a blacksmith, a paymaster, a carter, a soapmaker, a farmer, a liveryman, an engineer, a shoemaker, a housepainter, a florist, a yarn manufacturer, and a wagon builder.

The senior member of the group was named jury foreman. This was Linford Biles, the gray-whiskered, sixty-four-year-old widower whose house had nearly caught fire on the very day of Holmes's arrest when a shower of electrical sparks had rained onto his roof from the crossed wires overhead.

At precisely three P.M., following a one-hour lunch recess, District Attorney Graham began his opening address. His speech went on for close to an hour and forty-five minutes. All during this time, Holmes listened intently from the prisoner's dock, taking copious notes and occasionally consulting his volume of Stephen's *Digest of the Laws of Evidence*.

After rehearsing the technical details of the charge, Graham declared that, while it was within the jury's power to find one of four verdicts—manslaughter, murder in the second degree, murder in the first degree, or acquittal—there was, in reality, only "one verdict you will be able to find. Either this man in the dock willfully, deliberately, and premeditatedly killed Benjamin F. Pitezel, or he did not. If he did not, then of course, he is to be acquitted. But if he did, under the circumstances of the case, the evidence that he has committed it cannot, in my judgment, fall below that of the highest grade known to the law—murder of the first degree."

Graham then launched into a detailed account of the crime, beginning with the discovery of Pitezel's burned and blackened body. He described the exhumation of the corpse, the payment of the insurance policy, the division of the spoils between Holmes and Jeptha Howe. But greed, he asserted, was not Holmes's only motive for murdering his faithful accomplice. The alcoholic Pitezel, with his drink-loosened tongue and intimate knowledge of Holmes's many crimes, had become an active danger to his longtime employer.

Next, Graham told of Holmes's fateful encounter with Marion Hedgepeth, of the double cross that provoked the latter into betraying the insurance scheme to the police, and of Holmes's devious movements through the Midwest and up into Canada with the helpless Pitezel family in his power and the Pinkertons at his heels.

"This man had a great job on his hands," Graham said to the jury, his voice heavy with sarcasm. "He moved these people in three detachments. In one, he had himself and Georgiana Yoke, the beguiled woman he calls his wife. In another, he had Mrs. Pitezel, Dessie, and the baby. And in still another, he had Alice, Nellie, and Howard. He moved these three detachments separately, without any member of one encountering any member of the others. What a general! I am not surprised that this man undertakes to defend himself. I have no doubt that he will do it better than any lawyer that could be found. A man who could conduct three detachments and keep each one ignorant of the others is a general indeed."

For the most part, this story was familiar to the jurors, all of whom had admitted under questioning that they had kept up with the case in the newspapers. But Graham elicited some shocked reactions—and brought blushes to the cheeks of the ladies in the house—when he insinuated that, during the night they had spent in Philadelphia at Adella Alcorn's rooming house, Holmes had violated the innocence of Alice Pitezel.

"This man took Alice Pitezel, a fifteen-year-old girl, to 1905 North Eleventh Street," Graham said harshly, aiming an accusatory finger at Holmes, "and represented her as his sister, and they were given adjoining rooms. His sister! His sister! I will show you that he occupied the same room with that little girl at 1905 North Eleventh Street!"

Holmes—whose expression up to this point had been as blank as the court stenographer's—started at this charge and half-rose from his chair, as though he were about to raise an outraged objection. After a moment, however, he seemed to think better of it, settled back in his seat, and returned to taking notes.

Graham caused another sensation a bit later when he recounted Holmes's failed attempt to obliterate the rest of the Pitezel family with a bottle of nitroglycerin—a part of the story that had never been made public before.

"Holmes asked Mrs. Pitezel to handle an explosive that was sufficient to blow up a whole row of houses," Graham said, "in the hope that it might explode while she had it in her possession and kill her and the two children left to her. But no, she was not to die then and is living yet. Can it be that it was a providential preservation, in order that the links might be brought together and this man receive the punishment he deserves? Mrs. Pitezel, though a wreck of what she was, is still living and able to tell her story, as she will in a very short while tell you the whole pitiable story from beginning to end."

Graham concluded as he had begun, by repeating that "there is only one grade of guilt applicable to this crime, and that is murder in the first degree—the punishment for which is death."

It was almost four forty-five P.M. by the time the district attorney was finished. Approaching the bench, he held a brief consultation with Judge Arnold, who then adjourned court until ten the next morning. The bailiffs stepped to the dock to conduct the defendant from the room.

"With that," wrote the correspondent for the *Chicago Tribune,* "Holmes arose from his chair, and the last sensation of a day replete with extraordinary incidents occurred."

Speaking in a voice "vibrating with emotions," Holmes addressed the judge. "May it please Your Honor," he began, "I am forced to ask that certain privileges be accorded me in prison. They are not very extensive privileges." His cell, he explained, lacked sufficient light for him to work at night. Therefore, he would require a lamp, as well as "paper and writing materials," so "that I may be enabled to prepare my case."

Then, looking defiantly at the district attorney, he demanded that he be permitted "to interview a certain party—my wife!"

"Which wife?" Graham retorted.

Holmes drew himself up to his full height. "You well know whom I mean, Mr. Graham," he said indignantly.

"I don't know. I know you have a wife in New Hampshire and another in Wilmette, Illinois, and then there is a Miss Yoke in this city."

"That there shall be no mistake," Holmes said bitterly, "I mean the woman you insultingly call Miss Yoke. Can I send word to her? I would like to see her."

"She won't see you. You had the opportunity of seeing her in my office, but she shunned you."

"I never had! I say that I was legally married to this woman two years ago, and there has been no separation except that brought about by you."

"It is only her own choice," Graham said with a shrug. "It is a matter of indifference to me whether she sees you or not. But she has declined to see you."

"At least allow me to write and ask her, so that she may answer and I can read in her own handwriting that she doesn't want to see me."

"She told you so to your face," Graham said flatly. "In my presence."

"I beg to differ from you, sir," Holmes said, his face flushing with anger.

Here, Judge Arnold spoke up: "Mr. Holmes, you will be allowed to write a letter to her and one of the court officers will take it to her, and if there is an answer to it, he will bring it to you."

"I do not want it to be taken by any officer who is in any way connected with the district attorney," Holmes answered.

Now it was the judge's turn to grow angry. "Well, you can't get that. You can't have everything. You can't have the world. We have sworn officers of the court here. All you have to do is write her a letter and it will be taken to her by an officer."

Holmes directed an incensed look at Graham. "Will you answer me a direct question? Have you or have you not intercepted letters from me to her since last July? Haven't you done everything in your power to keep us apart? Answer yes or no."

"I don't know what right you have to address interrogations to me," Graham said huffily. "But I will say that I never addressed half a dozen words to her in my life!"

"Mr. Holmes," Judge Arnold interposed. "These are mere idle suspicions. You may write your letter. It will be taken by a court officer and no one but she shall see it."

"And," added the district attorney, "I will have her in court tomorrow morning, besides."

"I will see," concluded the judge, "that you get light and writing materials."

"I thank you, sir, for the privilege," said Holmes, bowing.

DEPRAVED

Judge Arnold brought down his gavel and adjourned court for the day.

Holmes's impassioned insistence that he and Georgiana had legally been wed struck many observers as genuine—the outraged response of a man whose wife's virtue had been called into question. But others, better versed in the law, saw a different—and far less gallant—motive for his indignant display.

Establishing the legitimacy of his marriage was a matter, not of honor, but of urgent self-interest to Holmes, who knew perfectly well that a wife cannot testify against her husband without his consent.

47

Holmes was on the aggressive. It hardly seemed that he was a defendant. . . . He was an orator, a prince at repartee, a lawyer, and a man fighting for his life all combined.

—*Philadelphia Inquirer,* October 30, 1895

The spectator gallery—a big wooden balcony comprising about five hundred seats—was entirely vacant on Tuesday. The announcement that only duly authorized individuals would be permitted access to the trial had kept the curious throngs away.

But if the gallery was empty, the lower part of the courtroom was overflowing. No one could recall a case in which an accused murderer had defended his own life in a trial, and the unprecedented spectacle had attracted a large legal crowd, from law students toting their distinctive green bags to such eminent attorneys as A. S. L. Shields, Joseph H. Shakespeare, Col. Wendell P. Bowman, and Mrs. Carrie Kilgore, the only female member of the Philadelphia bar.

A few prominent citizens had also exerted their influence to secure admission, among them Sheriff Clement and Select Councilman Bringhurst. Before the day was over, State Senator Becker also put in an appearance, admitting that "for once, curiosity had dragged him from his usual business."

Shortly before ten, the prisoner entered the courtroom through the entrance usually reserved for lawyers. Stepping briskly to the dock—which had been moved closer to the witness stand and directly in front of the jury box—he tossed his coat over the railing and took his seat.

Holmes had gotten only an hour of sleep. He had spent the rest of the night preparing his case and looked even more drawn than he had the day before. As soon as the proceedings began, however, he "took hold of his case with a vigor that was remarkable" (as the *Philadelphia Inquirer* reported). "In some points, the keenest lawyer could not have beaten him in his thrusts and parries. At times, Holmes would turn his volleys on the District Attorney and would assail him with darts that were covered in venom."

The sniping between Holmes and Graham began even before the first witness was questioned. Rising in the dock and addressing Judge Arnold, Holmes humbly requested that he be permitted "certain privileges or favors, even in addition to those so kindly granted me last night." The first was that he be provided with "drawings of the Callowhill Street house, showing all three floors and the stairway."

"We have plans of the whole house," said District Attorney Graham, "and you may have use of them at the proper time."

"Very well," Holmes continued. "I would also ask that a small quantity of this deadly liquid, which the district attorney has so boldly charged me with intending to use to exterminate the balance of the Pitezel family, be submitted to analysis, and if this is impossible, then a sample be turned over to someone whom I will furnish for that purpose. This is absolutely necessary, if Your Honor please, because the liquid in question is comparatively harmless. While it contains nitroglycerin, it is the commercial form of that preparation that is found in nearly every drugstore, and it could only do harm by being ignited, and even then to a limited extent."

"May I ask what deadly drug you refer to?" Graham said, assuming a baffled look. "I am at a loss to understand the allusion."

"In your address to the jury," Holmes replied, his voice quivering with resentment, "you charged me with using this deadly drug and intimated that you had a small quantity in your possession."

"Do you mean what I referred to as left in the house at Burlington, which you requested Mrs. Pitezel to carry from one part of the building to another?"

"That is what I mean."

Graham gave a little shrug. "That has never come into my possession, and I am unable to have it analyzed or give you any portion of it."

"Still, you were able to state it plainly," Holmes shot back.

"I will prove what I said," Graham replied coldly. "Your own statement said it was nitroglycerin."

"I do not deny that at all." Holmes glanced at the judge. "Then the only other thing I can ask here is that I be furnished with some recent work on toxicology and medico-jurisprudence."

Judge Arnold gazed curiously at Holmes. "Are you a physician?"

For a moment, Holmes seemed slightly taken aback, as though startled that the judge would be ignorant of such a well-publicized fact. "Why, yes, sir. And at present I have no one to furnish me with those things which are of vital importance to me."

"Perhaps Mr. Shoemaker or Mr. Rotan can get them for you, as we will give you the privilege of consulting these gentlemen," the judge replied.

Holmes nodded graciously toward the bench. "Very well. That will answer my purposes."

With these preliminaries disposed of, the examination of the first witness—the Pitezels' eldest daughter, Dessie—got under way.

Self-possessed and strikingly pretty in a dark gray dress, the seventeen-year-old girl occupied the stand for only a few minutes. Her testimony was a perfunctory matter of identifying a photographic portrait of her father. Graham, however, electrified the courtroom when—after showing the picture to the girl—he whirled around and held it directly in front of Holmes's eyes.

"Do you wish to look at it, sir?" he asked sternly.

As one eyewitness wrote, "it was a moment of drama— the accused murderer suddenly brought face-to-face with the counterpart presentment of his victim in the presence of his accusers."

But if Graham had hoped to unsettle Holmes, he was disappointed. The prisoner cast a brief, unblinking glance at the photograph, then turned and put a few simple questions to Dessie, who answered curtly before stepping down.

It was not until a short time later, when Eugene Smith took the stand, that Holmes truly went on the offensive. Under Graham's questioning, Smith—the carpenter and amateur inventor who had discovered Pitezel's body—reviewed his part in the affair, beginning with the day he had brought his model saw-set to "B. F. Perry's" patent shop on Callowhill Street and concluding with his trip to potter's field to help identify the corpse.

For the most part, Smith appeared self-assured on the stand. He betrayed his essential timidity, however, when he confessed that he had recognized Holmes on the ride to the graveyard but had failed to alert the authorities because he was afraid "to say anything." Though Holmes was under indictment only for the murder of Benjamin Pitezel, the spirits of Alice, Nellie, and Howard were a hovering presence throughout the trial; more than one observer, hearing Smith's testimony, was left with the rueful conclusion that the carpenter's diffidence had contributed, however unwittingly, to the children's deaths. Had Smith only possessed the confidence to speak up on that day, Holmes's part in the fraud would have been exposed right away, and the subsequent tragedy averted.

Taking up his cross-examination, Holmes quickly scored a minor point by compelling Smith to retract one of his statements. The carpenter had testified that, on his second visit to the patent dealer's, he had seen Holmes enter the office, then proceed upstairs after gesturing for "Perry" to follow. Standing in the dock, his pencil leveled accusingly at the witness, Holmes forced Smith to admit that, though he had seen the two men enter the stairwell, he had not actually observed them ascend to the second story.

However, since the floor plans made it clear that the stairway led nowhere else, this admission struck most of the audience as far less of a coup than Holmes's self-satisfied smile suggested.

As for the rest of the testimony, Holmes did his best to shake up the witness, but Smith stuck to his original statements. At one point—clearly hoping to bolster his contention that Pitezel had committed suicide—Holmes tried to get Smith to say that the patent dealer had appeared despondent. Smith, however, would have none of it: "It did not seem to me he had any care or trouble that I noticed."

The cross-examination ended with a heated exchange between Holmes and the district attorney. Under direct examination, Smith had testified that, after Dr. Mattern had failed to find the identifying marks on Pitezel's exhumed corpse, Holmes had "removed his coat, put on the doctor's gloves, pulled out a lancet, and went to work on the body." When Holmes began to harp on a seemingly insignificant detail— whether he had put on the rubber gloves before or after Mattern had gone off to wash his hands—Graham voiced an angry objection.

"That is not material," he exclaimed. "The prisoner has been allowed every latitude, but I object to these questions unless he tells what he means to show."

Holmes jabbed his pencil in Graham's direction. "I want to protest against the bloodthirsty way in which the district attorney and this witness are inclined to make it appear that I rushed to mutilate the dead body of my friend."

"Nobody has intimated that," interposed the judge.

"There was no bloodthirstiness on your part," said Graham, then added darkly, "Not at this time."

"No," Holmes retorted, "but *you* have been bloodthirsty at other times."

Following Smith's dismissal, Graham called the first of his medical witnesses, Dr. William Scott, the pharmacist who had been summoned to 1316 Callowhill Street to examine Pitezel's corpse. Before the district attorney could pose his first question, however, Holmes stood up and motioned that all the other witnesses be excluded from the room during Scott's testimony.

"I do not think it is just to my side of the case," he declared, "that these other witnesses should sit here and receive the full benefit of all the questions that have been asked, giving them time to consider them and arrange their answers."

"I will not agree to that," Graham replied.

"I am at a loss to understand," Holmes said with heavy sarcasm, "whether you make the rulings or whether the honorable judge does."

"Sometimes you and the district attorney settle matters without troubling me," interjected Judge Arnold, sounding slightly weary of the constant sniping between the two men. "If you ask me to exclude all the witnesses, the request will be denied. But witnesses pertaining to this part of the case—what took place at number 1316 Callowhill Street and at the exhumation of the body at the potter's field—will be directed to retire."

At a gesture from Graham, Assistant DA Thomas Barlow picked up a sheet of paper and read off the names of the relevant witnesses, who filed from the courtroom.

Holmes, however, was still unsatisfied and insisted on seeing the roster: "Not having a list of the witnesses, I am at a loss to know whether all have retired."

"I wish I could get the prisoner to understand that everybody is acting honestly in this case," Graham said impatiently.

Holmes ignored the remark. "Is Jeptha Howe here?" he demanded.

"Mr. Howe is in St. Louis," Graham replied, "but he may be here later."

"And in regard to my wife?"

"Which one?" blurted Graham.

Holmes's face flushed with anger. "The one whom you designate as Miss Yoke, thereby casting a slur upon her as well as myself."

"That is how she wants to be designated herself," Graham retorted. "The man who laid the foundation of the slur is the man who married her with two other wives living."

"I shall challenge you to prove that," said Holmes, his voice rising.

"That we shall do," Graham said with a thin smile.

Holmes took a moment to collect himself. When he spoke

again, his voice had returned to its normal volume, though it trembled slightly. "I ask if my wife is to be a witness and ask her to be excluded."

"If you are speaking of Miss Yoke—and that is the name she gave me, for she has the right to say what name she prefers," Graham answered, "if you mean Miss Yoke, I decline to inform you whether she will be examined as a witness or not. But she is not in the courtroom, if that is a matter of any satisfaction to you."

Expressing an ironic word of gratitude to Graham, Holmes reseated himself, and the examination of Dr. Scott proceeded.

Guided by Graham, the druggist described the condition both of the victim's body and the second-floor bedroom in which it lay. It was clear the lawyer wanted Dr. Scott's testimony to show that Pitezel's death could not have been caused by either chemical explosion or suicide.

Though he had gone to the house "expecting to find a man blown to death," Scott declared that the evidence was not consistent with such an accident. A shattered chemical bottle was near the body, but its fragments, instead of being "scattered all over the room," were lying inside the unbroken base. "It looked for all the world," Scott explained, "as though the bottle had been taken with force and crushed on the floor and the pieces fell inside of it." Similarly, the victim's corncob pipe was resting neatly beside the dead man's face, as though it had deliberately "been placed there."

The cadaver itself, though in a state of dreadful putrefaction, looked surprisingly serene. "The body laid very peaceful, quiet," Scott stated, "as though he had fallen into a sleep and life had passed away from him without a struggle."

Scott, who had attended the postmortem, went on to describe the findings, all of which—the drained heart, empty bladder, paralyzed sphincter, and congested, chloroform-odored lungs—pointed to one conclusion: "sudden death through chloroform poisoning." The examiners had also found a quantity of the chemical in the victim's stomach, though they decided that it had been "introduced there after death" since the organ showed no "inflammation or congestion, which would have been the result if chloroform had been taken in life."

"Could a person taking chloroform," Graham inquired, "have arranged his body as this body was found."

Scott's answer was an emphatic "No, sir."

"That could not be?"

"Impossible," Scott insisted.

"Why?"

"If taken by mouth, it would produce spasms—it would not cause death from shock immediately. If taken by inhalation, he would lose consciousness and not be able to govern his own willpower."

According to Holmes's statement of December 26, 1894, Pitezel had committed suicide on the third floor of the Callowhill Street house. Holmes claimed that he had dragged the corpse to the second-floor bedroom, where he had staged the phony accident. Seeking to refute this claim, Graham questioned Scott closely about the bodily contents involuntarily discharged by the victim at the moment of death.

The druggist testified that the dead man's bowels and bladder had been been emptied in the second-floor bedroom. In addition, a stream of noisome red fluid had "issued from his mouth and run onto the floor, filling the grain of the board." By contrast, the third floor contained no trace of any discharge.

Though this talk of excreta was so graphic that it made several jurors visibly uncomfortable, it appeared to have a very different effect on Holmes. Announcing that he had "not eaten anything today," he respectfully requested a lunch recess. Judge Arnold granted the motion, adjourning the court for an hour.

When the trial resumed at two-thirty, Holmes launched into a brisk cross-examination of Scott. He handled himself so professionally that even Judge Arnold nodded in approval at several points. Nevertheless, Holmes failed to elicit a single response that (as the *Chicago Tribune*'s writer put it) "was in the slightest degree in his favor."

By the time the next witness was called—the coroner's physician Dr. William K. Mattern—the pressure on Holmes was beginning to tell. Pleading exhaustion, he begged for a day's continuance; he did "not feel up to the strain" of cross-examining another major witness. But Graham would not agree to this motion and proceeded with his questioning of Mattern, whose testimony in regard to the autopsy findings confirmed Dr. Scott's.

When Holmes took over, it quickly became clear that—for all his shrewdness and skill—he had reached the limits of his legal abilities. He hammered away at Mattern in a desperate effort to find some vulnerable point in the physician's testimony. But everyone in the room could see that Holmes was flailing.

Nearly two hours into the cross-examination, Holmes began dwelling on such a small, insignificant detail—the precise size of the lancet he had used to excise Pitezel's neck mole during the postmortem at potter's field—that Graham could no longer contain his impatience. Rising, he angrily protested that Holmes was wasting time on irrelevancies. Judge Arnold concurred, and Holmes, looking chagrined, brought the cross-examination to a hasty end.

By the time Graham finished examining the next witness—Dr. Henry Leffman, professor of toxicology at the Women's Medical College of Pennsylvania and one of the country's leading analytic chemists—Holmes seemed like a defeated man. Leffman acknowledged that people had been known to kill themselves with chloroform. But he insisted that it would be impossible "for a man to administer chloroform to himself and then compose himself" in the peaceful attitude in which Pitezel's corpse had been found.

"Why?" asked Graham.

"No one is aware of the time when consciousness ceases," Leffman explained. "Judging from my own experience, I have been four times under the influence of anesthetics. There is a condition of confusion before true insensibility comes on, and it would be, I think, impossible for anyone to arrange his body in a perfectly composed condition like that entirely by his own act."

In cross-examining the witness, Holmes limited himself to a few dispirited questions. To the onlookers, he seemed like a different man from the one he had been in the morning, when he had argued and fought—according to one correspondent—with "the desperation of a cornered hyena." Now, wrote this reporter, "the hyena was almost a lamb."

When Judge Arnold announced his intention to continue the proceedings following a one-hour dinner recess, Holmes begged him to reconsider. "It is utterly impossible for me to attend three sessions without breaking down and becoming sick," he said plaintively. "I am subject to sick headaches, and I have been suffering with it all day. I think two sessions a day, at least for the next few days, will be sufficient."

"Well, we will hold a session tonight," answered the judge. "We'll look after the matter tomorrow."

The cavernous room was much emptier when the court reconvened at seven-thirty. Most of the audience had gone home for the night—unaware that the trial, already so full of dramatic turns, was about to take another one.

The evening session started slowly. Graham and his assistant ran late and kept the court waiting. After apologizing for his tardiness, the district attorney called for the next witness, but the crier misunderstood the name, and it took a few moments to straighten the matter out.

During this lull, Holmes suddenly arose and made a sensational announcement:

"Your Honor, partly on account of my physical condition, partly because I have been annoyed unnecessarily by reason of not being expeditious enough in examining witnesses, and partly because of my counsel's being criticized for allegedly deserting me, I have asked them to come here and consult with me. If they are willing to go on, I would like to know if the Court is willing that they should reenter the case."

"Oh, come now, Mr. Holmes," Graham scoffed. "Be frank for once. You know whether they are willing to come or not. You have been in consultation with them during the recess."

Holmes seemed flustered. "Well, yes," he stammered. "I have asked them to come here."

At that point—like actors responding to their cues—Rotan and Shoemaker strolled into the courtroom while the remaining audience members broke into an excited buzz. Walking directly to the bench, Rotan—his voice loud enough to be heard over the din—began addressing a long, involved explanation to Judge Arnold, who cut him short with a wave of a hand.

"No apology necessary," said the judge. "Go on."

And with that (wrote the *Philadelphia Inquirer*), "Holmes, the criminal lawyer," metamorphosed back into "Holmes, the accused criminal."

The evening provided one final bit of drama during Graham's examination of Adella Alcorn, the proprietress of the boardinghouse where Holmes and Alice Pitezel had passed the night of September 22, 1894, following the girl's identification of her father's corpse. The landlady testified that—after the pair had departed early the next morning—she had gone upstairs to clean their rooms.

"How many beds had been occupied?" Graham asked.

"Two."

"What did you find, if anything, in these rooms belonging to the prisoner?"

Mrs. Alcorn spoke up clearly. "A nightshirt."

"And what did you find besides that?"

By this point, it was obvious to everyone in the courtroom that Graham was trying to prove the charge he had made during his opening address: that Holmes had violated the purity of the fifteen-year-old girl. When Rotan raised a vehement objection, Graham rephrased his question:

"Did you find anything else there, without stating what it was?"

Mrs. Alcorn nodded. "Yes, sir."

"Belonging to the prisoner?"

Mrs. Alcorn shifted in her seat. "It was not there before he came, and I could not tell you who it belonged to, because it was not mine, and no one else had been in the room."

When Rotan objected again, Graham admitted that there was "some question in my own mind as to whether this is competent, and I do not want to state it in the presence of the jury. If counsel will come around at the side bar, I will tell Your Honor what I propose to prove, and then you can either admit it or reject it."

As the lawyers approached the bench, the audience—its

prurient interest piqued—puzzled over the mystery. Clearly, Mrs. Alcorn had discovered something suspicious, even shocking, in Holmes's bedroom. In light of her comment that "it was not mine," some observers speculated that the incriminating item was a female undergarment—one of the "unmentionables" of that Victorian time.

But the world would never learn what she had found. After a brief consultation with the attorneys, Judge Arnold rejected Graham's offer of proof. A few moments later, Mrs. Alcorn stepped down from the stand, leaving the audience—and the jurors—free to imagine the worst.

48

Never before, it is safe to say, has there been witnessed in any courtroom within this Commonwealth such a scene as was enacted yesterday in the trial of H. H. Holmes. Mrs. Carrie Pitezel was brought face to face with the man who, his accusers say, killed her husband, her two daughters, and her little son in cold blood. The meeting was more than the poor woman could stand. At the sight of several childish letters in the handwriting of her little ones, she broke down completely, and her piteous moans struck to the heart of everyone in the courtroom. Every heart except one.

—*Philadelphia Public Ledger*, October 31, 1895

The return of Rotan and Shoemaker meant that the trial had lost one of its most entertaining features—Holmes's spellbinding performance as his own defense attorney. Even so, day three turned out to be the dramatic high point of the proceedings, containing what everyone agreed was the single "most sensational scene yet enacted—a scene that moved many to tears, stirred the emotions of the jurors, and made even the judge and prosecutors wipe their eyes."

Until that scene took place, however, the day offered few diversions. A succession of witnesses was called to the stand, including O. LaForrest Perry and William E. Gary of the Fidelity Mutual Life Assurance Company. But their busi-

344

nesslike testimony, though important to the Commonwealth's case, had the spectators stifling yawns.

The audience stirred briefly to life when Orinton M. Hanscom, deputy superintendent of the Boston police, approached the stand. Hanscom was something of a celebrity,
having played a key role in the Lizzie Borden case as a
detective for the defense. But while he cut a dashing figure,
his testimony was as dry as the insurance officials'.

In the meantime, Holmes sat in his waist-high wire enclosure, assiduously taking notes, while a professional phrenol-
ogist, John L. Capen, M.D., studied him from a short
distance away. Dr. Capen was there as a representative of
The New York World, and his analysis of Holmes's features
appeared in the next day's edition. The wildly sensationalistic tone of this portrait was typical of the treatment Holmes
continued to receive in the popular press.

Holmes, according to this specialist, was

> a man with a keen but intensely repulsive face: a
> face shaped like a hatchet, like one of those old-
> fashioned hatchets. . . . The shape of the head is
> unusual, abnormal. The top of the head is flat, ex-
> cept for one sharp bump rising suddenly and
> sharply. It would be said to mean reverence by the
> usual phrenologist. But not reverence for human
> life—at all events, not in this case.
>
> The eyes are very big and wide open. They are
> blue. Great murderers, like great men in other
> walks of activity, have blue eyes. There are deep
> lines under the eyes that come from sleepless nights
> of troubled thought and helpless rage.
>
> Of the murderer's mouth not much can be seen,
> for the hair is as thick as the thickest fur. But one
> can see that the lips are very thin and the expres-
> sion so cruel and cold as to be not human.
>
> At first glance, the striking thing about the man
> is the skull, so abnormally shaped at the back; but
> it is not so abnormal as the murderer's ear. That
> ear—as small as a little girl's and twisted out of
> shape, so that the inner part sticks out beyond the

outer rim—would stamp the man as a criminal in the opinion of every student of criminology. It is a marvelously small ear, and at the top it is shaped and carved after the fashion in which old sculptors indicated deviltry and vice in their statues of satyrs.

He is made on a very delicate mold. To be a great murderer he needed all his cunning and trickery, for nature gave him neither the physical strength nor the animal brutality needed for violent killing. He has killed his friends, killed, cut up, and burned little children, and murdered women whom he pretended to love. But he probably never looked one of them in the face to murder him openly.

At the end of Hanscom's testimony, Assistant District Attorney Barlow was asked to read the transcript of the statement Holmes had made to the authorities following his arrest in Boston. A trained elocutionist, Barlow got to his feet and began to declaim the confession in a deep, dramatic voice.

He was halfway through the document when the door beside the crier's desk opened and a trio of dark-clad figures stepped into the courtroom. One was Dessie Pitezel, dressed in the same outfit she had worn the day before on the witness stand. The other was a stout, matronly woman, whose manner quickly made it clear that she was a professional nurse. In between these two stood a frail, deathly pale figure, garbed in funereal black.

Excited whispers ran through the audience. Carrie Pitezel was in the room.

The spectators in the rear craned their necks for a better look, but their view was obstructed by the district attorney, who walked over to have a brief, whispered conversation with the "much-talked-of widow" (as the newspapers called her). A few minutes later, Barlow reached the end of the document, and Graham called Mrs. Carrie Alice Pitezel to the stand.

On that day—Wednesday, October 30, 1895—Carrie was just three months shy of thirty-seven. But tragedy had drained every trace of youth from her face. Indeed, she might have accomplished her purpose without speaking a word, her very appearance seemed such damning proof of Holmes's villainy.

She was, wrote the correspondent for *The Philadelphia Inquirer,* "the very picture of human misery. Despair was written in every lineament of her colorless face. Big dark circles marked her eyes, and heavy lines furrowed her cheeks—the indelible evidence of ceaseless sorrow and worry."

As she settled into her place, Carrie cast a look of the most bitter hatred in the direction of the prisoner's dock. At that instant, Holmes looked up from his legal pad. The courtroom was as silent as death. In attempting to convey the tension of that moment, the *Inquirer* reached a new, melodramatic pitch:

"Face to face with the woman whose husband he is accused of murdering, whose children he is known to have separated from their mother, whether or not he was guilty of ending their lives; face to face with the woman who—if the theory of the prosecution is correct—will someday stand before him in the dread presence of a Higher Tribunal and join her innocent little ones in the awful denunciation, 'Thou art the man!' the prisoner Holmes sat calm and indifferent."

After glancing at Carrie for a moment, Holmes nonchalantly resumed his writing, while Graham approached the stand.

Carrie's testimony lasted several hours. Throughout that time, her voice was so choked and feeble that the court crier had to stand beside the box and repeat her answers. At various points she grew so faint that she had to be revived with smelling salts, administered by her hovering nurse. Several times during the afternoon, her physician, Dr. Thomas J. Morton, stopped by the courtroom to see how she was bearing up.

Meanwhile, Holmes was "the picture of busy contentment. He took notes of the proceedings. He occasionally read out of a book. At times, he chatted gaily with his attorneys." He seemed entirely indifferent to the heartrending spectacle taking place a few yards in front of him—even when virtually every other eye in the courtroom was moist with pitying tears.

Guided by the district attorney, the shattered woman told of her husband's move to Philadelphia to carry out the insurance fraud; of the newspaper notice of "B. F. Perry's" death; of Holmes's sudden appearance in St. Louis; of Alice's trip to identify the corpse; and of the settlement of the policy, whose proceeds immediately disappeared into the pockets of Holmes and Jeptha Howe.

Then in a broken, barely audible voice, punctuated by anguished sobs, she described how Holmes had taken away Alice, Nellie, and Howard, then kept her moving from city to city until—half-crazed with confusion and worry—she had found herself in the hands of the Boston police.

It was a familiar tale, whose details had been repeated endlessly in the press. But it gained renewed—and unbearably tragic—force coming directly from the lips of the tormented wife and mother.

Graham—who clearly regarded Mrs. Pitezel as his trump card—handled the examination so skillfully that the evening headlines described the session as a "field day for the Commonwealth." At one point, he stepped over to the prosecutor's table, picked up something in each hand, then returned to the witness box and held out the evidence for Carrie's inspection—two small, slightly faded pieces of cloth.

At a glance, they appeared to be unremarkable—as nondescript as dust rags. But there was nothing ordinary about them.

Many people, knowing where those scraps had come from, would have refused to lay a finger on them. Few could have held them in their hands, as Graham was doing, without feeling a tremor of unease—even dread.

They were swatches of Benjamin Pitezel's grave clothes, removed from his moldering body during a second exhumation conducted in early September.

"Mrs. Pitezel," Graham said somberly. "I show you portions of two garments taken from a corpse buried in potter's field, this city, but since laundered. Do you recognize the material?"

Carrie's bottom lip shook violently and she began to weep

into her handkerchief. It took a few moments before she regained enough control to speak again.

"That blue," she rasped. "It's the same color as my husband's trousers when I last saw him—when he left St. Louis." She pointed her quivering finger at Graham's other hand. "And that checked goods. I made him a shirt out of goods just like that."

It was a powerfully affecting moment, which produced its desired effect: several of the jury members seemed to be fighting back tears, and one or two cast openly baleful looks at the prisoner.

A few minutes later, Graham "struck to the heart" of every spectator in the room when he held up some of the letters that her homesick children had written but Holmes had never mailed.

"Mrs. Pitezel," Graham said, "I wish to show you these letters at this time solely for the purpose of identifying the handwriting. Look at them and hand them back to me." Graham passed her one of the letters, then asked, "Whose handwriting is that?"

Carrie's hands trembled as she examined the sheet. "Oh, my God, Mr. Graham. That's—" She could not finish the sentence. Overwhelmed with grief, she broke into racking sobs. It was not until her nurse hastened to her side and administered several spoonfuls of nerve medicine that Carrie was able to identify the handwriting as Alice's.

But the most harrowing moment was yet to come. Standing near the witness box, Graham asked Carrie if she had seen her husband since he had left St. Louis for Philadelphia in the summer of 1894.

"I have never seen my husband since the twenty-ninth of July," she answered softly.

"Have you seen or heard from Alice, Nellie, or Howard since this man got possession of them and took them away from you?"

Carrie dabbed at her eyes before replying. "No, sir. I have not heard from them."

"And have you not seen them since?"

At that moment, Rotan raised a strenuous objection to this line of questioning, insisting that it was incompetent, irrelevant, and would hopelessly prejudice the jurors against his client.

Judge Arnold, however, ruled the testimony admissible, and Graham repeated his question.

"Have you seen your children since?"

"I saw them in Toronto," Carrie answered in a broken voice. "In the morgue. Side by side."

The audience, straining to hear every word, had remained utterly silent during her reply. All at once, cries broke out throughout the courtroom, jury members wept openly, and Judge Arnold himself dug under his robe for his pocket handkerchief and began to pat his eyes.

Rotan objected again, though even he seemed shaken: "I cannot see what motive there is to bringing in these children." But his voice was uncharacteristically weak.

Graham's voice, by contrast, rang with indignation. "Was there not a motive for him to take Alice and put her out of the way—the girl that he sent to identify the father, and who knew that it *was* her father who was buried in the potter's field? Was there not a motive for him to kill that child? How can we tell but what those children together had talked over what had taken place? Was there not a motive for him to have destroyed the lives of all three of them?"

Swiveling, Graham pointed an accusing finger toward the prisoner's dock, where Holmes—his face registering nothing but blithe indifference—continued to scribble notes on his pad. Observing him through their tears, more than one of the spectators shook their heads in bewilderment and wondered yet again what manner of being he was.

One man, at least, believed he had an answer. That evening, during dinner recess, the correspondent for *The New York World* managed to secure an exclusive interview with the world-famous criminal.

Passing down a flight of stone steps to the basement of the courthouse, then through a long, dim tunnel lined with steel-barred cells, the reporter reached the apartment where Holmes took his meals and conferred with his lawyers during recesses.

The newsman found Holmes relaxed on a comfortable

leather lounge with his feet propped on a table. He was entertaining a visitor, a gentleman named McGarge—"a distinguished citizen of Philadelphia"—who was there purely out of curiosity. When the newsman entered, McGarge had just asked Holmes about the rigors of prison life.

Holmes conceded that the authorities had treated him with every consideration. Still, he lamented, he found his existence terribly "dull and wearying," particularly because of its unrelenting solitude. "If only I had company," he sighed. "Any living thing—even a bird or a mouse. Or a spider!"

Suddenly, Holmes addressed the guards posted outside his cell. "I fooled you boys once," he said with a low chuckle. "I had a live chicken in my cell, and I had it to keep me company for a whole month."

As the guards made incredulous noises, Holmes turned back to his visitors and proceeded to tell a remarkable tale. "You see, I was allowed to have food brought into the prison if I could pay for it, and I had some eggs that were not cooked. I saved one, and I hatched it."

Mr. McGarge offered a gentle expression of skepticism.

"It's true," Holmes insisted. "I wrapped the egg up in a coat and placed it beside the radiator, and it was born, all right. You cannot imagine the joy and satisfaction of bringing a life safely into the world to keep me company in that cell. That little chicken loved me, and I took care of it. I hid it away when the guards came around, and I had it a whole month. Then"—his voice suddenly grew husky with emotion—"then it died, as all the things we love die in the world."

As the two visitors returned to the courtroom a short while later, the newsman rendered his opinion that Holmes was a remarkable example of a "double personality." "It is most interesting as a study in human nature," he remarked, "to see the man who butchered and broiled little children hatching out a chicken and grieving over its death with undoubted sincerity."

Mr. McGarge, however, took a somewhat more cynical view of the matter, observing wryly that, sometime after hatching the egg, "Holmes doubtless had the chicken's life insured."

49

"I weep for you," the Walrus said:
   "I deeply sympathize."
With sobs and tears he sorted out
   Those of the largest size.
Holding his pocket handkerchief
   Before his streaming eyes.

—Lewis Carroll, "The Walrus and the Carpenter"

Public interest in the Holmes case continued to run high—particularly in Philadelphia, where the newspapers treated the trial as the greatest spectacle the city had witnessed since the Centennial of '76. On Thursday morning, October 31, the biggest crowd yet showed up at City Hall, pressing for admission. In spite of the police guards posted outside the courtroom, a surprising number of unauthorized individuals managed to wangle their way in—most of them (so the *Inquirer*'s correspondent noted) pretty young women whose only credentials were their "fetching smiles" and "fresh blue eyes."

The crowd was hoping for a show, and Holmes gave it to them. By the end of the day, however, the spectators were split over what they had seen. Some were convinced that it had been Holmes's most remarkable performance.

Others felt sure that, for once, he hadn't been acting at all.

Georgiana Yoke's long-awaited appearance was the occasion for Holmes's dramatic display. Before she could testify, however, Graham had to resolve the issue of her marital status. To that end, he first recalled William E. Gary, who had paid a visit to Holmes's residence in Wilmette as part of the insurance investigation.

"Whom did you see there?" asked Graham.

"Mrs. H. H. Holmes," answered Gary.

Graham handed him a photograph and asked him to identify it. It was a picture of Myrta Holmes.

Gary studied it for a moment before declaring, "That is Mrs. H. H. Holmes."

Gary went on to explain that, shortly after seeing Myrta, he had interviewed Holmes in Moyamensing. "I said to Mr. Holmes that I had called at Wilmette and had met his wife and found her a very bright and intelligent woman. He stated that she *was* a very intelligent woman. As I concluded my interview, Mr. Holmes requested me to wait a moment, stating that he wanted to write a letter to his wife if I could wait. I assented, and he retired to a stool and wrote a communication which he asked me to mail to Mrs. H. H. Holmes in Wilmette."

As it happened, Gary had taken the precaution of copying the letter before sending it off. After asking Gary to identify his copy, Graham offered it in evidence.

The letter read as follows:

Moyamensing Prison

Dear Mamma:

It is Thanksgiving Day. It finds me in my cell with the feeling strong upon me that I have nothing to be thankful for, not even my life. I took my chances and failed, and my principal regrets are the suffering and disgrace upon you and all others. I do not think I have to ask you to disbelieve the murder charges. . . . I expect a two years' sentence, but if I were free to-day I should never live again as in the past, either with you or anyone else, as I will never run the chances of degrading any woman further. . . . In a little time I will write you about the

353

property; only one-half page letters are allowed. Direct care of the superintendent if you wish to write.

H.

Graham then proceeded to read two more letters—the ones Holmes had written in September 1894 to Edwin Cass, head of Fidelity's Chicago office. In them, Holmes had repeatedly alluded to Myrta as "my wife."

Graham was still reading these letters aloud when the door behind the jury box opened and a young woman slipped into the room. Every head in the spectator section seemed to swivel at once in the direction of the captivating figure dressed in a stylish black gown, a black, broad-brimmed hat, trimmed with velvet, and harmonizing gloves.

Holmes looked over at her, too, and a peculiar, stricken expression passed over his face.

Just then, Graham finished reading the letters. Over Lawyer Rotan's objections, Judge Arnold announced his intention to allow Georgiana's testimony.

"I do not know of any stronger evidence that could be brought into court," said the judge, "than this testimony of the man against himself. He has, in his own declaration, made a statement of his marriage and of his wife in Wilmette. It is for the jury to say whether or not he was married to the lady at Wilmette, in which case the second marriage is absolutely void and null and does not require a divorce to make it so. There being testimony of a former marriage at the time he married this lady, she is entitled to testify against him."

With that, Georgiana Yoke stepped onto the stand, while the spectators sat transfixed by her charms. "Hers," wrote the *Inquirer*'s man, "was a face and form well calculated to win sympathy. Slender, delicate, refined, she looked the picture of tender innocence. Her cheeks were flushed, but the rosy tint was becoming—it well set off the head of flaxen hair. Her dainty lips twitched nervously. Her dreamy eyes were downcast. Not once were they turned toward the prisoner. Not for a glance were they lifted that way."

Suddenly, however, the crowd was distracted from its contemplation of this entrancing figure. Something extraordinary was going on in the prisoner's dock.

H. H. Holmes—"Holmes the brilliant, Holmes the fearless, the man who had sat without a tremor while Mrs. Pitezel was telling her horrible story, this being so apparently devoid of emotion"—was weeping uncontrollably.

The remarkable scene was described in the next morning's paper:

> For the first time since the trial began, Holmes's nerve seemed to have deserted him. The moment Miss Yoke ascended to the stand, his eyes filled with tears, and then he dropped his head upon his arm, which lay on the railing of the dock, and gave way to sobs. Two or three very audible moans escaped his lips, and it was several minutes before he could regain his composure.
>
> The sight of this man, who had stood the scorching arraignment of the district attorney and the pitifully tearful tales of the widow whose husband and children he is accused of murdering, in such an open and unreserved demonstration of grief was indeed a surprise to all who saw it. Tears were coursing down the prisoner's cheeks and his handkerchief was at his face.
>
> What horror and pathos had failed to do, a woman's face had done.

Afterward, some held to the opinion that the whole spectacle was a sham—that Holmes had been acting on the advice of his attorneys, who had urged him to display a bit of human emotion after his shockingly indifferent response to Mrs. Pitezel.

Others, however, contended that the outburst could not possibly have been faked. "The emotion," insisted one reporter, "could scarcely be assumed. The heaving chest, the panting lips, were too real for that. What memories the young woman's appearance called up to him, none could tell. Was it love—or was it fear—that moved the man?"

Whatever the case, Holmes's reaction brought murmurs of amazement from many in the audience. Judge Arnold banged for order, and Graham began his questioning, while Holmes dried up his tears, swallowed his sobs, and looked on glumly.

During Graham's examination, Georgiana recounted her experiences with Holmes. She gave particular attention to his odd behavior on the afternoon of September 2, 1894—the day of Pitezel's death—when he had returned, flushed and breathless, from his early-morning outing and insisted that they leave Philadelphia at once.

By that point in Georgiana's testimony, Holmes had regained enough self-composure to hold an urgent, whispered conference with his attorneys.

As soon as Graham had completed his questioning, Lawyer Rotan stood up and informed the judge that the defendant insisted on cross-examining the witness himself. Meeting with no objection, Holmes got slowly to his feet and leaned his hands on the dock rail.

For a moment, he seemed in danger of giving way to his tears again. He gulped hard and raised his handkerchief to his eyes. It was an affecting sight—though its authenticity was somewhat undermined by a remark he had let slip to his attorneys. As Holmes was rising from his seat, a newspaperman sitting close to the dock overheard him mutter, "I will now let loose the fount of emotion."

Though Holmes did his best to touch Georgiana's heart—appealing to her memories of their shared days of travel—the young woman remained utterly aloof. She refused to meet his gaze and replied to his queries in a tone of cool formality. The cross-examination turned out to be a brief and undramatic affair, notable only for the theatrical quavering of Holmes's voice, as though he were struggling at every moment to keep his emotions at bay.

Georgiana was succeeded on the stand by Detective Frank Geyer. The audience buzzed with excitement, expecting a dramatic, firsthand recitation of his celebrated hunt for the Pitezel children. They were in for a disappointment.

Geyer began by relating the details of an interview that he had conducted with the prisoner in the cell room of City

Hall on November 20, 1894—the day Holmes had been returned to Philadelphia following his arrest in Boston. After interrogating Holmes about Pitezel's death, Geyer had asked him "what became of the children." Holmes had proceeded to spin his now-familiar tall tale about turning them over to Minnie Williams.

At that point in Geyer's testimony, Graham turned toward the bench. "I propose, may it please the Court, to go on and prove the finding of the remains of these children."

Rotan leapt to his feet. "I insist that this is a matter which should not be discussed before the jury."

At the judge's direction, the bailiffs escorted the jury members from the room. As soon as they were out of earshot, Graham addressed the judge again:

"My offer is to prove the investigation concerning the whereabouts of the three children, and the finding of the body of Howard Pitezel in the house at Irvington in the suburbs of Indianapolis, and the finding of the body of Nellie and that of Alice at number 16 St. Vincent Street in the city of Toronto."

Graham took a step toward the bench, his thumbs hooked in his vest pockets. "It seems to me—and I have given the matter a great deal of earnest thought—that these things are so intimately connected with the occurrence at 1316 Callowhill Street that they constitute part of one and the same transaction. I am perfectly aware that the rule is—and it is a wise rule, too—that a man cannot be convicted of one offense by proving he committed another. But a line of authorities in Pennsylvania clearly indicate that the commission of other crimes may be proved for certain purposes. To make one criminal act a part of another, it must be shown that a connection between them must have existed in the mind of the actor.

"Surely," Graham asserted after an instant's pause, "there can be no greater or more pointed illustration of this proposition than this very case. Especially does this seem to be the case when we recall the fact that one of these children, whose bodies were found in the house in Toronto, was Alice Pitezel, the little girl who came on here and identified the dead body of the man as her father."

Graham's tone became more impassioned as he continued. "Holmes, if he had committed no crime, would have had no motive for the removal of that child. But having murdered her father, whom she identified, it became a part of his purpose to remove one of the elements that would menace him all the days of his life. He starts the wife, Mrs. Pitezel, with himself in flight, after taking the children from her, and moves her to various places. These are acts which he did in flight. Every act the man does in flight for the purpose of screening and protecting himself is evidence, since it grows out of the original crime, even if it be the commission of a new crime. He succeeds in getting rid of the three children in flight—a part of the continuous transaction.

"I submit these acts of his are connected together, spinning out of the same motive, resulting from the same thought. Indeed, we offer this evidence in support of the theory that this man intended to murder, not only the three children and the father, but also every member of that family."

As he brought his argument to a close, Graham introduced a pronounced note of deference into his voice, as though to communicate his utmost faith in Judge Arnold's sagacity. "I do not think I have anything further to add, but I earnestly urge what I have said upon Your Honor's attention. I believe this evidence to be admissible. I think I have clearly come within the scope of the general rule, and this evidence ought to go to the jury as part of the case."

With the audience sitting in rapt silence, Graham returned to his seat, while Rotan stood to present his reply.

"May it please this honorable Court," he began. "My associate and I recognize that now we have come to the most important part of the case, for it seems to me the outcome, to a very great extent, depends upon the admissibility of this particular evidence. As the district attorney has said, it is a well-known principle that when a man is on trial for the commission of a certain crime, evidence that he has committed another crime is inadmissible. From time to time, certain exceptions have grown up, but I have failed to find, in all the cases I have looked up, where the rule could be so broadened in scope to meet the proposed offer of evidence with respect to the alleged deaths of the three children in its application to the alleged death of the father."

Rotan quickly glanced at some notes he was clutching in one hand. "Justice Agnew, in *Shafner versus Commonwealth*, says that there must be a oneness of purpose, a sameness of purpose, and that if a number of deaths are caused apparently by an act of a defendant, it is necessary that the purpose must have been formed prior to the killing of any one of the deceased.

"Now, may it please Your Honor, applying that reasoning to this case, it will be necessary for Your Honor to believe, in order to admit this evidence, that Holmes had intended to take the life of every person who has died so far, and not only that—according to the argument of the district attorney—but also the life of Mrs. Pitezel and the life of the remaining child, Dessie. He could not have a motive for taking the lives of those who are dead without taking the lives of those who are living. It would break the connection."

Rotan paused for a moment, as though to let his point sink in. "Is it fair to assume that there is any evidence he intended to take the life of Mrs. Pitezel? Is there any evidence in the case to justify the assumption that he intended to take the life of Dessie?"

Rotan shook his head gravely. "My associate and I submit that there is nowhere evidence to indicate that Holmes had in mind any of these deaths. We therefore feel, from all the circumstances of the case, that Your Honor must not admit any evidence of this kind. It is the hinging part of the case, and we feel, as I say, that Your Honor should not admit it."

Though his oratorical skills were no match for Graham's, Rotan had argued effectively. Even before he was finished, however, Judge Arnold seemed to have reached a decision.

"The Commonwealth's argument," he declared as Rotan returned to his seat, "that the prisoner killed Alice Pitezel for the purpose of destroying her as a witness has nothing to support it. She was not a witness to the offense. Had she been a witness to her father's murder and then was killed, that, of course, would be evidence that could go in. But there is nothing of the kind here. All the little girl did was to identify her father a week or two after he was killed.

"To say that the murder of the girl at a subsequent time is competent in this trial—that would make an imaginary connection between the two acts. This prisoner is now on trial for the killing of Benjamin F. Pitezel in the city of Philadelphia, and that is the only case to be tried here. Evidence of his subsequent killing of these children elsewhere will not be admitted."

Leaning forward on his folded arms, Arnold directed his final words at Graham. "If he is not found guilty of the one murder for which he is indicted, he may be sent to Canada or Indiana. But he cannot be tried for these extraneous offenses now."

Arnold's ruling meant that nearly three dozen witnesses—from Detroit, Indianapolis, Toronto, Vermont, and elsewhere—had made the trip to Philadelphia for nothing. Excluded, too, was a boxful of gruesome evidence—including the charred bones of Howard Pitezel—that Graham was prepared to display.

The decision was a blow to the prosecution and a disappointment to the crowd. Rotan and Shoemaker, on the other hand, were visibly elated. They had scored a substantial victory—the first they could legitimately claim.

Indeed it seemed to infuse Holmes and his lawyers with a heady sense of confidence and prompted them to make a tactical move that would provide the final sensation of the trial.

50

Whereas the law is passionless, passion must ever
sway the heart of man.

—Aristotle, *Politics*

When Holmes entered the crowded courtroom at the start
of Friday's session, he seemed surprisingly relaxed—almost
chipper. "His step was firm and springy," observed the *Inquirer*'s man. "His eyes looked bright and confident. He
walked as though he had passed a restful night."

There were, according to the reporter, only two apparent
reasons for Holmes's buoyant mood: "Either his breakdown
of the day before had relieved the tension on his sadly-taxed
nerves, or the victory that his lawyers had gained had given
him renewed strength."

Whatever the case, he seemed to have recovered all his
old arrogance. He cast a defiant look around the courtroom
as he climbed into his wire pen.

The prosecution devoted the morning to tying up a few
loose ends. Both Carrie Pitezel and the coroner's physician
Dr. William Mattern were briefly recalled to the stand—the
former to identify her deceased husband's shirt cuffs, the
latter to confirm that involuntary fecal discharge can occur
only "at or immediately before death," not "after rigor mor-
tis sets in."

As soon as Dr. Mattern stepped down from the stand,
Graham rested the Commonwealth's case. By then it was
time for lunch.

When the court reconvened at two P.M., the room was jammed to overflowing. Those who couldn't find seats—men and women alike—occupied every inch of standing room, jostling for a clear view of the stand. They had come to watch the defense mount its case. According to rumor, Holmes was slated to appear as the star witness, perhaps that very afternoon.

Ten minutes went by, but the defense table and prisoner's dock remained empty. The crowd grew as restless as a theatrical audience waiting for a late curtain to rise. Finally, at 2:12 P.M., Holmes was taken to his place, followed a few minutes later by Rotan and Shoemaker. The former, looking flushed and nervous, offered a quick apology to the judge, who accepted it with a curt nod.

Three more tense minutes passed while Holmes's lawyers held a hushed conversation. Then Rotan stood and addressed the judge:

"May it please this honorable Court, the Commonwealth has all its evidence in, and we feel sure that the Commonwealth has failed to make out its case. It is incumbent upon the Commonwealth in all criminal cases, wherever tried, that they must prove that case beyond a reasonable doubt. We feel from the evidence that has been put in here that there exists that reasonable doubt.

"The Commonwealth has proved the fact that these men were intimate and that they came here for the purpose of carrying out an insurance fraud. But the medical testimony does not show that this man was killed by somebody else. It raises a doubt. It shows that it may possibly have been a suicide. We feel that the Commonwealth has not made out what is known as corpus delicti. They have proved that a man's body was found there, but they have not proved beyond a reasonable doubt that anybody killed him."

Rotan's voice had seemed a little shaky at the start, but he ended firmly. "That reasonable doubt the defense is entitled to, and we ask, may it please this honorable Court, that you give the jury binding instructions."

Rotan, in short, was asking the judge to direct a verdict of acquittal.

Before Judge Arnold could reply, Graham spoke up. "It is so ridiculous," he exclaimed, "that I will not argue it."

Judge Arnold seemed to concur: "I decline to make any such ruling. The jury must find a verdict for itself. I will not express any opinion."

After another hurried conference with Shoemaker, Rotan returned to his place and again addressed the judge:

"Your Honor, we have now reached the stage where it is incumbent upon the defense to decide what the defense shall be. As I said to the Court before, we feel we have not had enough time to properly prepare our defense, and we ask Your Honor to give us an hour or two in order that we may decide upon the outline of our defense. We have worked very hard in regard to other matters, and on account of the peculiar features of the case we ask the Court for a little time."

Making a small, exasperated sound, Judge Arnold agreed to a half-hour recess. As Holmes and his lawyers made their way from the room, a murmur went up from the crowd, which seemed to sense that something unanticipated, even extraordinary, was about to take place.

They were right.

Forty-five minutes later, well past Judge Arnold's allotted time, Holmes and his attorneys returned. As Shoemaker sat down at the defense table and Holmes took his place in the dock, Rotan approached the bench. And dropped a bombshell.

"May it please this honorable Court, Mr. Shoemaker and myself have just had a consultation with the defendant in reference to the defense. We feel that—owing to our inability to bring in a number of important witnesses from other places—it is advisable for us to close the case now, putting in no testimony whatsoever.

"We do this, Your Honor, also from the fact that we feel that the Commonwealth has failed utterly to make out its case."

It was the final and perhaps most astonishing turn in this unprecedented trial—"the last grand play," as one newspaper put it, "in a daring game which had for its stake a human life." The defense had decided to call no witnesses on

Holmes's behalf. It would submit its case on final argument alone.

When Rotan's meaning became clear to the crowd, they sent up a groan of disappointment—the sort of sound heard in Broadway houses when the management announces that, because of illness, the lead role will be played by an anonymous understudy instead of the legendary star. Judge Arnold banged for order, then adjourned the court until ten the next morning, when final arguments would be heard.

By seven o'clock on Saturday morning, the hallway outside the big courtroom was already mobbed. Men, women—even children—pushed, tugged, and elbowed each other in their struggle to work their way close to the entrance. When the big double doors were finally opened around nine forty-five, the crowd surged forward with a roar. Many of those who managed to make their way in did so at the cost of scratched cheeks and torn clothing.

For the first time since opening day, the big upstairs gallery was made available to spectators. In less than a minute, it was filled to capacity. A few of the female spectators had come equipped with opera glasses. Perched on the edge of their balcony seats, they held the little binoculars to their eyes and leaned forward for a good look at the defendant.

It did not require such intensive scrutiny to see that Holmes—for all his show of bravado—was suffering from a bad case of nerves. Sitting in his wire pen, he tried writing something on his ever-present notepad, but his fingers shook so badly that he was forced to abandon the effort.

Shortly before ten, District Attorney Graham—whose final speech was expected to be the highlight of the session—strode into the room, trailed by a large, mostly female retinue. After showing his lady friends to their seats, he took a moment to find places for the rest of his party, whose members included former DA William B. Mann—himself a legendary orator—and such luminaries as General Louis Wagner, Major Moses Veale, and Christopher L. Flood.

Almost predictably, Holmes's counsel supplied some last-minute melodramatics. At ten-fifteen A.M. Judge Arnold had begun to drum his fingers on the bench when Lawyer Rotan rushed in to announce that he had just received word that his partner was ill. Promising to "make as much haste as possible," he hurried from the courtroom.

He was back in five minutes. "May it please Your Honor," he said, breathing as raggedly as though he had returned at a jog. "I have gone over to a drugstore, where I found Mr. Shoemaker under the care of a physician, who says that he is in a complete state of nervous prostration. I know that he has been ill for the last day or two. But Mr. Shoemaker says he is willing to leave the entire matter in charge of the Court—that if the Court feels that the case should go on, he has no objection at all. I express the sentiment myself, but at the same time, of course"—here, the ruddy-faced young lawyer paused to catch his breath—"I recognize that the defendant is by law allowed the right to have two speeches."

A brief dispute followed in which Rotan insisted on his right to make both the opening and closing statements, with the Commonwealth's final remarks sandwiched in between. Judge Arnold disagreed with this interpretation, asserting that it was the prosecution's right to present the closing argument.

Graham settled the matter with a gesture that struck the crowd as supremely generous. Standing, he gave a gracious nod in his opponent's direction. "In view of the fact that Mr. Shoemaker is ill," he declared, "and that Mr. Rotan is here by himself, I propose on behalf of the Commonwealth to voluntarily waive my right to close the case. I will make the opening speech to the jury and leave Mr. Rotan the closing argument."

With that, Graham gathered up a sheaf of papers, drew himself to his full, imposing height, and stepped before the jury box.

Graham had a well-deserved reputation as a spellbinder, and his final statement—combining clear, compelling logic with passionate oratory—amply demonstrated his skills. "Gentlemen of the jury," he began in his deep, resonant voice. "I am quite sure that it is with a feeling of relief that you see the end of this trial rapidly approaching, and that you—who have been taken from your homes, your places of business, and practically imprisoned during the whole length of the proceedings—are now to be released and permitted to return and resume your usual places and duties in society.

"I propose to ask you now to join with me in reasoning for a little while about the evidence which you have heard—the testimony in this case. I am going to ask you to give me your best attention, and your best thought, while I try to refresh your recollection and aid your reason in reaching the right conclusion from the evidence.

"The Commonwealth of Pennsylvania wants no victim. The Commonwealth of Pennsylvania does not ask for the conviction of this man—though he may be covered with the evidence of guilt in other matters—unless, in this specific case now on trial, the testimony that you have heard points indubitably to his guilt and authorizes his conviction. I ask your attention to the evidence because I propose to say to you that, after a careful perusal of it, my mind is forced to the conclusion that I must press upon you the discharge of a great, and perhaps to you, a trying duty.

"The task laid before me is this: I must point out from the evidence the facts which prove conclusively that this prisoner at the bar murdered Benjamin F. Pitezel at number 1316 Callowhill Street on the second day of September 1894 so conclusively that there will not be a single doubt lurking in your mind, so positively that you will feel under your oaths as jurors that there is but one course left open for you, and that is to find the verdict pointed out to you in the opening of this case—the highest known to the law—a verdict of murder in the first degree."

Graham's recap followed a straightforward, chronological course, beginning with Monday's first witnesses. He paid particular attention to the medical experts, whose testimony had clearly proven that the victim had been poisoned by chloroform, not killed by an accidental explosion. "While the broken jar and other evidences of an explosion were present," Graham stated, "they were artificially produced by somebody with the intention to deceive. There was no explosion."

Moreover, the testimony both of the medical witnesses

and of the merchants who had sold Pitezel his cigars and whiskey on the evening before his death contradicted the allegation of suicide. "This man who was out the night before, apparently happy, and making provision for the next day, not intending to die but intending to have some of the things he considered necessary for his comfort—Holmes claims has committed suicide. This man who was writing to his wife, 'I am coming out to see you, and if I can make arrangements to conduct business in Philadelphia, I am going to bring you and the children to Philadelphia, and we'll live there'—this man, Holmes says, committed suicide. All the surroundings in this case deny that he thought of suicide, and the story that Holmes tells is absolutely impossible and is rebutted by the evidence."

Taking up Holmes's claim that he had moved the body from the third floor to the second, Graham appealed to the jurors' common sense. "The first question I ask is, why did he not leave him on the third-story floor? What necessity was there for bringing him down to the second story? Could he not just as well have burned and disfigured him up there on the third-story floor as he could have on the second story?

"Gentlemen," Graham said gravely, "that body was never on the third-story floor. The relaxation of the involuntary muscles, and the involuntary discharges from the person, took place at or immediately before dissolution. These discharges were found on the second-story floor, not on the third-story floor, clearly indicating that death took place where the body was found. This is a very significant fact."

Having established that "the dead man had been poisoned" and that "the poison had *not* been self-administered," Graham reviewed "the second step in the progress of the case"—namely, the identification of the victim. "The Commonwealth must show, for we can assume nothing, that the dead man was Benjamin F. Pitezel, the man named in the indictment as the subject of this murder." To accomplish that end, the Commonwealth had summoned a host of witnesses, beginning with Coroner Ashbridge.

"Why Coroner Ashbridge?" Graham asked, his voice taking on a sudden, mournful note. "We could not call Alice

Pitezel, the child who identified him before the coroner. We could not call her to prove that the stiff and disfigured corpse upon which her young eyes gazed at the potter's field was the body of her dead father. We could not produce her for that purpose, for the mother has told us that the last she saw of her was her dead body in the morgue in the city of Toronto."

Graham shook his head sadly before continuing. "No, that piece of evidence the Commonwealth could not produce. But the Commonwealth proceeds formally and in an orderly manner to establish to your satisfaction that this body was the body of Benjamin F. Pitezel."

Besides the witnesses Graham had called, there was other, even more convincing evidence of the corpse's identity. "Not only have these half dozen people said Perry and Pitezel were the same, but we go to the grave itself, and from its dark recesses we bring forth silent but persuasive testimony on the question of identity. Pieces of the clothing from the dead body were taken by the doctor. Here is a piece of the shirt that this man wore. Poor Mrs. Pitezel was called back to that stand, and you may remember the broken sobs with which she exclaimed, 'Oh, that's Benny's shirt that he took with him when he left St. Louis for Philadelphia.' That burned fragment is part of the clothing that the wife identifies as that of her husband. Buried with the body, deep down in that dark grave, it comes forth to the living light to proclaim that the body resting there is the body of Holmes's friend, Benjamin F. Pitezel."

Having shown that it was Pitezel who had died at the Callowhill Street address and that he "was not self-destroyed but destroyed by a second person in that house," the Commonwealth was next obliged to prove that the killer was Holmes. Accordingly, Graham proceeded with a detailed synopsis of the insurance conspiracy, of Holmes's financial motives for eliminating his partner, and of his suspicious behavior on the day of Pitezel's death, when the defendant, "in the company of his wife, practically fled from the city of Philadelphia."

With withering scorn, Graham described Holmes's initial statements to the police. "They are marvelous productions in the line of fiction. They are wonderful statements, with scarcely an element of truth in them. The facility with which this man could utter one falsehood after another must be apparent to you in your observation of this testimony, and from the statements you have heard, not only from the officials but from the lips of this pure, good woman whom he called his wife, Miss Yoke.

"Think of it!" Graham cried, his voice ringing with indignation. "Think of it! Think of the deception and the falsehood! Think of his deceit to her! He meets her in St. Louis. He is going to engage her as his wife. He then tells her the story of a fictitious uncle, with his millions, or whatever the estate may have been, and who requested that he, H. H. Holmes, should take the name of Henry Mansfield Howard, and thenceforth be known as his heir. He enters into one of the most sacred relations in life with deception and deceit upon him. He marries her as Henry Mansfield Howard. During all of his journeys, he never once places his own name upon the register of a hotel. Lies supply the place of truth at every point, and false registry is the order of his journey at every hotel."

Swiveling away from the jury box, Graham stabbed an accusing finger in the direction of the prisoner, who seemed to quail before the thrust. "Upon every step, from point to point, as we go through this evidence, we find Mudgett, alias Holmes, a fabricator and a falsifier!"

Graham turned back to the jurors. "But this is a digression, so I ask your attention to his statement again. He tells you that a body was substituted. Was there a body substituted? Don't you believe with me that this man"—here, Graham held up the photograph of Pitezel he had shown to Dessie on the second day of the trial—"was the man who was buried in potter's field? Don't you think that this is the man whose body was found in the second-story room? Lie number one. But he says, 'B. F. Pitezel is down in South America and he has little Howard with him.'

"Oh, gentlemen, that is an awful, a frightful statement. What fearful twisting and destruction of the truth! Pitezel in South America! He had seen the body taken up out of the potter's field and made little Alice testify that it was the body of the father. Down in South America! It is a wonder that the lie did not scorch his lips, as the flames scorched the dead body of Pitezel and consumed the flesh. Little Howard with his father in South America! Gentlemen, think of it, and then recall in that connection the broken utterances of that poor woman Mrs. Pitezel, as she was about to leave the stand, when she said—in answer to the question, where did you see Howard last?—'I last saw little Howard's belongings in the coroner's office in Indianapolis.' Little Howard in South America with his father? God help such a liar!"

Graham paused for a moment, as though to recover his composure after being swept away by the force of his outrage. When he spoke again, his voice seemed weighted down with a terrible pathos.

"Then comes the story of Mrs. Pitezel. Gentlemen, you remember that story. I am not going to weary you by its repetition. In all the fifteen years of my service in this office, I do not remember a story that stirred my heart or moved my sensibilities like the broken sentences of that woman when, with evident suffering in every line and mark upon her face, in the supreme effort that she made to control herself and to avoid breaking down, she told that pitiful, yet marvelous, story, of how this man led her from place to place in the pursuit of her husband. That was a strange story, gentlemen. If you and I had read it in fiction, we would say, perhaps, that the novelist had overstated the facts, that he had overdrawn the story and made it stronger than our imagination or fancy could tolerate."

In spite of his promise not to "weary" the jurors with a repetition of the tale, Graham, in fact, went on to recall it at some length. "Was ever power over a family more complete than this man's?" he marveled. "Every letter intercepted—no communication between them. Not one syllable from child to mother. Not one syllable from mother to child. Did I speak wrongfully, gentlemen, or was I cruel in making the statement when I said that this was a man of steel, with a heart of stone? Anyone that would take these children's letters addressed to their mother and hide and conceal them may justly be charged with being heartless, and with being cruel beyond comparison.

"He is the jailer of the family. He suppresses their mail. But"—and here Graham allowed a grim smile to play about his lips—"he does not destroy it. For in almost every case of villainy and criminality, somehow or other, whether it be providential for the detection and punishment of the rascal or not, I cannot tell, but somehow, the villain overreaches himself in his efforts at concealment, and here and there a telltale fact comes to light and points the unerring finger of accusation at him, saying, 'That's the guilty man.' Yes, this is a marvelous story, and the conclusion of it is not less marvelous than the rest."

Graham wound up his address by retracing the steps of his argument, marking out a path that could lead to only one possible conclusion. "See how far in our progress we have come. We have established that this is Benjamin F. Pitezel. We have established that he has died of chloroform poisoning. We have established that it was not self-administered but administered by a second person. We have shown that Holmes was there in the house on that fateful Sunday alone with the dead man. We have shown that every story told by him to explain his presence was false. We have shown that his allegation of suicide was false. We have shown the effort at concealment when there was no other object unless it be that the defendant knew he had committed a murder and was telling these falsehoods, one after the other, to conceal it.

"Upon no other hypothesis can his conduct be explained than that he was concealing the crime of murder. That is what made him flee from city to city. That is what made him take his wife with him upon this wonderful journey. That is what made him take the children along. That is what made him conceal the letters. And that is what made him shut off communication between the different members of that household.

"This man was fleeing from the shadow of murder. That was the crime he was seeking to avoid. That was what he was fleeing from. It was the menace of pursuit and detection that made him take this journey, which, if it had not been interrupted at Boston, would only have terminated when he reached Berlin with his alleged wife, Miss Yoke."

The speech ended quietly, as though—having marshaled such compelling evidence of the defendant's guilt—Graham had no further need of eloquence. "Now this strange story is drawing to a close. It has been dramatic in its incidents, but those incidents have nothing to do with the case. The fact that this man appears without counsel and then with counsel has nothing to do with his guilt or innocence. The simple question is: Has the Commonwealth of Pennsylvania, as it is bound to do, made out its case beyond a fair and reasonable doubt? If you believe it has, then your duty is to find a verdict of murder of the first degree against this man. There is no middle ground. If this man was poisoned, then there was purpose to kill, and it was a willful, premeditated, and deliberate murder, and this prisoner is responsible in the highest form of verdict you can render."

Thanking them for their "patient and earnest attention," the district attorney bowed to the jurors and returned to his seat. The murmured approbation of the crowd made it clear that—had such demonstrations been permitted in the courtroom—Graham, like any virtuoso, would have been rewarded with a standing ovation.

51

And when the jury returned its verdict, Justice cried, "Amen!"

—Frank P. Geyer, *The Holmes-Pitezel Case*

Rotan's closing argument did not get under way until three P.M., following a one-hour lunch recess. His speech was a good deal briefer than the district attorney's, and not nearly as accomplished. Still, the young lawyer won praise from his listeners for an able performance in the face of overwhelming odds.

Aware that he was battling not only against Graham but also against the unbridled allegations of the press, Rotan began by reminding the jurors that Holmes was entitled to the presumption of innocence. In doing so, Rotan displayed his own flair for dramatic metaphor:

"While there may have been opinions formed by you from the newspapers in reference to this case, you have promised to put all that aside as unreliable. You have come here, and after looking at this defendant, by the law you must say, 'This man is to my mind an innocent man.' This man, as you look upon him, is as though he were clothed in armor. This armor is that presumption of innocence with which the law surrounds him, and while all the poisonous influences which you may have found in the papers, and all the condemning evidence in this case, beat up against and pierce that armor, the presumption is not removed until the whole armor is shattered and falls clanging to the ground."

Cleverly (and necessarily, since the defense had made no case of its own), Rotan used the Commonwealth's witnesses to his own advantage. Far from challenging their testimony, he freely conceded its truth, while arguing that it only served to bolster the defense's position—that Pitezel had taken his own life.

He admitted that the dead man was Benjamin Pitezel; that Pitezel and Holmes were not only intimate friends but co-conspirators in the insurance fraud; that Holmes had visited the Callowhill Street house on the day of the death; that Pitezel's stomach contained several ounces of chloroform; and that Holmes had kept Carrie on the move by pretending that her husband was still alive.

Nevertheless, he insisted, "if you look at the evidence, you will see by analyzing it carefully that every fact in the case is more consistent with the theory of suicide than it is with the crime of murder."

In essence, Rotan's argument consisted of a series of questions designed to elicit that "reasonable doubt" on which he hoped to win an acquittal. Why, he asked, would Holmes—the purported criminal mastermind—have made it so hard for himself to collect the insurance money if he had intended to murder Pitezel from the start? Why was the insurance policy made payable to Carrie instead of to Holmes? Why would Holmes have introduced chloroform into the corpse's stomach, thereby making it appear as though Pitezel had poisoned himself? "Can you imagine a man killing another in a manner which would show that there was suicide when the policy contained a clause against suicide?"

And there were other weak links in the Commonwealth's supposedly flawless chain of evidence. How could Holmes—"a weak, light, frail man, effeminate in his manner, effeminate in his strength"—have overcome a "strong, muscular, powerfully built" individual such as Pitezel, who outweighed him by at least twenty-five pounds? According to the district attorney, Pitezel had drunk himself into a stupor the evening before and was still unconscious when Holmes arrived at Callowhill Street. But the Commonwealth's own medical experts had testified that there was "nothing in the stomach to show that there was alcohol in any considerable amount, nothing in the brain to show that there was alcohol there.

"What then could it have been?" exclaimed Rotan. "Could it have been that Pitezel was asleep? The defendant never left the boardinghouse on North Fifteenth Street until half-past ten or eleven o'clock in the morning, and it took from twenty to twenty-five minutes at the very least to come down to Thirteenth and Callowhill. This would bring it to ten or twenty minutes of eleven. Is it likely that the man would have been asleep at that time? Is there anything to show that he was lying in bed? He was lying on the floor. Would a man naturally lie on the floor to go to sleep? It is not natural to infer that when a man goes to a room he lies down on the floor, and you find him there asleep at half-past ten or twenty minutes of eleven on Sunday morning."

Rotan acknowledged that Holmes had manipulated Carrie Pitezel by promising her that she would soon be reunited with her husband. But here, too, he argued, there was nothing to suggest that Holmes was guilty of any crime worse than insurance fraud.

Why," asked Rotan, "was Holmes taking this woman around with him—to Toronto, Detroit, Prescott, Ogdensburg? It was evidently his intention to make for the seacoast and get them all out of the country. Since Mrs. Pitezel knew of the insurance conspiracy, Holmes could not very well have left her in St. Louis, or at the home of her parents in Galva, since she would have been found readily by the police and would have been a witness against him in the fraud.

"If Holmes had stated to Mrs. Pitezel that Pitezel was dead, what would have been the result? In the first place, she would have broken down, and in the second place, she might have said, 'My husband being dead, I will travel no further.' Thus, he kept holding out this inducement for her to travel. He was exercising control over her to keep her moving with him, to get her and all of them out of the country so that, if the fraudulent collection of the insurance money were found out, he would be safe and the witnesses against him out of reach."

Finally, asked Rotan, why—if Holmes had murdered Pitezel—did he return voluntarily to Philadelphia when he could have been taken to Texas to face the far less serious charge of horse theft? "Now the Commonwealth would have you believe they lynch men in Texas for stealing horses, and Holmes was afraid of that. But do they really lynch men, except by mobs, except when horse thieves are caught in the act? Would they lynch a man arrested three thousand miles away and brought back by due process of law, months later, long after the tempers involved had had full opportunity to cool down?

"No. Holmes returned to Philadelphia voluntarily to face whatever charges faced him in Philadelphia. And if he had killed Pitezel, surely he must have known he had done it. And he must have known, too, if he had done it, he would one day be found out. But he returned—fearlessly—and his fearlessness was the product of his innocence of murder."

Bringing his argument to a close, Rotan demonstrated his agility by paying tribute to Graham's superior eloquence while reminding the jurors that it was their solemn duty to base their decision on hard evidence, not highflown oratory.

"This man," he said, gesturing toward the prisoner's dock where Holmes sat plucking nervously at his chin hairs, "has been assailed for a long time in this and other matters. He has been indicted here for murder, and the case is now going to you for your most earnest consideration. I shall expect that only in regard to the testimony given from the witness stand is this man to be judged, and I want you not to be influenced by the magnificent oration and the masterly way in which the Commonwealth, represented by our learned district attorney, has presented the facts in his speeches. He is handy and adept at that—he is a master hand. We, to an extent, are greatly inexperienced, never having had such opportunities for experience, and, I may say, probably never will attain the height which the district attorney has in conducting cases of this kind.

"I only ask that you will not prejudice this case on account of any speech made by him. You should not be influenced by that."

Rotan spoke his final words with all the assurance he

could muster. "I now let this case go to you with a great deal of confidence—so much confidence that we have not put in a defense. We feel that the Commonwealth has failed in removing that reasonable doubt to which the prisoner is entitled, and that we can safely rely upon this case going to you and your rendering a verdict of not guilty."

Immediately following Rotan's speech, Judge Arnold gave his charge to the jury. He began by reiterating a point Graham had made in his opening address—that, while the jurors had it in their power to find Holmes guilty of second-degree murder or manslaughter, neither of those verdicts "would be in accord with the evidence. In my judgment, the case is one in which there should be a verdict either of murder in the first degree or a verdict of acquittal."

Since the Commonwealth's case had been built entirely on circumstantial evidence, Judge Arnold spent some time defining that concept: "The word *circumstantial* leads some persons to believe that the evidence is inconclusive and imperfect, but this is not so. The difference between circumstantial and direct evidence is that direct evidence is more immediate—the evidence of the eyesight, generally—and requires fewer witnesses than a chain of circumstances which leads to but one conclusion."

To clarify the point, the judge provided a vivid example. "Suppose, while walking along the street, you hear something behind you that sounds like a pistol shot. You turn and find a man running past you, with others in pursuit. You join in the chase and see the man arrested. You walk back with him under arrest, and on the way back you find a pistol with a chamber discharged, and still warm and smoking. Further on, you come upon a man who has been killed by a pistol shot. What is the inference that you draw from those facts? And is not that inference irresistible? Yet, you did not see the pistol fired.

"Now in the case of killing by means of poison, experience shows that nearly all such cases are proved by circumstantial evidence only. Poisoning is generally a secret act, and unless the party using the poison has someone to assist him, who afterwards confesses and testifies, direct evidence cannot be obtained.

"In the present case, the defendant is accused of killing Benjamin F. Pitezel by means of poison. Three questions must be considered and determined and answered by you in order to reach a verdict of guilty of murder as charged in the indictment.

"The first question is: Is Benjamin F. Pitezel dead? The second is: Did he die a violent death? And the third is: If he died a violent death, did he commit suicide or did the defendant kill him?"

Judge Arnold then spent over an hour reviewing the "sum and substance" of the testimony in the case from his handwritten notes. Outside the courtroom windows, the somber daylight faded. The gray fall sky had darkened to black by the time he brought his remarks to a close.

"In all criminal cases, gentlemen, it is essential that the defendant shall be convicted by evidence which persuades the jury of the guilt of the prisoner beyond a reasonable doubt. If, after considering the testimony, you are unable to come to the conclusion that he is guilty—if there is a doubt about it and you hesitate, or if you are not fairly satisfied by the evidence of his guilt—he is entitled to the benefit of the doubt and should be acquitted."

Removing his pince-nez reading glasses and laying down his sheaf of notes, the judge gazed gravely at the jurors. "Consider this defendant's case calmly, considerately, patiently. I have no doubt that if you will do that, if you adhere to the evidence, you will have no trouble in reaching a righteous verdict."

It was almost six P.M. when the jurors were escorted to the deliberation room by a contingent of court officers. As soon as they were under lock and key, Graham—following through on a promise he had made to the press corps a few days earlier—led the reporters into his office and allowed them to examine a cache of evidence that (as one of the newsmen wrote) "left no doubt that Holmes was a scoundrel unworthy of human form."

These grisly items—barred from the trial by Judge Arnold's ruling in regard to the Pitezel children—included Howard's charred jawbone and several of his teeth, the stove in which the boy had been incinerated, and the spade Holmes had used to bury the bodies of Alice and Nellie.

Graham also displayed Benjamin Pitezel's skull, which (along with the samples of clothing identified by Carrie) had been removed from the corpse during the recent exhumation. Graham had been ready to introduce the skull into evidence, but had refrained when the defense admitted that the dead man was Pitezel.

As the relics were being passed from hand to hand, Graham noticed an unfamiliar individual examining Pitezel's skull with an intensity that surpassed even that of the journalists. Making his way through the crowd, Graham confronted this gentlemen, who turned out to be none other than C. A. Bradenburgh, proprietor of the "Holmes Museum" at Ninth and Arch streets. Bradenburgh—who had been raking in money during the past few months by displaying a substitute skull among his other replicas—made it clear to the district attorney that he was willing to offer a handsome sum for the original. Would the Commonwealth be interested in such a transaction?

"Indeed not!" cried the outraged attorney, snatching the skull out of the impresario's hands and showing him unceremoniously to the door.

Holmes, meanwhile, had been led to the basement cell to await the verdict. Though he showed little appetite for the dinner he was offered, he seemed, on the whole, remarkably self-possessed for a man whose fate was hanging in the balance. He chatted with his jailers and passed some time idly flipping a coin—thumbing it into the air, catching it in his palm, and slapping it over onto the back of his opposite hand.

When one of his guards, Charles Wood, asked him what he was doing, Holmes replied that he was trying to predict the verdict. "Tails, convicted," Holmes said with a wry smile. "Heads, acquitted."

Altogether, Holmes flipped the coin ten times. It came up heads—"not guilty"—every time but one.

Holmes wasn't the only one playing guessing games. Back in the courtroom—where most of the crowd had remained in place, afraid of losing their seats if they left them—lawyers and laymen alike argued and even wagered over the outcome.

Interestingly, the consensus matched the prediction of Holmes's tossed coin. The majority agreed that, for all Graham's skill, the Commonwealth had failed to make its case beyond a reasonable doubt.

One old-timer, however—the ancient court clerk, William Henszey, who had been observing juries for more years than even he could remember—stuck to a different opinion. The twelve men who held Holmes's life in their hands were going to send him to the gallows, Henszey declared.

He had seen it in their faces.

At precisely eight forty-five a bustle in the courtroom made it clear that the jury was about to return. Judge Arnold entered first, followed by Graham and his assistant, Thomas Barlow. Next came Rotan and Shoemaker, the latter bundled in an overcoat and shivering as though afflicted with an ague.

Finally, the prisoner was ushered in and led to the dock.

The silence in the packed courtroom was almost oppressive. Every eye was turned to Holmes, who stood erect in the dock, one hand encircling the opposite wrist behind his back. He displayed no obvious signs of agitation—though spectators sitting directly behind him could see, from the whiteness of his knuckles, just how tightly he was squeezing his wrist.

A moment later, the jury filed in. Not one of them looked in Holmes's direction as they took their places in the box.

When Holmes saw the expression on their faces, his own face went white. He let out a few dry coughs, raising a trembling hand to his lips.

"Gentlemen of the jury," Clerk Henszey intoned, "have you reached a verdict?"

When the foreman replied that they had, Henszey looked at the judge. "Your Honor, the jury has agreed."

Judge Arnold nodded, and again Henszey turned to the jurors. "Gentlemen of the jury, in announcing your verdict, you will please rise and remain standing until the court hath recorded it."

The jurymen arose in a body.

"Gentlemen of the jury, how say you?" asked the gravel-voiced clerk. "Do you find the prisoner at the bar, Herman W. Mudgett, guilty of the felony of murder, whereof he stands indicted, or not guilty."

Without hesitation the foreman replied, "Guilty of murder in the first degree."

Holmes drew his lips tight to steady their quivering. Then he sank into his seat while—at Rotan's request—Clerk Henszey polled the jurors, who confirmed their condemning verdict one by one.

Afterward, one of the jurors told a reporter that he and his colleagues had arrived at their decision before the door of the deliberation room had closed behind them. But—believing it improper to send a man to the gallows without even the appearance of due consideration—they had decided to take their dinner and discuss the evidence before delivering their judgment.

As soon as the trial was formally adjourned, Holmes was led down to the basement holding room. A mob of newsmen quickly gathered outside the iron-barred door, pleading for a comment.

"I can't say very much," Holmes replied hoarsely. "I scarcely know what to add to what I have already said."

Shortly afterward, he was escorted into a van and returned to Moyamensing. By the time he was back in his cell, he had found something he wanted to say. Seated at his small writing desk, he composed a formal statement, which ran the next morning in newspapers throughout the country:

It is not safe for a man in my position to criticize the verdict which has been rendered concerning me. Many able lawyers who have followed this trial have declared that the evidence is not sufficient to convict. I, who know my own innocence of the charge brought against me, know, of course, that no evidence *could* be brought. I know that I am innocent and, while lack of time and money to prepare my case have brought about this temporary defeat of justice, I know that I shall be acquitted and vindicated in the end.

I have been told and I have been warned that for me to tell the truth would be dangerous. A plain denial, I was told, would be more convincing than any explanation, however truthful. I believed, however, as I still believe, that an innocent man cannot be convicted under our laws and that he could certainly not be convicted for telling the truth.

I am aware that a higher tribunal must pass upon my sentence before it can be confirmed. I know that this higher tribunal must, in the face of my innocence, give me a new trial. At this new trial I shall have had time, at least, to prepare my defense and to refute the web of false contortions spun by the ambitious lawyers who have prosecuted and persecuted me.

I did not murder Pitezel. He committed suicide. I am innocent of the charge against me. I cannot possibly be condemned for a crime which I did not commit.

Early in my life I was thrown much into the company of an old man, upon whom I grew to look at almost as an oracle. Often he would say to me: "He that seeks sympathy receives ridicule." Bearing this in mind, and in no sense wishing to appear before the public as a martyr, yet more for the sake of others than myself, I ask that for a time at least I be dealt with leniently, for in the name of Almighty

DEPRAVED

God and in the names of those who are near and
dear to me, I state that I have not taken a
human life.

That was what Holmes had to say on the day his trial
ended. But it was not his final word.

A few months later, he would issue another, very different
statement. And its publication would send shock waves
across America.

383

52

I was born with the devil in me. I could not help the fact that I was a murderer, no more than the poet can help the inspiration to sing.... I was born with the Evil One standing as my sponsor beside the bed where I was ushered into the world, and he has been with me since.

—From the confession of H. H. Holmes

On Friday morning, April 10, 1896, *THE PHILADELPHIA INQUIRER* carried a half-page announcement for a sensational coming attraction, scheduled to appear in its Sunday edition:

HOLMES CONFESSES MANY MURDERS

The Most Fearful and Horrible Murderer Ever Known in the Annals of Crime

FIRST AND ONLY COMPLETE CONFESSION

The Most Remarkable Story of Murder and Inhuman Villainy Ever Made Public

CONVICTION LIES IN EVERY LINE

The only way to describe it is to say that it was written by Satan himself or one of his chosen monsters

Printed in the center of the ad was a facsimile letter, penned in Holmes's flowing hand: "The following statement was written by me in Philadelphia County Prison for the *Philadelphia Inquirer* as a true and accurate confession in all particulars. It is the only confession of my fearful crimes I have made or will make. I write it fully appreciating all the horror it contains & how it condemns me before the world."

Having spent so much time protesting his innocence and proclaiming himself a scapegoat for a politically ambitious district attorney, Holmes seemed to have undergone an extraordinary change of heart. Presumably, he was eager to unburden himself before coming face-to-face with his Maker. But those with a firsthand knowledge of Holmes's profoundly manipulative nature perceived other, less pious, motives behind this remarkable turnabout.

Holmes, to begin with, had nothing to lose. Three weeks after the jury brought in its verdict, the Pennsylvania Supreme Court had turned down his appeal for a new trial. On November 30, he had been sentenced to hang. By the time *The Philadelphia Inquirer* trumpeted the news of the upcoming confession, Holmes's execution had been set for Thursday, May 7.

On the other hand, Holmes had a great deal to gain by publicizing his atrocities. In mid-March, he had received a visit from representatives of newspaper czar William Randolph Hearst, who reportedly offered him $7,500 for exclusive rights to his confession—a considerable sum in 1896 dollars. Even with the gallows looming, Holmes had an eye for the main chance. By all accounts, he had always been a good provider for his Wilmette wife, Myrta, and their little daughter, Lucy. Hearst's money would make a substantial bequest—and Holmes, for his part, was prepared to give good value in return.

But money was only part of the story. Holmes had another, even more powerful inducement, more in keeping with his uniquely perverse aspirations. As early as October 30, a newspaper reporter, visiting the notorious criminal in his cell, had noted Holmes's desperate "ambition to be great in some way—and his models of greatness, if one may judge from his talk, are old-time villains of high degree."

And indeed, immediately after the end of Holmes's trial, District Attorney Graham had prophesied to reporters "that Holmes will confess fully when he finds all hope of escape is gone. His pride in his criminal career is unbounded. In his most despondent moods, he would always cheer up when told by Mr. Barlow and myself that we considered him the most dangerous man in the world. It is our confident belief that, before he dies, he will make such confession as will give him the highest possible rank as a wholesale criminal."

It was a remarkably astute prediction. For on Sunday, April 12, 1896, Holmes displayed himself before the world as the most monstrous criminal of his day, a psychopathic killer whose record of slaughter would remain unmatched until the latter half of our own century and the dawning of the era he foreshadowed—the Age of the Serial Killer.

During the police investigation of the Castle, when hysteria over the "archfiend" was at its height, newspapers had bandied about all sorts of figures. Estimates of his victims ranged from a half dozen to several hundred.

The final number he admitted to on Sunday, April 12, was a great deal smaller than the most frenzied guesses, though certainly enough to mark him as the most prolific murderer of his day.

Twenty-seven people—men, women, and children.

Before providing the hideous details of his crimes, Holmes offered a few prefatory comments. The nature of these remarks suggests that, besides being a reader of Mark Twain and Robert Louis Stevenson, Holmes was familiar with the work of Edgar Allan Poe, especially the famous short story "William Wilson," whose narrator begins by describing his transformation from a "trivial" criminal into the most infamous villain of his age, "an object for the scorn—for the horror—for the detestation of my race." Wilson's "record of unpardonable crime" is so painful for him to set down that he contemplates his rapidly approaching death with relief.

Holmes begins his confession in a strikingly similar vein. "A word as to the motives that have led to the commission of these many crimes and I will proceed to the most distaste-

ful task of my life, the setting forth in all its horrid naked-
ness the recital of the premeditated killing of twenty-seven
human beings ... thus branding myself as the most detest-
able criminal of modern times—a task so hard and distaste-
ful that, beside it, the certainty that in a few days I am to
be hanged by the neck until I am dead seems but a pastime."

In spite of his promise, however, Holmes does not offer
any motives for his crimes. Instead, he describes an extraordinary metamorphosis that has taken place during the past
two years.

"I am convinced that since my imprisonment I have
changed woefully and gruesomely from what I was formerly
in feature and figure. My features are assuming a pronounced Satanical cast. I have become afflicted with that
dread disease, rare but terrible, with which physicians are
acquainted, but over which they have no control whatsoever.
That disease is a malformation or distortion of the osseous
parts. ... My head and face are gradually assuming an elon-
gated shape. I believe fully that I am growing to resemble
the devil—that the similitude is almost completed.

"In fact, so impressed am I with this belief, that I am
convinced I no longer have anything human in me."

After reading the narrative that followed this amazing
declaration, his readers were undoubtedly inclined to agree.

Though evidence strongly suggests otherwise, Holmes in-
sists that he was innocent of murder until 1886, when he
killed his first victim, Dr. Robert Leacock of Baltimore, "a
friend and former schoolmate," whose life was "insured for
a large sum," which Holmes made a failed attempt to collect.
Until that time, writes Holmes, he had "never sinned so
heavily by thought or deed. Later, like the man-eating tiger
of the tropical jungle, whose appetite for blood has once
been aroused, I roamed about the world seeking whom I
could destroy."

Another physician, a man named Russell, became
Holmes's second victim. Russell, a tenant of the Castle, had
fallen behind in his rent. During a heated quarrel over the
matter, Holmes "struck him to the floor with a heavy chair,"
and "with one cry for help, ending in a groan of anguish,

[Russell] ceased to breathe." Russell's corpse became the first of many that Holmes sold to an acquaintance at a medical college for $25 to $45 apiece.

Julia Conner and her four-year-old daughter, Pearl, were next. Holmes is titillatingly vague about Julia's murder, writing only that she died "to a certain extent due to a criminal operation." He did away with the little girl to eliminate her as a potential witness. "The death of Pearl," he writes, "was caused by poison. . . . It was done as I believed the child was old enough to remember of her mother's death."

The fifth murder was the cold-blooded killing of a man identified only as Rodgers, a fellow tenant at a rooming house in West Morgantown, Virginia, where Holmes was "boarding for a few weeks" during a business trip. "Learning that the man had some money, I induced him to go on a fishing trip with me, and, being successful in allaying his suspicions, I finally ended his life by a sudden blow upon the head with an oar."

Victim number six also died of a fractured skull—though in this case, Holmes claims, the fatal blow was struck by an accomplice. The victim was a "Southern speculator" named Charles Cole. "After considerable correspondence, this man came to Chicago, and I enticed him into the Castle, where, while engaging him in conversation, a confederate struck him a most vicious blow upon the head with a piece of gas pipe." Cole's skull was so damaged that the corpse was "almost useless" as a medical specimen. As for the unnamed accomplice, Holmes says only that "he was fully as guilty as myself and, if possible, more heartless and bloodthirsty, and I have no doubt is still engaged in the same nefarious work."

The seventh victim was a domestic named Lizzie, who worked in the Castle restaurant. Holmes's underling, Pat Quinlan—a married man with several small children—had become infatuated with the young woman. Afraid that the indispensable Quinlan might quit his employ and run off with the girl, Holmes "thought it wise to end [her] life. . . . This I did by calling her to my office and suffocating her in the vault, she being the first victim that died therein. Before her death, I compelled her to write letters to her relations and to Quinlan, stating that she had left Chicago for a Western state and would not return."

Throughout the Castle investigation, Holmes had been compared to the folktale character Bluebeard—the legendary lady-killer who butchered each of his successive brides when she opened a forbidden door and discovered the dead bodies of her predecessors. Holmes's account of his next crimes made this analogy seem more apt than ever.

These murders occurred immediately after Lizzie's killing—indeed, on the very evening that Holmes was getting the corpse of Quinlan's sweetheart ready for transport to a medical college. Among the tenants of the Castle at that time were a gentleman named Frank Cook, his wife, Sarah, and the latter's niece, Miss Mary Haracamp of Hamilton, Canada, who, shortly after her arrival in Chicago, had entered Holmes's employ as a stenographer.

For reasons he fails to explain, "Mrs. Cook and her niece had access to all the rooms in the Castle by means of a master key." On the evening in question, Holmes was upstairs "busily preparing my last victim for shipment" when "the door suddenly opened and Mrs. Cook and her niece stood before me. It was a time for quick action, rather than for words of explanation on my part, and before they had recovered from the horror of the sight, they were within the fatal vault, so lately tenanted by the dead body."

What made this crime even more abhorrent was the fact that "Mrs. Cook, had she lived, would have soon become a mother." Counting the unborn child, Holmes's murder tally had now reached ten.

Emeline Cigrand became victim number eleven. For the first time, Holmes confirmed what the police had suspected for months—that he had murdered the lovely young woman by suffocating her in his vault. He had done this, he claimed, because Emeline had become engaged to another man—an "attachment that was particularly obnoxious to me, both because Miss Cigrand had become almost indispensable in my office work and because she had become my mistress as well as stenographer."

On the morning of her marriage day, Emeline dropped by Holmes's office to bid him good-bye. Tricking her into his vault, he slammed the door behind her, then promised to release her if she wrote a letter to her fiancé, calling off the wedding. "She was very willing to do this and prepared to leave the vault upon completing the letter, only to learn that the door would never again be opened until she had ceased to suffer the tortures of a slow and lingering death."

Holmes then goes on to describe a botched attempt at a triple murder. Apparently hard up for money and eager to collect "the ninety dollars that my agent for disposing of 'stiffs' would have given me for the bodies," he had attempted to kill three young women who worked in his restaurant. Late one night, he snuck into the room they shared in the Castle and attacked them in their beds. "That these women lived to tell of their experience ... is due to my foolishly trying to chloroform all of them at the same time. By their combined strength they overpowered me and ran screaming into the street, clad only in their night robes." Holmes reveals that he "was arrested the next day but was not prosecuted."

Adding these intended victims to Mrs. Pitezel and her two surviving children, whose lives he had also attempted to take, Holmes feels justified in claiming (whether with pride or contrition, it is impossible to say) "thirty-three [victims] instead of twenty-seven, as it was through no fault of my own that they escaped."

Holmes was more successful with his next victim, "a very beautiful young woman named Rosine Van Jossand." After living with her "for a time" in the Castle, he poisoned her "by administering ferro-cyanide of potassium" and then buried her remains in the basement.

Holmes's claim that his bloodlust grew stronger with each new death seemed borne out by the sadistic cruelty of his next killing. The victim was a onetime Castle employee named Robert Lattimer, who knew "of certain insurance work I had engaged in" and made the mistake of trying to blackmail Holmes. "His own death and the sale of his body was the recompense meted out to him. I confined him within the secret room and slowly starved him to death.... Finally, needing its use for another purpose, and because his pleadings had become almost unbearable, I ended his life. The partial excavation in the walls of this room found by the police was caused by Lattimer's endeavoring to escape by tearing away the solid brick and mortar with his unaided fingers."

Asphyxiation, slow starvation, and chloroform poisoning—Holmes's favorite methods of destruction—were used to eliminate several more Castle victims: a woman identified only as "Kate ———"; a "young Englishman" who had been Holmes's partner in various real-estate schemes; a wealthy widow "whose name has passed from my memory"; and a "man who came to Chicago to visit the Columbian Exposition." For the sake of either convenience or variety, however, he occasionally employed other methods as well. He dispatched two women—a Miss Anna Betts and Julia Conner's sister, Gertie—by substituting poison for prescription medicines. And he claims to have killed a man named Warner—the "originator" of the patented "Warner Glass Bending Process"—in an especially gruesome way.

"It will be remembered," Holmes writes, "that the remains of a large kiln made of firebrick was found in the Castle basement. . . . It was so arranged that in less than a minute after turning on a jet of crude oil atomized with steam, the entire kiln would be filled with a colorless flame, so intensely hot that iron would be melted therein." Holmes had presumably constructed this kiln because he was interested in going into the glass-bending business himself, and it was under the pretext of getting "certain minute explanations of the process" from the inventor that he managed to lure Warner into the oven. As soon as Warner was inside, Holmes "closed the door and turned on both the oil and steam to their full extent. In a short time, not even the bones of my victim remained."

Victims twenty-one and twenty-two were the Williams sisters. At long last, Holmes gave up pretending that Minnie Williams was alive and admitted that his lurid tale of sororicide was a lie.

Retracting his earlier aspersions—his portrayal of Minnie as a mentally unstable strumpet who had run off to London to open a massage parlor after murdering her sister in a jealous rage—Holmes apologizes for the "wrongs I have heaped upon her name" and attests to her "pure and Christian life.... Prior to her meeting me in 1893, she was a virtuous woman." Soon after her arrival in Chicago, Minnie came to work for Holmes, and it wasn't long before he had persuaded her "to give me $2,500 in money and to transfer to me by deed $50,000 worth of Southern real estate." He also induced her "to live with me as my wife, all this being easily accomplished owing to her innocent and child-like nature, she hardly knowing right from wrong in such matters."

Correctly perceiving her younger (and far shrewder) sister, Nannie, as a potential threat to his schemes, Holmes invited her to Chicago, brought her to the Castle, and killed her in the vault. "It was the footprint of Nannie Williams," he writes, "that was found upon the painted surface of the vault door, made during her violent struggles before death." Minnie's murder followed shortly thereafter. According to this version, Holmes took her on a trip to Momence, Illinois, where—in an abandoned house on the outskirts of town— he poisoned her and buried her body in the basement.

But Holmes hadn't finished with the Williams family. After Minnie's death, he "found among her papers an insurance policy made out in her favor by her brother, Baldwin Williams of Leadville, Colorado. I therefore went to that city early in 1894 and, having found him, took his life by shooting him, it being believed I had done so in self-defense."

Of all his sins, Holmes professes the deepest remorse for those he committed against Minnie. "Because of her spotless life before she knew me, because of the large amount of money I defrauded her of, because I killed her sister and brother, because, not being satisfied with all this, I endeavored after my arrest to blacken her good name ... for all these reasons this is without exception the saddest and most heinous of any of my crimes."

Unsurprisingly, Holmes devotes the most space to the crime he had been condemned for. After two years of denying his guilt, he finally admits to Benjamin Pitezel's murder. In fact, he goes even further. For reasons that can only be surmised—a perverse desire to live up to his satanic billing, a showman's willingness to give his public their money's worth, or possibly a sincere need to confess his most heinous sins—he portrays himself as infinitely more cruel than even his prosecutors had suggested.

"It will be understood," Holmes states, "that from the first hour of our acquaintance, even before I knew he had a family who would later afford me additional victims for the gratification of my bloodthirstiness, I intended to kill him." He is at pains to exonerate his late accomplice of any involvement in murder, declaring that Pitezel "neither knew of nor was a party to the taking of any human life." Investing the victim with a dimension of innocence, this revelation only adds to the horror of the crime.

And indeed that crime, as Holmes here describes it, was far more horrific than anyone had suspected:

> Pitezel left his home for the last time late in July, 1894, a happy, light-hearted man, to whom trouble or discouragements of any kind were almost unknown. We then journeyed together to New York and later to Philadelphia, where the fatal house upon Callowhill Street in which he met his death September 2, 1894, was hired.... Then came the waiting from day to day until I should be sure of finding him in a drunken stupor at midday.... After thus preparing I went to the house, quietly unlocked the door, and stole noiselessly within and to the second-story room, where I found him insensibly drunk, as I had expected.
>
> Only one difficulty presented itself. It was necessary for me to kill him in such a manner that no struggle or movement of his body should occur.... I overcame this difficulty by first binding him hand and foot, and having done this I proceeded to burn him alive by saturating his clothing and his face with benzine and igniting it with a match. So horrible was this torture that in writing of it, I have been tempted to attribute his death to some more humane means—not with a wish to spare myself,

but because I fear that it will not be believed that one could be so heartless and depraved.

Holmes's description of the death of little Howard Pitezel is equally shocking. After making his preparations—"purchasing the drugs I needed to kill the boy," then stopping at "the repair shop for the long knives I had previously left there to be sharpened"—Holmes "called [Howard] into the house and insisted that he go to bed at once, first giving him the fatal dose of medicine. As soon as he had ceased to breathe, I cut his body into pieces and by the combined use of gas and corncobs proceeded to burn it with as little feeling as though it had been some inanimate object. . . . To think that I committed this and other crimes for the pleasure of killing my fellow beings, to hear their cries for mercy and pleas to be allowed even sufficient time to pray and prepare for death—all this is now too horrible for even me, hardened criminal that I am, to again live over without a shudder. Is it to be wondered at that since my arrest my days have been those of self-reproaching torture and my nights of sleepless fear? Or that even before my death, I have commenced to assume the form and features of the Evil One himself?"

As for his final victims, Alice and Nellie Pitezel, Holmes confirms the theory that he murdered the girls by locking them in his trunk, inserting a rubber tube into the hole he had bored for that purpose, then connecting the opposite end of the tube to a gas jet and asphyxiating them. "Then came the opening of the trunk and the viewing of their little blackened and distorted faces, then the digging of their shallow graves in the basement of the house, the ruthless stripping off of their clothing and the burial without a particle of covering save the cold earth."

He also confirms the truth of the insinuation made during the trial—that he had "ruined" Alice Pitezel. The deaths of the two girls, he writes, "will seem to many to be the saddest of all, both on account of the terribly heartless manner in which it was accomplished and because in one instance, that of Alice, the oldest of these children, her death was the least of the wrongs suffered at my hands."

As though recognizing that he has damned himself beyond

the hope of human forgiveness, Holmes refrains from offering a conventional closing word of repentance. "It would now seem a very fitting time for me to express regret or remorse. . . . To do so with the expectation of even one person who has read this confession to the end believing that in my depraved nature there is room for such feelings is, I fear, to expect more than would be granted."

By the time this extraordinary document was syndicated in the papers, Holmes's notoriety had spread around the world. (At one point in the confession he notes with apparent pride that his name is known "even in South Africa, where the case was recently given considerable prominence in a local issue.") Under the circumstances, it is not surprising that this shocking catalog of bloodshed and torture was a major sensation.

Within a few days of its publication, it was also the object of a heated controversy. For all its apparently brutal candor, there was a significant problem with it. Parts of it were demonstrably untrue.

For one thing, Holmes's insistence that he had undergone such a frightening physical metamorphosis that he was "thankful I am no longer allowed a [looking] glass" had no basis in fact. His jailers and visitors attested that—except for his Vandyke beard, which he had shaved—his appearance hadn't changed at all since his trial.

There was an even more troubling anomaly. Immediately after the confession appeared, a number of his presumed victims came forward to refute his claims. These included the supposedly incinerated Mr. Warner and Holmes's former employee Robert Lattimer, whose death struggles had been so graphically described. A third "victim" was known to have died in a train wreck. At the same time, Holmes was strongly suspected of having done away with other tenants of the Castle whose names he had failed to include in his confession.

District Attorney Graham offered the most convincing explanation for these inconsistencies. "The confession," he told reporters, "is a mixture of truth and falsehood. Holmes never could help lying."

Whether Holmes's lies were compulsive or calculated, they had the effect of insuring that his crimes would forever be surrounded by mystery and ambiguity. Like the bone pile found in the Castle cellar, whose jumble of human and animal remains made it impossible for the police to sort out the truth, his final statement was as much camouflage as confession.

53

No Respite for Holmes.
The Devil is Going to Get His Due.

—*Boston Globe*, May 2, 1896

Even with death approaching, Holmes's audacity remained undiminished. During the last week of April—shortly after he had publicly confessed to the murder of more than two dozen people—he applied to Governor Hastings for executive clemency. The governor declined to oblige.

Holmes was undeterred. For a man who claimed to view his coming execution as a boon—a release from his days and nights of "self-reproaching torture"—he seemed desperately eager to gain, if not a pardon, then at least a temporary reprieve. On April 30—exactly one week before his scheduled hanging—he sent a letter to Thomas Fahy, Carrie Pitezel's Philadelphia attorney. In it, Holmes laid out a complicated financial transaction relating to the encumbrances on his Chicago property. Holmes assured Fahy that he could work out a deal with his creditors that would yield at least $2,000, which he proposed "at once to place in escrow for Mrs. Pitezel's benefit." In addition, he offered Carrie "one-third of what we can realize from [the sale of] the block at Sixty-third Street."

The only catch was that these matters couldn't be resolved for several weeks—until the eighteenth of May at the earliest—which meant that Carrie would have to intercede on his behalf by petitioning Governor Hastings for a respite.

Holmes concluded his letter with an extraordinary remark. "I have tried to make matters as easy for Mrs. Pitezel as I could," wrote the man who had slain her husband and three young children. "I would also beg Mrs. Pitezel to remember that, while she may think me unfit to live, I am certainly unfit to die, and in return for what I can do for her, should like an opportunity to read and otherwise try and prepare myself for death."

When Carrie—recognizing this proposal as a flagrant bribe—refused to rise to the bait, Holmes made one last bid for borrowed time. He composed another, even more remarkable, letter, this one to his old nemesis, Detective Frank Geyer. In it, Holmes claimed that his recently published confession contained an inaccurate version of the murders of Alice, Nellie, and Howard Pitezel. "I continue to accept responsibility for the children's deaths," he wrote, "and yet I myself did not kill them. I had a confederate and directed him to do the job." Holmes offered to aid Geyer in the apprehension of this mysterious "confederate" in exchange for a reprieve.

But Geyer, like Carrie Pitezel, wouldn't bite. He was determined to see Holmes swing and had no intention of putting off that satisfaction.

By Wednesday, May 6, Holmes, the master schemer, had finally run out of ploys. And out of time.

Holmes had concluded his letter to Carrie by pleading for "an opportunity to read and otherwise try and prepare myself for death." The reading he referred to was, of course, the Bible.

Back in November, on the day his death sentence was formally passed, Holmes had been interviewed by a reporter from *The Philadelphia Public Ledger,* who asked if he intended to seek succor from "spiritual advisers." Holmes had shaken his head emphatically in reply. "I am a fatalist," he declared. "Whatever is to be is to be. I have no worries about the hereafter."

As the weeks went by, however, a change seemed to come over him. He became increasingly introspective. Coiled in a corner of his cell was a heavy iron chain used to restrain unruly prisoners: the free end was linked to a leg manacle, the other attached to an iron staple in the floor. One day, shortly after the publication of Holmes's confession, a guard looked through the bars of the cell and saw the chain laid out in the shape of a cross. A few days later, Holmes announced that he had converted to Roman Catholicism. By the final week of his life, he was receiving regular visits from the Reverend Father Dailey of the Church of the Annunciation.

And indeed, after he failed in his last feverish efforts to gain a reprieve, Holmes seemed possessed by a newfound serenity. On the night before his execution, he sat at his writing table until just past midnight, composing letters to relatives, business associates, and the surviving family members of several of his victims. At twelve-fifteen A.M., he laid down his pen, arranged his papers into tidy stacks, and began to undress, folding his clothes with his usual care. After performing his nightly devotions, he stretched out on his cot, turned his back to the light glowing dimly outside his cell door, and was asleep within minutes.

He slept soundly until six the next morning when the day watch, John Henry, came on duty.

"Harry!" the guard called softly through the bars of the door.

Holmes stirred slightly.

"Harry, it's time to get up."

Rousing himself, Holmes sat up and greeted the guard. "Is it six already?"

"Yes. How do you feel?"

Holmes considered the question a moment. "Pretty solemn."

"Are you nervous?"

Smiling slightly, Holmes rose from his cot and stuck his left hand through the bars of the door, fingers spread. "See if I tremble."

Henry would later tell reporters that the hand was "as steady as an iron bar."

After ordering a breakfast of toast, eggs, and coffee, Holmes began to dress "as unconcernedly" (according to

Henry's account) "as a man might do who had a thousand more toiletries to make before he died."

It was traditional for condemned men at Moyamensing to go to their deaths in a new suit of clothes. Holmes, however, had refused to follow this custom. Instead, he put on an outfit he had worn many times before—a light gray serge suit with lapelled vest and cutaway coat. He did make one modification. In place of his collar and tie, he knotted a white handkerchief loosely about his neck.

By then, Samuel Rotan had arrived, looking considerably more agitated than his client. After greeting the young lawyer warmly, Holmes sat him down for a last, earnest talk. The subject was Holmes's burial plan.

His career as a corpse peddler had left Holmes with a terror of ending up on someone else's dissection table. This was not an idle fear, since several prominent physicians had already declared their interest in autopsying the brain of the extraordinary criminal. There was also good reason for Holmes to believe that his body might prove irresistibly attractive to some ghoulish huckster, intent on putting it on public display. Rotan had recently been approached by one such individual, who had offered him a considerable sum—as much as $5,000, according to news reports—for the remains of the world-famous "Murder Demon."

Holmes had devised an elaborate scheme to protect his corpse from grave robbers. He was determined that his body would never be violated, either by the probing tools of science or the prurient gaze of the crowds.

At that very moment, an enormous crowd was gathered outside the great, grim walls of Moyamensing, although they had no hope of seeing the actual execution. Admission to the hanging was strictly limited to ticket holders. Requests had poured in from as far away as San Francisco—over four thousand in all. Only sixty tickets had been issued, however, each filled out with the witness's name.

The bulk of the crowd had come simply to be part of the great event. A line of city policemen was there to keep order, but the crowd was generally well behaved—laughing, chatting, exchanging crude jokes. A holiday atmosphere prevailed.

At precisely nine-thirty A.M., the small doorway set into the great wooden gate creaked open. Clutching their tickets, the witnesses forced their way through the crowd, then filed past the ferret-eyed gateman into the damp prison yard. In the end, at least twenty unauthorized individuals—relatives and friends of various prison workers—managed to gain entrance, bringing the total number of witnesses to slightly more than eighty.

Besides a score of newspapermen, the spectators included such prominent figures as Dr. N. MacDonald, the famous criminologist from Washington, D.C., Sheriff S. B. Mason of Baltimore, and Prof. W. Rasterly Ashton of Philadelphia's Medico-Chirurgical College. Also in attendance were Detective Frank Geyer and L. G. Fouse, president of the Fidelity Mutual Life Assurance Company.

For fifteen minutes or so, the group milled about the cobblestoned courtyard, where executions were conducted in earlier times. Moyamensing Prison had been constructed in 1771, and above the entranceway hung a grim reminder of that bygone era—part of an antique English gibbet. Puzzled by the rusty, iron-hooped device roughly shaped like a human being, one of the younger reporters asked about its function. He was told that long ago—in a presumably less civilized age—the bodies of the hanged were placed inside those cagelike contraptions, then suspended from high poles at crossroads until nothing but skeletons remained.

Suddenly, the door to the prison office opened. Among the fourscore witnesses were twelve sheriff's jurors, there to certify to the time, place, and manner of death of the prisoner. The jury members included three ex-sheriffs and four doctors. By a curious coincidence, another juror—Samuel Wood, a yarn manufacturer of Germantown—had also been a member of the jury at Holmes's trial.

The dozen men were summoned into the big prison office, where Sheriff Clement—a white-whiskered man in a frock coat purchased specially for this occasion—administered the oath. Afterward, the rest of the spectators were admitted to the office. For the next ten minutes, they stood about restlessly, eyeing the wall clock and filling the room with to-bacco smoke.

At precisely ten o'clock, Sheriff Clement's assistant, Mr. Grew, appeared in the room. "Hats off, gentlemen," he commanded. "And no smoking. Witnesses will please form a double line, jurors in front, and head towards that door." He gestured toward the doorway he had just come through, which opened onto the main cellblock of the prison. "You will please preserve perfect order."

Hats were removed, cigarettes and cigars extinguished underfoot. The eighty men silently arranged themselves into a double column. Then the solemn procession moved through the far doorway and into the cellblock, shoe soles scuffling on the asphalt floor.

Sunshine poured down from a big skylight, illuminating the long, whitewashed corridor with its triple-tiered cells on either side. Halfway down the corridor loomed the gallows, surrounded by a group of uniformed guards. Approaching it, the witnesses suddenly broke from their line, jostling for the best positions from which to view the execution.

More than fifty men had died on that particular gallows, which dated from the decade before the Civil War. Its railed platform stood eight feet above the ground and was painted so dark a green that it looked almost black. It might have been a speaker's stand—except for its double-doored trap and the crossbar overhead from which dangled a surprisingly slender length of rope. In the clear light, the spectators could count the seven spirals of the hangman's knot above the noosed end.

After their indecorous struggle for the best vantage points, the witnesses grew silent. Sparrows trilled in the outside courtyard as the tense spectators gazed upward, scanning the three tiers of heavily barred cells for the one that held Holmes.

After polishing off his breakfast, Holmes took paper and pen in hand for the final time and composed a brief note of gratitude to Rotan. When Fathers Dailey and MacPake arrived a few moments later, Holmes gave himself into their care. The two priests had just finished administering last rites when prison superintendent Perkins and his assistant, Alexander Richardson, appeared at the cell door.

"Are you ready?" Perkins asked the kneeling prisoner.

Holmes nodded once and got to his feet. Clasping a crucifix in both hands, he stepped into the corridor, Perkins and Sheriff Clement in front, the two white-robed priests at his sides, Rotan and Richardson bringing up the rear.

Clustered in front of the gallows, the spectators could not see the solemn party approach from the opposite side. But they could hear the chanting of the priests—a mournful drone that grew louder every moment. Suddenly, shoe soles scraped on the wooden steps of the gallows and Sheriff Clement and Superintendent Perkins materialized on the platform. A moment later, they moved briskly to one side, making room for Holmes.

Stepping up to the railing, the great criminal gazed serenely down at the crowd. In the strong morning light, his wavy hair appeared almost blond, as did his long flowing mustache. The witnesses were struck by the neatness of his attire: his brushed suit, creased trousers, polished, square-toed shoes. Holding his crucifix before him, his expression calm and untroubled, he looked like a clergyman about to deliver a homily to his Sabbath congregation.

"Gentlemen, I have a very few words to say," he began in his silken voice. "I would make no remarks at this time were it not for my feeling that by not speaking I would acquiesce in my execution by hanging. I wish to say at this instant that the extent of my misdoing in taking human life consists in the killing of two women. They died at my hands as the result of criminal operations. I only state this so that there shall be no misunderstanding of my words hereafter. I am not guilty of taking the lives of the Pitezel family, the three children or the father, Benjamin F. Pitezel, for whose death I am now to be hanged. This is all I have to say."

Later, one of Holmes's intimates—an attorney, R. O. Moon—revealed that, on the day prior to the execution, Holmes had confided to him that the "two women" were Julia Conner and Emeline Cigrand.

After making this astonishing statement—essentially an

utter retraction of the sworn confession he had published only a few weeks before—Holmes bowed politely and briefly embraced Rotan, who turned and hurried down the scaffold steps, clearly overcome with emotion. Holmes, meanwhile—hitching up his trouser legs to preserve the creases—knelt briefly between the chanting priests.

Rising again, he handed his crucifix to Father MacPake and positioned himself directly over the trap. Assistant Superintendent Richardson leaned toward him and whispered something in his ear. Nodding, Holmes removed the white handkerchief from his neck, fastened the top button of his coat, then held his hands out in front of him.

Richardson swiftly drew one of Holmes's arms behind his back, then the other. The audience heard a sharp click—handcuffs closing about the condemned man's wrists. Then Richardson took something that looked like a black satin bag and pulled it over Holmes's head.

"Make it quick, Alex," Holmes said, his voice muffled by the fabric.

Coolly, Richardson slipped the noose around Holmes's neck, lifting up the bottom of the black hood to draw the rope tight. By then, Sheriff Clement and Superintendent Perkins had melted out of sight. The priests were still kneeling by the top step, intoning the Miserere.

Pulling out his white pocket handerchief, Richardson gave a signal that the spectators couldn't see. Almost at once, a bolt clicked and the trapdoor crashed open.

The black-hooded figure plummeted, bounced upward, dropped again, then spun slowly at the end of the taut-drawn rope, its head cocked grotesquely to one side. Its fingers clenched, its chest and shoulders heaved, and its feet jerked in a weird, rhythmic motion, as though the dangling body were walking in the air.

"My God," a deputy sheriff named Saybolt gasped, then fainted into the arms of the man standing beside him. Several other spectators blanched and turned away.

As the body spiraled in a shaft of sunlight, the prison physician—Dr. Benjamin F. Butcher—stepped onto a little stool provided by a guard and placed his ear against Holmes's chest.

"Still beating," he announced.

Though the force of the fall had broken Holmes's neck and yanked the noose so tight that the hemp was embedded in his flesh, his heart continued to work for another fifteen minutes. From time to time, his body would shake and his limbs twitch convulsively. Finally, the movements subsided.

At precisely 10:25 A.M.—Thursday, May 7, 1896—H. H. Holmes was pronounced dead.

In the opinion of the sheriff's jury, death had come "instantaneously." The hanged man, they declared with authority, "had not suffered any pain."

In the end, after years of being demonized by the press—denounced as "Satan or one of his chosen monsters"—Holmes was granted not only human status but even a measure of respect. Trumpeting his execution in their morning editions, newspapers from New York City to San Francisco made note of his fortitude and courage in the final moments of his life. But it was *The Chicago Tribune*—a paper that had spent months accusing Holmes of the most diabolical acts—that paid him the ultimate tribute.

Holmes had met his death, read the headline, "like a man."

Epilogue

The Holmes Curse

Slightly less than two hours after Holmes's execution, undertaker John J. O'Rourke drove his wagon up to the rear of Moyamensing. In the bed of the wagon lay a plain pine coffin. Within minutes, Holmes's body had been bundled out of the prison and placed in the box. O'Rourke immediately returned to his house and pulled the wagon around back where two assistants awaited. On the grass beside them sat an oversize casket and five barrels of portland cement.

The coffin was taken down from the bed of the truck and the big casket loaded on. Then—in accordance with Holmes's instructions—O'Rourke and his assistants poured a ten-inch layer of freshly mixed cement into the bottom of the casket. Holmes's corpse—still dressed in the suit he was hanged in—was laid in the cement and his face covered with a silk handkerchief. More cement followed, O'Rourke packing it tightly over the body.

When the casket was filled to the top, the lid was nailed down. Then the casket was driven to Holy Cross Cemetery in Delaware County and transferred to a vault, where it was guarded overnight by two Pinkertons.

The following afternoon, Friday, May 8, a crowd of over one hundred men, women, and children watched as two dozen burly laborers hauled the cement-filled casket up a wooden ramp and onto a furniture wagon. It was driven to a double grave, dug to a depth of ten feet, which Samuel Rotan had purchased earlier that day for $24. As the casket was lowered carefully down a wooden slide to the bottom of the hole, Father MacPake spoke a few words over it.

When the brief service was finished, the gravediggers covered the casket with another layer of sand and cement, two feet thick. Then they picked up their spades and began shoveling in the dirt.

Holmes's final wish had been fulfilled. His corpse was encased in several tons of rock-hard cement. It would take an unusually determined grave robber—one armed with drills, dynamite, and a derrick—to get at his remains.

But if Holmes's body was imprisoned forever, his malevolent soul was another matter. Though his fortitude in the face of death had gained him the grudging admiration of the press, he continued to live on in the public mind as a creature of supernatural evil. In the months following his execution, this perception seemed confirmed by a bizarre series of misfortunes that befell many of the people involved in his case. It was as if Holmes's demonic spirit had risen from the grave to take vengeance on those who had conspired against him.

In rapid succession, Dr. William K. Mattern—the coroner's physician who had been a major witness against him—died of blood poisoning; both Coroner Ashbridge and Judge Arnold suffered life-threatening illnesses; Superintendent Perkins of Moyamensing committed suicide; Peter Cigrand—the father of Holmes's murdered mistress, Emeline—was horribly burned in a gas explosion; and Detective Frank Geyer was stricken with a serious malady.

Not long afterward, a fire gutted the office of O. LaForrest Perry, the claims manager for Fidelity Mutual, who had been so instrumental in Holmes's apprehension. All the furnishings and appurtenances in Perry's office were destroyed by the flames, except for three framed mementos: the original copy of Holmes's arrest warrant, plus two photographic portraits of the world-famous criminal. When Perry's secretary saw these unscathed souvenirs hanging on the wall above the charred ruins of his desk, she begged him to destroy them. By then, people had already begun talking about "the Holmes Curse."

Even those who had given succor to the archcriminal did not seem immune from it. Several weeks after the hanging, the Reverend Father Henry J. MacPake—the young, gentle-faced priest who had helped administer last rites to Holmes and then officiated at his funeral—was found dead in the rear yard of St. Paul's Academy on Christian Street. The coroner named uremia as the cause of death. That, however, did not explain the heavy bruises on the young priest's face and head. Or the bloody stains on the backyard fence and the mysterious footprints on the ground beside the corpse.

Yet it was the tragic death of Linford Biles that caused even skeptics to wonder if there might be some truth to all the talk about Holmes's "malignant influence."

On a Saturday morning some weeks after the execution, Biles—the sixty-five-year-old paymaster who had served as the jury foreman—was awakened by a commotion below his bedroom window. Looking outside, he saw a small crowd gathered on the street. They were gesturing upward and shouting something about a fire.

Throwing on his clothes, Biles hurried onto the sidewalk. Up on the roof, a bluish flame shot skyward. Biles instantly guessed its source—the crisscrossing wires strung over his house had touched, sparked, and ignited his shingles. Those wires had given him trouble before.

Within minutes, Biles had run back inside his house, hurried upstairs, and climbed onto the roof, intending somehow to move the wires away from the shingles. When his daughter saw what he was up to, she roused her brother, urging him to climb onto the roof and bring their father back inside before he hurt himself "fooling with" the wires.

The young man did as he was told. Seconds later, the spectators below heard a strange thudding sound on the roof—then an ominous silence. By then the police had arrived. Climbing onto the roof, they found the bodies of the father and son stretched out side by side. The younger Biles was still breathing, but the father—who had accidentally come in direct contact with the live wires—had been electrocuted. His left hand was scorched, his forehead blackened, his left foot badly burned.

As news of the tragedy spread, neighbors gathered outside the house. One of these was Mrs. Crowell, an old woman who had been present two years before when the same wires had nearly started a major fire. She had sensed something sinister on that occasion and had feared that Mr. Biles would come to a bad end. Now that her dark presentiment had been realized, she could only shake her head in wonder.

"I read in the papers where Holmes said he was starting to look like the devil," the old woman told a reporter for *The Philadelphia Times* who had arrived to investigate reports that the "curse" had claimed another victim. "Now I'm thinking he didn't just look like the devil but really was one in fact."

In the coming years, other men who'd had dealings with Holmes would meet violent ends. One of these was Marion Hedgepeth.

For informing on Holmes, Hedgepeth had expected a pardon. An official word of gratitude was all he received. On the very day of Holmes's execution, Hedgepeth was transported to the Missouri State Penitentiary to begin his twenty-five-year sentence. "This is what a life of graft got me," he said, scowling, as the deputies led him inside.

Still, the "Handsome Bandit" had his loyal supporters, who immediately began campaigning for his release, sending petitions to the governor that praised Hedgepeth as a "friend to society" who had "helped exterminate a horrible monster." As the years went by, newspapers periodically printed stories about Hedgepeth's jailhouse rehabilitation. According to these inspiring accounts, the former highwayman spent much of his free time reading the Bible and composing letters to his mother.

He wrote other letters, too, including one to William Pinkerton, in which he urged his former nemesis to help him win a pardon: "Here I am, a broken old man, with an incurable disease, just waiting to die. . . . If I ever am released, I will flee back to the arms of my poor old mother."

Finally, on July 4, 1906, Hedgepeth's prayers were answered. He was pardoned by Governor Folk. Speaking to a crowd of well-wishers outside the prison gates, the formerly dashing outlaw—now white-haired and toothless—told the crowd that "I shall go to Colorado if I can get that far. If I cannot, then in the arms of my poor old mother and four devoted sisters, I shall give up my miserable and misspent life."

Back home in Missouri, however, Hedgepeth seemed less inclined simply to curl up and die. He managed to finagle employment as an informer for the Pinkertons, working under the direction of F. H. Tillotson, general manager of the agency's Kansas City branch. Many of the detectives were openly distrustful of Hedgepeth, but Tillotson stood firm in his belief that "Hedgepeth is honest in his endeavor for reformation . . . and can be trusted to do anything we ask of him."

An ability to read character is a requirement for a good detective and Tillotson was first-rate. That his judgment in this case proved so unsound was less a mark of his deficiencies than of Hedgepeth's exceptional cunning.

In September 1907, Hedgepeth was arrested for blowing a safe in Omaha, Nebraska. He was found guilty and sentenced to ten years in jail. Released after only two, largely because he was dying of tuberculosis, he immediately assembled a new gang and held up a Chicago saloon at midnight of New Year's Eve, 1910. As Hedgepeth was stuffing the loot in a burlap sack, a policeman walked through the door. Hedgepeth went for his gun, but the policeman drew first.

Hedgepeth died with a bullet in the chest.

Gradually, the stories about the Holmes Curse faded. But on March 7, 1914, nearly twenty years after the notorious "multimurderer" was put to death, a disquieting article appeared in *The Chicago Tribune*. "HOLMES CASTLE" SECRETS DIE, read the headline.

The story reported the suicide of Pat Quinlan, former caretaker of the Castle and suspected accomplice in Holmes's crimes. At the time of his suicide, Quinlan was living on a farm near Portland, Michigan. He had killed himself by taking strychnine, and his death—as the newspaper noted—meant that "the mysteries of Holmes' Castle" would remain forever unexplained.

As to the reason for Quinlan's suicide, no one could fully explain it, though his relatives offered a suggestive clue.

Something seemed to be haunting him, they told the police. For several months before he swallowed strychnine, Pat Quinlan could no longer sleep.

Sources and Acknowledgments

When I began researching this book in the fall of 1990, I was amazed (and a little daunted) by the sheer mass of material printed about Holmes from the day of his arrest until his bizarre interment in several tons of cement. Given the enormous fascination he exerted on the American public, it seemed inexplicable that this extraordinary criminal had been so thoroughly forgotten by everyone except the most hard-core true-crime enthusiasts. Meanwhile, his English contemporary, Jack the Ripper, had achieved the immortality of a true pop myth.

Part of the Ripper's appeal, no doubt, derives from the mystery of his identity, which continues to tantalize armchair detectives everywhere. But the answer to Holmes's current obscurity also lies, I believe, in the nature of his crimes.

Though the precise number of his victims will never be known—estimates range into the hundreds—it seems certain that, at the very least, he murdered nine people over a period of years (Ben Pitezel and his three children, Julia and Pearl Conner, Emeline Cigrand, and the two Williams sisters), thus qualifying as America's first serial killer. Still, with his "Castle of Horror," chloroform, and chemical vats, he often seems like a figure from a different era, a creature out of gothic romance or Victorian nightmare. (His contemporaries described him as a real-life Jekyll and Hyde.) Moreover, though he was certainly a psychopath (at the time of

414

his execution, reports began to surface that he had originally fled New Hampshire after mutilating his own son by Clara Lovering), it is hard to determine the degree to which his crimes were motivated by sexual sadism. By contrast, the Ripper—the blade-wielding lust-murderer stalking women in the night—speaks more directly to the anxieties and obsessions of our own age.

In any event, the newspapers of his day served as my primary source material. The Holmes case was front-page news from coast to coast, though it was covered most exhaustively in the two cities directly involved with his crimes, Chicago and Philadelphia. He also received lavish attention from the New York City press (indeed, *The New York World* seemed to enjoy a particularly privileged relationship with Holmes, who supplied the paper with a steady stream of exclusive statements during his trial).

For my reconstruction of Holmes's early life, education, and criminal career; of the building, exploration, and destruction of the Castle; of the insurance swindle and investigation into Pitezel's death; of Holmes's arrest, trial, execution, and burial—for these and other parts of the story (Marion Hedgepeth's early exploits, for example, and my epilogue on the Holmes Curse), I relied primarily on the following newspapers: *The Philadelphia Inquirer, The Philadelphia Public Ledger, The Philadelphia Times, The Chicago Tribune, The Chicago Inter Ocean, The Chicago Times-Herald, The New York Times, The New York World,* and *The New York Herald.*

My re-creation of Geyer's celebrated hunt for Alice, Nellie, and Howard Pitezel also drew on these newspapers, though my major source was Geyer's own book, *The Holmes-Pitezel Case* (Philadelphia: Publisher's Union, 1896). As far as can be determined, only a single copy exists of *Holmes's Own Story* (Philadelphia: Burk & McFethridge Co., 1895). It is preserved in the Rare Books Division of the Library of Congress and formed the basis of my chapter on that fascinating, if wildly unreliable, autobiography. My description of the trial drew heavily on the official transcript, published in book form as *The Trial of Herman W. Mudgett,*

Alias, H. H. Holmes, For the Murder of Benjamin F. Pitezel (Philadelphia: George T. Bisel, 1897).

Other books from that era which, if nothing else, provided insight into both the public's obsession with Holmes and the often scandalous journalistic standards of the time were Robert L. Corbitt, *The Holmes Castle* (Chicago: Corbitt & Morrison, 1895), *Holmes, the Arch-Fiend, or: A Carnival of Crime* (Cincinnati: Barclay & Co., ca. 1895), and—arguably the most egregious "true crime" book ever published—*Sold to Satan, Holmes—A poor wife's sad story, not a mere rehash, but something new and never before published. A living victim* (Philadelphia: Old Franklin Publishing House, ca. 1895).

Holmes's story has been told (usually inaccurately) in many histories of crime, going back to Matthew Pinkerton's *Murder in All Ages* (Chicago: A. E. Pinkerton and Co., 1898). In addition to Pinkerton's book, I consulted the following volumes: Thomas S. Duke, *Celebrated Criminal Cases of America* (San Francisco: The James H. Barry Co., 1910); H. B. Irving, *A Book of Remarkable Criminals* (New York: George H. Doran Co., 1918); Allan Churchill, *A Pictorial History of American Crime, 1849–1929* (New York: Holt, Rinehart & Winston, 1964); Robert Jay Nash, *Bloodletters and Badmen* (New York: M. Evans, 1973); Carl Sifratis, *The Encyclopedia of American Crime* (New York: Facts on File, 1982); and James D. Horan and Howard Swiggett, *The Pinkerton Story* (New York: G.P. Putnam Sons, 1951). The latter also contains a good deal of useful information on Marion Hedgepeth's incorrigible life.

The lurid doings at Holmes's Sixty-third Street Castle form a colorful chapter in the annals of Chicago crime. I found useful, often vivid, material in Herbert Ashbury, *The Gem of the Prairie: An Informal History of the Chicago Underworld* (New York: Alfred A. Knopf, 1940); Stephen Longstreet, *Chicago 1860–1919* (New York: David McKay, 1973); and Finis Farr, *Chicago: A Personal History of America's Most American City* (New Rochelle, N.Y.: Arlington House, 1973).

For my chapter on the Chicago Fire, I drew on Robert Cromie, *The Great Chicago Fire* (New York: McGraw Hill,

1958), and David Lowe, ed., *The Great Chicago Fire: In Eyewitness Accounts and Contemporary Photographs and Illustrations* (New York: Dover Books, 1979). I based my discussion of the "Keeley cure" on information in Mark E. Lender and James Kirby Martin, *Drinking in America: A History* (New York: Free Press, 1982). My chapter on Jack the Ripper derives partly from Donald Rumbelow, *The Complete Jack the Ripper* (Boston: New York Graphic Society, 1975). My descriptions of the Chicago World's Fair made use of material from contemporary newspaper sources as well as from David Borg, *Chicago's White City of 1893* (Lexington, Ky.: University Press of Kentucky, 1976), and Arthur Schlesinger, *The Rise of the City: 1878–1898* (New York: Macmillan, 1933).

Since the 1950s, Holmes has been the subject of several books besides this one. One of the best is also the most difficult to find: Charles Boswell and Lewis Thompson's *The Girls in Nightmare House* (New York: Fawcet Publications, 1955), a lively, well-researched (though long-out-of-print) paperback whose lurid title and cover illustration belie the authors' unsensationalized approach. I am also indebted to David Franke's scholarly *The Torture Doctor* (New York: Hawthorn Books, 1972), as I am to David Franke himself, who supplied me with several useful leads. Holmes appears in fictionalized guise in Robert Bloch's thriller *American Gothic* (New York: Simon & Schuster, 1974) and is the subject of Allan Eckert's admirable, exhaustively researched novel *The Scarlet Mansion* (Boston: Little Brown and Company, 1985).

Thanks to Allan Eckert I became acquainted with the person to whom this book is dedicated, Mildred Voris Kerr. The daughter of Dessie Pitezel and granddaughter of Carrie and Benjamin, this extraordinary (indeed inspiring) woman quickly became not just a generous source of knowledge but a friend. Her death at age 89 in April, 1993, took everyone by surprise. She was a person of such remarkable vitality that—to those who had the privilege of knowing her—it seemed as though she might go on enjoying life forever.

HAROLD SCHECHTER

For various forms of assistance, kindness, and support, I would also like to thank Ward Childs, Jennifer Ericson, Eileen Flanagan, Suzanne Katz, Allen Koenigsberg, Catharine Ostlind, Richard and Alice Pisciotta, Ralph Pugh, Sylvia Reid, Patterson Smith, Loretto Szucs, Peter M. Vanwingen, and Mike Wilk.

Finally—my deepest gratitude, as ever, to Linda Marrow.

HAROLD SCHECHTER

This respected true crime historian brings his immense knowledge to this ultimate encyclopedia of serial killers.

This comprehensive resource of mass murders proves why Harold Schechter is the source to turn to for true crime!

A TO Z ENCYCLOPEDIA OF SERIAL KILLERS

Pocket Books Trade Paperback
0-671-02074-9

HAROLD SCHECHTER

"America's principle chronicler of its greatest psychopathic killers" (*The Boston Book Review*) once again
brings readers into the minds of one of history's
most notorious serial killers in

In 1891, Jane Toppan, a proper New England
matron, embarked on a profession as a private-duty
nurse. Selfless and good-natured, she beguiled
Boston's most prominent families. They had no
idea what they were welcoming into their homes.

FATAL
The Poisonous Life of a Female Serial Killer
Pocket Star Books
0-671-01450-1

Visit
❖ Pocket Books ❖
online at

....

www.SimonSays.com

....

Keep up on the latest new
releases from your favorite
authors, as well as author
appearances, news, chats,
special offers and more.

SIMON & SCHUSTER
A VIACOM COMPANY
www.SimonSays.com

Pocket
Books